Becker Professional Education, a global leader in professional education, has ~   erials
for the ACCA for more than 20 years. Thousands of students studyin~ '
succeeded in their professional examinations studying with its Plat.
Central and Eastern Europe and Central Asia.

Nearly half a million professionals have advanced their careers throug~   ~cation's
courses. Throughout its 60-year history, Becker has earned a strong tra   ~ent success through
world-class teaching, curriculum and learning tools.

Becker Professional Education has been awarded ACCA Approved Content Provider Status for its ACCA
materials, as well as materials for the Diploma in International Financial Reporting (DipIFR).

We provide a single solution for individuals and companies in need of global accounting certifications and
continuing professional education.

Becker Professional Education's ACCA Study Materials

All of Becker's materials are authored by experienced ACCA lecturers and are used in the delivery of classroom
courses.

Study Text: Gives complete coverage of the syllabus with a focus on learning outcomes. It is designed to be
used both as a reference text and as part of integrated study. It also includes the ACCA Syllabus and Study
Guide, exam advice and commentaries and a Study Question Bank containing practice questions relating to
each topic covered.

Revision Question Bank: Exam style and standard questions together with comprehensive answers to
support and prepare students for their exams. The Revision Question Bank also includes past examination
questions (updated where relevant), model answers and alternative solutions and tutorial notes.

Revision Essentials Handbook*: A condensed, easy-to-use aid to revision containing essential technical
content and exam guidance.

*Revision Essentials Handbook are substantially derived from content reviewed by ACCA's examining team.

Becker Professional Education
is an ACCA approved content provider

BECKER
PROFESSIONAL EDUCATION®

ACCA

FINANCIAL REPORTING F7
STUDY TEXT

September 2017 to June 2018 Edition

BECKER
PROFESSIONAL EDUCATION®

This training material has been prepared and published by Becker Professional Development International Limited: www.becker.com/acca

ISBN: 978-1-78566-385-7

Title: Becker is and will remain the owner of all title, ownership rights, intellectual property, and all other rights and interests in and to the Materials that are subject to the terms of this Agreement. The Materials are protected by the copyright laws of the United States and international copyright laws and treaties.

Termination: The license granted under this Agreement commences upon your receipt of these Materials. This license shall terminate the earlier of: (i) ten (10) business days after notice to you of non-payment of or default on any payment due Becker which has not been cured within such 10-day period; or (ii) immediately if you fail to comply with any of the limitations described above; or (iii) upon expiration of the examination period for which the Materials are valid as specified on your order confirmation and in the title of the course package. For example, Materials marked, "For Examinations to August 2018," are valid for examinations from September 2017 to August 2018 and the license to these Materials terminates at the end of August 2018. All online packages and Materials will be removed after the relevant examination period and you will no longer have access to the online packages or Materials. In addition, upon termination of this license for any reason, you must delete or otherwise remove from your computer and other device any Materials you downloaded, including, but not limited to, any archival copies you may have made. The Title, Exclusion of Warranties, Exclusion of Damages, Indemnification and Remedies, Severability of Terms and Governing Law provisions, and any amounts due, shall survive termination of the license.

Your Limited Right to Terminate this License and Receive a Refund: You may terminate this license for the in-class, online, and self-study Programs in accordance with Becker's refund policy at https://becker.com/ACCA.

Exclusion of Warranties: YOU EXPRESSLY ASSUME ALL RISK FOR USE OF THE MATERIALS. YOU AGREE THAT THE MATERIALS ARE PROVIDED TO YOU "AS IS" AND "AS AVAILABLE" AND THAT BECKER MAKES NO WARRANTIES, EXPRESS OR IMPLIED, WITH RESPECT TO THE MATERIALS, THEIR MERCHANTABILITY OR FITNESS FOR A PARTICULAR PURPOSE AND NO WARRANTY OF NONINFRINGEMENT OF THIRD PARTIES' RIGHTS. NO DEALER, AGENT OR EMPLOYEE OF BECKER IS AUTHORIZED TO PROVIDE ANY SUCH WARRANTY TO YOU. BECAUSE SOME JURISDICTIONS DO NOT ALLOW THE EXCLUSION OF IMPLIED WARRANTIES, THE ABOVE EXCLUSION OF IMPLIED WARRANTIES MAY NOT APPLY TO YOU. BECKER DOES NOT WARRANT OR GUARANTEE THAT YOU WILL PASS ANY EXAMINATION.

Exclusion of Damages: UNDER NO CIRCUMSTANCES AND UNDER NO LEGAL THEORY, TORT, CONTRACT, OR OTHERWISE, SHALL BECKER OR ITS DIRECTORS, OFFICERS, EMPLOYEES, OR AGENTS BE LIABLE TO YOU OR ANY OTHER PERSON FOR ANY CONSEQUENTIAL, INCIDENTAL, INDIRECT, PUNITIVE, EXEMPLARY OR SPECIAL DAMAGES OF ANY CHARACTER, INCLUDING, WITHOUT LIMITATION, DAMAGES FOR LOSS OF GOODWILL, WORK STOPPAGE, COMPUTER FAILURE OR MALFUNCTION OR ANY AND ALL OTHER DAMAGES OR LOSSES, OR FOR ANY DAMAGES IN EXCESS OF BECKER'S LIST PRICE FOR A LICENSE TO THE MATERIALS, EVEN IF BECKER SHALL HAVE BEEN INFORMED OF THE POSSIBILITY OF SUCH DAMAGES, OR FOR ANY CLAIM BY ANY OTHER PARTY. Some jurisdictions do not allow the limitation or exclusion of liability for incidental or consequential damages, so the above limitation or exclusion may not apply to you.

Indemnification and Remedies: You agree to indemnify and hold Becker and its employees, representatives, agents, attorneys, affiliates, directors, officers, members, managers, and shareholders harmless from and against any and all claims, demands, losses, damages, penalties, costs or expenses (including reasonable attorneys' and expert witnesses' fees and costs) of any kind or nature, arising from or relating to any violation, breach, or nonfulfillment by you of any provision of this license. If you are obligated to provide indemnification pursuant to this provision, Becker may, in its sole and absolute discretion, control the disposition of any indemnified action at your sole cost and expense. Without limiting the foregoing, you may not settle, compromise, or in any other manner dispose of any indemnified action without the consent of Becker. If you breach any material term of this license, Becker shall be entitled to equitable relief by way of temporary and permanent injunction without the need for a bond and such other and further relief as any court with jurisdiction may deem just and proper.

Confidentiality: The Materials are considered confidential and proprietary to Becker. You shall keep the Materials confidential and you shall not publish or disclose the Materials to any third party without the prior written consent of Becker.

Severability of Terms: If any term or provision of this license is held invalid or unenforceable by a court of competent jurisdiction, such invalidity shall not affect the validity or operation of any other term or provision and such invalid term or provision shall be deemed to be severed from the license. This Agreement may only be modified by written agreement signed by both parties.

Governing Law: This Agreement shall be governed and construed according to the laws of the State of Illinois, United States of America, excepting that State's conflicts of laws rules. The parties agree that the jurisdiction and venue of any dispute subject to litigation is proper in any state or federal court in Chicago, Illinois, U.S.A. The parties hereby agree to waive application of the U.N. Convention on the Sale of Goods. If the State of Illinois adopts the current proposed Uniform Computer Information Transactions Act (UCITA, formerly proposed Article 2B to the Uniform Commercial Code), or a version of the proposed UCITA, that part of the laws shall not apply to any transaction under this Agreement.

F7

Contents

Contents

Introduction

ABOUT THIS STUDY TEXT

This Study Text has been specifically written for the Association of Chartered Certified Accountants fundamentals level examination, F7 *Financial Reporting.*

It provides comprehensive coverage of the core syllabus areas and is designed to be used both as a reference text and as an integral part of your studies to provide you with the knowledge, skill and confidence to succeed in your ACCA studies.

About the author: Phil Bradbury is Becker's lead tutor in international financial reporting and has more than 17 years' experience in delivering ACCA exam-based training.

How to Use This Study Text

You should start by reading through the syllabus, study guide and approach to examining the syllabus provided in this introduction to familiarise yourself with the content of this exam.

The sessions which follow include the following features:

Focus	These are the learning outcomes relevant to the session, as published in the ACCA Study Guide.
Session Guidance	Tutor advice and strategies for approaching each session.
Visual Overview	A diagram of the concepts and the relationships addressed in each session.
Definitions	Terms are defined as they are introduced and larger groupings of terms will be set forth in a Terminology section.
Illustrations	These are to be read as part of the text. Any solutions to numerical Illustrations are provided.
Exhibits	These extracts of external content are presented to reinforce concepts and should be read as part of the text.
Examples	These should be attempted using the pro forma solution provided (where applicable).
Key Points	Attention is drawn to fundamental rules, underlying concepts and principles.
Exam Advice	These tutor comments relate the content to relevance in the examination.
Commentaries	These provide additional information to reinforce content.
Session Summary	A summary of the main points of each session.
Session Quiz	These quick questions are designed to test your knowledge of the technical content. A reference to the answer is provided.
Study Question Bank	A reference to recommended practice questions contained in the Study Question Bank. As a minimum you should work through the priority questions after studying each session. For additional practice you can attempt any remaining questions.
Example Solutions	Answers to the Examples are presented at the end of each session.

SYLLABUS

Aim

To develop knowledge and skills in understanding and applying accounting standards and the theoretical framework in the preparation of financial statements of entities, including groups and how to analyse and interpret those financial statements.

Main Capabilities

On successful completion of this exam, candidates should be able to:

A. Discuss and apply a conceptual and regulatory framework for financial reporting

B. Account for transactions in accordance with International accounting standards

C. Analyse and interpret financial statements

D. Prepare and present financial statements for single entities and business combinations in accordance with International accounting standards

Position in the ACCA Qualification

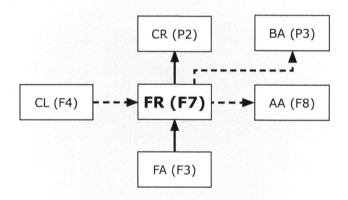

Relational Diagram of Main Capabilities

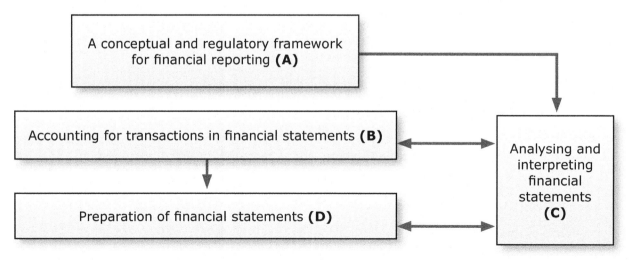

Rationale

The financial reporting syllabus assumes knowledge acquired in F3 *Financial Accounting*, and develops and applies this further and in greater depth.

The syllabus begins with the conceptual framework for financial reporting with reference to the qualitative characteristics of useful information and the fundamental bases of accounting introduced in the F3 syllabus within the Knowledge module. It then moves into a detailed examination of the regulatory framework of accounting and how this informs the standard setting process.

The main areas of the syllabus cover the reporting of financial information for single companies and for groups in accordance with generally accepted accounting principles and relevant accounting standards.

Finally, the syllabus covers the analysis and interpretation of information from financial reports.

Detailed Syllabus

A. The Conceptual and Regulatory Framework for Financial Reporting

1. The need for a conceptual framework and the characteristics of useful information

2. Recognition and measurement

3. Regulatory framework

4. The concepts and principles of groups and consolidated financial statements

B. Accounting for Transactions in Financial Statements

1. Tangible non-current assets

2. Intangible assets

3. Impairment of assets

4. Inventory and biological assets

5. Financial instruments

6. Leasing

7. Provisions and events after the reporting period

8. Taxation

9. Reporting financial performance

10. Revenue

11. Government grants

12. Foreign currency transactions

C. Analysing and Interpreting Financial Statements of Single Entities and Groups

1. Limitations of financial statements

2. Calculation and interpretation of accounting ratios and trends to address users' and stakeholders' needs

3. Limitations of interpretation techniques

4. Specialised, not-for-profit, and public sector entities

D. Preparation of Financial Statements

1. Preparation of single entity financial statements

2. Preparation of consolidated financial statements including an associate

EXAMINABLE DOCUMENTS

Title		Study Session
IAS 1	Presentation of Financial Statements	3
IAS 2	Inventories	6
IAS 7	Statement of Cash Flows	26
IAS 8	Accounting Policies, Changes in Accounting Estimates and Errors	4
IAS 10	Events After the Reporting Period	16
IAS 12	Income Taxes	17
IAS 16	Property, Plant and Equipment	7
IAS 20	Accounting for Government Grants and Disclosure of Government Assistance	9
IAS 21	The Effects of Changes in Foreign Exchange Rates	24
IAS 23	Borrowing Costs	8
IAS 27	Separate Financial Statements	19
IAS 28	Investments in Associates and Joint Ventures	23
IAS 32	Financial Instruments: Presentation	18
IAS 33	Earnings per Share	27
IAS 36	Impairment of Assets	13
IAS 37	Provisions, Contingent Liabilities and Contingent Assets	15
IAS 38	Intangible Assets	11
IAS 40	Investment Property	10
IAS 41	Agriculture	6
IFRS 3	Business Combinations	19, 20, 21, 22
IFRS 5	Non-current Assets Held for Sale and Discontinued Operations	12
IFRS 7	Financial Instruments: Disclosures	18
IFRS 9	Financial Instruments	18
IFRS 10	Consolidated Financial Statements	19, 20, 21, 22
IFRS 13	Fair Value Measurement	2
IFRS 15	Revenue from Contracts with Customers	5
IFRS 16	Leases	14
Other Statements		
	The Conceptual Framework for Financial Reporting	2

ACCA Support

For examiner's reports, guidance and technical articles relevant to this exam see
www.accaglobal.com/gb/en/student/exam-support-resources/
fundamentals-exams-study-resources/f7.html

The ACCA study guide offers more detailed guidance on the depth and level at which the examinable documents will be examined and should therefore be read in conjunction with the examinable documents list. The ACCA's Study Guide which is reproduced as follows is referenced to the Sessions in this Study Text.

ACCA STUDY GUIDE

A. The Conceptual and Regulatory Framework for Financial Reporting	Ref.
1. The need for a conceptual framework and the characteristics of useful information	2
a) Describe what is meant by a conceptual framework for financial reporting.	
b) Discuss whether a conceptual framework is necessary and what an alternative system might be.	
c) Discuss what is meant by relevance and faithful representation and describe the qualities that enhance these characteristics.	
d) Discuss whether faithful representation constitutes more than compliance with accounting standards.	3
e) Discuss what is meant by understandability and verifiability in relation to the provision of financial information.	2
f) Discuss the importance of comparability and timeliness to users of financial statements.	
g) Discuss the principle of comparability in accounting for changes in accounting policies.	4
2. Recognition and measurement	2
a) Define what is meant by 'recognition' in financial statements and discuss the recognition criteria.	
b) Apply the recognition criteria to:	
i) assets and liabilities.	
ii) income and expenses.	
c) Explain and compute amounts using the following measures:	
i) historical cost	
ii) current cost	
iii) net realisable value	
iv) present value of future cash flows	
v) fair value	
d) Discuss the advantages and disadvantages of the use of historical cost accounting.	
e) Discuss whether the use of current value accounting overcomes the problems of historical cost accounting.	
f) Describe the concept of financial and physical capital maintenance and how this affects the determination of profits.	
3. Regulatory framework	
a) Explain why a regulatory framework is needed including the advantages and disadvantages of IFRS over a national regulatory framework.	1
b) Explain why accounting standards on their own are not a complete regulatory framework.	1
c) Distinguish between a principles based and a rules based framework and discuss whether they can be complementary.	2
d) Describe the IASB's Standard setting process including revisions to and interpretations of Standards.	1
e) Explain the relationship of national standard setters to the IASB in respect of the standard setting process.	1

(continued on next page)

		Ref.
4.	**The concepts and principles of groups and consolidated financial statements**	**19**
a)	Describe the concept of a group as a single economic unit.	
b)	Explain and apply the definition of a subsidiary within relevant accounting standards.	
c)	Using accounting standards and other regulation, identify and outline the circumstances in which a group is required to prepare consolidated financial statements.	
d)	Describe the circumstances when a group may claim exemption from the preparation of consolidated financial statements.	
e)	Explain why directors may not wish to consolidate a subsidiary and when this is permitted by accounting standards and other applicable regulation.	
f)	Explain the need for using coterminous year ends and uniform accounting polices when preparing consolidated financial statements.	
g)	Explain why it is necessary to eliminate intra-group transactions.	**20**
h)	Explain the objective of consolidated financial statements.	**20**
i)	Explain why it is necessary to use fair values for the consideration for an investment in a subsidiary together with the fair values of a subsidiary's identifiable assets and liabilities when preparing consolidated financial statements.	**21**
j)	Define an associate and explain the principles and reasoning for the use of equity accounting.	**23**

B.	**Accounting for Transactions in Financial Statements**	**Ref.**
1.	**Tangible non-current assets**	**7**
a)	Define and compute the initial measurement of a non-current asset (including borrowing costs and an asset that has been self-constructed).	**7, 8**
b)	Identify subsequent expenditure that may be capitalised, distinguishing between capital and revenue items.	
c)	Discuss the requirements of relevant accounting standards in relation to the revaluation of non-current assets.	**7**
d)	Account for revaluation and disposal gains and losses for non-current assets.	**7**
e)	Compute depreciation based on the cost and revaluation models and on assets that have two or more significant parts (complex assets).	**7**
f)	Discuss why the treatment of investment properties should differ from other properties.	**10**
g)	Apply the requirements of relevant accounting standards to an investment property.	**10**
2.	**Intangible non-current assets**	**11**
a)	Discuss the nature and accounting treatment of internally generated and purchased intangibles.	
b)	Distinguish between goodwill and other intangible assets.	
c)	Describe the criteria for the initial recognition and measurement of intangible assets.	
d)	Describe the subsequent accounting treatment, including the principle of impairment tests in relation to goodwill.	
e)	Indicate why the value of purchase consideration for an investment may be less than the value of the acquired identifiable net assets and how the difference should be accounted for.	**21**
f)	Describe and apply the requirements of relevant accounting standards to research and development expenditure.	**11**

(continued on next page)

	Ref.

3. Impairment of assets — 13

a) Define, calculate and account for an impairment loss.

b) Account for the reversal of an impairment loss on an individual asset.

c) Identify the circumstances that may indicate impairments to assets.

d) Describe what is meant by a cash generating unit.

e) State the basis on which impairment losses should be allocated, and allocate an impairment loss to the assets of a cash generating unit.

4. Inventory and biological assets — 6

a) Describe and apply the principles of inventory valuation.

b) Apply the requirements of relevant accounting standards for biological assets.

5. Financial instruments — 18

a) Explain the need for an accounting standard on financial instruments.

b) Define financial instruments in terms of financial assets and financial liabilities.

c) Explain and account for the factoring of receivables.

d) Indicate for the following categories of financial instruments how they should be measured and how any gains and losses from subsequent measurement should be treated in the financial statements:

   i) amortised cost

   ii) fair value through other comprehensive income (including where an irrevocable election has been made for equity instruments that are not held for trading)

   iii) fair value through profit or loss

e) Distinguish between debt and equity capital.

f) Apply the requirements of relevant accounting standards to the issue and finance costs of:

   i) equity

   ii) redeemable preference shares and debt instruments with no conversion rights (principle of amortised cost)

   iii) convertible debt

6. Leasing — 14

a) Account for the right of use assets and lease liabilities in the records of the lessee.

b) Explain the exemption from the recognition criteria for leases in the records of the lessee.

c) Account for sale and leaseback agreements.

7. Provisions and events after the reporting period — 15

a) Explain why an accounting standard on provisions is necessary.

b) Distinguish between legal and constructive obligations.

c) State when provisions may and may not be made and demonstrate how they should be accounted for.

d) Explain how provisions should be measured.

e) Define contingent assets and liabilities and describe their accounting treatment and required disclosures.

f) Identify and account for:

   i) warranties/guarantees

   ii) onerous contracts

   iii) environmental and similar provisions

   iv) provisions for future repairs or refurbishments.

(continued on next page)

	Ref.
g) Events after the reporting period.	**16**
i) distinguish between and account for adjusting and non-adjusting events after the reporting period	
ii) Identify items requiring separate disclosure, including their accounting treatment and required disclosures	
8. Taxation	**17**
a) Account for current taxation in accordance with relevant accounting standards.	
b) Explain the effect of taxable temporary differences on accounting and taxable profits.	
c) Compute and record deferred tax amounts in the financial statements.	
9. Reporting financial performance	
a) Discuss the importance of identifying and reporting the results of discontinued operations.	**12**
b) Define and account for non-current assets held for sale and discontinued operations.	**12**
c) Indicate the circumstances where separate disclosure of material items of income and expense is required.	**3**
d) Account for changes in accounting estimates, changes in accounting policy and correction of prior period errors.	**4**
e) Earnings per share (eps)	
i) calculate the eps in accordance with relevant accounting standards (dealing with bonus issues, full market value issues and rights issues)	**27**
i) explain the relevance of the diluted eps and calculate the diluted eps involving convertible debt and share options (warrants)	
10. Revenue	**5**
a) Explain and apply the principles of recognition of revenue:	
i) Identification of contracts	
ii) Identification of performance obligations	
iii) Determination of transaction price	
iv) Allocation of the price to performance obligations	
v) Recognition of revenue when/as performance obligations are satisfied.	
b) Explain and apply the criteria for recognising revenue generated from contracts where performance obligations are satisfied over time or at a point in time.	
c) Describe the acceptable methods for measuring progress towards complete satisfaction of a performance obligation.	
d) Explain and apply the criteria for the recognition of contract costs.	
e) Apply the principles of recognition of revenue, and specifically account for the following types of transaction:	
i) principal versus agent	
ii) repurchase agreements	
iii) bill and hold arrangements	
iv) consignments	
f) Prepare financial statement extracts for contracts where performance obligations are satisfied over time.	
11. Government grants	
a) Apply the provisions of relevant accounting standards in relation to accounting for government grants.	**11**

(continued on next page)

	Ref.
12. Foreign currency transactions	**24**
a) Explain the difference between functional and presentation currency and explain why adjustments for foreign currency transactions are necessary.	
b) Account for the translation of foreign currency transactions and monetary/ non-monetary foreign currency items at the reporting date.	

C. Analysing and Interpreting Financial Statements of Single Entities and Groups	**Ref.**
1. Limitations of financial statements	**25**
a) Indicate the problems of using historic information to predict future performance and trends.	
b) Discuss how financial statements may be manipulated to produce a desired effect (creative accounting, window dressing).	
c) Explain why figures in a statement of financial position may not be representative of average values throughout the period for example, due to:	
i) seasonal trading	
ii) major asset acquisitions near the end of the accounting period.	
d) Explain how the use of consolidated financial statements might limit interpretation techniques.	
2. Calculation and interpretation of accounting ratios and trends to address users' and stakeholders' needs	**25**
a) Define and compute relevant financial ratios.	
b) Explain what aspects of performance specific ratios are intended to assess.	
c) Analyse and interpret ratios to give an assessment of an entity's/group's performance and financial position in comparison with:	
i) previous period's financial statements	
ii) another similar entity/group for the same reporting period	
iii) industry average ratios.	
d) Interpret financial statements to give advice from the perspectives of different stakeholders.	
e) Discuss how the interpretation of current value based financial statements would differ from those using historical cost based accounts.	**2**
3. Limitations of interpretation techniques	**25**
a) Discuss the limitations in the use of ratio analysis for assessing corporate performance.	
b) Discuss the effect that changes in accounting policies or the use of different accounting polices between entities can have on the ability to interpret performance.	
c) Indicate other information, including non-financial information, that may be of relevance to the assessment of an entity's performance.	
d) Compare the usefulness of cash flow information with that of a statement of profit or loss or a statement of profit or loss and other comprehensive income.	**26**
e) Interpret a statement of cash flows (together with other financial information) to assess the performance and financial position of an entity.	**26**
f) i) explain why the trend of eps may be a more accurate indicator of performance than a company's profit trend and the importance of eps as a stock market indicator	**27**
ii) discuss the limitations of using eps as a performance measure.	**27**
4. Specialised, not-for-profit and public sector entities	**25**
a) Explain how the interpretation of the financial statement of a specialised, not-for-profit or public sector organisation might differ from that of a profit-making entity by reference to the different aims, objectives and reporting requirements.	

(continued on next page)

D.	Preparation of Financial Statements	Ref.
1.	**Preparation of single entity financial statements**	
a)	Prepare an entity's statement of financial position and statement of profit or loss and other comprehensive income in accordance with the structure and content prescribed within IFRS and with accounting treatments as identified within syllabus areas A, B and C.	3
b)	Prepare and explain the contents and purpose of the statement of changes in equity.	3
c)	Prepare a statement of cash flows for a single entity (not a group) in accordance with relevant accounting standards using the direct and the indirect method.	26
2.	**Preparation of consolidated financial statements including an associate**	
a)	Prepare a consolidated statement of financial position for a simple group (parent and one subsidiary and associate) dealing with pre and post acquisition profits, non-controlling interests and consolidated goodwill.	20, 22, 23
b)	Prepare a consolidated statement of profit or loss and consolidated statement of profit or loss and other comprehensive income for a simple group dealing with an acquisition in the period and non-controlling interest.	22
c)	Explain and account for other reserves (e.g. share premium and revaluation surplus).	21
d)	Account for the effects in the financial statements of intra-group trading.	21, 22
e)	Account for the effects of fair value adjustments (including their effect on consolidated goodwill) to:	21
	i) depreciating and non-depreciating non-current assets	
	ii) inventory	
	iii) monetary liabilities	
	iv) assets and liabilities not included in the subsidiary's own statement of financial position, including contingent assets and liabilities	
f)	Account for goodwill impairment.	21
g)	Describe and apply the required accounting treatment of consolidated goodwill.	21
h)	Explain and illustrate the effect of the disposal of a parent's investment in a subsidiary in the parent's individual financial statements and/or those of the group (restricted to disposals of the parent's entire investment in the subsidiary).	22

Approach to Examining the Syllabus

The syllabus may be assessed by paper-based or computer-based examinations (CBE). The examination will be structured in three sections.

All questions are compulsory. It will contain both computational and discursive elements. Some questions will adopt a scenario/case study approach.

Time allowed: 3 hours

- Section A of the exam comprises 15 objective test (OT) questions of 2 marks each.
- Section B of the exam comprises three 10-mark case-based questions. Each case has five OT questions of 2 marks each.
- Section C of the exam contains two 20-mark questions.

The CBE format introduces many time saving efficiencies compared to the paper-based exam. So to provide an equal assessment, students will have **3 hours 15 minutes** to complete the paper-based exams, compared to 3 hours allowed for sessions CBEs. For further details see the section *Exam time—providing an equal assessment* at www.accaglobal.com/gb/en/student/changes-to-exams/f5-f9-session-cbe.html

In CBE there may be instances where extra questions appear for the purpose of quality assurance. In such cases an extra 20 minutes will be allowed.

Section A and B questions will be selected from the entire syllabus. OT questions in paper-based examination will contain multiple-choice questions (MCQs) only. Computer-based examinations (CBE) will contain a variety of OT types. More detail on the differences between paper-based exams and CBEs can be found in the later Exam Technique section.

Section C questions will mainly focus on the following syllabus areas but a minority of marks can be drawn from any other area of the syllabus:

- Analysing and interpreting the financial statements of single entities and groups (syllabus area C)

- Preparation of financial statements (syllabus area D)

Questions on topic areas that are also included in F3 will be examined at an appropriately greater depth in this exam.

Candidates will be expected to have an appreciation of the need for specified accounting standards and why they have been issued. For detailed or complex standards, candidates need to be aware of their principles and key elements.

Guide to Examination Assessment

ACCA reserves the right to examine anything contained within the study guide at any examination session. This includes knowledge, techniques, principles, theories and concepts as specified.

For financial accounting examinations ACCA publishes *examinable documents* once a year to indicate exactly what regulations could potentially be assessed within identified examination sessions.

The documents listed as examinable are the latest that were *issued* prior to 1st September 2016 and will be examinable in the September 2017 to June 2018 examination sessions.

Regulations issued in accordance with the above dates may be examinable even if the *effective* date is in the future.

EXAMINATION TECHNIQUE—PAPER-BASED EXAM

Reading and Planning Time

ACCA recommends that you use the additional 15 minutes allowed for the paper-based exam in reading and planning:

- To read and plan Section C questions, in particular.

- To rank the questions in Section B according to their level of difficulty. Attempting the easiest of these questions first and the most difficult last should help keep your confidence high during the exam.

- Although you may use your calculator throughout the exam, when reading and planning, it is more effective to carefully read requirements and note down your ideas for any discursive elements of the Section C questions.

Time Allocation

▦ The time available for the exam is 180 minutes and this has to be allocated between the three sections.

▦ 54 minutes should be allocated to Section A so each MCQ should take, on average, just 3.6 minutes. Although the more theoretical MCQs may take only seconds to answer, those requiring detailed calculations might take as long as 5 minutes.

▦ 54 minutes should also be allocated to Section B.

▦ Allocating 1.8 minutes per mark means that each 20-mark scenario-based question should be given 36 minutes.

▦ Manage your time strictly to ensure you attempt all parts of all questions.

Section A

▦ These objective test (OT) questions consist of:

   ● a "stem" (the question);

   = a "key" (the correct answer); and

   = 3 "distractors" (plausible but incorrect answers).

Illustration 1 Answering an OT Question

On 1 January 20X6 a company purchased a plant. The invoice showed:

	$
Cost of plant	48,000
Delivery to factory	400
One-year warranty covering breakdown during 20X6	800
	49,200

Modifications to the factory building costing $2,200 were necessary to enable the plant to be installed.

What amount should be capitalised for the plant in the company's records in accordance with IAS 16 _Property, Plant and Equipment_?

A. $48,000
B. $48,400
C. $50,600
D. $51,400

Solution

Step 1

Start by reading the question in **bold**. This tells you what you have to do:

   ■ amount of capital cost to be recognised

Step 2

Write down or think about anything that will help you (e.g. a T a/c, formula, "pro forma" calculation or statement from an IFRS):

   ■ costs attributable to bringing the asset to the _location_ and _condition necessary_ for intended use

Step 3

Solve:

   ■ 48,000 + 400 + 2,200 = 50,600; the warranty is a running cost that must be expensed to profit or loss

Step 4

Select the appropriate box on your answer sheet:

   ■ C.

Exam Advice

- Approximately half of the questions in Section A will be non-computational. The time pressure for such items is relatively low, allowing more time for computational items.

- Ignore the answers, A, B, C and D, when doing calculations.

- It is not unusual for one of the distractors to be a number that will be calculated before reaching the final solution. Especially under exam pressure you may think you have the correct answer before you have completed the calculation.

- If you do not (or cannot) calculate an amount that corresponds to any of the amounts offered do not select one that stands out as disproportionate to the others; it is more likely to be a distractor than the key.

- If you are getting close to the end of your time allocation for Section A and you still have a few questions left to answer—guess! If you have time at the end of the exam you can still come back and check them. Avoid leaving questions unanswered before you move to the remaining sections as you will **not** be allowed to complete the OT answer sheet when the exam time is up.

Section B

- Each set of five OT questions will be based around a "case" or short scenario.

- Typically two from each set of five OT questions will be computational.

- Although the questions will be scenario based not all of the questions will rely on details in the scenario. For example, a scenario includes reference to impairment and one or both of the non-computational questions require knowledge of the relevant accounting standard with no specific application to the scenario.

- Each OT question is independent and therefore can be answered in any order.

- As for Section A, ensure that you select an answer for every part of every question; there is no negative marking.

Section C

Numerical Requirements

- Before starting a computation, picture your route. Do this by noting down the steps you are going to take and imagining the layout of your answer.

- Write clearly in **black** ink and leave space.

- A columnar layout is often appropriate and it helps to avoid mistakes and is easier for the marker to follow.

- Include all your workings and **cross-reference** them to the face of your answer.

- If you are not sure how to interpret something in the question then state your assumed interpretation.

- If you later notice a mistake in your answer, show the correction but it is *not* worthwhile spending time amending the consequent effects of it. The marker will *not* penalise you for errors caused by an earlier mistake.

- If you cannot perform a particular calculation but it is needed in a later step, make a sensible guess and continue (e.g. if necessary, state an assumed return on capital employed and use this assumed figure when analysing the results of a company).

Written Requirements

Planning

- Read the requirement carefully to identify exactly what is required and how many separate points you are being asked to address.

- Note down *relevant* thoughts on your plan—this may be on the question paper.

- Give your plan a structure that you can follow when you write up the answer.

Presentation

- Use headings and subheadings to give your answer structure and to make it easier to read.
- Use short paragraphs for each point that you are making.
- Separate paragraphs by leaving a line of space between each.
- Write legibly using a good-quality **black** pen.
- Use bullet points where this seems appropriate (e.g. for a list of advantages/ disadvantages). However, each bullet point *must* read on from an introduction to the list or be complete in itself. You must not write in "note form".

Style

- Long philosophical debate does not impress markers.
- More points briefly explained tend to score higher marks than just one or two points explained in detail.
- Ensure your comments are relevant to the specifics of the scenario. For example, inventory turnover is likely to be irrelevant to a company which provides services rather than goods.
- Appropriate comments on amounts that have been calculated incorrectly will be given credit.
- If you could not complete the calculations required for comment then *assume* an answer to the calculations. As long as your comments are consistent with a sensible assumption (e.g. it must not contradict information in the question) you will be awarded the marks for the comments.
- As you write, refer back to the requirement to ensure that you are addressing it. "Knowledge dumping" on a topic will not earn any marks if it does not address the requirement.

EXAMINATION TECHNIQUE—COMPUTER-BASED EXAM

Many of the comments made above regarding paper-based exams also apply to CBEs, in particular the points on time allocation and how generally to approach the questions in each section. However there are some important differences in the OT question types used in CBEs and how responses to long-form questions should be constructed.

OT Types

In addition to single-answer multiple choice question type, the CBE will also contain OT questions drawn from the following types:

- Multiple response—more than one correct answer
- Pull down list—drop down menu
- Fill in the blank—number entry
- Hot area—selecting area(s) in an image
- Hot spot—selecting one point in an image
- Drag and drop—matching

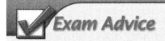 Exam Advice

Illustrations of all the types relevant to this exam can be found in Becker's *Objective Test Question Practice* booklet which is also included in Becker's *Revision Question Bank*.

Constructed Response Questions

Although the scenarios and requirements will be the same as for the paper-based exam, candidates must construct their answers using either a:

- blank spreadsheet;
- blank word processing document;
- pre-formatted spreadsheet; or
- template.

The most common forms of input will be a blank spreadsheet or blank word processing document.

Answers to these questions will be marked by subject matter experts and therefore workings for computational requirements must be shown. However, no marks are awarded for formatting and hence a candidate can focus on the content of an answer rather than how it looks.

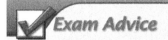

When attempting long-form questions during your revision try out the constructed response workspace referenced at the end of this section to input your answer.

CBE Functionality

During the live exam the following online functionality will include:

- Timer—with a warning when only 15 minutes remain.
- Scratch pad—although the exam centre will also provide physical note paper. The scratch pad/physical notes will **not** be marked.
- Symbols—for selection of currency symbols.
- A calculator with standard and scientific modes—candidates can also bring a physical calculator to the exam.
- Help/Formulae/Tables—which include a guide to the spreadsheet and word processing functions.
- Navigator/Item Review Screen—shows each question's status as:
  - "Complete"—however this does not guarantee that all parts of a question have been completed.
  - "Incomplete"—the question has been viewed but not attempted.
  - "Unseen"—the question has not been viewed.
  - "Flagged for review"—where the candidate has used the flag function.

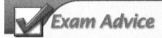

You are strongly urged to use the following ACCA resources that are available to help candidates familiarise themselves with the CBE style and functionality in preparation for the exam:

- Your Guide to ACCA CBEs (pdf and video);
- Full specimen exam;
- Extra constructed response questions;
- Constructed response workspace.

All are available at www.accaglobal.com/uk/en/student/exam-support-resources/ fundamentals-exams-study-resources/f7/specimen-exams.html

xix

International Financial Reporting Standards

FOCUS

This session covers the following content from the *ACCA Study Guide.*

A. The Conceptual and Regulatory Framework for Financial Reporting

3. Regulatory framework

a) Explain why a regulatory framework is needed, also including the advantages and disadvantages of IFRS over a national regulatory framework. ☐

b) Explain why accounting standards on their own are not a complete regulatory framework. ☐

d) Describe the IASB's standard setting process, including revisions to and interpretations of Standards. ☐

e) Explain the relationship of national standard setters to the IASB in respect of the standard setting process. ☐

Session 1 Guidance

■ **Read** through this session carefully, taking into account why the IASB was created and its standing today in the world of financial reporting.

■ **Keep** up-to-date on the IASB's work plan by regularly visiting the IASB website www.iasb.co.uk (s.2.4).

(continued on next page)

VISUAL OVERVIEW

Objective: To introduce sources of authority in international financial reporting.

ACCOUNTING PRINCIPLES
- What is GAAP?
- Sources of GAAP
- Statute and Standards
- European Union
- IFRS v Local GAAP

IASB
- Background
- Objectives
- Standard Setting
- Projects and Work Plan

IFRS
- GAAP Hierarchy
- General Purpose Financial Statements
- International Harmonisation

Session 1 Guidance

▉ **Understand** how the IASB functions and its role in harmonising accounting throughout the world (s.3.3).

▉ **Note** that all listed companies within the European Union (EU) are now required to file their consolidated accounts under IFRS.

1   Accounting Principles

1.1   What is GAAP?

- GAAP (generally accepted accounting principles) is a general term for a set of financial accounting standards and reporting guidelines used to prepare accounts in a given environment.*
- The term may or may not have legal authority in a given country.
- It is a dynamic concept. It changes with time in accordance with changes in the business environment.

1.2   Sources of GAAP

1.2.1   Regulatory Framework

- The body of rules and regulations, from whatever source, which an entity must follow when preparing accounts in a particular country for a particular purpose, for example:
  - Statute (e.g. Companies Acts)
  - Accounting standards.
- Statements issued by professional accounting bodies which lay down rules on accounting for different issues, for example:
  - International Financial Reporting Standards (IFRSs)
  - Financial Reporting Standards (UK FRSs)
  - Financial Accounting Standards (US FASs).

1.2.2   Other Sources

- Best practice, that is, methods of accounting developed by companies in the absence of rules in a specific area.
- Industry groups, such as:
  - The Oil Industry Accounting Committee (OIAC)
  - British Bankers' Association (BBA).

1.3   Role of Statute and Standards

- Some countries have a very legalistic approach to drafting financial statements. The legal rules are detailed and specific and the system is more geared to the production of a profit figure for taxation purposes.
- Some countries adopt an approach by which statute provides a framework of regulation and standards then fill in the blanks. For example in the UK:
  - **Statute:**   Companies Acts 2006;
  - **Standards:** Financial Reporting Standards (FRSs)
    Statements of Standard Accounting Practice (SSAPs)
    Urgent Issues Task Force consensus pronouncements (UITFs).
- Some countries have relatively little in the way of statute and rely largely on standards (e.g. the US).*
- At present there are a number of working parties trying to converge US GAAP and IFRS standards and eliminate or minimise the differences between them.

Commentary

*UK GAAP, US GAAP are more specific statements.

Key Point

The structure of US GAAP is very much rules-based, whereas that of IFRS is principles-based.

Commentary

*Although there is no accounting statute as such in the US, a body of the federal government called the Securities and Exchange Commission (SEC) oversees the accounting regulations issued by the profession. The SEC can veto accounting treatments and demand that regulation be enacted in new areas.

- The SEC now allows companies which prepare their accounts in accordance with IFRS to list their shares on US stock markets without providing a reconciliation to US GAAP.

1.4 Role of the European Union

- The common industrial policy of the EU calls for the creation of a unified business environment, including harmonisation of financial reporting.
- This is pursued though the issue of directives to member states. These are instructions to enact legislation in specified areas.
- New member states of the EU (and aspiring applicants) include the provisions of the EU directives into their own legislation in preparation for membership.
- The EU originally stated that IFRSs were compatible with EU directives. There is considerable divergence, however, in GAAP between member states.

 **Key Point**

Further to the IOSCO endorsement (International Organisation of Securities Commissions; see later), **all listed EU companies** were required to publish consolidated financial statements in compliance with IFRS with effect from 1 January 2005.

- Additionally, member states are allowed to extend the application of IFRSs to:
  - unlisted companies;
  - individual accounts of publicly traded companies; and
  - other companies and limited liability partnerships.

1.5 IFRS v Local GAAP

- Over the past 10 years, many countries have adopted IFRS as their accounting framework with local GAAP either disappearing or only being used for private entities.
- Other countries in which no local GAAP existed have adopted IFRS "upfront" and no form of local GAAP is required.
- There are advantages for countries adopting IFRS as their GAAP but, at the same time, there are disadvantages.

1.5.1 Advantages

✔ One international model for all.

✔ Improved quality and credibility provides access to global funds.

✔ Reduces training costs; accountants only need to learn one model.

✔ Recognised globally.

1.5.2 Disadvantages

✗ Cost to convert from local GAAP.

✗ Reluctance to change.

✗ May be a requirement for both statutory and IFRS accounts.

✗ Perception of difficulty.

2 IASB

2.1 Background

- The International Accounting Standards Board (IASB) was formed to take over the work of the International Accounting Standards Committee (IASC) in April 2001.
- The IASC was an independent private sector body set up by accountancy bodies in 1973.
- The IASC had complete autonomy in the setting of international accounting standards and in the issue of discussion documents on international accounting issues from 1981.

2.2 Objectives

- The IASB's Mission Statement sets out its objectives: To develop, in the public interest, a single set of high-quality, understandable and enforceable global reporting standards that require high-quality, transparent and comparable information in financial statements.*
    - to promote the use of rigorous application of those standards;
    - to take account of the needs of a range of sizes and types of entities in diverse economic settings (e.g. emerging economies); and
    - to promote and facilitate adoption of IFRSs through the convergence of national accounting standards and IFRS.

*In other words, the IASB's objective is to assist participants in the world's capital markets and other users of financial statements in making economic decisions.

2.3 Standard Setting

- IFRSs are developed through an international *due process* which involves:*
    - accountants, financial analysts and other users of financial statements;
    - the business community;
    - stock exchanges;
    - regulatory and legal authorities;
    - academics; and
    - other interested individuals and organisations throughout the world.

*The International Forum of Accounting Standard Setters (IFASS) (formerly known as National Standard-setters, NSS) is a grouping of national accounting standard-setters from around the world, plus other organisations that have a close involvement in financial reporting issues.

▦ Due process normally involves the following steps (those in bold are required under the terms of the IFRS Foundation's Constitution):

> Identification and review of associated issues and consideration of the application of the Framework to the issues.

> Study of national accounting requirements and practice and an exchange of views with national standard setters.

> **Consultation with the IFRS Advisory Council about adding the topic to the IASB's agenda.**

> Formation of an advisory ("working") group to advise the IASB.

> Publishing a discussion document ("paper", i.e. DP) for public comment.

> **Publishing an exposure draft (ED) for public comment.***

> **Consideration of all comments received within the comment period.**

> If considered desirable, holding a public hearing and conducting field tests.

> **Approval of a standard by at least 10 votes of the IASB.***

*Commentary

*A basis for conclusions is usually included within an ED and the published standard.

*Commentary

*Any dissenting opinions ("alternative views") of IASB board members must be included within an ED and the published standard. The basis of the IASB's conclusions, which summarises the Board's considerations, is also published for comment.

2.3.1 Discussion Papers

▦ The IASB may develop and publish discussion documents, usually called discussion papers, for public comment.

▦ A discussion paper:

- sets out the problem, the scope of the project and the financial reporting issues;
- discusses research findings and relevant literature; and
- presents alternative solutions to the issues under consideration and the arguments and implications relative to each.

▦ Following the receipt and review of comments, the IASB develops and publishes an exposure draft, which is also for public comment.

2.3.2 Exposure Draft

▓ An exposure draft invites comment on any aspect of specific questions and the proposed IFRS.

▓ It sets out the proposed standards and transitional provisions.

2.3.3 Voting

Key Point

The publication of a Standard, an exposure draft or a final IFRIC interpretation requires approval by 10 of the IASB's 16 members (nine if fewer members are sitting).

▓ All other decisions, including the issue of a discussion paper, require a simple majority of the IASB members present at a meeting (which must be attended by at least 60% of the members).

2.3.4 Comment Period

▓ Within the IASB's constitution, the comment period is for a "reasonable period".*

▓ Typically this is for 90 or 120 days. The minimum comment period for an exposure draft is 60 days.

2.4 Projects and Work Plan

2.4.1 Work Plan

▓ The IASB's current work plan includes:

  ● the Conceptual Framework; and
  ● principles of disclosure.

▓ The IASB now also issues an annual improvement standard which is intended to deal with non-urgent, minor amendments to standards. The changes are split into two types, those resulting in accounting changes and those which are terminology or editorial changes.

2.4.2 Public Information

▓ The aim of the IASB is to make its deliberations, activities and intentions as transparent and open as possible.

▓ Extensive information on the IASB and its activities is available on the IASB's website. This includes all discussion documents, exposure drafts, public comments, current activities and timetables of IASB and IFRS IC meetings.

▓ IASB and IFRS IC meetings are open to the public and may be received as a webcast through the IASB website.

▓ IASB Update and IFRS IC Update are issued after every IASB and IFRS IC meeting detailing the issues discussed and the conclusions reached.

▓ Various publications are issued from time to time to assist in the understanding of the work of the IASB and in IFRS.*

*Commentary

*A "reasonable period" must allow, for example, for the translation of documents.

Exam Advice

The improvements standard is not an examinable document in its own right.

*Commentary

*An example publication, "IFRS—A Briefing for Chief Executives, Audit Committees and Boards of Directors provides summaries of all current IFRSs in "non-technical language".

3   International Financial Reporting Standards

Key Point

IFRSs are a major international GAAP. They are widely used and accepted as a basis for the preparation of financial statements across many jurisdictions.

3.1   GAAP Hierarchy

*Commentary

- In descending order of authoritativeness:
    - IFRS, including any appendices that form part of the Standard*
    - Interpretations
    - Appendices to an IFRS that do not form part of the Standard
    - Implementation guidance issued by the IASB.
- All Standards and Interpretations issued under the previous constitution (i.e. IASs and SICs) continue to be applicable unless and until they are amended or withdrawn.

*The term *IFRSs* includes all standards and interpretations approved by the IASB and IASs and SICs issued by the IASC.

3.2   General Purpose Financial Statements

- IFRSs apply to the published financial statements of all profit-oriented entities (i.e. those engaged in commercial, industrial and financial activities).
- Entities may be corporate or organised in other forms (e.g. mutual cooperatives or partnerships). IFRSs may also be appropriate to not-for profit activities, government business enterprises and other public sector entities.
- IFRSs apply to all "general purpose financial statements" (i.e. those aimed at the common information needs of a wide range of users).
- IFRSs apply to both individual entity and consolidated financial statements.
- Any limitation on the applicability of specific IFRSs is made clear in the "scope" section to the standard.
- An IFRS applies from a date specified in the standard and is not retroactive unless indicated to the contrary.
- Some standards give a choice of accounting policies:
    - IAS 16 *Property, Plant and Equipment* allows assets to be subsequently measured using a cost or revaluation model (*Session 7*).
    - IFRS 3 *Business Combinations* allows non-controlling interest to be measured in one of two ways (*Session 22*).

3.3   Role in International Harmonisation

- The IASB has had considerable influence on the harmonisation of financial reporting:
    - through adoption by multinationals and local regulators; and
    - through working with the International Organisation of Securities Commissions (IOSCO).

3.3.1 Adoption

▨ IFRSs are used:

- as national requirements or as the basis for national requirements;
- as an international benchmark for countries developing their own requirements;
- by regulatory authorities and companies; and
- by large multinationals for the purpose of raising finance on international capital markets.

3.3.2 IOSCO

▨ The members of the International Organisation of Securities Commissions are securities commissions and other stock exchange regulators. Harmonisation of financial reporting standards has been high on IOSCO's agenda for many years.

▨ In 1993, IOSCO agreed a list of core standards needed for use in financial statements for listing purposes.

▨ Although many were already dealt with by IASs, the IASC needed to amend some existing standards, complete existing projects and start new ones (e.g. on financial instruments). This was IASC's "core program".

▨ The "core program" was completed in 1999 and in 2000, IOSCO endorsed the "IASC 2000 standards" for use in the preparation of financial statements for cross-border offerings and listings.

▨ This endorsement meant that IOSCO recommended that its members allow entities quoted on the stock exchanges of the world to adopt IFRS for filing purposes. (It was not binding.)

3.3.3 Use Around the World

▨ More than 120 countries are reported to be either permitting or requiring the use of IFRS, for example:

- Bahrain, Chile, Georgia and Guatemala—all listed companies, including domestic, **must** follow IFRS.
- European Union, European Economic Area member states— all domestic listed companies were required to adopt IFRS on or before 1 January 2005.

▨ IFRS financial statements are not currently permitted in, for example, China, Pakistan, Iran, Egypt or Indonesia. However, China has substantially converged national standards to IFRS.*

*The range and extent of use of IFRS varies around the world. Clearly this is constantly changing.

3.3.4 Convergence

▨ The IASB Constitution envisages a "partnership" between the IASB and National Standard Setters (NSSs) as they work together to achieve the convergence of accounting standards world-wide.*

▨ Convergence is a gradual process by which local GAAP approaches and is replaced with IFRS. As a step-by-step transition process it:

- gives more time for preparation; and
- reduces the potentially negative effect on companies trading their shares.

*NSSs include the accounting standards boards of Australia (AASB), Germany (DRSC), UK (ASB) and US (FASB).

- The main effects on financial statements of adopting IFRS include:
  - greater use of fair value as a measurement basis;
  - considerably greater disclosure; and
  - the need for more narrative to explain its complexities.
- Major areas of differences between local GAAP and IFRS may be classified, for example, between those which are:
  - fully related to day-to-day accounting (e.g. IAS 16 *Property, Plant and Equipment*);
  - partially related to day-to-day accounting (e.g. IAS 19 *Employee Benefits*); and
  - related to consolidation (e.g. IFRS 3 *Business Combinations*).

Summary

- IFRS is a principles-based set of accounting standards. They are widely used for the preparation of financial statements across many jurisdictions.

- IFRSs apply to the published financial statements of all profit-oriented entities.

- All listed EU companies were required to publish consolidated financial statements in compliance with IFRS with effect from 1 January 2005.

- Recently, many countries have adopted IFRS as their accounting framework with local GAAP either disappearing or used only for private entities.

- Publication of a Standard, exposure draft or final IFRIC requires approval by 10 of the IASB's 16 members.

Session 1 Quiz

Estimated time: 15 minutes

1. State two sources of GAAP. (1.2)
2. Give three advantages to countries adopting IFRS. (1.5)
3. State the objectives of the IASB as set out in its mission statement. (2.2)
4. State the purpose of a discussion paper. (2.3.1)
5. State how long the comment period is for an exposure draft of a new accounting standard (IFRS). (2.3.4)
6. State how long the comment period is for an exposure draft of a new IFRS. (2.3.4)
7. State the GAAP hierarchy. (3.1)
8. Name the body that the acronym IOSCO stands for. (3.3)

Study Question Bank

Estimated time: 25 minutes

Priority		Estimated Time	Completed
Q1	Standard Setting Process	25 minutes	

Conceptual Framework

FOCUS

This session covers the following content from the *ACCA Study Guide.*

A. The Conceptual and Regulatory Framework for Financial Reporting

1. The need for a conceptual framework and the characteristics of useful information

a) Describe what is meant by a conceptual framework for financial reporting.

b) Discuss whether a conceptual framework is necessary and what an alternative system might be.

c) Discuss what is meant by relevance and faithful representation and describe the qualities that enhance these characteristics.

e) Discuss what is meant by understandability and verifiability in relation to the provision of financial information.

f) Discuss the importance of comparability and timeliness to users of financial statements.

2. Recognition and measurement

a) Define what is meant by "recognition" in financial statements and discuss the recognition criteria.

b) Apply the recognition criteria to:
   i)   assets and liabilities
   ii) income and expenses

c) Explain the following measures and compute amounts using:
   i)   historical cost
   ii) current cost
   iii) net realisable value
   iv) present value of future cash flows
   v)   fair value

d) Discuss the advantages and disadvantages of the use of historical cost accounting.

e) Discuss whether the use of current value accounting overcomes the problems of historical cost accounting.

f) Describe the concept of financial and physical capital maintenance and how this affects the determination of profits.

3. Regulatory framework

c) Distinguish between a principles-based and a rules-based framework and discuss whether they can be complementary.

C. Analysing and Interpreting Financial Statements

2. Calculation and interpretation of accounting ratios and trends to address users' and stakeholders' needs

e) Discuss how the interpretation of current value based financial statements would differ from those using historical cost-based accounts.

VISUAL OVERVIEW

Objective: To set out the concepts underlying the preparation and presentation of financial statements for external users.

PURPOSE AND SCOPE
- Purpose
- Principles v Rules
- Scope
- Financial Statements
- Application
- Users and Information Needs
- The Future

GENERAL PURPOSE FINANCIAL REPORTING
- Objective and Usefulness
- Limitations
- Financial Statements
- Going Concern

QUALITATIVE CHARACTERISTICS
- "Economic Phenomena"
- Fundamental Characteristics
- Relevance
- Faithful Representation
- Enhancing Characteristics
- Cost Constraint

ELEMENTS OF FINANCIAL STATEMENTS
- Definitions
- Recognition
- Measurement Bases

CONCEPTS OF CAPITAL AND CAPITAL MAINTENANCE
- Historical Cost
- Capital
- Capital Maintenance
- Analysing Accounts
- Current Value Accounting

FAIR VALUE
- Background
- Terminology
- Non-financial Assets
- Valuation Techniques
- Hierarchy of Inputs
- Disclosure

Session 2 Guidance

■ **Understand** the importance of the conceptual framework (s.1).

■ **Learn** the fundamental characteristics of useful information. (s.3.2).

■ **Know** the definitions of elements given in the Framework (s.4.1).

■ **Apply** the recognition criteria to elements that should be included in the financial statements (s.4.2).

■ **Learn** the hierarchy of inputs is applied in the fair valuation process (s.6.5).

■ **Read** the technical article "The need for and an understanding of the conceptual framework".

1 Purpose and Scope

1.1 Purpose

- Primarily, the purpose of the Framework is to assist the Board of IASB in:
  - developing future IFRSs and reviewing existing IFRSs; and
  - promoting harmonisation of regulations by providing a basis for reducing the number of alternative accounting treatments permitted by IFRSs.
- Other purposes are:
  - to assist **national standard-setting bodies** in developing national standards;
  - to assist **preparers** of financial statements in applying IFRSs and in dealing with topics which have yet to form the subject of an IFRS;
  - to assist **auditors** in forming an opinion as to whether financial statements conform with IFRSs;
  - to assist **users** of financial statements in interpreting information contained in financial statements prepared in conformity with IFRSs; and
  - to provide those who are interested in the work of IASB with information about how IFRSs are formulated (published in a "basis of conclusion").*

> ***Commentary**
>
> *In short, the Framework provides a conceptual foundation for the preparation and appraisal of accounting standards.

1.2 Principles v Rules

> **Key Point**
>
> A conceptual framework lays down the building blocks for the accounting standards.
>
> The IASB's Framework sets out the principles of how to account for transactions and events without being too prescriptive in giving rules.

- Those using US GAAP follow a rules-based set of regulations (i.e. a rule for every type of transaction). If there is no rule for a particular transaction then a new rule is prescribed.*
- Under a principles-based conceptual framework there are no strict rules but a set of guidelines to assist in the preparation and understanding of financial statements.
- A conceptual framework is a relatively new concept in accounting. Before such frameworks existed there was basically nothing to bind together the entire system of financial reporting.*
- The alternative to a conceptual framework is a formal set of rules for every transaction. The problem with such a system is that people will try to circumvent those rules. In financial accounting and reporting this is known as "creative accounting".

> ***Commentary**
>
> *Most other GAAPs have some similar form of conceptual framework. For example, US GAAP has a conceptual framework (even though it is rules based). UK GAAP calls its framework a "Statement of Principles".
>
> *Without a conceptual framework, inconsistencies in accounting practices made it extremely difficult to make comparisons between entities or even within a single entity over more than one accounting period.

- Although consistency might be improved by applying a rigid set of rules, the system would require a new rule for every new transaction. The new rule would be independent of other rules and might conflict with existing rules for similar transactions.
- Using a conceptual framework allows a degree of flexibility and interpretation by the user but ensures that the user stays within the bounds of the framework.
- The IASB's Framework defines the elements of financial statements and the characteristics which should be embodied in those financial statements.

1.3   Scope

- Objective of financial statements
- Underlying assumption
- Qualitative characteristics of useful information
- Definition, recognition and measurement of elements
- Concepts of capital and capital maintenance.

1.4   Financial Statements

1.4.1   Included

- Statement of financial position
- Statement of profit or loss and other comprehensive income
- Statement of changes in equity
- Statement of changes in financial position (e.g. a statement of cash flows)
- Integral notes, other statements and explanatory material.

1.4.2   Not Included

- Reports by directors
- Statements by chairman
- Discussion and analysis by management and similar items included in a financial or annual report.

1.5   Application

- The Framework applies to financial statements of all commercial, industrial and business reporting entities, whether public or private.

1.6   Users and Their Information Needs

Users	Information Needs
Investors and their advisers	• Risk and return of investment: — for decision-making (buy, hold or sell?) — to assess ability to pay dividends.
Employees and their representatives	• Stability and profitability of employers. • Ability to provide remuneration, retirement benefits and employment opportunities.
Lenders	• Whether loans and interest will be paid when due.
Suppliers and other trade creditors	• Whether amounts owing will be paid when due.
Customers	• Continuance—important for long-term involvement with, or dependence on, the entity.
Governments and their agencies	• Allocation of resources and, therefore, activities of entities. • Information to regulate activities, determine taxation policies and as the basis for national income and similar statistics.
Public	• Contribution to the local economy, including the number of employees and the patronage of local suppliers. • Trends and recent developments in prosperity and range of activities.

1.7   The Future

▓ The Framework was first published more than 30 years ago, and there are a number of areas where it conflicts with IFRS. In these cases, the standard always takes precedence over the framework document.

   The IASB is in the process of producing a new framework document. The project has been broken down into phases. In September 2010 the IASB completed Phase A of the project by publishing the "Objectives and Qualitative Characteristics" chapters of the new *Conceptual Framework for Financial Reporting*.

2   General Purpose Financial Reporting

2.1   Objective and Usefulness

▓ To provide information about the financial position, performance and changes in financial position of a reporting entity that is useful to a wide range of users in making economic decisions.

▓ To show the results of management's stewardship (i.e. accountability for resources entrusted to it).*

▓ Existing and potential investors, lenders and creditors ("primary users") mostly need to rely on published financial information, as they cannot obtain it directly.

***Commentary**

*"Management" in the Framework also encompasses any governing board.

2.2   Limitations

✗   Financial reports cannot meet all the information needs of primary users. Those users must therefore consider other sources of information (e.g. economic conditions, political events and industry outlooks).

✗   IFRSs are developed to meet the information requirements of primary users. Although other users may find them useful they do not specifically aim to meet their needs.

✗   Financial reports do not purport to show the value of the reporting entity.

✗   Financial reports are based largely on estimates, judgements and models.

2.3   Financial Position, Performance and Changes in Financial Position

2.3.1   Economic Resources, Claims and Changes

Financial reports provide information on an entity's financial position, its financial performance and the changes in its financial position.

This information enables users to evaluate:

   ● the ability of an entity to generate cash and cash equivalents; and

   ● the timing and certainty of their generation.*

*Commentary

*The statement of financial position provides information about "economic resources" and "claims" against the company. Information about the effects of transactions which change those resources and claims are provided in the other financial statements (e.g. a rights issue of shares in the statement of cash flows).

Financial Position	Financial Performance	Changes in Financial Position
Financial position is affected by: ● economic resources controlled; ● financial structure; ● liquidity and solvency; and ● capacity to adapt to changes.	In particular, profitability, which can be used to: ● predict capacity to generate cash flows from an existing resource base; and ● form judgements about effectiveness with which additional resources might be employed.	Used to: ● evaluate investing, financing and operating activities; ● assess ability to generate cash flows; and ● indicate how cash is obtained and spent and the cost of financing it.

STATEMENT OF FINANCIAL POSITION	STATEMENT OF PROFIT OR LOSS AND OTHER COMPREHENSIVE INCOME	STATEMENT OF CASH FLOWS

2.3.2 Accrual Accounting

Key Point

Financial reporting is reflected by accrual accounting as this provides a better basis for assessing performance than cash receipts and payments.

- Under accrual accounting, effects of transactions and other events are:
  - recognised when they occur, not as cash is received or paid;*
  - recorded in the accounting records and reported in the financial statements of the periods to which they relate.
- Financial statements prepared on the accrual basis inform users of obligations to pay cash in the future and of resources that represent cash to be received in the future.

2.4 Underlying Assumption of Going Concern

- There is only one "underlying assumption" of financial statements: going concern.

Key Point

Going concern is the assumption that an entity will continue in operation for the foreseeable future.

- Therefore, there is neither intention nor need to liquidate or curtail materially the scale of operations.*

***Commentary**

*The accrual basis gives rise to the "matching" concept—that expenses are recognised on the basis of a direct association between costs incurred and earning of income.

***Commentary**

*The going concern assumption, which concerns the basis of preparation, is presumed to apply unless users of financial statements are told otherwise (i.e. in the notes to the financial statements).

3 Qualitative Characteristics

3.1 "Economic Phenomena"

- "Economic phenomena" in the Framework refers to economic resources, claims against the entity and the effects on these of transactions, conditions and other events.

3.2 Fundamental Qualitative Characteristics

- Fundamental qualitative characteristics are **relevance** and **faithful representation**.
- Other enhancing characteristics are:
  - comparability;
  - verifiability;
  - timeliness; and
  - understandability.

Key Point

Qualitative characteristics of financial statements are the attributes which make information provided therein useful to primary users.

3.3   Relevance

- This quality concerns the decision-making needs of users. Relevance helps users:
  - to evaluate past, present or future events (i.e. has a predictive value); and
  - to confirm or correct their past evaluations (i.e. has a confirmatory value).*
- Relevance of information is affected by:

Its Nature	Materiality
• Nature alone may be sufficient to determine relevance.	• Depends on size of item or error judged in the specific circumstances of its omission or misstatement. • It provides a threshold or cut-off point rather than being a primary qualitative characteristic.

- Both nature and materiality may be important (e.g. amounts of inventories held in each main category).*

Commentary

*For example, the fact that Azure AG sold a property for $4 million is one piece of information. That it sold it to another company which is owned by Azure's chief executive officer is another piece of information.

Commentary

*Predictive and confirmatory values are inter-related (e.g. the same information may confirm a previous prediction and be used for a future prediction).

Definition

Materiality— information is material if its omission or misstatement could influence the economic decisions of users taken based on the financial statements.

3.4   Faithful Representation

- Useful information must represent faithfully what it purports to represent (or could be reasonably expected to represent).
- To faithfully represent the economic phenomena may mean that on occasions the financial statements must do more than just follow accounting standards. If a transaction is outside the scope of all standards the transaction still has to be reflected in the financial statements.*
- Faithful representation encompasses:
  - neutrality (i.e. free from bias);
  - completeness (within bounds of materiality and cost)— an omission can cause information to be false or misleading and thus unreliable; and
  - accuracy (i.e. free from error).*

Commentary

*There is no specific standard on accounting for a Van Gogh painting, but an entity must faithfully represent the fact that it has acquired a painting.

Commentary

*An earlier version of the framework emphasised the concept of "substance over form" (i.e. precedence of economic reality over legal form). This concept is now embedded in the characteristic of "faithful representation". IAS 8 still requires an entity to reflect the economic substance of a transaction when it differs to the legal form.

3.5 Enhancing Characteristics

3.5.1 Comparability

▦ Users need to be able to compare financial statements of:
  - an entity *through time*—to identify trends in financial position and performance; and
  - *different* entities—to evaluate relative financial position, performance and changes in financial position.

▦ Comparability requires *consistent* measurement and display of the financial effect of like transactions and other events.*

▦ An implication of this is that users must be informed of the accounting policies employed, any changes in those policies and the effects of such changes.

▦ Financial statements must show corresponding information for preceding periods.

*Consistent measurement, for example, means adopting the same initial measurement and subsequent measurement rules for intangible assets as for tangible assets.

3.5.2 Verifiability

▦ This means that knowledgeable, independent observers could reach a consensus that a particular representation has the fundamental quality of faithfulness.

▦ Verification may be:
  - direct (e.g. through physical inspection); or
  - indirect (e.g. using a model, formula or technique).*

*Verifiability relates not only to single point estimates but also to ranges of outcomes and related probabilities.

3.5.3 Timeliness

▦ Information needs to be available in time for users to make decisions.*

3.5.4 Understandability

▦ Users are assumed to have a reasonable knowledge of business and economic activities and accounting and a willingness to study information with reasonable diligence (i.e. they are expected to have a level of financial expertise).

▦ Information about complex matters should not be excluded on the grounds that it may be too difficult for certain users to understand.

*Older information is generally less useful (but may still be useful in identifying and assessing trends).

3.6 Cost Constraint

▦ The cost of providing information should not exceed the benefit obtained from it.

▦ This cost, though initially borne by the reporting entity, is ultimately borne by the users (e.g. through lower returns on their investment).

▦ Users also incur costs (e.g. in analysing and interpreting information).

▦ Benefits are most difficult to quantify and assess:
  - the better the quality of information, the better decision-making should be;
  - confidence in the efficiency of capital markets lowers the cost of capital.

4 Elements of Financial Statements

4.1 Terminology

Financial statement elements: the broad classes of the financial effects of transactions grouped according to their economic characteristics.

Asset:
- a resource *controlled* by the entity;*
- as a result of *past* events;
- from which *future economic benefits* are expected to flow.

Liability:
- a *present obligation* of the entity;*
- arising from past events;
- settlement of which is expected to result in an outflow of resources embodying economic benefits.

Equity:
- the residual interest;
- in the *assets* of the entity;
- after deducting all its *liabilities.**

Income:*
- increases in economic benefits during the accounting period;
- in the form of inflows (or enhancements) of assets or decreases of liabilities;
- which result in increases in equity;
- other than those relating to contributions from equity participants.

Expenses:
- decreases in economic benefits during the accounting period;
- in the form of outflows (or depletions) of assets or incurrences of liabilities;
- which result in decreases in equity;
- other than those relating to distributions to equity participants.

> ***Commentary**
>
> *An asset does not have to be owned to be controlled (e.g. an asset acquired under lease is controlled but not owned).
>
> *A possible obligation is not a recognised liability; it is contingent and will be disclosed in the financial statements.
>
> *Equity is defined in terms of other items in the statement of financial position; it amounts to the "balancing figure".

> ***Commentary**
>
> *The Framework defines assets, liabilities and equity, and the definitions for income and expenses follow on from those. Therefore, it may be said that the Framework considers the perspective of the statement of financial position.

Illustration 1 A Transaction and Elements Affected

An entity purchases, on credit, goods for resale.

- A liability is created:
  - Present obligation to repay the supplier.
  - Past event in purchasing the goods.
  - Outflow of economic benefits when the supplier is paid.
- The goods meet the definition of an asset:
  - Control the use of the goods.
  - Past event is the purchasing of the goods.
  - Inflow of economic benefits when the goods are sold.

The goods are then sold for cash.

- Cost of sale (an expense) is recognised as there has been a decrease in inventory assets.
- Income in the form of revenue is recognised from the sale of goods.
- Assets have increased in the form of the receipt of cash.

4.2 Recognition

4.2.1 Meaning of Recognition

- The process of incorporating in the statement of financial position or statement of profit or loss and other comprehensive income an item which meets the definition of an element and satisfies the criteria for recognition.*
- It involves the depiction of the item in words and by a monetary amount and the inclusion of that amount in the statement of financial position or statement of profit or loss and other comprehensive income totals.
- Items which satisfy the recognition criteria must be recognised.
- The failure to recognise such items is not rectified by disclosure of the accounting policies used nor by notes or explanatory material.

***Commentary**

*One factor to consider in assessing whether an item meets a definition of an element is "substance over form" (i.e. the underlying substance and economic reality, not merely legal form). For this reason, leases are generally treated as assets acquired (see *Session 14*).

4.2.2   Recognition Criteria*

- Items are recognised when it is probable that any future economic benefit associated with the item will flow to or from the entity; and
- The item has a cost or value that can be **measured** with reliability.

*An element may meet the definition of an element, but if it does not meet the two recognition criteria it cannot be included in the financial statements.

4.3   Measurement Bases

	Assets	**Liabilities**
Historical Cost	• The amount paid (or the fair value of the consideration given) to acquire them at the time of their acquisition. • Land is the best example of an asset measured at historical cost, and would be valued at the invoice price of the purchase.	• The amount received in exchange for the obligation.
Current Cost	• The amount which would have to be paid if the same or an equivalent asset were acquired currently. • A financial asset is a good example of an asset measured at current cost; its value would be based on the market price of the instrument.	• The undiscounted amount which would be required to settle the obligation currently.
Realisable (Settlement) Value	• The amount which could currently be obtained by selling the asset in an orderly disposal. • Inventory may be valued at net realisable value (see *Session 6*).	• At settlement values (i.e. the undiscounted amounts expected to be paid to satisfy the liabilities in the normal course of business).
Present Value	• Present discounted value of the future net cash inflows which the item is expected to generate in the normal course of business.	• Present discounted value of the future net cash outflows which are expected to be required to settle the liabilities in the normal course of business. • The liability element of a compound instrument is a good example of a liability measured at the present value of future cash flows (see *Session 18*).

5 Concepts of Capital and Capital Maintenance

5.1 Historical Cost Accounting

- Historically, accounting is based on what an item had cost (i.e. historical cost). As economies have advanced, however, there has been concern that historical cost accounting does not reflect the modern economics of today's transactions.

5.1.1 Advantages of Historical Cost

✔ Easy to understand and follow.

✔ Objective evidence of transactions.

✔ Used throughout the world.

5.1.2 Disadvantages of Historical Cost

✗ Current revenues are matched with historical costs.

✗ Value of the assets in the statement of financial position do not equate to the economic benefits to be earned from their use.

✗ Holding gains are not separated from operating gains. Holding gains are gains made merely by holding onto an asset.

Illustration 2 Holding and Operating Gain

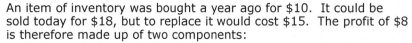

An item of inventory was bought a year ago for $10. It could be sold today for $18, but to replace it would cost $15. The profit of $8 is therefore made up of two components:

1. a holding gain of $5 ($15 − $10); and

2. an operating gain of $3 ($18 − $15).

✗ Historical cost accounting does not reflect the general rise in prices (inflation) which affects an economy.

5.2 Concepts of Capital*

5.2.1 Financial Concept

- Capital is synonymous with the *net assets* or *equity*.

5.2.2 Physical Concept

- Capital is regarded as the *productive capacity* based, for example, on units of output per day.

*Commentary

*This section of the old framework has still to be updated by the IASB.

5.3   Concepts of Capital Maintenance and the Determination of Profit

▨ The wealth of a company is measured by its ability to maintain a level of capital. A number of capital maintenance theories have been used by accountants over the past 40 years.

5.3.1   Financial Capital Maintenance

▨ Profit is earned only if the financial (or money) amount of the net assets at the end of the period exceeds the financial (or money) amount of net assets at the beginning of the period (after excluding any distributions to/contributions from owners during the period). There are two theories based on financial capital maintenance:

1. "Money" concept, which is historical cost accounting;

2. "Real term" concept, which considers the effect of a general level of inflation. This method is called Current Purchasing Power (CPP) accounting and in its simplest form would uplift asset, liability, revenue and cost figures to reflect levels of inflation in the economy.

5.3.2   Physical Capital Maintenance

▨ Profit is earned only if the physical productive capacity (or operating capability) at the end of the period exceeds the physical productive capacity at the beginning of the period (after excluding any distributions to/contributions from, owners during the period). Current Cost Accounting (CCA) is an accounting model used in the past to reflect changes in the operating capabilities of an entity. This method applies specific changes in value to each component of the operations of an entity.

▨ The effect of both real-term and physical capital maintenance concepts would be to reduce the level of distributable profits of an entity, taking account of either inflation or specific price-level changes. By reducing profit levels it insures that the capital of an entity is at least as much at the end of the year as it was at the beginning of the year.

Illustration 3 Current Cost Accounting

Start a period with one item of inventory which cost $200 and is sold for $250:

General inflation	5%
Specific inflation	10%

Capital Maintenance

	Financial capital		Operating capital
	Money	Real	
Net assets at end	250	250	250
Net assets at start	(200)	(210)	(220)
	50	40	30

Statement of Profit or Loss

Revenue	250	250	250
Cost of sales	(200)	(200)	(200)
	50	50	50
Inflation adjustment	**—**	**(10)**	**(20)**
	50	40	30

Statement of Financial Position

Total net assets	250	250	250
Shareholders' funds:			
B/fwd	200	200	200
Inflation reserve	**—**	**10**	**20**
Retained earnings	50	40	30
	250	250	250

Analysis

- Capital maintenance and holding gains are concepts which are inter-linked.
- If a company fails to consider inflation it may make decisions which will harm it. This company could pay out $50 as a dividend. This would erode its capital base in real terms.
- Even if a company does include the effects of general inflation (in this case by setting aside 5% x 200 = $10 as a "non-distributable" reserve), but suffers specific inflation in excess of general inflation, it will erode its capacity to operate.

5.4 Analysing Accounts

- When analysing accounts, care must be taken in respect of the base information being used. Accounts based on historical costs will give totally different results than those based on current costs.

 **Key Point**

In times of rising prices, profitability will be higher using historical cost accounting rather than current cost accounting; current cost accounting seeks to eliminate any holding gains.

- The use of CPP accounting eliminates the effect of inflation from the base figures, and uses a common time-based unit of currency.

- Inventory holding days is affected by whether inventory is measured on historical or current costs.

5.5   Is Current Value Accounting the Answer?

- Over the past 30 years, the accounting profession has attempted to introduce some form of current value accounting model.*

- In the 1970s and 1980s, UK GAAP had a compulsory standard requiring accounts to incorporate a current cost accounting model into their financial statements, as well as their historical cost accounts.

- Implementing current value accounting models has invariably caused problems and has never achieved the backing of the preparers and analysts who prefer the more conservative approach of historical cost accounting.

- Although some current values are easily obtained (e.g. replacement cost of inventory), the calculation of "value-in-use" (see *Session 13*) can be very subjective (and therefore less reliable). Valuations may be almost impossible to verify and comparisons between companies made even more difficult. The majority of users may not understand what the figures represent.

- Under IFRS today, there is no formal model of current cost accounting; however, a number of standards do require some assets and liabilities to be measured at fair value, such as financial instruments. Some accountants believe that fair value accounting is current cost accounting by another name.

- Although current value accounting seeks to provide more relevant financial information than historical cost accounting, it opens up new problems and issues which are probably greater than those under historical cost accounting.

*Commentary

*For example, before 2005 there was a voluntary International Accounting Standard on using a form of CPP accounting.

6   Fair Value

6.1   Background

- When the Framework document was first issued, the concept of fair value was not widely used in accounting and so was not incorporated into the Framework as a measurement basis.

- Over the past 10 to 15 years the use of fair value in accounting has become far more widespread, with many IFRSs now requiring or allowing the use of fair value.

- When the IASB issued new standards which required or allowed the use of fair value, there was no consistency between each standard as to how fair value should be measured.

- In May 2011, the IASB issued IFRS 13 *Fair Value Measurement*, which prescribes *how* fair value should be measured, when the use of fair value is required or permitted by another standard.*

Key Point

IFRS 13 does **not** specify *when* an entity should use fair value, but *how* it is used.

*Commentary

*If an entity holds investment property, it is IAS 40 which allows the use of fair value but IFRS 13 which specifies how fair value is measured.

6.2   Terminology

Fair value: the price which would be received to sell an asset or paid to transfer a liability in an orderly transaction between market participants at the measurement date.*

- When measuring fair value all characteristics of the asset (or liability) which market participants would take into account should be reflected in the valuation. This could include the condition or location of the asset and any restrictions on its use.

- The definition is market based and is not entity specific. It reflects factors which market participants would apply to the asset (or liability), not the factors which a specific entity would necessarily apply.

Active market: a market in which the transaction for the asset or liability takes place with sufficient frequency and volume to provide pricing information on an ongoing basis.

Highest and best use: the use of a non-financial asset by market participants which would maximise the value of the asset or the group of assets and liabilities within which the asset would be used.

6.3   Non-financial Assets

- **Fair value** measurement of a non-financial asset (e.g. an investment property) reflects its highest and best use.

- **Highest and best use** takes into account:*
  - the use which is physically possible;
  - what is legally allowed; and
  - the financial feasibility of using the asset.

- Taking account of the **highest and best use** may need to assume that the asset will be combined with, or complement, other assets (or liabilities) available to market participants.*

6.4   Valuation Techniques

- IFRS 13 assumes that the transaction will occur in the principal market for the asset (or liability), if one exists. If there is no principal market then the standard requires the valuation to be based on the most advantageous market.

- Unless proved otherwise, the market place will be presumed to be the one in which the entity transacts on a regular basis.

- The objective of the standard is to estimate the price at which the asset (or liability) could exit the entity in an orderly transaction. Three common techniques which would give an accurate estimate are considered.

6.4.1   Market Approach

- This approach uses prices, and other information, generated in a market place which involves identical or comparable assets or liabilities.

6.4.2   Cost Approach

- This approach reflects the amount which would be required to replace the service capacity of the asset (current replacement cost).

*The definition of **fair value** is based on an "exit price" (i.e. taking the asset or liability out of the entity) rather than an "entry price" (i.e. bringing the asset or liability into the entity).

*_Highest and best use_ does not reflect illegal activities in the use of the asset but does reflect what is economically viable (considering any financial constraints).

*If an entity uses a stand-alone asset but its best use would be in combination with other assets, **fair value** is based on this best use (i.e. irrespective of its current use.

6.4.3   Income Approach

▧ This approach considers future cash flows and discounts those cash flows to a current value. Models which follow an income approach include:

 ◦ present value; and
 ◦ option pricing models (e.g. Black-Scholes-Merton).

6.5   Hierarchy of Inputs

▧ The techniques used to estimate fair values should maximise observable inputs wherever possible. The standard lays down a hierarchy (order) with the intention of increasing consistency of usage and comparability in the measurement of fair values and their related disclosures.

6.5.1   Level 1 Inputs

▧ These are quoted prices in active markets for identical assets or liabilities which the entity can access at the measurement date.*

6.5.2   Level 2 Inputs

▧ These are inputs other than quoted prices which are observable for the asset or liability, either directly or indirectly.

▧ These would include prices for similar, but not identical, assets or liabilities which were then adjusted to reflect the factors specific to the measured asset or liability.

6.5.3   Level 3 Inputs

▧ These are unobservable inputs for the asset or liability.

▧ For example:

 ◦ a valuation of a decommissioning liability assumed in a business combination;
 ◦ use of internal data as part of the calculation of cash flows relating to a cash-generating unit.

6.6   Disclosure

▧ The disclosure requirements of IFRS 13 are very extensive and depend on whether level 1, 2 or 3 inputs are being used in the measurement techniques. The disclosures required are of a quantitative and qualitative nature.

▧ The standard also distinguishes between measurements of a recurring nature and those of a non-recurring nature.

▧ Disclosures include the following:

 ◦ the reason for using fair value;
 ◦ the level of hierarchy used;
 ◦ description of techniques used for level 2 or 3 inputs;
 ◦ for non-financial assets, disclosure is required if the highest and best use differs from what the entity is using; and
 ◦ for level 3 inputs, a reconciliation of the opening and closing balances and any amounts included in profit or loss for the period.

Exam Advice

Option pricing is not examinable in F7.

*Commentary

*Level 1 inputs should be used wherever possible. The use of level 3 inputs should be kept to a minimum.

Exam Advice

The disclosures listed here are only a selection of those required as the examiner is not expected to require extensive knowledge in this area.

Session 2 Quiz
Estimated time: 20 minutes

1. Name the FOUR components of a set of financial statements, as laid out in the Framework. (1.4)

2. The Framework mentions various user groups for whom financial statements are prepared. One such group is employees. Name the other SIX user groups. (1.6)

3. The objective of a set of financial statements is to show information about three areas to the users, to enable them to make economic decisions. List the THREE areas. (2)

4. Describe what the Framework refers to as "economic phenomena". (3.1)

5. Explain the elements of financial statements. (4.1)

6. Define "asset" in the Framework. (4.1)

7. List the FOUR fundamental qualitative characteristics which should apply to the information shown in the financial statements. (3.2)

8. Name the TWO criteria which must be satisfied for an item to be recognised (included) in the financial statements (the recognition criteria). (4.2)

9. Describe TWO advantages and TWO disadvantages of historical cost accounting. (5.1)

10. Define fair value. (6.2)

Study Question Bank
Estimated time: 30 minutes

Priority		Estimated Time	Completed
Q3	Laidlaw	30 minutes	
Additional			
Q2	Hughes and Custom Cars		

Summary

- Objectives of general purpose financial statements:
  - to provide information about the financial position, performance and changes in financial position; and
  - to show the results of stewardship/accountability of management.
- Financial statements reflect the underlying assumption that the entity is a *going concern*.
- There are **two fundamental** qualitative characteristics—*relevance* and *faithful representation*.
- There are **four enhancing** characteristics—comparability, verifiability, timeliness and understandability.
- Elements of financial statements are assets, liabilities, equity, income and expenses.
- Recognition means incorporating in the financial statements an item which meets the definition of an element and satisfies the recognition criteria:
  - probable future economic benefit; and
  - reliable measurement.
- Measurement involves assigning monetary amounts. Bases include:
  - historical cost (most common but often combined with other bases);
  - current cost;
  - net realisable (settlement) value; and
  - present value (discounted).
- IFRS 13 prescribes the techniques to be used for measuring fair values; it does not state when to use fair values.
- Level 1 inputs should be maximised and level 3 inputs minimised.

IAS 1 *Presentation of Financial Statements*

FOCUS

This session covers the following content from the *ACCA Study Guide.*

A. The Conceptual and Regulatory Framework for Financial Reporting

1. The need for a conceptual framework and the characteristics of useful information

d) Discuss whether faithful representation constitutes more than compliance with accounting standards. ☐

B. Accounting for Transactions in Financial Statements

9. Reporting financial performance

c) Indicate the circumstances where separate disclosure of material items of income and expense is required. ☐

D. Preparation of Financial Statements

1. Preparation of single entity financial statements

a) Prepare an entity's statement of financial position and statement of profit or loss and other comprehensive income in accordance with the structure and content prescribed within IFRS and with the accounting treatments as identified within syllabus areas A, B and C. ☐

b) Prepare and explain the contents and purpose of the statement of changes in equity. ☐

Session 3 Guidance

- **Understand** the need for faithful representation and how this is achieved (s.2.1–2.3) and the additional disclosure that is necessary when financial statements are prepared other than on a going concern basis (s.2.4).

- **Learn** the minimum line items which must be shown in the financial statements (s.4.5, s.5.2). The examiner may well ask you to produce a statement of profit or loss using either the "nature of expense" or "function of expense" method (s.5.5).

(continued on next page)

VISUAL OVERVIEW

Objective: To describe general purpose financial statements and to set out presentation considerations, guidelines for structure and minimum content requirements.

STRUCTURE AND CONTENT	FINANCIAL STATEMENTS	OVERALL CONSIDERATIONS
• "Disclosure" • Identification • Reporting Date and Period • Terminology	• IAS 1 • Representation • Objectives • Components • Supplementary Statements	• Faithful Representation • Emphasis • Departure From IFRS • Going Concern • Accrual Basis • Consistency • Materiality and Aggregation • Offsetting • Comparative Information

STATEMENT OF FINANCIAL POSITION	STATEMENT OF COMPREHENSIVE INCOME	STATEMENT OF CHANGES IN EQUITY	NOTES TO THE FINANCIAL STATEMENTS
• Current v Non-current • Current Assets • Current Liabilities • Overall Structure • Presenting Elements	• Presentation • Profit or Loss • Other Comprehensive Income • Material Items • Analysis of Expenses	• A Separate Statement • Structure • Reclassification	• Structure • Accounting Policies • Estimation Uncertainty

Session 3 Guidance

■ **Understand** what is meant by "offsetting" (s.2.8).

■ **Learn** the criteria for recognising assets and liabilities as current (s.4.2, s.4.3).

■ **Understand** what is presented in the statement of changes in equity and why (s.6).

1 Financial Statements

1.1 IAS 1

1.1.1 Objective

- To prescribe the content of general purpose financial statements to ensure comparability with:
  - the entity's own financial statements; and
  - financial statements of other entities.
- To achieve this the standard sets out:
  - overall considerations for the presentation;
  - guidelines for the structure; and
  - minimum requirements for content of financial statements.

1.1.2 General Purpose Financial Statements

- General purpose financial statements are those intended to meet the needs of users who are not in a position to demand reports tailored to specific information needs.
- The financial statements may be presented separately or in another public document (e.g. annual report or prospectus).

1.1.3 Application

- To financial statements of individual entities and consolidated financial statements of groups.
- To all types of entities, including banks, insurance and other financial institutions.
- To entities with a profit objective (including public sector business entities).

1.1.4 Terminology

- "IFRSs" is a generic term which encompasses all standards (IFRSs and IASs) and interpretations (IFRICs and SICs).
- "IAS", "IFRS", "IFRIC" and "SIC" are specific terms for individual pronouncements (e.g. IAS 2 *Inventory*).

1.2 Representation

- Financial statements are a *structured* financial representation of:
  - financial position of an entity; and
  - transactions undertaken by an entity.

1.3 Objectives of Financial Statements

 **Key Point**

The objective of financial statements is to provide information useful to a wide range of users in making economic decisions about:*

- financial position;
- performance; and
- cash flows.

 ***Commentary**

*The Framework (see *Session 2*) is also relevant to the objectives of financial statements.

- To show the results of management's stewardship.
- To meet this objective, financial statements provide information about an entity's:
  - assets;
  - liabilities;
  - equity;
  - income and expenses including gains and losses; and
  - cash flows.

1.4 Components

- A complete set of financial statements includes:*
  - statement of financial position;
  - statement of profit or loss and other comprehensive income;
  - a statement of changes in equity;
  - statement of cash flows;
  - accounting policies and explanatory notes.

1.5 Supplementary Statements

- Entities also may present additional information on a voluntary basis. For example:
  - Environmental reports
  - Value added statements
  - A review by management (management commentary) to include financial and other information.
- Such additional statements presented are **outside** the scope of IFRSs.

Commentary

*A complete set of financial statements should also include comparable figures for the previous period, meaning there will be two statements of financial position, etc. However, if an entity changes an accounting policy or amends a prior period error, then a third statement of financial position must be presented for comparison purposes.

2 Overall Considerations

2.1 Faithful Representation and Compliance With IFRSs

- Financial statements should "present fairly":
  - financial position;
  - financial performance; and
  - cash flows.
- Achieved by appropriate application of IFRSs (and any necessary additional disclosures).
- Inappropriate accounting treatments are *not* rectified by;
  - disclosure of accounting polices used; or
  - notes or explanatory material.

2.2 Emphasis

Key Point

In virtually all circumstances, fair presentation is achieved by **compliance** in all material respects with applicable IFRSs. Compliance with IFRSs must be **disclosed.**

▣ Fair presentation requires:

  ● selection and application of **appropriate accounting policies; and**

  ● presentation of information (including accounting policies) in a manner which provides relevant, reliable, comparable and understandable information.

▣ Additional disclosures when the requirements of IFRSs are insufficient to enable users to understand the effect of particular transactions on the financial position and performance of the entity.

▣ Where an IFRS is applied before its effective date, that fact must be disclosed.

2.3 Departure From IFRS

▣ In *extremely* rare circumstances, if compliance would be misleading, and therefore departure from a standard is necessary to achieve a fair presentation, the entity must disclose:*

  ● That management has concluded that the financial statements fairly present the entity's financial position, performance and cash flows.

  ● That it has complied in all material respects with applicable IFRSs except that it has departed from a standard in order to achieve a fair presentation.

  ● The standard from which the entity has departed, the nature of departure, including the treatment that the standard would require together with the reason why that treatment would be misleading in the circumstances and the treatment adopted.

  ● The financial effect of the departure on the entity's profit or loss, assets, liabilities, equity and cash flows for each period presented.

Commentary

*Departures from IFRS are often referred to as "true and fair override" (i.e. that a "true and fair" view takes precedence).

2.4 Going Concern

▣ It is management's responsibility:

  ● to assess the entity's ability to continue as a going concern (considering all information available for the foreseeable future);

  ● to prepare financial statements on a going concern basis (unless management considers that it is probable that the entity will be liquidated/cease trading); and

  ● to disclose material uncertainties which may affect the going concern concept.

▣ The degree of consideration depends on the facts in each case. If the entity has a history of profitable operation and ready access to financial resources, detailed analysis may not be required before a conclusion is reached.

▣ In other cases management may need to consider a wide range of factors, such as:

  ● current and expected future profitability;

  ● debt repayment schedules; and

  ● sources of finance.

▣ Foreseeable future is at least, but not limited to, 12 months from the end of the reporting period.

Key Point

That an entity is a going concern is the only underlying assumption (see *Session 2*).

▦ When financial statements are **not** prepared on a going concern basis, that fact must be disclosed, together with the basis on which the financial statements have been prepared and the reason for departing from the going concern concept.

2.5 Accrual Basis of Accounting

2.5.1 Concept

▦ Assets, liabilities, equity, income and expenses are:
- recognised when they occur (*not* as cash or its equivalent is received or paid); and
- recorded in the accounting records and reported in the financial statements of the periods to which they relate.

2.5.2 "Matching" Concept

▦ Expenses are recognised on the basis of a *direct association* between:
- costs incurred; and
- earning of specific items of income.

2.6 Consistency of Presentation

▦ Presentation and classification of items in financial statements should be retained from one period to the next.

▦ IFRS does allow for changes in presentation and/or classification but only in the following circumstances:
- The change will result in a more appropriate presentation (e.g. if there is a significant change in the nature of operations).
- A change is required by a financial reporting standard or an interpretation.

2.7 Materiality and Aggregation*

Definition

Materiality—omissions or misstatements of items are material if they could, individually or collectively, influence the economic decisions of users taken based on the financial statements. Materiality depends on the size and nature of the omission or misstatement judged in the surrounding circumstances. The size or nature of the item, or a combination of both, could be the determining factor.

▦ **Materiality** provides that the specific disclosure requirements of IFRSs need not be met if a transaction is not material.

Material Items	Immaterial Amounts
▦ Present separately in financial statements.	▦ Aggregate with amounts of similar nature or function (in the financial statements or the notes).
▦ Material items which have different characteristics should not be aggregated together.	▦ Need not be presented separately.

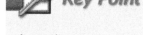
Key Point

An entity must prepare its financial statements (except the statement of cash flows) under the accrual basis of accounting.

***Commentary**

*Considerations apply to the financial statements as a whole; this includes the disclosure notes.

2.8   Offsetting

▨ Assets and liabilities, and income and expenses, cannot be offset unless another standard or interpretation requires or allows the use of offsetting.*

▨ Offsetting, except when the offset faithfully represents a transaction, would detract from the ability of users to understand the events which occurred and would inhibit the assessment of future cash flows.

▨ An allowance of bad or irrecoverable debts against receivables is not seen as offsetting.

▨ The standard does allow some netting off of items within the statement of profit or loss and other comprehensive income. For example:

  ⊙ Gains/losses on the sale of non-current assets are reported after deducting the carrying amount from the amount of consideration on disposal.

  ⊙ Expenditure related to a recognised provision, where reimbursement occurs from a third party, may be netted off against the reimbursement.

  ⊙ Gain/losses relating to a group of similar transactions will be reported on a net basis (e.g. foreign exchange gains and losses). Any material gain or loss should be reported separately.

Commentary

*IAS 12 *Income Taxes* requires a tax liability to be offset against a tax asset under certain conditions.

2.9   Comparative Information

▨ One year's prior period results must be included as part of current period financial statements for comparison purposes.

Numerical information in the previous period	Narrative and descriptive information in the previous period
■ DISCLOSE *unless* an IFRS permits/requires otherwise.	■ INCLUDE when relevant to understanding *current* period's financial statements (e.g. re legal disputes).

▨ When the presentation or classification of items in the financial statements is amended:

  ⊙ if practicable, restate comparatives and disclose the nature, amount and reason for restatement;

  ⊙ if impracticable, disclose the reason for not restating and the nature of the changes which would otherwise have been made.

▨ If the entity has changed an accounting policy or reflected a prior period error, then a third statement of financial position is presented as at the beginning of the prior financial year.

3 Structure and Content

3.1 "Disclosure"

▨ IAS 1 uses the term in a broad sense, encompassing items presented in each of the financial statements as well as in the notes to the financial statements.

3.2 Identification of Financial Statements

▨ Financial statements must be clearly identified and distinguished from other information in the same published document (e.g. annual report or prospectus).

3.2.1 Importance

▨ IFRSs apply only to the financial statements and not to other information so users must be able to distinguish information prepared using IFRSs from other information not subject to accounting requirements.

3.2.2 Information to Be Prominently Displayed (and Repeated Where Necessary)

▨ Component of the financial statements presented (e.g. statement of financial position).

▨ Name of reporting entity.

▨ Whether financial statements cover an individual entity or a group.

▨ End of reporting period or the period covered by the financial statements (as appropriate).

▨ Presentation currency.

▨ Level of precision used (e.g. 000, millions, etc).

3.3 Reporting Date and Period

▨ Financial statements should be presented at least annually.

▨ In exceptional circumstances where an entity's end of reporting period changes and the statements are presented for a period longer or shorter than a year, the entity discloses:

   ◦ the reason for using a period other than one year; and

   ◦ the fact that comparative amounts for the statement of profit or loss and other comprehensive income, changes in equity, statement of cash flows and related notes are **not** comparable.

3.4 Terminology

▨ The standard applies a terminology which is consistent with all other standards but it does not prohibit the use of other terms as long as the meaning is clear (e.g. non-current assets can still be termed "fixed" assets).

4 Statement of Financial Position

4.1 The Current/Non-current Distinction

▓ Current and non-current assets and current and non-current liabilities should be presented as separate classifications in the statement of financial position, unless a presentation based on liquidity order provides more relevant and reliable information. This may be the case for financial institutions.

▓ Whichever method is adopted, if a classification includes amounts which will be settled or recovered in less than 12 months and more than 12 months, the amounts more than 12 months must be disclosed.

▓ A separate classification:

- distinguishes net assets which are continuously circulating as working capital from those used in long-term operations;
- highlights assets expected to be realised within the current *operating cycle* and liabilities due for settlement in the same period.

▓ Other useful information:

- maturity dates of trade and other receivables and payables;
- inventories expected to be recovered more than one year from the end of the reporting period.

4.2 Current Assets

> ### Key Point
>
> An asset is classified as "current" when it satisfies **one** of the following criteria:
>
> ■ it is expected to be realised, or is intended for sale or consumption, in the normal course of the operating cycle; or
>
> ■ it is held primarily for trading purposes;
>
> ■ it is expected to be realised within 12 months of the end of the reporting period; or
>
> ■ it is cash or cash equivalent which is not restricted in use.

▓ There are two conceptual views of the term "current": the liquidity approach and the operating cycle approach.

▓ All other assets are classified as "non-current".

4.2.1 Liquidity Approach

▓ Classification of assets and liabilities into current and non-current is intended to give an approximate measure of an entity's liquidity (i.e. its ability to carry on its activities on a day-to-day basis without encountering financial constraints).*

4.2.2 Operating Cycle Approach

▓ Classification is intended to identify those resources and obligations which are continuously circulating.*

*Criterion: will items be realised or liquidated in the near future?

*Criterion: will items be consumed or settled within the entity's normal operating cycle?

| Exhibit 1 | DISCLOSURE OF SIGNIFICANT ACCOUNTING POLICIES |  |

The following is an extract from the notes to the Consolidated Financial Statements 2015 of Daimler AG.

Presentation. Presentation in the consolidated statement of financial position differentiates between current and non-current assets and liabilities. Assets and liabilities are classified as current if they are expected to be realized or settled within one year or within a longer and normal operating cycle. Deferred tax assets and liabilities as well as assets and provisions for pensions and similar obligations are generally presented as non-current items.

The consolidated statement of income is presented using the cost-of-sales method.

4.3 Current Liabilities

 **Key Point**

A liability is classified as "current" when:*
- it is expected to be settled in the normal course of the operating cycle;
- it is held primarily for trading purposes;
- it is due to be settled within 12 months of the end of the reporting period; and
- the entity does not have an unconditional right to defer settlement for at least 12 months after the end of the reporting period.

 ***Commentary***

*An option to convert a liability into equity at a later date does not affect its classification.

- All other liabilities are classified as "non-current".
- Refinancing of a long-term loan, falling due within 12 months, after the end of the reporting period will still require the loan to be classified as a current liability.
- Any refinancing or restructuring of loan payments after the end of the reporting period will qualify for disclosure as a non-adjusting event in accordance with IAS 10 *Events after the Reporting Period.*

4.4 Overall Structure

- There is no prescribed format although IAS 1 presents a format as an illustration.
- There are two main types of format found in practice. They are expansions of two different expressions of the accounting equation:

  - Net assets (assets − liabilities) = Capital
  - Assets = Capital + Liabilities

- Either format in *Illustration 1* would be consistent with IAS practice.

Illustration 1 Acceptable Formats

IAS 1 Suggested Format		UK Format		
Assets	$			$
Non-current assets	50	Non-current assets		50
Current assets	40	Current assets	40	
		Current liabilities	(30)	
		Net current assets		10
		Total assets less current liabilities		60
		Non-current liabilities		(10)
Total assets	90			50
Balances to:		*Balances to:*		
Equity and Liabilities				
Capital and reserves	50	Capital and reserves		50
Non-current liabilities	10			
Current liabilities	30			
	90			50

4.5   Presentation of Assets, Liabilities and Equity

- Certain items **must** be shown in the statement of financial position. The requirements for these "line items" are:*

  - Property, plant and equipment
  - Investment property
  - Intangible assets
  - Financial assets (other than equity accounted investments, trade and other receivables and cash balances)
  - Assets and assets included in disposal groups classified as held for sale
  - Investments accounted for under the equity method
  - Biological assets
  - Inventories
  - Trade and other receivables
  - Cash and cash equivalents
  - Trade and other payables
  - Liabilities included in disposal groups classified as held for sale
  - Current tax assets or liabilities
  - Deferred tax assets or liabilities
  - Provisions
  - Financial liabilities (other than trade and other payables and provisions)
  - Non-controlling interest, to be presented as part of equity
  - Issued equity capital and reserves.*

*Line items can be aggregated if deemed to be immaterial.

*The order of the "line items" which must appear in the statement of financial position is not prescribed.

▨ An entity should disclose, either in the statement of financial position or in the notes, further sub-classifications of the line items presented classified in a manner appropriate to the entity's operations.

▨ The detail provided in sub-classifications depends on specific requirements of other IFRSs and the size, nature and amounts involved. The disclosures will vary for each item.

▨ Typically, companies will present the main headings in the statement of financial position and the detail in the notes to the accounts.

5 Statement of Comprehensive Income

5.1 Presentation

▨ All items of income and expense recognised in a period must be presented either:

- in a *single* statement of profit and loss and other comprehensive income; or
- in *two* statements:

  1. a statement displaying line items of **profit or loss** (separate "income statement"); and

  2. a second statement beginning with profit or loss and displaying items of **other comprehensive income**.

▨ Both **profit or loss** and **total comprehensive income** must be attributed, separately, to:

- non-controlling interests; and
- owners of the parent.*

*Disclosure of the separate attribution of both **profit or loss** and **total comprehensive income** is required in the relevant statement(s).

5.2 Profit or Loss

▨ The requirement for line items in the statement of profit or loss includes:

- revenue;
- gains and losses arising from the derecognition of financial assets measured at amortised cost (IFRS 9);*
- finance costs;
- share of profits and losses of associates and joint ventures accounted for under the equity method;
- tax expense;
- a single amount for the total of discontinued operations (see IFRS 5); and
- **profit or loss** (i.e. the total of income less expenses, excluding the items of other comprehensive income (see s.5.3).*

*Other gains and losses associated with financial assets, including impairment, are detailed in *Session 18*.

*ALL items of income and expense in a period MUST be included in profit or loss unless an IFRS requires or permits otherwise.

5.3   Other Comprehensive Income

▨ Other comprehensive income relates to items of income and expense which are not recognised in profit or loss; they include:

- changes in revaluation surplus;*
- changes in fair value of financial assets designated at fair value through other comprehensive income;
- certain exchange differences; and
- the deferred tax implications related to these items.

▨ Each item of other comprehensive income is presented as a line item and classified by nature (including any share of other comprehensive income of associates and joint ventures accounted for using the equity method).

▨ Items are grouped between those which:

- **will not** be reclassified to profit and loss subsequently; and
- **will** be reclassified to profit or loss at a future point in time.

▨ Items of other comprehensive income may be presented either:

- **net** of related tax effects (see *Illustration 2*); or
- **before** related tax effects. In this case tax effects must be allocated and shown separately for the two groups (see *Illustration 3*).

*Commentary

*Reclassification adjustments do not arise on changes in a revaluation surplus (IAS 16 *Property, Plant and Equipment*).

Exam Advice

Be aware of where gains and losses are included, making the distinction between profit and loss and other comprehensive income.

| Illustration 2 | Comprehensive Income Net of Related Tax Effects* | | |

Year ended 31 December 20X8	Before-tax amount	Tax (expense) benefit	Net-of-tax amount
Items which will not be reclassified in profit or loss:			
Gains of property revaluation	x	(x)	x
Investments in equity instruments	(x)	x	(x)
Actuarial gains (losses) on defined benefit pension plans	(x)	x	(x)
Share of other comprehensive income of associates	x		x
	x	x	x
Items which may be reclassified subsequently to profit or loss:			
Exchange differences on translating foreign operations	x	(x)	x
Cash flow hedges	x	(x)	x
	x	x	x
Other comprehensive income	x	(x)	x

*Commentary

*The income tax relating to each item must be disclosed in the notes if not in the statement of other comprehensive income.

Illustration 3 Comprehensive Income Before Related Tax Effects*		
Year ended 31 December	**20X8**	**20X7**
Items which will not be reclassified in profit or loss:		
Investments in equity instruments	(x)	x
Gains of property revaluation	x	x
Actuarial gains (losses) on defined benefit pension plans	x	(x)
Share of other comprehensive income of associates	x	x
Income tax relating to items that will not be reclassified	(x)	(x)
	x	(x)
Items that may be reclassified subsequently to profit or loss:		
Exchange differences on translating foreign operations	x	(x)
Cash flow hedges	x	(x)
Income tax relating to items that may be reclassified to profit or loss	(x)	x
Other comprehensive income for the year	x	(x)

*Commentary

*Using the format in *Illustration 3* the income tax relating to each item must be disclosed in the notes.

5.4   Material Items

▨ The nature and amount of material items of income or expense should be disclosed separately. For example:

- ◦ write-downs of assets (and reversals thereof);
- ◦ costs of restructurings;
- ◦ asset disposals;
- ◦ discontinued operations; and
- ◦ legal settlements.

5.5   Analysis of Expenses

▨ An entity should provide an analysis of expenses using a classification based on either:

- ◦ nature; or
- ◦ function.*

Key Point

Although IFRS requires the disclosure of material events and transactions it does not allow items to be classified as extraordinary or exceptional in nature.

*Commentary

*Although the analysis of expenses can be performed either in the statement of profit or loss or in the notes, the former is encouraged.

Nature of Expenditure Method

- Expenses are aggregated by nature, for example:
  - depreciation/amortisation;
  - materials consumed;
  - employee benefit expense.

Advantages

- ✔ Simple to apply in many small entities.
- ✔ No arbitrary allocations of costs across functions.
- ✔ More objective.
- ✔ Less judgement is required.

Function of Expenditure Method*

- Classifies expenses as:
  - cost of sales;
  - distribution;
  - administrative activities.

Advantage

- ✔ Provides more relevant information to users.

Disadvantage

- ✗ Cost allocation can be arbitrary and involves considerable judgement.

*Commentary

*The "function of expenditure" method is also called the "cost of sales" method, as it classifies expenses according to their function within cost of sales.

Illustration 4 Alternative Classifications*

BY NATURE	$	BY FUNCTION	$
Revenue	x	**Revenue**	x
Other income	x	Cost of sales	(x)
Changes in inventories of finished goods and work in progress	x/(x)	Gross profit/(loss)	x
		Other income	x
Work performed by entity and capitalised	x	Distribution costs	(x)
Raw materials and consumables used	(x)	Administrative expenses	(x)
Staff costs	(x)		
Depreciation and amortisation expense	(x)		
Other expenses	(x)	Other expenses	(x)
Finance cost	(x)	Finance cost	(x)
Share of profit from associates	x	*Share of profit* from associates	x
Profit before tax	x	**Profit before tax**	x

*Commentary

*Entities classifying expenses by function must disclose additional information on the nature of expenses, including depreciation and amortisation expense and staff costs.

6   Statement of Changes in Equity

6.1   A Separate Statement

- An entity should present as a separate component of its financial statements, a statement showing:*
  - total comprehensive income for the period, showing separately the total amounts attributable to owners of the parent and to non-controlling interest;
  - for each component of equity, the effects of retrospective application or retrospective restatement (per IAS 8 *Accounting Policies, Changes in Accounting Estimates and Errors*);
  - the amounts of transactions with owners in their capacity as owners, showing separately contributions and distributions; and
  - for each component of equity, a reconciliation between the carrying amount at the beginning and the end of the period, disclosing each change separately.

*Commentary

*Components of equity include each class of contributed equity and the accumulated balance of each class of other comprehensive income and retained earnings. Changes in equity reflect the increase or decrease in net assets. Except for changes resulting from transactions with owners, the overall change clearly represents the total amount of income and expense, including gains and losses, generated by the entity's activities.

Key Point

In addition an entity should present, either in the statement of changes in equity or in the notes, dividends recognised as distributions to owners during the period and the related amount per share.

6.2   Structure

- The requirements are most easily satisfied in a columnar format with a separate column for each component of equity:*

*Commentary

*A full year's comparative information must also be shown in the statement of changes in equity.

	Attributable to owners of the parent[1]				Non-controlling interest $	Total equity $
	Share capital $	Share premium $	Revaluation[2] surplus $	Retained earnings $		
Balance at 1 January	x	x	x	x	x	x
Change in accounting policy				(x)	(x)	(x)
Restated balance	x	x	x	x	x	x
Changes in equity for period						
Issue of share capital	x					x
Dividends				(x)		(x)
Total comprehensive income for the year			x	x	x	x
Transfer to retained earnings			(x)	x		
Balance at 31 December	x	x	x	x	x	x

Notes:

[1] A column showing the sub-total of amounts attributable to equity holders of the parent should also be included.

[2] A translation reserve might similarly be presented as a separate column.

6.3 Reclassification

▦ This is a transaction reported within other comprehensive income which is later reported again within profit or loss, usually when the item is realised. IFRSs may require or prohibit this.

▦ Reclassifying to profit or loss is prohibited for surpluses on the revaluation of property, plant and equipment (IAS 16 *Property, Plant and Equipment*). If the asset is sold the surplus may be taken to retained earnings as a reserve transfer.

▦ Cumulative gains and losses on financial assets voluntarily measured at fair value through other comprehensive income are not reclassified through profit or loss; but financial assets measured at fair value through other comprehensive income due to the business model of an entity are reclassified through profit or loss when the asset is derecognised.*

▦ The IASB's decisions about reclassification have been made on an ad hoc basis.

Commentary

*Details of this are covered in *Session 18*.

7 Notes to the Financial Statements

7.1 Structure

7.1.1 Objectives of Notes to the Financial Statements

- To present information about:
  - the basis of preparation of the financial statements; and
  - specific accounting policies selected and applied for significant transactions and events.
- To disclose information required by IFRSs which is not presented elsewhere.
- To provide additional information necessary for a fair presentation of the financial statements.

7.1.2 Presentation

- Notes should be presented in a systematic manner.*
- Each item in each of the financial statements should be cross-referenced to notes.
- The normal order of presentation is as follows:
  - Statement of compliance with IFRSs.
  - Statement of measurement basis and accounting policies applied.
  - Supporting information for items presented in each financial statement in the order in which each line item and each financial statement is presented.
  - Other disclosures, including:
    - contingencies, commitments and other financial disclosures; and
    - non-financial disclosures.

7.2 Disclosure of Accounting Policies

- Matters to be disclosed in respect of significant accounting policies:
  - measurement basis (or bases) used; and
  - each specific accounting policy that is significant to a fair presentation.
- Disclosure is required of judgements management has made in the process of applying an entity's accounting policies which have the most significant effect on amounts recognised.

7.3 Key Sources of Estimation Uncertainty

- Disclosure must be made about key assumptions concerning the future and key sources of estimation uncertainty at the end of the reporting period which have a significant risk of causing a material adjustment to the carrying amount of assets and liabilities within the next financial year.
- Disclosure should include information about the nature of the assets and liabilities and their carrying amounts at the end of the reporting period.

Exam Advice

The topic "Notes to the Financial Statements" tends to receive less emphasis from the examiners than the other topics covered in this Study Session.

*Commentary

*IAS 1 does not require a specific order. It could be based around the issues most relevant to the entity or grouped by measurement feature (e.g. fair value).

Summary

- IAS 1 prescribes the basis for presentation of *general purpose financial statements*.
- A complete set of financial statements includes **four** statements and notes, including a summary of accounting policies.
- Fair presentation is **presumed** by application of IFRSs, with additional disclosure (if necessary).
- Inappropriate accounting policies are **not** rectified by disclosure.
- Going concern is presumed. Significant uncertainties must be disclosed.
- Accrual basis is required (except for cash flow information).
- Consistency must be retained unless a change is justified (must disclose).
- Material items must be presented separately. Dissimilar items may be aggregated (if individually immaterial).
- Assets and liabilities, and income and expenses, may not be offset unless required or permitted by an IFRS.
- Comparative information is required unless another standard requires otherwise.
- Statement of financial position must normally be classified (current v non-current). Note, disclosure must separate longer-term amounts.
- All assets/liabilities other than current assets/liabilities are non-current.
- Minimum items are specified for the financial statements. Additional line items may be needed for fair presentation.
- "Profit or loss" describes the bottom line of the statement of profit or loss.
- All items of income/expense recognised in a period must be included in profit or loss (unless an IFRS requires otherwise).
- Other comprehensive income includes changes in unrealised gains and losses (e.g. on revaluation).
- Comprehensive income may be presented as one or two statements. Allocations to non-controlling interests and owners must be shown.
- No item may be presented as "extraordinary item" but material items may be disclosed separately.
- A separate statement of changes in equity must include the effects of retrospective application and dividends **recognised** as distributions.

Session 3 Quiz
Estimated time: 20 minutes

1. List the components of a set of financial statements according to IAS 1. (1.4)
2. State under what circumstances a company may decide not to comply with a relevant IFRS/IAS. (2.3)
3. Define materiality. (2.7)
4. An asset is classified as a current asset if it meets any one of FOUR criteria. List those FOUR criteria. (4.2)
5. Name the items which must be shown in the statement of profit or loss and other comprehensive income. (5.2)
6. Explain the purpose of the statement of changes in equity. (6.1)
7. Name the items which must be shown in the statement of changes in equity and may not be shown in the notes to the financial statements instead. (6.1)
8. Describe the main objectives of the notes to the financial statements. (7.1.1)

Study Question Bank
Estimated time: 40 minutes

Priority		Estimated Time	Completed
Q5	Pricewell	**40 minutes**	
Additional			
Q4	Cayman		

Accounting Policies

FOCUS

This session covers the following content from the *ACCA Study Guide.*

A. The Conceptual and Regulatory Framework for Financial Reporting

1. The need for a conceptual framework and the characteristics of useful information

g) Discuss the principle of comparability in accounting for changes in accounting policies. ☐

B. Accounting for Transactions in Financial Statements

9. Reporting financial performance

d) Account for changes in accounting estimates, changes in accounting policy and the correction of prior period errors. ☐

Session 4 Guidance

■ **Understand** the distinction between a change in accounting estimate (s.2.2) and a change in accounting policy (*Illustration 3*).

■ **Learn** what is meant by a prior period error (s.2.2).

■ **Understand** when a company needs to change its financial statements retrospectively as opposed to when it should apply changes from the present point in time going forward (s.3, s.4, s.5).

(continued on next page)

VISUAL OVERVIEW

Objective: To explain the need for guidance on reporting performance and to prescribe the classification, disclosure and accounting treatment of certain items in the statement of profit or loss and other comprehensive income.

```
                    ┌─────────────────────────┐
                    │  FINANCIAL STATEMENTS   │
                    │  • Purpose              │
                    │  • Disaggregation       │
                    │  • Reporting Aspects    │
                    │    of Performance       │
                    └─────────────────────────┘
                                 │
                    ┌─────────────────────────┐
                    │    IAS 8 TERMINOLOGY    │
                    └─────────────────────────┘
                                 │
        ┌────────────────────────┼────────────────────────┐
┌──────────────────┐  ┌──────────────────────┐  ┌──────────────────────┐
│ ACCOUNTING       │  │ CHANGES IN           │  │ PRIOR PERIOD ERRORS  │
│ POLICIES         │  │ ACCOUNTING ESTIMATE  │  │ • Accounting         │
│ • Selection and  │  │ • Estimation         │  │   Treatment          │
│   Application    │  │ • Accounting         │  │ • Disclosures        │
│ • Consistency    │  │   Treatment          │  │                      │
│ • Changes        │  │ • Disclosure         │  │                      │
│ • Disclosure     │  │                      │  │                      │
└──────────────────┘  └──────────────────────┘  └──────────────────────┘
```

 **Financial Statements**

1.1 Purpose

Key Point

The objective of financial statements is to provide information about the financial **position**, **performance** and **cash flows** of an entity which is useful to a wide range of users in making economic decisions.

▨ The economic decisions taken by users of financial statements require an evaluation of the ability of an entity to generate cash and cash equivalents and the timing and certainty of their generation.

▨ Users are better able to evaluate this ability to generate cash and cash equivalents if they are provided with information which focuses on the financial position, performance and cash flows of an entity.

▨ Information about the performance of an entity, in particular its profitability, is required in order to:

- assess potential changes in the economic resources it is likely to control in the future;
- predict its capacity to generate cash flows from its existing resource base; and
- form judgements about the effectiveness with which the entity might employ additional resources.

▨ Information about variability of performance is important in this respect.

1.2 Disaggregation

▨ In order to make economic decisions, users of the accounts need to understand the composition of figures in as much detail as possible. There is a trend in reporting to provide more detailed information about the composition of key elements of the financial statements.*

▨ For example:

- disclosure of material and unusual items which are part of ordinary activities;
- information on discontinued operations; and
- segmental reporting.

▨ Users can use such information to make better-quality forecasts regarding the entity.

 **Commentary**

*Such information is typically analysed in the notes to the financial statements.

1.3   Reporting Aspects of Performance

Relevant standards are:

- IAS 8 *Accounting Policies, Changes in Accounting Estimates and Errors*
- IAS 1 *Presentation of Financial Statements*
- IFRS 8 *Operating Segments*
- IAS 7 *Statement of Cash Flows*
- IFRS 5 *Non-current Assets Held for Sale and Discontinued Operations.*

In considering the reporting of financial performance, the following areas need to be covered:*

- The form and content of the statement of profit or loss and other comprehensive income:
    - Structure (IAS 1)
    - Items to be included (IAS 1)
    - Classification of material items (IAS 1)
    - Disclosures for discontinued operations (IFRS 5).
- Other statements of performance:
    - Statement of cash flows (IAS 7)
    - Statements showing changes in equity (IAS 1).

Exam Advice

IFRS 8 is a "disclosure" standard and is not examinable in F7.

Commentary

*All the areas concerning financial performance should be incorporated into an understanding of how international GAAP provides information to enable users to understand performance.

2   IAS 8 Terminology

Accounting policies: specific principles, bases, conventions, rules and practices applied in preparing and presenting financial statements.

Change in accounting estimate: an adjustment to the carrying amount of an asset or liability (or the amount of annual consumption of an asset) which:

- results from a current assessment of expected future benefits and obligations.
- These changes arise due to new information or developments and are not corrections of errors.
- Examples include:
    - a receivable balance that becomes irrecoverable;
    - a change in the estimated useful life of a depreciable asset.

Prior period errors: omissions and misstatements, relating to the financial statements of previous periods which arose from a failure to use, or the misuse of, information which:

- was available when the financial statements were authorised for issue;
- could reasonably be expected to have been obtained and taken into account when the financial statements were prepared and presented.
- Errors may include the effects of mathematical mistakes, mistakes in the application of accounting policies, oversights and fraud.

3 Accounting Policies

3.1 Selection and Application

- When an IFRS applies to a transaction, the accounting policy (or policies) applied to that transaction is determined by applying the relevant IFRS and any relevant implementation guidance issued by the IASB.

 **Key Point**

- If there is no applicable IFRS for a transaction, management must use its judgement in developing and applying an accounting policy which will provide information that:
  - is relevant to the economic decision-making needs of users;
  - is reliable;
  - represents faithfully;
  - reflects the economic substance of the transaction;
  - is neutral; and
  - is complete in all material aspects.

- Management may consider:
  - requirements of accounting standards dealing with similar transactions;
  - the definitions and recognition criteria in the Framework;
  - recent pronouncements of other standard-setting bodies which use a similar conceptual framework; and
  - any other accounting literature denoting best practice in a particular industry.

Illustration 1 Absence of a Specific Accounting Standard

Kitty has recently purchased a Van Gogh painting to display in a client reception area, with the hope that it will lead to more contracts and that the painting will appreciate.

There is no specific accounting standard that deals with these types of asset, but IAS 40 *Investment Property* does deal with a particular type of asset which is held for capital appreciation.

It would therefore seem appropriate to use IAS 40 as justification to value the painting at fair value year on year.

Exhibit 1   HERITAGE ASSETS

The following is an extract from the Notes to the Consolidated Financial Statements of the Victoria & Albert Museum Annual Report and Accounts 2014–2015.

1. Accounting policies
e) Heritage assets
Additions to the collection are capitalised and recognised in the Balance Sheet at the cost or value of the acquisition, where such a cost or valuation is reasonably obtainable. Such items are not depreciated as they are deemed to have indefinite lives; items are not revalued as a matter of course unless significantly impaired. To date no impairments have occurred of capitalised items.

3.2   Consistency

Illustration 2   Inventory Valuation

IAS 2 *Inventories* requires inventory to be valued at the lower of cost and net realisable values. In identifying cost, it allows two possible formulae—first-in, first-out (FIFO) and weighted average. The same cost formula must be applied to similar items of inventory, but a different cost formula can be applied to a different classification of inventory.

Key Point

The selection and application of accounting policies to transactions of a similar nature must be **consistent**.

3.3   Changes in Accounting Policy

3.3.1   When

Key Point

- An entity can *only* change an accounting policy if:*
  - it is *required* to do so by an IFRS (i.e. a *mandatory* change); or
  - the change would result in the financial statements providing *more relevant and reliable information* (i.e. a *voluntary* change).

- If an entity decides to adopt the revaluation model of IAS 16 *Property, Plant and Equipment* this is a change in accounting policy.*

3.3.2   How

- A new or revised IFRS generally contains "transitional provisions" which should be applied to any change of accounting policy.
- If there are *no* transitional provisions, or if the change in policy is *voluntary*, then a change in policy is applied *retrospectively*.

Commentary

*As many users of financial statements are interested in analysing trends in an entity's financial statements it would not be appropriate if the entity could change its accounting policy whenever it wanted to.

Commentary

*Note, however, that this adoption of the revaluation model is accounted for in accordance with the more specific requirements of IAS 16 and not IAS 8.

■ **Retrospective application** means that:

● the *opening* balance of each affected part of equity for the *earliest* period presented is adjusted; and

● the comparative amounts are disclosed for each prior period as if the new policy had *always been applied*.

■ If it is not practicable to apply the effects of a change in policy to prior periods then IAS 8 allows that the change be made from the earliest period for which retrospective application is practicable.*

3.3.3 IAS 1 Presentation

 Key Point

Under IAS 1, when a change of policy occurs, or a prior period error is rectified, an additional statement of financial position must be presented for the previous year end (i.e. three statements).

 *Commentary

*"Practicable" is widely used in financial reporting and auditing. It means that something can be put into practice. It is not the same as "practical". It may not be practical to do something, but if it can be done it is practicable.

3.4 Disclosure

3.4.1 Change Due to New IFRS

■ Title of new IFRS and the nature of the change in policy.

■ When applicable, that the change is made in accordance with the IFRS's transitional provisions, a description of those provisions and the effect that the provisions might have on future periods.

■ For the current period and each prior period presented, the amount of the adjustment for each line item affected in the financial statements.

■ The amount of the adjustment relating to periods before those presented.

■ If retrospective restatement is not practicable, the circumstances that led to the existence of the condition and a description of how and from when the change has been applied.

3.4.2 Voluntary Change in Policy

■ Nature of the change in policy.

■ Reasons why the new policy provides more reliable and relevant information.

■ For the current period and each prior period presented, the amount of the adjustment for each line item affected in the financial statements.

■ The amount of the adjustment relating to periods before those presented.

■ If retrospective restatement is not practicable, the circumstances that led to the existence of the condition and a description of how and from when the change has been applied.

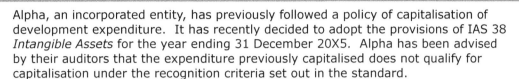

Illustration 3   Change in Accounting Policy

Alpha, an incorporated entity, has previously followed a policy of capitalisation of development expenditure. It has recently decided to adopt the provisions of IAS 38 *Intangible Assets* for the year ending 31 December 20X5. Alpha has been advised by their auditors that the expenditure previously capitalised does not qualify for capitalisation under the recognition criteria set out in the standard.

The notes to the accounts for the year ended 31 December 20X5 in respect of the deferred development expenditure was as follows:

	$
Balance at 1 January 20X5	$1,000
Additions	500
Amortisation	(400)
Balance at 31 December 20X5	1,100

During the year ended 31 December 20X6, the company has expensed all expenditure in the period on projects, in respect of which, expenditure had previously been capitalised, and no amortisation has been charged in the statement of profit or loss in 20X6.

The following are extracts from the draft accounts for the year ended 31 December 20X6.

Statement of profit or loss	**20X6**	**20X5** *(as previously published)*
	$	$
Revenue	1,200	1,100
Expenses	(800)	(680)
Profit for the year	400	420

Statement of changes in equity (extract)	$	$
Balance as at 1 January	3,000	2,580
Profit for the year	400	420
Balance as at 31 December	3,400	3,000

Required:

Show how the statement of profit or loss and statement of changes in equity would appear in the financial statements for the year ended 31 December 20X6, processing the necessary adjustments in respect of the change in accounting policy by applying the new policy retrospectively.

Illustration 3 Change in Accounting Policy (continued)

Solution

Statement of profit or loss	20X6	20X5 (as restated)
	$	$
Revenue	1,200	1,100
Expenses	(800)	(780)
Profit for the year	400	320

Statement of changes in equity (extract)	$	$
Balance as at 1 January 20X6 As previously stated	3,000	2,580
Prior period adjustment	(1,100)	(1,000)
Balance at beginning of year, as adjusted	1,900	1,580
Profit for the year	400	320
Balance as at 31 December 20X6	2,300	1,900

Notes:

1. The entity amortised $400 in 20X5 but spent $500. The policy would have been to write off the amount of expenditure directly to the statement of profit or loss; therefore, the entity needs to adjust last year's figures by an extra $100 expense.

   The adjustment against last year's statement of profit or loss ($100) has the effect of restating it to what it would have been if the company had been following the same policy last year. This is important because the statement of profit or loss as presented will be prepared on a comparable basis.

2. The balance left on the deferred expenditure account at the end of the previous year ($1,100) is written off against the accumulated profit which existed at that time.

   This $1,100 is made up of an amount which arose last year (the difference between the amount spent ($500) and the amount amortised ($400), and the balance which existed at the beginning of the previous year ($1,000)).

   These amounts are written off against last year's profit and the opening balance on the accumulated profit last year, respectively.

4 Changes in Accounting Estimate

4.1 Estimation

▦ Many items recognised in the financial statements must be measured with an element of estimation attached to them:

- trade receivables are measured after allowing for estimated irrecoverable amounts;
- inventory is measured at lower of cost and net realisable value with allowance made for obsolescence, etc;
- a provision under IAS 37 is often only a "best estimate" of future economic benefits to be paid out;
- non-current assets are depreciated; the charge takes into account the expected pattern of consumption of the asset and its expected useful life. Both the depreciation method (reflecting the consumption pattern) and useful life are estimates.

4.2 Accounting Treatment

 Key Point

When a change in circumstances occurs which affects the estimates previously made, the effect of that change is recognised *prospectively* in the current and future (where relevant) periods' profit or loss.

▦ A change in estimate is not an error or a change in accounting policy and therefore does not affect prior period statements.

▦ If the change in estimate affects the measurement of assets or liabilities then the change is recognised by adjusting the carrying amount of the asset or liability.

4.3 Disclosure

▦ The nature and amount of a change in estimate which has an effect in the current period or is expected to have an effect in future periods.

▦ If it is not possible to estimate the effects on future periods, then that fact must be disclosed.

5 Prior Period Errors

5.1 Accounting Treatment

▦ The amount of the correction of an error which relates to prior periods is reported by:

- adjusting the opening balance of retained earnings; and
- restating comparative information.

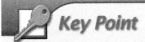

Key Point

The financial statements of the current period are presented as if the error had been corrected in the period in which the error was originally made. However, an entity does not reissue the financial statements of prior periods.

- If it is not practicable to determine the period-specific effects of an error on comparative information for prior periods presented, the opening balances are restated for the earliest period which is practicable.

Illustration 4 Prior Period Error Accounting Treatment

In the year ended 31 December 20X6, a prior period error of $12 million is identified. Of this error, $2 million relates to 20X6; $3 million relates to 20X5; $4 million relates to 20X4; and $3 million relates to 20X3.

The opening retained earnings as of 1 January 20X5 will be adjusted by the sum of the error for 20X3 and 20X4 of $7 million; 20X5's profits will be adjusted for the error of $3 million; and the $2 million relating to 20X6 will be reflected in that year's profit or loss.

5.2 Disclosures

- Nature of the error.
- For each prior period presented the amount of the correction for each line item affected in the financial statements.
- The amount of the correction at the beginning of the earliest period presented.
- If retrospective restatement is not practicable, the circumstances which led to the existence of the condition and a description of how and from when the error has been corrected.

Summary

- Changes in accounting policies are not changes in estimates.
- Changes in accounting estimates are not corrections of errors.
- A change in policy may be required by a standard or be voluntary.
- A change in estimate is accounted for prospectively.
- Changes in accounting policy are accounted for retrospectively unless a new/revised standard specifies otherwise (in transitional provisions).
- The correction of prior period errors is accounted for retrospectively.
- Retrospective application means:
  - adjusting opening balances in equity (e.g. retained earnings) for the earliest prior period presented; and
  - restating comparative amounts.

Session 4 Quiz
Estimated time: 15 minutes

1. When no accounting standard exists for a particular transaction, a company develops and applies an accounting policy for the transaction type. List the characteristics/qualities of the information resulting from the policy. (3.1)

2. Specify the circumstances under which a company may change an accounting policy. (3.3.1)

3. Explain the meaning of retrospective application of a change in accounting policy. (3.3.2)

4. Suppose a company changes an accounting policy voluntarily. Describe the information related to the change it must disclose in the financial statements. (3.4.2)

5. State when a change in an accounting estimate should be made. (4.2)

6. Describe the disclosures required to report prior period errors. (5.2)

Study Question Bank
Estimated time: 40 minutes

Priority		Estimated Time	Completed
Q6	Perseus	40 minutes	
Additional			
Q7	Tunshill		

Session 5

IFRS 15 *Revenue from Contracts with Customers*

FOCUS

This session covers the following content from the *ACCA Study Guide.*

B. Accounting for Transactions in Financial Statements

10. Revenue

a) Explain and apply the principles of recognition of revenue: ☐
   i) Identification of contracts
   ii) Identification of performance obligations
   iii) Determination of transaction price
   iv) Allocation of the price to performance obligations
   v) Recognition of revenue when/as performance obligations are satisfied.

b) Explain and apply the criteria for recognising revenue generated from contracts where performance obligations are satisfied over time or at a point in time. ☐

c) Describe the acceptable methods for measuring progress towards complete satisfaction of a performance obligation. ☐

d) Explain and apply the criteria for recognition of contract costs. ☐

e) Apply the principles of recognition of revenue, and specifically account for ☐ the following types of transactions:
   i) principal versus agent
   ii) repurchase agreements
   iii) bill-and-hold arrangements
   iv) consignments.

f) Prepare financial statement extracts for contracts where performance obligations are satisfied over time. ☐

Session 5 Guidance

- **Learn** the five steps of the revenue recognition process (s.1).
- **Understand** the criteria that indicate that a performance obligation is satisfied over time (s.2.1).
- **Know** the indicators of transfer of control in order to **identify** when revenue is recognised when a performance obligation is satisfied at a point in time (s.2.2).
- **Understand** when to recognise a contract liability, contract asset and/or receivable (s.2.3).

(continued on next page)

VISUAL OVERVIEW

Objective: To understand the principles that govern the recognition of revenue from contracts with customers.

```
                    ┌─────────────────────────────┐
                    │      PRINCIPLES OF          │
                    │   REVENUE RECOGNITION       │
                    │                             │
                    │  • IFRS 15                  │
                    │  • Contracts With Customers │
                    │  • Performance Obligations  │
                    │  • Transaction Price        │
                    │  • Allocate Price           │
                    │  • Recognise Revenue        │
                    └─────────────────────────────┘
```

```
┌──────────────────────┐   ┌──────────────────────┐   ┌──────────────────────┐
│    PERFORMANCE       │   │   RECOGNITION OF     │   │ SPECIFIC TRANSACTIONS│
│    OBLIGATIONS       │   │   CONTRACT COSTS     │   │                      │
│                      │   │                      │   │  • Principal v Agent │
│ • Satisfied Over Time│   │ • Incremental Costs  │   │  • Repurchase        │
│ • At a Point in Time │   │ • Costs to Fulfil    │   │    Agreements        │
│ • Presentation       │   │   Contract           │   │  • Bill-and-Hold     │
│                      │   │                      │   │    Arrangements      │
│                      │   │                      │   │  • Consignments      │
└──────────────────────┘   └──────────────────────┘   └──────────────────────┘
```

```
┌──────────────────────┐
│ MEASURING PROGRESS   │
│ TOWARDS COMPLETION   │
│                      │
│ • Output Methods     │
│ • Input Methods      │
│ • Cost Recognition   │
└──────────────────────┘
```

Session 5 Guidance

■ **Learn** how to apply the output and input methods used to measure progress towards completion when a performance obligation is satisfied over time (s.3).

■ **Learn** when to recognise as assets or expenses the costs to obtain a contract and the costs to fulfil a contract (s.4).

■ **Know** how to apply the principles of revenue recognition to principal versus agent transactions, repurchase agreements, bill-and-hold arrangements and consignments (s.5).

■ **Read** the technical article "Revenue revisited".

1 Principles of Revenue Recognition

1.1 IFRS 15

IFRS 15 *Revenue from Contracts with Customers* outlines the five steps of the revenue recognition process:

Step 1	Identify the contract(s) with the customer
Step 2	Identify the separate performance obligations
Step 3	Determine the transaction price
Step 4	Allocate the transaction price to the performance obligations
Step 5	Recognise revenue when (or as) a performance obligation is satisfied

- The core principle of IFRS 15 is that an entity recognises revenue from the transfer of goods or services to a customer in an amount that reflects the consideration that the entity expects to be entitled to in exchange for the goods or services.

1.2 Identify Contracts With Customers

Definition

Contract—an agreement between two or more parties that creates enforceable rights and obligations. Contracts can be written, verbal or implied based on an entity's customary business practices.

Customer—a party that has contracted with an entity to obtain goods or services that are an output of the entity's ordinary activities in exchange for consideration.

- The revenue recognition principles of IFRS 15 apply only when a contract meets **all** of the following criteria:*
  - the parties to the contract have **approved** the contract;
  - the entity can identify each party's **rights** regarding the goods or services in the contract;
  - the **payment terms** can be identified;
  - the contract has **commercial substance**; and*
  - it is **probable** that the entity will collect the **consideration** due under the contract.

1.3 Identify Performance Obligations

Definition

Performance obligation—a promise to transfer to a customer:

- a good or service (or bundle of goods or services) that is distinct; **or**
- a series of goods or services that are substantially the same and are transferred in the same way.

*Commentary

*These are assessed at the beginning of the contract and, if the contract meets them, they are **not** reassessed unless there is a significant change in circumstances that makes the contract rights and obligations unenforceable. If a contract does not initially meet the criteria, it can be reassessed at a later date.

*Commentary

*Commercial substance means that the risk, timing or amount of future cash flows is expected to change as a result of the contract.

If a promise to transfer a good or service is not distinct from other goods and services in a contract, then the goods or services are combined into a single performance obligation.

Key Point

A good or service is distinct if **both** of the following criteria are met:

1. The customer can benefit from the good or service on its own or when combined with the customer's available resources; and
2. The promise to transfer the good or service is separately identifiable from other goods or services in the contract.*

*Commentary

*A transfer of a good or service is **not** separately identifiable if the good or service:

- is not integrated with other goods or services in the contract; or
- does not modify or customise another good or service in the contract; or
- does not depend on or relate to other goods or services promised in the contract.

Illustration 1   Identify Performance Obligations (I)

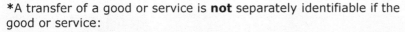

Tanner is building a multi-unit residential complex. It enters into a contract with a customer for a specific unit that is under construction. The goods and services to be provided in the contract include procurement, construction, piping, wiring, installation of equipment and finishing.

Analysis

Although the goods and services provided by the contractor are distinguishable, they are not distinct in this contract because the goods and services cannot be separately identified from the promise to construct the unit. Tanner will integrate the goods and services into the unit, so all the goods and services are accounted for as a single performance obligation.

Illustration 2   Identify Performance Obligations (II)

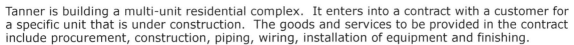

A software developer, Jackson, enters into a contract with a customer to transfer a software licence, perform installation and provide software updates and technical support for five years. Jackson sells the licence, installation, updates and technical support separately. Jackson determines that each good or service is separately identifiable because the installation does not modify the software and the software is functional without the updates and technical support.

Analysis

The software is delivered before the installation, updates and technical support and is functional without the updates and technical support, so the customer can benefit from each good or service on its own. Jackson also has determined that the software licence, installation, updates and technical support are separately identifiable. On this basis, there are four performance obligations in this contract:

1. Software licence
2. Installation service
3. Software updates
4. Technical support

1.4 Determine the Transaction Price

Definition

Transaction price—the amount of consideration to which an entity is entitled in exchange for transferring goods or services.

- The transfer price does not include amounts collected for third parties (i.e. sales taxes or VAT).
- The effects of the following must be considered when determining the transaction price:
  - the time value of money;*
  - the fair value of any non-cash consideration;
  - estimates of variable consideration;
  - consideration payable to the customer.*

*Commentary

*The time value of money does not need to be considered if the length of the contract is less than one year.

*Commentary

*Consideration payable to the customer is treated as a reduction in the transaction price unless the payment is for goods or services received from the customer.

Exam Advice

Variable consideration is not examinable at F7.

Example 1 Time Value of Money

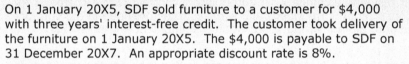

On 1 January 20X5, SDF sold furniture to a customer for $4,000 with three years' interest-free credit. The customer took delivery of the furniture on 1 January 20X5. The $4,000 is payable to SDF on 31 December 20X7. An appropriate discount rate is 8%.

Required:

Determine the transaction price for the sale of the furniture and calculate the interest income to be recognised over the three years.

Solution

	$
Transaction price:	
Interest income	
20X5:	
20X6:	
20X7:	

1.5 Allocate the Transaction Price

- The transaction price is allocated to all separate performance obligations in proportion to the stand-alone selling price of the goods or services.

Definition

Stand-alone selling price—the price at which an entity would sell a promised good or service separately to a customer.

- The best evidence of stand-alone selling price is the observable price of a good or service when it is sold separately.
- It should be estimated if it is not observable.

The allocation is made at the beginning of the contract and is not adjusted for subsequent changes in the stand-alone selling prices.

Example 2 Allocating Transaction Price

Jackson enters into a contract with a customer to transfer a software licence, perform installation, and provide software updates and technical support for five years in exchange for $240,000. Jackson has determined that each good or service is a separate performance obligation. Jackson sells the licence, installation, updates and technical support separately, so each has a directly observable stand-alone selling price:

	$000
Software licence	150
Installation service	60
Software updates	40
Technical support	50
	300

Required:

Allocate the $240,000 transaction price to the four performance obligations.

Solution.

	$000
Software licence	
Installation service	
Software updates	
Technical support	
Total	

1.6   Recognise Revenue

- Recognise revenue when (or as) a performance obligation is satisfied by transferring a promised good or service (an asset) to the customer.
- An asset is transferred when (or as) the customer gains control of the asset.
- The performance obligation will be satisfied over time or at a point in time.

2 Performance Obligations

2.1 Satisfied Over Time

- A performance obligation is satisfied over time if **one** of the following criteria is met:
  - The customer receives and consumes the benefits of the goods or services while the contract is being fulfilled (e.g. service contracts, such as a cleaning service or a monthly payroll processing service).
  - Performance creates or enhances an asset that the customer controls during that creation or enhancement.
  - Performance does not create an asset which the supplier has an alternative use for and the supplier has an enforceable right to payment for performance completed to date (e.g. a construction contract).
- Revenue is recognised over time by measuring progress towards complete satisfaction of the performance obligation.
- Output methods and input methods (described in s.3) can be used to measure progress towards completion.*
- Revenue for a performance obligation satisfied over time can only be recognised if progress can be reasonably estimated.
- Revenue is recognised to the extent of costs incurred if there is no reasonable estimate of progress but costs are expected to be recoverable..

2.2 Satisfied at a Point in Time

- A performance obligation that is not satisfied over time is satisfied at a point in time.
- Revenue should be recognised at the point in time when the customer obtains control of the asset.
- Indicators of the transfer of control include:
  - the customer has an obligation to pay for an asset;
  - the customer has legal title to the asset;
  - the entity has transferred physical possession of the asset;
  - the customer has the significant risks and rewards of ownership;
  - the customer has accepted the asset.

Commentary

*A single method of measuring progress should be applied to each performance obligation and the same method should be used for similar performance obligations in similar circumstances.

Illustration 3   Satisfaction of Performance Obligations (I)

Tanner is building a multi-unit residential complex. It enters into a contract with a customer for a specific unit that is under construction. The contract has the following terms:

- The customer pays a non-refundable security deposit upon entering the contract.
- The customer agrees to make progress payments during construction.
- If the customer fails to make the progress payments, the entity has the right to all of the contract consideration if it completes the unit.
- The terms of the contract prevent the entity from directing the unit to another customer.

Analysis

This performance obligation is satisfied over time because:

- The unit does not have an alternative future use to Tanner because it cannot be directed to another customer.
- Tanner has a right to payment for performance to date because it has a right to all of the contract consideration if it completes the unit.

Illustration 4   Satisfaction of Performance Obligations (II)

Tanner is building a multi-unit residential complex. It enters into a contract with a customer for a specific unit that is under construction. The contract has the following terms:

- The customer pays a deposit upon entering the contract that is refundable if the entity fails to complete the unit in accordance with the contract.
- The remainder of the purchase price is due upon completion of the unit.
- If the customer defaults on the contract before completion, Tanner only has the right to retain the deposit.

Analysis

This performance obligation is satisfied at a point in time because it is not a service contract, the customer does not control the unit as it is created and the entity does not have an enforceable right to payment for performance completed to date (i.e. the entity only has a right to the deposit until the unit is completed).

2.3   Statement of Financial Position Presentation

- A contract asset or contract liability should be presented in the statement of financial position when either party has performed in a contract.

Definition

Contract liability—an entity's obligation to transfer goods or services to a customer for which the entity has received consideration from the customer or consideration is due from the customer (i.e. the customer pays or owes payment before the entity performs).

Contract asset—an entity's right to consideration in exchange for goods or services that the entity has transferred to the customer (i.e. the entity performs before the customer pays).

- In addition, any unconditional right to consideration should be presented separately as a receivable in accordance with IFRS 9 *Financial Instruments*.*

> ***Commentary***
>
> *A right to consideration is unconditional if only the passage of time is required before payment is due.

Illustration 5   Contract Liability and Receivable

On 1 January, Anderson enters into a non-cancellable contract with Tanner for the sale of an excavator for $350,000. The excavator will be delivered to Tanner on 1 April. The contract requires Tanner to pay the $350,000 in advance on 1 February and Tanner makes the payment on 1 March.

Required:

Prepare the journal entries that would be used by Anderson to account for this contract.

Solution

On 1 February, Anderson recognises a receivable because it has an unconditional right to the consideration (i.e. the contract is non-cancellable):

Dr	Receivable	350,000	
	Cr	Contract liability	350,000

On 1 March, when Tanner makes the payment Anderson recognises the cash collection:

Dr	Cash	350,000	
	Cr	Receivable	350,000

On 1 April, Anderson recognises revenue when the excavator is delivered to Tanner:

Dr	Contract liability	350,000	
	Cr	Revenue	350,000

Illustration 6   Contract Asset and Receivable

On 1 January, Anderson enters into a contract with Tanner for the sale of two excavators for $350,000 each. The contract requires one excavator to be delivered on 1 February and states that the payment for the delivery of the first excavator is conditional on the delivery of the second excavator. The second excavator is delivered on 1 June.

Required:

Prepare the journal entries that would be used by Anderson to account for this contract.

Solution

On 1 February, Anderson recognises a contract asset and revenue when it satisfies the performance obligation to deliver the first excavator:

Dr	Contract asset	350,000	
	Cr	Revenue	350,000

A receivable is not recognised on 1 February because Anderson does not have an unconditional right to the consideration until the second excavator is delivered.

On 1 June, Anderson recognises a receivable and revenue when it satisfies the performance obligation to deliver the second excavator:

Dr	Receivable	700,000	
	Cr	Contract asset	350,000
	Cr	Revenue	350,000

3 Measuring Progress Towards Completion

3.1 Output Methods

- Output methods recognise revenue on the basis of the value to the customer of the goods or services transferred to date relative to the remaining goods or services promised.
- Examples of output methods include:
  - Surveys of performance completed to date*
  - Appraisals of results achieved
  - Milestones achieved
  - Time elapsed
  - Units produced or delivered.

> ***Commentary**
>
> *The value of "work certified" to date may be a measure used to identify the degree of completion and therefore revenue to be recognised in profit or loss.

- Output methods should only be used when the output selected represents performance towards complete satisfaction of the performance obligation.*

> ***Commentary**
>
> *A disadvantage of output methods is that the outputs used may not be available or directly observable. When this is the case, an input method may be necessary.

3.2 Input Methods

- Input methods recognise revenue on the basis of the efforts or inputs to satisfy the performance obligation relative to the total expected inputs.
- Examples of input methods include:
  - Labour-hours worked
  - Costs incurred
  - Time elapsed
  - Resources consumed.
- Revenue can be recognised on a straight-line basis if inputs are used evenly throughout the performance period.

> ### Illustration 7 Straight-Line Basis
>
> A health club enters into a contract with a customer for one year of unlimited health club access for $75 per month. The health club determines that the customer simultaneously receives and consumes the benefits of the club's performance, so the contract is a performance obligation satisfied over time. Because the customer benefits from the club's services evenly throughout the year, the best measure of progress towards complete satisfaction of the performance obligation is a time-based measure. Revenue will be recognised on a straight-line basis throughout the year at $75 per month.

3.3 Cost Recognition

- Costs are recognised in the same proportion that applies to the recognition of revenue, except for the following:
  - Abnormal costs (e.g. to rectify an error in the production or service process) are expensed as incurred; and
  - Input costs that are not proportionate to the construction process.
- If an incurred cost is not proportionate to the progress in the satisfaction of the performance obligation that cost shall be excluded when measuring the progress of the contract. A cost incurred that is **not** proportionate to the progress towards completion is **excluded** from the measurement of progress.
- In this situation revenue will be recognised to the extent of the actual cost incurred in respect of that component.

> ### Illustration 8 Non-proportionate Costs
>
> Jethro is constructing a property for a customer for a contract price of $4 million. Construction of the property is a single performance obligation satisfied over time.
>
> The total costs of the contract are expected to be $3 million, of which $1 million is for the elevators to be included in the property. The elevator is a distinct component of the contract and the customer obtains control of the elevator before the property itself has been completed.
>
> Costs incurred to date are $1.4 million of which $1 million is in respect of the elevator. Revenue is recognised based on the input costs incurred to date.
>
> Jethro will recognise revenue as follows:
>
> | | |
> |---|---:|
> | Elevator | $1,000,000 |
> | Other ($400/_{2,000}$ × ($4m − $1m)) | $600,000 |
>
> Total revenue recognised is $1.6 million with costs recognised of $1.4 million.

Example 3 Output and Input Methods

Tanner is building a multi-unit residential complex. In the prior year, Tanner entered into a contract with a customer for a specific unit that is under construction. Tanner has determined that the contract is a single performance obligation satisfied over time. Tanner gathered the following information for the contract during the year.

Tanner Co—Year Ended 31 December	
	$
Costs to date	1,500
Future expected costs	1,000
Work certified to date	1,800
Expected sales value	3,200
Revenue taken in earlier periods	1,200
Cost taken in earlier periods	950

(handwritten: {2,500 beside Costs to date and Future expected costs)

Required:

Calculate the figures to be included in the statement of profit or loss in respect of revenue and costs for the year ended 31 December on both:

(i)   a sales basis (an output method); and

(ii)   a cost basis (an input method).

Solution

(a)   Calculate total expected profit

	$
Revenue	3,200
Less: Contract costs to date	(1,500)
Future expected costs	(1,000)
Total expected profit	700

(b)   Measure of progress towards completion

Sales basis =   1,800/3,200 = 56.25%   Cost basis =   1,500/2,500 = 60%
                OUTPUT   INPUT

(c)   Calculate revenue/costs for the year

	(1) To date	(2) Prior year	$	(1) To date	(2) Prior year	$
Revenue	3,200 × 56.25% = 1,800	1,800 − 1,200	600	3,200 × 60% = 1,920	1,920 − 1,200	720
Cost of sales	2,500 × 56.25% = 1,416	1,416 − 950	(466)	2,500 × 60% = 1,500	1,500 − 950	550
Profit			144			170

(1)   Calculate attributable revenue and costs to date.

(2)   Deduct any revenue and costs taken in earlier periods.

Example 4 **Statement of Financial Position Presentation**

Following on from *Example 3*:

The contract is expected to take three years to complete and the customer has contracted to pay $1,000 at the end of each of the first two years and the balance on completion.

Example 3 shows the position at the end of the second year; a contract asset of $200 was recognised at the end of the first year. The customer paid the first two instalments when they fell due.

Required:

Determine the figures to be included in the statement of financial position at the end of the second year using both:

(i)   a sales basis; and

(ii)   a cost basis.

4 Recognition of Contract Costs

4.1   Incremental Costs of Obtaining a Contract

Incremental costs of obtaining a contract—costs to obtain a contract that would not have been incurred if the contract had not been obtained.

- The incremental costs of obtaining a contract, such as sales commissions, are recognised as an asset if the entity expects to recover them.
- Costs to obtain the contract that would have been incurred regardless of whether the contract was obtained are charged to expense when incurred.

Illustration 9 Incremental Costs

Jackson enters into a contract with a customer to transfer a software licence, perform installation, and provide software updates and technical support for three years in exchange for $240,000. In order to win this contract, Jackson incurred the following costs:

	$000
Legal fees for drawing up the contract	10
Travel costs to deliver proposal	20
Commissions to sales employee	12
Total	42

Required:

Determine which costs should be recognised as an asset and which should be expensed.

Solution

The travel costs should be expensed because they would have been incurred even if the developer did not get the contract.

The legal fees and sales commissions should be recognised as assets because they are costs of obtaining the contract, assuming that the developer expects to recover them.

4.2   Costs to Fulfil a Contract

■ Costs incurred to fulfil a contract that are not within the scope of another standard should be recognised as an asset if they meet **all** of the following criteria:

  ● They relate directly to a contract;

  ● They generate or enhance the resources of the entity; and

  ● They are expected to be recovered.

■ Costs that must be expensed when incurred include:

  ● General and administrative costs;

  ● Cost of wasted materials, labour or other resources; and

  ● Costs that related to satisfied performance obligations.

Example 5 Recognition of Contract Costs

Jackson enters into a contract with a customer to transfer a software licence, perform installation and provide software updates and technical support for three years in exchange for $240,000. In order to fulfil the technical support portion of the project, Jackson purchases an additional workstation for the technical support team for $8,000 and assigns one employee to be primarily responsible for providing the technical support for the customer. This employee also provides services for other customers. The employee is paid an annual salary of $30,000 and is expected to spend 10% of his time supporting this customer.

Required:

Determine which costs should be recognised as an asset and which should be expensed.

5 Specific Transactions

5.1 Principal v Agent

▨ When an entity uses another party to provide goods or services to a customer, the entity needs to determine whether it is acting as a principal or an agent.

| **Principal** | The entity controls the good or service before it is transferred to the customer. | Revenue = Gross consideration |
| **Agent** | The entity arranges for the other party to provide the good or service. | Revenue = Fee or commission* |

Commentary

*The fee or commission may be the net consideration that the entity retains after paying the other party the consideration received in exchange for the good or service.

▨ Indicators that an entity is an agent and does not control the good or service before it is provided to the customer include:

- Another party is responsible for fulfilling the contract;
- The entity does not have inventory risk;
- The entity does not have discretion in establishing prices for the other party's goods or services;
- The consideration is in the form of a commission; and
- The entity is not exposed to credit risk.

F7 Financial Reporting

Illustration 10   Principal or Agent

On 1 January, Anderson enters into a contract with Tanner for the sale of an excavator with unique specifications. Anderson and Tanner develop the specifications and Anderson contracts with a construction equipment manufacturer to produce the equipment. The manufacturer will deliver the equipment to Tanner when it is completed.

Anderson agrees to pay the manufacturer $350,000 upon delivery of the excavator to Tanner. Anderson and Tanner agree to a selling price of $385,000 that will be paid by Tanner to Anderson. Anderson's profit is $35,000.

Anderson's contract with Tanner requires Tanner to seek remedies for defects from the manufacturer, but Anderson is responsible for any corrections due to errors in specifications.

Required:

Determine whether Anderson is acting as principal or agent in its contract with Tanner.

Solution

Anderson is acting as principal in the contract based on the following indicators:

- Anderson is responsible for fulfilling the contract because it is responsible for ensuring that the excavator meets specifications.
- Anderson has inventory risk because it is responsible for correcting errors in specifications, even though the manufacturer has inventory risk during production.
- Anderson has discretion in establishing the selling price.
- Anderson's consideration is in the form of profit, not commission.
- Anderson has credit risk for the $385,000 receivable from Tanner.

5.2 Repurchase Agreements

Definition

Repurchase agreement—a contract in which an entity sells an asset and also promises or has the option to repurchase the asset.

- There are three forms of repurchase agreements:
  1. An entity's obligation to repurchase the asset (a forward);
  2. An entity's right to repurchase the asset (a call option);
  3. An entity's obligation to repurchase the asset at the customer's request (a put option).

5.2.1 Forward or Call Option

- When an entity has an option or right to repurchase an asset, the customer does not obtain control of the asset and the entity accounts for the contract as either:
  - a **lease** if the entity can or must repurchase the asset for **less** than the original selling price; or
  - a **financing arrangement** if the entity can or must repurchase the asset for an amount **greater than or equal to** the original selling price.

- If the repurchase agreement is a financing arrangement, the entity will:

  - continue to recognise the asset;

  - recognise a financial liability for any consideration received from the customer; and

  - recognise as interest expense, which increases the financial liability, equal to the difference between the amount of consideration received from the customer and the amount of consideration to be paid to the customer.

Illustration 11   Repurchase Agreement

On 1 January, Anderson enters into a contract with Tanner for the sale of an excavator for $350,000. The contract includes a call option that gives Anderson the right to repurchase the excavator for $385,000 on or before 31 December. Tanner pays the entity $350,000 on 1 January. On December 31 the option lapses unexercised.

Required:

Explain how Anderson should account for the transaction on 1 January, during the year and on 31 December.

Solution

Anderson should account for the transaction as a financing arrangement because the repurchase price is greater than the original selling price.

On 1 January, Anderson recognises a financial liability of $350,000:

Dr Cash	350,000	
Cr Financial liability		350,000

During the year, Anderson recognises interest expense of $35,000, the difference between the repurchase price of $385,000 and the cash received of $350,000.

Dr Interest expense	35,000	
Cr Financial liability		35,000

On 31 December, when the option lapses, Anderson derecognises the liability and records a sale:

Dr Financial liability	385,000	
Cr Revenue		385,000

5.2.2 Put Option

- If an entity has an obligation to repurchase the asset at the customer's request for **less than** the original selling price, the entity accounts for the contract as either:

  - a **lease**, if the customer has a significant economic incentive to exercise the right; or

  - a **sale with a right of return,** if the customer does not have a significant economic incentive to exercise the right.

- If the repurchase price is **equal to or greater than** the original selling price, the entity accounts for the contract as either:

  - a **financing arrangement**, if the repurchase price is more than the expected market value of the asset; or

  - a **sale with a right of return**, if the repurchase price is less than or equal to the expected market value of the asset and the customer does not have a significant economic incentive to exercise the right.

Example 6 Put Option

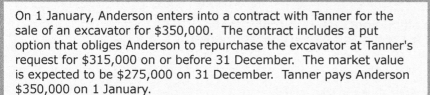

On 1 January, Anderson enters into a contract with Tanner for the sale of an excavator for $350,000. The contract includes a put option that obliges Anderson to repurchase the excavator at Tanner's request for $315,000 on or before 31 December. The market value is expected to be $275,000 on 31 December. Tanner pays Anderson $350,000 on 1 January.

Required:

Determine whether Anderson should account for this transaction as a lease, a financing arrangement or a sale with a right of return.

5.3 Bill-and-Hold Arrangements

Definition

Bill-and-hold arrangement—a contract in which the entity bills a customer for a product that it has not yet delivered to the customer.

- Revenue cannot be recognised in a bill-and-hold arrangement until the customer obtains control of the product.

- Generally, control is transferred to the customer when the product is shipped to the customer or delivered to the customer (depending on the terms of the contract).*

- For a customer to have obtained control of a product in a bill-and-hold arrangement, **all** of the following criteria must be met:

  - There must be a substantive reason for the bill-and-hold arrangement (e.g. the customer has requested because it does not have space for the product);

  - The product has been separately identified as belonging to the customer;

  - The product is currently ready for transfer to the customer; and

  - The entity cannot use the product or direct it to another customer.

Commentary

*In some contracts, the customer obtains control of the product without taking physical possession of the contract.

Illustration 12   Bill-and-Hold Arrangements

On 1 January, Anderson enters into a contract with Tanner for the sale of an excavator and spare parts. The manufacturing lead time is six months. On 1 July, Tanner pays for the machine and spare parts, but only takes possession of the machine. Tanner inspects and accepts the spare parts, but requests that the parts be stored in Anderson's warehouse because Tanner does not have a place to store the parts and its premises are very close to Anderson's warehouse.

Anderson expects to store the spare parts in a separate section of its warehouse for three years. The parts are available for immediate delivery to Tanner. Anderson cannot use the spare parts or transfer them to another customer.

Required:

Identify the performance obligation(s) in this contract and determine when revenue is recognised on each performance obligation.

Solution

There are three performance obligations in this contract:

1. Promise to provide the excavator.
2. Promise to provide spare parts.
3. Custodial services related to the spare parts.

Tanner obtains control of the spare parts on 1 July because all of the criteria are met (i.e. there is a substantive reason for Anderson to hold the spare parts, the parts are separately identified and ready to transfer and Anderson cannot use the parts or transfer them to another customer).

Anderson recognises revenue for the excavator and spare parts on 1 July when the excavator is transferred to Tanner and Tanner has obtained control of the spare parts.

Anderson recognises revenue on the custodial services over the three years for which the service is provided.

5.4   Consignments

- When an entity delivers its product to a dealer or distributor for sale to end customers, the entity needs to determine whether the contract is a sale or a consignment arrangement.

Sale	The dealer or distributor has obtained control of the product.	Recognise revenue when the product is shipped or delivered to the dealer or distributor (depending on the terms of the contract).
Consignment	The dealer or distributor has not obtained control of the product.	Recognise revenue when the dealer or distributor sells the product to a customer, or when the dealer or distributor obtains control of the product (i.e. after a specified period of time expires).

▨ The following are indicators of a consignment arrangement:

  ⦿ The entity controls the product until a specified event occurs, such as the sale of the product to a customer or until a specified period expires.

  ⦿ The entity can require the return of the product or transfer the product to another party.

  ⦿ The dealer does not have an unconditional obligation to pay the entity for the product (although it might be required to pay a deposit).

Illustration 13 **Car Dealership Arrangement**

FMC, a large multinational car manufacturer, delivers cars to a car dealer on the following terms:

■ Legal title passes on sale to the public;

■ The car dealer must pay for the car when legal title passes. The price to the car dealer is determined on the date FMC delivers the cars to the dealership;

■ FMC can require the return of the cars and, if not sold by the car dealer, can transfer the cars to another dealer.

Required:

Determine whether FMC should account for the delivery of the cars to the car dealer as a sale or a consignment arrangement.

Solution

FMC should account for the delivery of cars to the car dealer as a consignment arrangement because the dealer has not obtained control of the cars, as evidenced by the fact that FMC can require the return or transfer of the cars and the dealer does not have an unconditional obligation to pay FMC for the cars.

Revenue should not be recognised until the dealer sells a car.

Session 5 Quiz

Estimated time: 25 minutes

1. State the FIVE steps in the revenue recognition process. (1.1)

2. Name the THREE criteria that are used to determine whether a performance obligation is satisfied over time. (2.1)

3. Explain the difference between output methods and input methods used to measure progress towards completion. (3.1, 3.2)

4. State the criteria for recognising contract costs. (4.1, 4.2)

5. State FIVE indicators that an entity is an agent. (5.1)

6. Name the THREE forms of repurchase agreements. (5.2)

7. State the THREE criteria that must be met for control to transfer in a bill-and-hold arrangement. (5.3)

8. State THREE indicators of a consignment arrangement. (5.4)

Study Question Bank

Estimated time: 40 minutes

Priority		Estimated Time	Completed
Q8	Merryview	30 minutes	
Q9	Mocca	10 minutes	

Summary

- The five steps of the revenue recognition process are:
  1. identify the contract(s);
  2. identify the separate performance obligation(s);
  3. determine the transaction price;
  4. allocate the transaction price;
  5. recognise revenue.
- A contract is an agreement between parties that creates enforceable rights and obligations.
- A promise to transfer a good or service that is not distinct from other goods and services must be combined into a single performance obligation.
- The transaction price is allocated in proportion to the stand-alone selling price of the goods and services.
- Input or output methods can be used to measure progress towards completion.
- When a performance obligation is satisfied at a point in time, revenue is recognised when the customer takes control of the asset.
- A contract asset or liability is presented in the financial statements when either party has performed in a contract.
- Incremental costs of obtaining a contract are recognised as assets.
- An entity is a principal when it controls the good or service in a contract before it is transferred to the customer.
- An entity is an agent when it arranges for another party to provide a good or service.
- An option or right to repurchase an asset gives rise to a lease or a financing arrangement.
- An obligation to repurchase an asset for less than the original selling price gives rise to a lease or a sale with a right of return.
- An obligation to repurchase an asset for not less than the original selling price gives rise to a financing arrangement or a sale with a right of return.
- Revenue cannot be recognised in a bill-and-hold arrangement until the customer takes control of the product.
- Revenue is recognised in a consignment arrangement when the dealer or distributor sells the product to a customer or takes control of the product.

Solution 1—Time Value of Money

The transaction price is $3,175 ($4,000 \times 1/(1.08)^3$) because the time value of money must be considered when determining the transaction price. Interest income will also be recognised as follows:

20X5: $3,175 \times 8\% = \$254$

20X6: ($3,175 + \$254) \times 8\% = \$274$

20X7: ($3,175 + \$254 + \$274) \times 8\% = \$297$

Solution 2—Allocating Transaction Price

		$000
Software licence	$(240 \times {}^{150}/_{300})$	120
Installation service	$(240 \times {}^{60}/_{300})$	48
Software updates	$(240 \times {}^{40}/_{300})$	32
Technical support	$(240 \times {}^{50}/_{300})$	40
Total		240

Solution 3—Output and Input Methods

(a) Calculate total expected profit

	$
Revenue	3,200
Less: Contract costs to date	(1,500)
Future expected costs	(1,000)
Total expected profit	700

(b) Measure of progress towards completion

Sales basis	Cost basis
$\dfrac{1,800}{3,200} = 56.25\%$	$\dfrac{1,500}{2,500} = 60\%$

(c) Calculate revenue and costs for the year

	To date	Prior* year	$	To date	Prior year	$
Revenue	$3,200 \times 0.5625$ = 1,800	1,800 − 1200 =	600	$3,200 \times 0.6$ = 1,920	1,920 − 1200 =	720
Cost of sales	$2,500 \times 0.5625$ = 1,406	1,406 − 950 =	(456)	$2,500 \times 0.6$ =1,500	1,500 − 950 =	(550)
Profit			144			170

*Commentary

*The revenue and costs recognised at end of the first year have been assumed to be the same using both sales and costs basis for simplicity. In practice this is unlikely to be the case.

Solution 4—Statement of Financial Position Presentation

(i) Sales basis

Dr	Contract asset	600	
	Cr Revenue		600

Revenue recognised for the period.

Dr	Cash	1,000	
	Cr Contract asset		800
	Cr Contract liability		200

Cash received $1,000 is offset against the contract asset of $800 ($200 opening balance plus $600 recognised in second year) to leave a contract liability of $200.

Contract costs of $1,500 have been incurred to date but only $1,406 has been expensed to profit or loss. This leaves $94 work in progress (asset) to include in inventories.

(ii) Cost basis

Dr	Contract asset	720	
	Cr Revenue		720

Revenue recognised for the period.

Dr	Cash	1,000	
	Cr Contract asset		920
	Cr Contract liability		80

Cash received $1,000 is offset against the contract asset of $920 ($200 opening balance plus $720 recognised in second year) to leave a contract liability of $80.

There is no work in progress using the cost method as all costs are expensed to profit or loss as incurred.

Solution 5—Recognition of Contract Costs

The additional workstation should be recognised as an asset under IAS 16 *Property, Plant and Equipment.*

The cost of the employee assigned to the contract should be recognised as payroll expense because, although the costs are related to the contract and are expected to be recovered, the employee was already working for the developer and therefore the costs do not generate or enhance the resources of the developer.

Solution 6—Put Option

The transaction should be accounted for as a lease because:

- Anderson has an obligation to repurchase the excavator for less than the original selling price; and
- Tanner has a significant economic incentive to exercise the option because the repurchase price is greater than the market value expected on 31 December.

Inventory and Biological Assets

FOCUS

This session covers the following content from the *ACCA Study Guide.*

B. Accounting for Transactions in Financial Statements

4. Inventory and biological assets

a) Describe and apply the principles of inventory valuation. ☐

b) Apply the requirements of relevant accounting standards for biological assets. ☐

Session 6 Guidance

■ **Pay attention** to the effect of using different pricing methods and how the financial statements can be altered by changing from one valuation model to another. IAS 2 *Inventories* is a straightforward standard.

■ **Know** how to explain the methods of valuing inventory including FIFO and average cost (s.2.4).

(continued on next page)

VISUAL OVERVIEW

Objective: To describe the accounting treatment of inventories including biological assets.

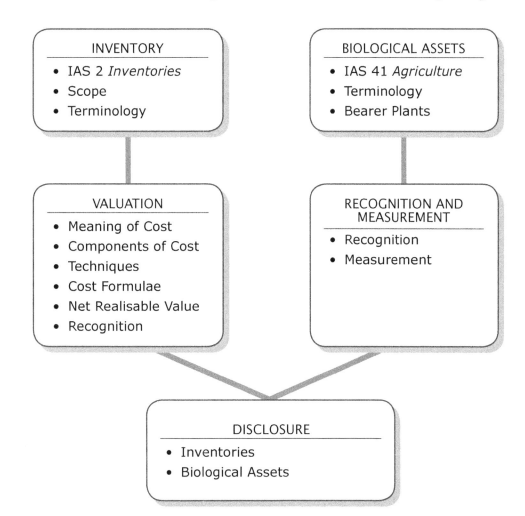

INVENTORY
- IAS 2 *Inventories*
- Scope
- Terminology

BIOLOGICAL ASSETS
- IAS 41 *Agriculture*
- Terminology
- Bearer Plants

VALUATION
- Meaning of Cost
- Components of Cost
- Techniques
- Cost Formulae
- Net Realisable Value
- Recognition

RECOGNITION AND MEASUREMENT
- Recognition
- Measurement

DISCLOSURE
- Inventories
- Biological Assets

Session 6 Guidance

■ **Be able** to calculate net realisable value (s.2.5).

■ **Understand** that biological assets can arise other than by purchase (e.g. through procreation) and undergo physical transformation (s.3.2).

■ **Be able** to measure biological assets at fair value and account for gains and losses arising (s.4.2).

1 Inventory

1.1 IAS 2 *Inventories*

- The primary issue in accounting for inventories is the amount of cost to be recognised as an asset and carried forward until related revenue is recognised.
- IAS 2 provides guidance on:
  - cost determination;
  - subsequent recognition as expense (including any write-down to net realisable value); and
  - cost formulae which may be used to assign costs to inventories.

1.2 Scope

- All inventories *except*:*
  - financial instruments (IAS 32 and IFRS 9); and
  - biological assets related to agricultural activity and agricultural produce at the point of harvest (IAS 41).
- The measurement provisions of IAS 2 do *not* apply to:
  - agricultural produce after harvest and minerals and mineral products measured at net realisable value in accordance with well-established industry practices; and
  - inventories held by commodity broker-traders measured at fair value less costs to sell.

*Commentary

*The inventories listed here as exceptions are entirely outside the scope of IAS 2. Some inventories are within the scope of the standard with regard to disclosure, but not measurement.

1.3 Terminology

Definition

Inventories—assets which are:

- held for resale in the ordinary course of business (e.g. merchandise purchased by retailer);
- in the process of production for resale (e.g. finished goods, work in progress, raw materials); or
- in the form of materials or supplies to be consumed in the production process or rendering of services.

Net realisable value—the estimated selling price in the ordinary course of business less the estimated cost of completion, and estimated costs necessary to make the sale.

2 Recognition and Measurement

Key Point

Inventories are measured at the *lower* of *cost* AND *net realisable value*.

2.1 Meaning of Cost

Key Point

Cost includes all costs involved in bringing the inventories to their present location and condition.

- Components of cost include:
  - purchase costs;
  - costs of conversion; and
  - other costs.

2.2 Components of Cost

Purchase Costs	Conversion Costs	Other Costs
• Purchase price; • Import duties/non-refundable taxes; • Transport/handling; • *Deduct* trade discounts/rebates.	• Direct production costs; • Production overheads based on normal capacity (i.e. expected on average under normal circumstances); • Joint product costs (*deduct* net realisable value of by-products).	• Non-production overheads only if incurred in bringing inventories to present location and condition (e.g. storage in whiskey distillers) and specific design costs; • Borrowing costs in limited circumstances (see IAS 23).

- The following expenditures are *excluded*:
  - abnormal amounts of wasted materials, labour and other production costs;
  - storage costs unless necessary to the production process;
  - administrative overheads; and
  - selling costs.
- For service providers, the cost of inventories consists primarily of labour including supervisory personnel and attributable overheads.*

*Commentary

*Profit margins or non-production costs which are often factored into prices charged by service providers are excluded from inventory cost.

2.3 Techniques for Measurement of Cost

▦ Two costing methods can be used for convenience if results approximate actual cost:

Standard Cost*	Retail Method*
• Takes into account normal levels of materials, labour, efficiency and capacity utilisation. • Standards must be regularly reviewed and revised as necessary.	• For inventories of large numbers of rapidly changing items with similar margins. • Reduces sales value by appropriate percentage gross margin. • This is a practical means of measurement for financial reporting purposes.

*Commentary

*Standard cost is a management tool which may need to be adapted to conform to IAS 2.

*An average percentage for each retail department is often used.

2.4 Cost Formulae

2.4.1 Specific Identification

▦ Specific identification of individual costs is required for:*

  ◦ items not ordinarily interchangeable; and

  ◦ goods/services produced and segregated for specific projects.

2.4.2 Formulae

▦ Formulae are permitted where specific identification of individual costs to individual items is not practicable.

▦ Only two formulae are permitted:

  1. First-in, first-out (FIFO)

  2. Weighted average.*

*Commentary

*Specific identification is not practicable in many businesses.

*In practice, weighted average formulas are likely to produce similar results when price changes are small and infrequent and there is a fairly rapid turnover of inventories.

FIFO Formula	Weighted Average Formula
• Assumes that items purchased (or manufactured) first are sold first. • Therefore inventory at period end is most recently purchased or produced. • Used, for example, for: — cars on a production line; — retail produce with a "sell by" (or "best before") date.	• Determined from weighted average cost of: — items at beginning of the period; and — cost of similar items purchased/produced during the period. • May be calculated on a periodic basis or on each additional shipment. • Used for like items used in production/sold without regard to when received.

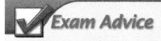 Exam Advice

Knowledge of these formulae is assumed from F3 *Financial Accounting* and detailed calculations will not be required in the F7 exam.

Example 1 Freya

Freya sets up in business on 1 September buying and selling CD players. These were purchased during the month as follows.

	Quantity	Price per unit
5 September	200	$150
16 September	80	$185

On 24 September, Freya sold a consignment of 250 CD players for $50,000.

Required:

Calculate (a) gross profit and (b) total value of closing inventory using each of the following inventory valuation methods:

(i) FIFO

(ii) Weighted average cost.

Solution

(a) Gross profit

	(i) FIFO	(ii) Weighted average
	$	$
Proceeds	50,000	50,000
Less: Cost		
Gross profit		

(b) Closing inventory value

(i)   FIFO

(ii)   Weighted average

2.4.3 Consistency

Key Point

An entity must use the same cost formula for all inventories having a similar nature and use in the entity.

▨ Different cost formulae may be used for inventories which have different characteristics.

2.5 Net Realisable Value

2.5.1 Need For

▨ Costs of inventories may not be recoverable due to:
- damage;
- obsolescence;
- decline in selling price; or
- an increase in estimated costs to completion/to be incurred.

▨ Any necessary write-down to net realisable value is usually on an item-by-item basis.*

> ***Commentary***
>
> *Assets are not carried in excess of amounts expected to be realised from their sale or use.

2.5.2 Considerations

▨ Estimates of net realisable value take into consideration:
- fluctuations of price or cost relating to events after the period end; and
- the purpose for which inventory is held.

2.5.3 Materials

▨ Materials for use in production are not written down to below cost unless the cost of finished products will exceed net realisable value.

2.5.4 Timing

▨ A new assessment is made of net realisable value in each subsequent period. When circumstances causing write-down no longer exist (e.g. selling price increases), write-down is reversed. Note that reversals are rare in practice.

Example 2 Net Realisable Value

Barnes is trying to calculate the year-end inventories figure for inclusion in his accounts. Details of his three stock lines are as follows.

Product	Cost	Realisable value	Selling expenses
	$	$	$
Alpha	100	120	25
Beta	50	60	5
Omega	75	85	15

Required:

Calculate the value of closing inventory which Barnes should use for his accounts.

Solution

		$
Alpha		
Beta		
Omega		
Closing Inventory		

2.6   Recognition

2.6.1   As an Expense

 **Key Point**

When inventories are sold, their carrying amount is recognised as an expense in the period in which related revenue is recognised.

▢ Any write-down to net realisable value and all losses are recognised in the period the write-down/loss occurs.

▢ Any reversal of any write-down is recognised as a *reduction* in expense in the period the reversal occurs.

▢ Inventories allocated to asset accounts (e.g. self-constructed property, plant or equipment) are recognised as an expense during the useful life of an asset.

2.6.2   As an Asset

▢ Although mentioned in IFRS 15 *Revenue from Contracts with Customers*, it is appropriate to consider here the "substance over form" issue of "consignment inventory".

▢ A consignment sale is one under which the recipient (buyer) undertakes to sell the goods on behalf of the shipper (seller).

▢ The IFRS 15 issue is whether and when revenue should be recognised in the accounts of the shipper. An implication of this is which party should record the inventory as an asset?

▢ This issue is very common in the automotive industry. Consignment inventory is held by the dealer but legally owned by the manufacturer.

- Who records the asset will depend on whether it is the dealer or the manufacturer who bears the risks and benefits of the rewards of ownership.
- Treatment—is the inventory an asset of tthe dealer at delivery?
  - **If yes**—the dealer recognises the inventory in the statement of financial position with the corresponding liability to the manufacturer.
  - **If no**—do not recognise inventory until transfer of title has crystallised (manufacturer recognises inventory until then).

3 Biological Assets

3.1 IAS 41 *Agriculture*

- IAS 41 prescribes the accounting treatment and the presentation and disclosures related to agricultural activity, including:
  - biological assets except for bearer plants;
  - agricultural produce at the point of harvest; and
  - related government grants.
- It does not deal with land or intangible assets related to agricultural activity, which are addressed in IAS 16 and IAS 38, respectively.

Exam Advice

Only biological assets are examinable.

3.2 Terminology

Biological asset: a living animal or plant.

Biological transformation: includes the processes of growth, degeneration, production and procreation that give rise to qualitative and quantitative changes in a biological asset.

Harvest: the detachment of produce from a biological asset or the cessation of a biological asset's life.

Agricultural produce: the product harvested from a biological asset.

Fair value: the price that would be received to sell an asset (or paid to transfer a liability) in transaction between market participants at the measurement date.

3.3 Bearer Plants

Bearer plants, which are used solely to grow produce (e.g. apple trees or grape vines), are accounted for under IAS 16 *Property, Plant and Equipment*.

- The fair value measurement model of IAS 41 was deemed inappropriate to bearer plants.*
- A bearer plant is measured at accumulated cost until maturity which is then depreciated over the plant's useful life.

*Commentary

*Because, for example, they "mature" and are not for sale.

4 Recognition and Measurement

4.1 Recognition

- A biological asset should be recognised when, and only when:
  - the asset is controlled as a result of a past event;
  - it is probable that future economic benefits associated with the asset will flow to the entity; and
  - fair value can be measured reliably.*

*Commentary

IAS 41 presumes that fair value can be measured reliably.

4.2 Measurement

4.2.1 At Fair Value Less Costs to Sell

- A biological asset should be measured at its fair value less costs to sell:*
  - on initial recognition; and
  - at the end of each reporting period.

*Commentary

*IFRS 13 applies to the measurement of fair value.

Illustration 1 Fair Value

A farmer owns a dairy herd at 1 January 20X6. The number of cows in the herd is 100. The fair value of the herd at this date is $5,000. The fair values of 2-year-old animals at 31 December 20X5 and 3-year-old animals at 31 December 20X6 are $60 and $75, respectively.

Separating out the value increases of the herd into those relating to price change and those relating to physical change gives the following valuation:

	$
Fair value at 1 January 20X6	5,000
Increase due to price change (100 × ($60 − $50))	1,000
Increase due to physical change (100 × ($75 − $60))	1,500
Fair value at 31 December 20X6	7,500

4.2.2 Gains and Losses

- A gain or loss arising on initial recognition of a biological asset is included in profit or loss for the period in which it arises.

Illustration 2 Initial Recognition Gain or Loss

A newborn calf is immediately recognised as a biological asset. There is no direct cost of "buying" the calf so measuring it at fair value less costs to sell will result in a gain (as long as fair value exceeds costs to sell). This gain is recognised immediately in profit or loss.

If costs to sell exceed fair value, a loss must be recognised immediately in profit or loss.

Exam Advice

Calculations of the analysis of a change in fair value are not expected. This is included in part (b) of *Example 3* for completeness.

- Any changes in fair value less costs to sell arising at the end of each reporting period are similarly recognised in profit or loss for the period.

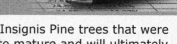

Example 3 Changes in Fair Value

As at 31 December 20X6, a plantation consists of 100 Insignis Pine trees that were planted 10 years earlier. Insignis Pine takes 30 years to mature and will ultimately be processed into building material for houses or furniture.

Only mature trees have established fair values by reference to a quoted price in an active market. The fair value (inclusive of current transport costs to get 100 logs to market) for a mature tree of the same grade as in the plantation is:

As at 31 December 20X6:	171
As at 31 December 20X7:	165

The appropriate discount rate is 6% per annum.

Required:

(a) Estimate the fair value of the plantation as at:

    (i) 31 December 20X6; and

    (ii) 31 December 20X7

(b) Analyse the gain between the two period ends:

    (i) a price change; and

    (ii) a physical change.

Solution

(a) Estimate of Fair Value

    (i) 31 December 20X6

    Mature plantation =

    Immature plantation =

    (ii) 31 December 20X7

    Mature plantation =

    Immature plantation =

(b) Analysis of Gain

    (i) Price change

    Reflects the change in price on the biological asset over the period.

                                                                                                    $

    Prior year estimate restated at *current* price

    Less

    Prior year estimate (at prior year price)

    Gain/(Loss)

    (ii) Physical change

    Reflects the change in the state of maturity of the biological asset at current price.

                                                                                                    $

    Current year estimate (at current price)

    Less

    Prior year estimate restated at *current* price

    Gain/(Loss)

4.2.3 Reliable Measurement Presumption

- The presumption that fair value can be measured reliably can be rebutted **only** on *initial recognition* when:
  - a quoted market price is not available; and
  - alternative estimates are clearly unreliable.
- In this case, the biological asset should be valued at cost less accumulated depreciation (in accordance with IAS 16) and any impairment losses (in accordance with IAS 36).
- When fair value can be measured reliably the asset will be carried at fair value less costs to sell.

5 Disclosure

5.1 Inventories

- Accounting policies adopted in measuring inventories including cost formula used.
- Carrying amounts:
  - Total carrying amount—in appropriate classifications (e.g. merchandise, raw materials, work in progress, finished goods).
  - Carrying amount at fair value less costs to sell.
  - Carrying amount of inventories pledged as security for liabilities.
- Expense in the period:
  - The amount of inventories recognised as an expense.
  - The amount of any write-down.
  - Any reversal of write-down recognised as income, and the circumstances leading to the reversal.

▦ The amount of inventories recognised as an expense during the period is often referred to as "cost of sales":

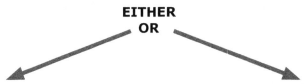

| Cost of inventories recognised as an expense:* | Operating costs, applicable to revenues, recognised as an expense, classified by nature.* |

▦ Cost of inventories recognised as an expense:*
  ◦ measurement of inventory sold;
  ◦ unallocated production overheads;
  ◦ abnormal production costs.

▦ Operating costs, applicable to revenues, recognised as an expense, classified by nature.*

▦ Costs recognised as an expense for:
  ◦ raw materials and consumables;
  ◦ labour costs; and
  ◦ other operating costs.

▦ Net change in inventories.

Commentary

*This corresponds to the "cost of sales" or "by function" format of the statement of profit or loss and other comprehensive income.

*Corresponding to the "by nature format of the statement of profit or loss and other comprehensive income.

5.2 Biological Assets

▦ The carrying amount of biological assets is presented *separately* in the statement of financial position.

▦ Disclosures include:
  ◦ The methods and assumptions used in determining fair value.
  ◦ A reconciliation of changes in the carrying amount between the beginning and the end of the current period.
  ◦ The aggregate gain or loss arising that is recognised in profit or loss.

▦ Separate disclosure of physical changes and price changes in the market is encouraged.

Summary

- Value at lower of cost AND net realisable value (NRV).
- NRV is selling price less cost to complete and sell.
- Cost includes all costs to bring inventories to their present condition and location.
- If specific cost is not determinable, use FIFO or weighted average.
- Cost of inventory is recognised as an expense in the period in which the related revenue is recognised.
- Any write-down is charged to expense. Any reversal in a later period is credited to income by reducing that period's cost of goods sold.
- Biological assets are living assets that undergo transformation.
- Under IAS 41 biological assets are measured at fair value less costs to sell.
- If fair value cannot be measured reliably IAS 16 (and IAS 36) apply.
- A gain or loss arising in a period can be analysed between physical and price changes. Disclosure of this is encouraged.

Session 6 Quiz
Estimated time: 20 minutes

1. Name the types of inventory within the scope of IAS 2. (1.2)
2. Explain how inventories are measured. (2.4)
3. List items which could be included in the cost of inventory. (2.1, 2.2)
4. Give the TWO formulas for valuing inventory under IAS 2. (2.4.2)
5. Explain why the cost of inventory may not be recoverable. (2.5)
6. Define biological transformation. (3.2)
7. Explain how a gain or loss can arise on initial recognition of a biological asset. (4.2.2)
8. State the circumstances under which the fair value presumption of IAS 41 can be rebutted. (4.2.3)
9. State how biological assets are measured if there is no reliable fair value. (4.2.3)

Study Question Bank
Estimated time: 25 minutes

Priority		Estimated Time	Completed
Q10	Sampi	25 minutes	

EXAMPLE SOLUTIONS

Solution 1—Freya

(a) Gross profit

	(i) FIFO	(ii) Weighted average
	$	$
Proceeds	50,000	50,000
Less: Cost (W)	(39,250)	(40,000)
Gross profit	10,750	10,000

Working

	Units		Unit price	$		Units		Unit price	$
FIFO	200	x	150	30,000	Weighted	200	x	150	30,000
	50	x	185	9,250	average	80	x	185	14,800
				39,250		280			44,800
					Therefore	1			160
					Therefore	250			40,000

(b) Closing inventory value

(i) FIFO   30 x 185 = $5,550
(ii) Weighted average   30 x 160 = $4,800

Solution 2—Net Realisable Value

			$
Alpha	NRV	120 − 25 =	95
Beta	Cost		50
Omega	NRV	85 − 15 =	70
Closing Inventory			215

Solution 3—Changes in Fair Value

(a) **Estimate of Fair Value**

(i) 31 December 20X6

The mature plantation would have been valued at 17,100.

The estimate for the immature plantation is $\dfrac{17,100}{1.06^{20}} = 5,332$

(ii) 31 December 20X7*

The mature plantation would have been valued at 16,500.

The estimate for the immature plantation is $\dfrac{16,500}{1.06^{19}} = 5,453$

(b) **Analysis of Gain**

The gain identified in (a) is analysed as follows:

(i) Price change

Reflects the change in price on the biological asset over the period.

		$
Prior year estimate restated at *current* price $\dfrac{16,500}{1.06^{20}}$	=	5,145
Less		
Prior year estimate (at prior year price) per (a)(i)		5,332
Loss		(187)

(ii) Physical change

Reflects the change in the state of maturity of the biological asset at current price.

	$
Current year estimate (at current price) per (a)(ii)	5,453
Less	
Prior year estimate restated at *current* price per (b)(i)	5,145
Gain	308

Commentary

*The difference in fair value of the plantation between the two period ends is \$121 (\$5,453 − \$5,332) which will be reported as a gain in profit or loss.

IAS 16 *Property, Plant and Equipment*

FOCUS

This session covers the following content from the *ACCA Study Guide.*

B. Accounting for Transactions in Financial Statements

1. Tangible non-current assets

a) Define and compute the initial measurement of a non-current asset (including borrowing costs and an asset that has been self-constructed). ☐

b) Identify subsequent expenditure that may be capitalised, distinguishing between capital and revenue items. ☐

c) Discuss the requirements of relevant accounting standards in relation to the revaluation of non-current assets. ☐

d) Account for revaluation and disposal gains and losses for non-current assets. ☐

e) Compute depreciation based on the cost and revaluation models and on assets that have two or more significant parts (complex assets). ☐

Session 7 Guidance

- **Learn** the definitions (s.1.3).
- **Revise** the importance of the distinction between capital and revenue expenditure in the preparation of financial statements (s.2.2).
- **Understand** areas relating to IAS 16 *Property, Plant and Equipment,* such as recognition, measurement—both initial and subsequent, depreciation, revaluation and subsequent expenditure.

(continued on next page)

VISUAL OVERVIEW

Objective: To prescribe the accounting treatment for tangible non-current assets.

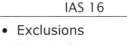

IAS 16
- Exclusions
- Terminology

RECOGNITION
- Criteria
- Capital v Revenue

INITIAL MEASUREMENT AT COST
- Components of Cost
- Exchange of Assets

SUBSEQUENT COSTS
- Running Costs
- Part Replacement
- Major Inspection or Overhaul

DISCLOSURE
- For Each Class
- Others
- Revaluations

DERECOGNITION
- Accounting Treatment
- Derecognition Date

MEASUREMENT AFTER RECOGNITION
- Accounting Policy
- Cost Model
- Revaluation Model

REVALUATIONS
- Fair Value
- Frequency
- Accumulated Depreciation
- Increase/Decrease
- Subsequent Accounting

DEPRECIATION
- Accounting Standards
- Depreciable Amount
- Depreciation Methods
- Non-depreciation

RECOVERY OF CARRYING AMOUNT
- Impairment
- Compensation

Session 7 Guidance

■ **Understand** the accounting treatment for subsequent expenditure paying particular attention to complex assets and major overhaul or inspection costs (s.4).

■ **Work through** the issues that arise in accounting for property, plant and equipment such as depreciation, revaluations and disposals (s.6, s.7).

1 IAS 16

1.1 Exclusions

IAS 16 does not apply to:

- biological assets which relate to agricultural activity (IAS 41); or
- mineral rights and reserves such as oil, natural gas and similar non-regenerative resources.

1.2 Terminology

Property, plant and equipment—tangible assets which:

- are held for use in the production or supply of goods or services or for rental or for admin purposes; and
- are expected to be used during more than one period.

Depreciation—the systematic allocation of a depreciable amount of an asset over its useful life.

Depreciable amount—the cost (or other amount substituted for cost) less its **residual value.**

Useful life—either the period of time over which an asset is expected to be used, or the number of production or similar units expected to be obtained from the asset.

Cost—the amount of cash/cash equivalents paid or the fair value of other consideration given to acquire an asset at the time of its acquisition or construction.*

Residual value—an estimate of the amount which would currently be obtained from the disposal of the asset, after deducting the estimated costs of disposal, if the asset was already of the age and in the condition expected at the end of its **useful life.**

Carrying amount—the amount at which an asset is recognised in the statement of financial position after deducting any accumulated depreciation and accumulated impairment losses.

Impairment loss—the amount by which the **carrying amount** of an asset exceeds its recoverable amount.

*Fair value is as defined in IFRS 13 *Fair Value Measurement.*

2 Recognition

2.1 Criteria

An item of **property, plant and equipment** is recognised when:

- it is *probable* that *future economic benefits* associated with the asset will flow to the entity, (satisfied when risks and rewards have passed to the entity); and
- the **cost** of the asset to the entity can be *measured reliably.**

In certain circumstances, it is appropriate to allocate the total expenditure on an asset to its component parts and account for each component separately.

*Reliable measurement is usually readily satisfied because an exchange transaction evidencing purchase identifies cost. For a self-constructed asset, a reliable measurement of cost can be made from transactions with third parties for the acquisition of materials, labour and other inputs used.

2.2   Capital Expenditure v Revenue Expenditure

 *Key Point*

In determining whether an item of expenditure should be recognised in the cost of asset, it is important to distinguish whether it should be included in:

■ the statement of financial position ("capital expenditure"); or

■ profit or loss ("revenue expenditure").

2.2.1   Capital Expenditure

Capital expenditure is incurred in:

▨ acquiring property and equipment intended for long-term use (benefits future accounting periods); and

▨ increasing the revenue-earning capacity of an existing non-current asset (by increasing efficiency or useful life).

Items of capital expenditure (except for the cost of land) will ultimately be expensed to profit or loss (through **depreciation**) as the asset is "consumed" through its use.

2.2.2   Revenue Expenditure

Revenue expenditures is incurred in the daily running (operation) of the business.

Examples include:

▨ buying or manufacturing goods which are sold and providing services;

▨ selling and distributing goods;

▨ administration costs; and

▨ repairing long-term assets.

Revenue expenditure is charged to profit or loss immediately. Thus, they are *matched* with the revenues of the accounting period.

Illustration 1   Capital Expenditure and Revenue Expenditure Examples

(i) $27,000 spent on acquiring new car for a sales executive is capital expenditure.

(ii) An annual road (or vehicle) tax of $1,800 included in the purchase price of (i) should be excluded from the amount capitalised as it is a revenue expense (a "running" cost).

(iii) $10,000 on the purchase of a second-hand delivery vehicle will be capital cost (that it is not a new asset which is purchased is irrelevant).

(iv) $12,000 spent on the refurbishment (i.e. renovation) of (iii) to bring it into use also will be capital.

(v) $1,000 monthly rental for hire of a vehicle is revenue expenditure.

---

3 Initial Measurement at Cost

 **Key Point**

Property, plant and equipment is initially measured at cost.

3.1 Components of Cost

- Purchase price, including import duties and non-refundable purchase taxes (after deducting trade discounts and rebates.)
- Directly attributable costs of bringing the asset to location and working condition, for example:
  - employee benefits (e.g. wages) arising directly from construction or acquisition;
  - costs of site preparation;
  - initial delivery and handling costs;
  - installation and assembly costs;
  - costs of testing proper functioning (net of any sale proceeds of items produced);
  - professional fees (e.g. architects and engineers); and
  - borrowing costs for qualifying assets in accordance with IAS 23 (see *Session 8*).
- An *initial* estimate of dismantling and removal costs (i.e. "decommissioning") the asset and restoring the site on which it is located. The obligation for this may arise either:
  - on acquisition of the item; or
  - as a consequence of using the item other than to produce inventory.

3.2 Exchange of Assets

- Cost is measured at fair value of asset received, which is equal to fair value of the asset given up (e.g. trade-in or part-exchange) adjusted by the amount of any cash or cash equivalents transferred. Except when:
  - the exchange transaction lacks commercial substance; or
  - the fair value of neither the asset received nor the asset given up is reliably measurable.
- Whether an exchange transaction has commercial substance depends on the extent to which the reporting entity's future cash flows are expected to change as a result of the transaction.

4 Subsequent Costs*

*Commentary

4.1 Running Costs

▨ The carrying amount of an item of property, plant and equipment does not include the costs of day-to-day servicing of the item.

*The issue is whether this is capital or revenue expenditure.

Key Point

Servicing costs (e.g. labour and consumables) are recognised in profit or loss as incurred.

▨ Often described as "repairs and maintenance", running costs are made to restore or maintain future economic benefits.

4.2 Part Replacement

▨ Some items (e.g. aircraft, ships, gas turbines, etc) are a series of linked parts which require regular replacement at different intervals and so have different useful lives.*

▨ The carrying amount of an item of property, plant and equipment recognises the cost of replacing a part when that cost is incurred, if the recognition criteria are met.

▨ The carrying amount of replaced parts is derecognised (i.e. treated as a disposal).

*Commentary

*"Complex asset" is a term commonly used to describe assets which have more than one major component with different useful lives.

Illustration 2 A Component Asset

An airline is required by law to replace its engines every five years. The engines may be identified as assets with a separate life from the rest of the aeroplane and written off to zero over five years. After five years, the engines will be replaced and the cost of the new replacement engines will then be added to the cost of the aeroplane, and this cost will then be depreciated over the next five years. The rest of the aeroplane will be depreciated over the plane's useful life, which will probably be longer than five years. This is an example of a "component" asset.

4.3 Major Inspection or Overhaul Costs

▨ Major inspections for faults, regardless of whether parts are replaced, may be a condition for continuing to operate an item of property, plant and equipment (e.g. a ship).

▨ On initial recognition, inspection costs are estimated; this amount is depreciated over the period to the first inspection. This amount is part of the original cost recognised and is not an additional component of cost.

▨ Any remaining carrying amount of the cost of the previous inspection (as distinct from physical parts) is derecognised.

▨ The amount capitalised will be depreciated over the period to the next major inspection, when the costs incurred at that point will be capitalised.

Key Point

The cost of each major inspection performed is recognised in the carrying amount, as a replacement, if the recognition criteria are satisfied.

Illustration 3 Capitalising Overhaul Costs

A shipping company is required by law to bring all ships into dry dock every five years for a major inspection and overhaul. Overhaul expenditure might at first sight seem to be a repair to the ships but it is actually a cost incurred in getting the ship back into a seaworthy condition. As such the costs must be capitalised.

A ship which cost $20 million with a 20-year life must have a major overhaul every five years. The estimated cost of the overhaul at the five-year point is $5 million.

The depreciation charge for the first five years of the assets life will be as follows:

	Overhaul	Capital
Cost	5	15
Years	5	20
Depreciation per year	1	0.75

Total accumulated depreciation for the first five years will be $8.75, and the carrying amount of the ship at the end of year 5 will be $11.25 million.

The actual overhaul costs incurred at end of year 5 are $6 million. This amount will now be capitalised into the costs of the ship, to give a carrying amount of $17.25 million.

The depreciation charge for years 6 to 10 will be as follows:

	Overhaul	Capital
Cost	6	11.25
Years	5	15
Depreciation per year	1.2	0.75

Annual depreciation for years 6 to 10 will now be $1.95 million. This process will be continued for years 11 to 15 and years 16 to 20. By the end of year 20, the capital cost of $20 million will have been depreciated plus the actual overhaul costs incurred at years 5, 10 and 15.

5 Measurement After Recognition

5.1 Accounting Policy

 Key Point

An entity may choose between the cost model and the revaluation model. The same policy, however, must be applied to each entire class of property, plant and equipment.

▪ Classes include land, land and buildings, factory plant, aircraft, vehicles, office equipment, fixtures and fittings, etc.

5.2   Cost Model

Carry at cost less any accumulated depreciation and any accumulated **impairment losses.**

5.3   Revaluation Model

- Carry, at a revalued amount, the fair value at the date of the revaluation less any subsequent accumulated depreciation and any accumulated impairment losses.
- Fair values must be reliably measurable.
- All revalued assets are still depreciated, unless the asset is land.

6   Revaluations

6.1   Fair Value

- Only those assets whose fair value can be measured reliably may be revalued; they are carried at fair value at the revaluation date less any subsequent depreciation and impairment losses.
- Fair value is assessed using the fair value hierarchy in IFRS 13 *Fair Value Measurements.* The basis of the hierarchy is as follows:
  - **Level 1 inputs**—quoted prices in active markets for identical assets which the entity can access at the measurement date.
  - **Level 2 inputs**—inputs other than quoted prices (included in level 1) which are observable for the asset, either directly or indirectly.
  - **Level 3 inputs**—unobservable inputs for the asset.

6.2   Frequency

- Revaluations must be made sufficiently regularly to ensure that there is no material difference between the carrying amount and fair value at the end of the reporting period.
- Frequency depends on movements in fair values. When fair value differs materially from carrying amount, a further revaluation is necessary.
- Items in a class may be revalued on a rolling basis over a short period of time, provided that revaluations are kept up-to-date.

6.3   Accumulated Depreciation

- At the date of the revaluation, accumulated depreciation is either:
  1. restated proportionately with the change in gross carrying amount so that the carrying amount after revaluation equals its revalued amount; or
  2. eliminated against gross carrying amount and the net amount restated to the revalued amount.

Example 1 Accumulated Depreciation

	$
Cost	1,000
Accumulated depreciation	(250)
Carrying amount	750

Required:
Determine the accounting entries required to restate the net amount at a revalued amount of:
(a) $1,100
(b) $ 900.

Solution

	(a) $	(b) $
Cost		
Accumulated depreciation		
Carrying amount		

(a)	$	$
Dr Cost		
Dr Accumulated depreciation		
Cr Revaluation reserve		

(b)	$	$
Dr Accumulated depreciation		
Cr Cost		
Cr Revaluation reserve		

6.4   Increase/Decrease

- On an asset-by-asset basis:
  - An increase is credited directly to a revaluation reserve and included in "other comprehensive income".
  - A revaluation increase, however, must be taken to profit or loss to the extent that it reverses a revaluation decrease on the asset which was previously recognised as an expense.
  - A decrease is recognised as an expense in profit or loss for the period.
  - A revaluation decrease, however, must be charged directly against any related revaluation surplus to the extent that it is covered by that surplus.

Illustration 4 Revaluation Model

An asset was purchased for $100 on 1 January 20X1. The entity adopted the revaluation model for subsequent measurement of the asset.

	Asset	Revaluation surplus	Profit or loss	
1.1.20X1	100	—	—	
	20	20 Cr		The surplus is taken to revaluation reserve.
31.12.20X1	120	20 Cr		
1.1.20X2	120	20 Cr		A deficit is taken to the profit or loss unless it reverses a surplus held on the asset.
	(15)	(15) Dr	—	
31.12.20X2	105	5 Cr		
1.1.20X3	105	5 Cr		Again the deficit is taken to revaluation reserve but only to the extent it reverses the previously recognised surplus with the rest to profit or loss.
	(9)	(5) Cr	4 Dr	
31.12.20X3	96	—		
1.1.20X4	96	—		That part of the surplus which reverses the previously expensed deficit is taken to the profit or loss. The rest is taken to revaluation reserve.
	15	11 Cr	4 Cr	
31.12.20X4	111	—		

▨ For simplicity, annual depreciation has been excluded from *Illustration 4*. However, depreciation would be charged each year before the revaluation adjustment is made.

▨ The revaluation surplus may be transferred directly to retained earnings when the surplus is realised. Realisation occurs as the asset is consumed or disposed of.

▨ However, it is not reclassified (i.e. it is not included in profit or loss on disposal).

6.5 Subsequent Accounting

6.5.1 Transfer to Retained Earnings

▨ IAS 16 allows, but does not require, an entity to make a transfer from the revaluation surplus to retained earnings as the asset is used.*

Commentary

*A transfer to retained earnings lies within equity (shown in the statement of changes in equity) and cannot be made through profit or loss. See *Illustration 5*.

Key Point

If the transfer is made over the remaining life of the asset then the transfer to retained earnings will be an annual transfer based on the difference in depreciation charge under historical cost and the revalued amount.

Illustration 5 Extract from Statement of Changes in Equity

	Share capital $	Share premium $	Revaluation surplus $	Retained earnings $	Total $
Balance at 31 December 20X6	x	x	x	x	x
Changes in equity for 20X7					
Issuance of share capital	x	x			x
Dividends (paid and declared)				(x)	(x)
Total comprehensive income for the year			x/(x)	x/(x)	x/(x)
Transfer to retained earnings			(x)	x	
Balance at 31 December 20X7	x	x	x	x	x

- The transfer is the *difference* between the annual depreciation expense based on the revalued amount and the annual depreciation expense based on historic cost.
- This portion of the revaluation surplus is deemed to be realised (and is now available for distribution as a dividend to shareholders)

6.5.2 Disposal

- The revaluation surplus may be transferred directly to retained earnings when the surplus is realised (e.g. on disposal of the asset or during the asset's remaining useful life).

7 Depreciation

7.1 Accounting Standards

- The **depreciable amount** is allocated on a systematic basis over the useful life of the asset. Note that the term "depreciable amount" is based on the cost or revalued amount.
- Depreciation method, useful life and **residual value** must be reviewed at least *annually,* at each financial year end.

Key Point

If expectations differ from previous estimates, the change(s) are accounted for as a change in accounting estimate (in accordance with IAS 8).

- The depreciation method should reflect the pattern in which the asset's economic benefits are consumed.
- The depreciation charge for each period is recognised as an expense unless it is included in the carrying amount of another asset (e.g. in inventory).
- Each part of an item of property, plant and equipment which is significant (in relation to total cost) is depreciated separately.

7.2 Depreciable Amount

7.2.1 Useful Life

▥ Factors to be considered:

- Expected usage assessed by reference to expected capacity or physical output.
- Expected physical wear and tear (depends on operational factors such as the number of shifts, repair and maintenance programmes, etc).
- Technical obsolescence arising from:
  — changes or improvements in production; or
  — change in market demand for product or service output.
- Legal or similar limits on the use (e.g. expiry dates of related leases).
- Asset management policy may involve disposal of assets after a specified time; therefore, useful life may be shorter than economic life.

▥ Repair and maintenance policies may also affect useful life (e.g. by extending it or increasing residual value) but do not negate the need for depreciation.

7.2.2 Depreciation Period

▥ Depreciation commences when an asset is available for use.

▥ Depreciation ceases when an asset is derecognised (e.g. scrapped or sold) or when the asset is classified as held for sale in accordance with IFRS 5.

Example 2 Useful Life

An asset costing $1,000 was estimated to have a useful life of 10 years and residual value $200. After two years, useful life was revised to four remaining years. Calculate the depreciation charge for each of the first three years.

Solution

	Year 1 $	Year 2 $	Year 3 $
Cost	1,000	1,000	1,000
Accumulated depreciation	_____	_____	_____
Carrying amount	_____	_____	_____
Charge for year			

7.2.3 Land and Buildings

▥ These are separable assets and are dealt with separately for accounting purposes, even when they are acquired together.

- Land normally has an unlimited useful life and is therefore not depreciated.
- Buildings normally have a limited useful life and are depreciable assets.

7.3   Depreciation Methods

7.3.1   Examples

▨ Straight-line ➲ a constant charge over useful life.

▨ Reducing/diminishing balance ➲ a decreasing charge over useful life.

▨ Units of production ➲ a charge based on expected use or output.

7.3.2   Annual Review

▨ The method should be reviewed annually. Any change will be reflected in the depreciation charge in profit or loss in the current and future periods (IAS 8).

7.4   Non-depreciation

7.4.1   Background

▨ Many argue that certain assets should not be subject to the general rule that all assets must be depreciated.

▨ In some jurisdictions, companies have adopted a policy not to depreciate certain assets.

7.4.2   Arguments for This Approach

✔ Assets are maintained to a very high standard. This maintenance cost is charged to the profit or loss in lieu of depreciation.

✔ The residual value is at least equal to the carrying amount (e.g. due to high maintenance).

✔ Assets have a very long useful economic life, such that depreciation is immaterial.

✔ The asset is not currently in use.

7.4.3   IAS 16

▨ The standard requires depreciation to be charged in all circumstances, but a case can be made for "non-depreciation" on the grounds that the residual value is greater than the carrying amount of the asset (i.e. depreciation is zero).

8 Recovery of Carrying Amount

8.1 Impairment

- To determine whether an item of property, plant and equipment is impaired an entity applies IAS 36 *Impairment of Assets.*
- Impairment losses are accounted for in accordance with IAS 36.

8.2 Compensation

- In certain circumstances, a third party will compensate an entity for an impairment loss (e.g. insurance for fire damage or compensation for compulsory purchase of land for a motorway).
- Such compensation must be included in the profit or loss when it becomes receivable. Recognising the compensation as deferred income or deducting it from the impairment or loss or from the cost of a new asset is not appropriate.

9 Derecognition

9.1 Accounting Treatment

- Statement of financial position—eliminate on disposal or when no future economic benefits are expected from use ("retirement") or disposal.
- Profit or loss—recognise gain or loss (difference between estimated net disposal proceeds and carrying amount) unless a sale and leaseback (IFRS 16). Gains are **not** classified as revenue.
- See IFRS 5 for treatment of non-current held for sale.

9.2 Derecognition Date

- The derecognition date is the date the recipient takes control of the asset (assuming that the performance obligation has been satisfied in accordance with IFRS 15).

10 Disclosure

10.1 For Each Class

▨ Measurement bases used for determining gross carrying amount.

▨ Depreciation methods used.

▨ Useful lives or the depreciation rates used.

▨ Gross carrying amount and accumulated depreciation at the beginning and end of the period. Accumulated impairment losses are aggregated with accumulated depreciation.

▨ A reconciliation of carrying amount at the beginning and end of the period showing:

- additions (i.e. capital expenditure);
- disposals;
- acquisitions through business combinations;
- increases or decreases resulting from revaluations;
- impairment losses (i.e. reductions in carrying amount);
- reversals of impairment losses;
- depreciation; and
- other movements.

10.2 Other Disclosures

▨ Existence and amounts of restrictions on title, and property, plant and equipment pledged as security.

▨ Expenditures on account of property, plant and equipment in the course of construction.

▨ Contractual commitments for the acquisition of property, plant and equipment.

▨ Compensation from third parties for items impaired, lost or given up which is included in profit or loss, if not disclosed separately in profit or loss.

10.3 Items Stated at Revalued Amounts

▨ Effective date of revaluation.

▨ Whether an independent valuer was involved.

▨ Carrying amount of each class of property, plant and equipment which would have been included in the financial statements had the assets been carried under the cost model.

▨ Revaluation surplus, indicating movement for the period and any restrictions on distribution of balance to shareholders.

Session 7 Quiz
Estimated time: 20 minutes

1. Define "property, plant and equipment". (1.3)

2. Name the recognition criteria for capitalising expenditure on property, plant and equipment. (2.1)

3. Explain how new items of property, plant and equipment are measured. (3)

4. Explain how the replacement of a major part of an asset is accounted for. (4.2)

5. If a company decides to use the revaluation model to value a class of assets, state how the value of those assets will be shown in future statements of financial position. (5.3)

6. If a company decides to use the revaluation model, state how often the assets must be revalued. (6.2)

7. Explain how the revaluation model accounts for an increase in value. (6.4)

8. List factors to be considered when identifying the useful life of an asset. (7.2.1)

9. Give the arguments which have been used for the non-depreciation of assets. (7.4.2)

10. Give the circumstance under which an asset should be de-recognised. (9.1)

Study Question Bank
Estimated time: 25 minutes

Priority		Estimated Time	Completed
Q11	Fam	**25 minutes**	
Additional			
Q12	Flightline		

Summary

- An item of property, plant and equipment is recognised when:
  - it is *probable* that future economic benefits will flow from it; and
  - its cost can be *measured reliably.*
- Initial measurement is at cost.
- Subsequently, use:
  - depreciated (amortised) cost—"cost model";
  - up-to-date fair value—"revaluation model".
- Property (except land) and plant and equipment are depreciated on a systematic basis over their useful lives:
  - base is cost less estimated residual value (or revalued amount);
  - method should reflect the consumption of economic benefits; and
  - useful life should be reviewed annually (and any change reflected in the current period and *prospectively*).
- Significant costs to be incurred at the end of an asset's useful life are reflected by:
  - recognising as a cost element (if IAS 37 liability criteria are met); or
  - reducing the estimated residual value.

  In either case, the amount is effectively expensed over the life of the asset.
- Revaluations should be made with sufficient regularity.
- The *entire class* to which a revalued asset belongs must be revalued.
- Revaluation gains are recognised in other comprehensive income and accumulated in equity (unless reversing a previous charge to profit or loss).
- Decreases in valuation are charged to profit or loss (unless reversing a revaluation surplus).
- When a revalued asset is sold/disposed of, any remaining revaluation surplus is transferred directly to retained earnings (not through profit or loss).
- Gain/loss on retirement/disposal is calculated by reference to the carrying amount.
- Required disclosures include:
  - reconciliation of movements;
  - items pledged as security;
  - capital commitments;
  - if assets are revalued, historical cost amounts; and
  - change in revaluation surplus.

EXAMPLE SOLUTIONS

Solution 1—Accumulated Depreciation

	(a)	(b)
	$	$
Cost	1,100	900
Accumulated depreciation	0	0
Carrying amount	1,100	900

	$	$		$	$
Dr Cost	100		Dr Accumulated depreciation	250	
Dr Accumulated depreciation	250		Cr Cost		100
Cr Revaluation reserve		350	Cr Revaluation reserve		150

Solution 2—Useful Life

	Year 1	Year 2	Year 3
	$	$	$
Cost	1,000	1,000	1,000
Accumulated depreciation	(80)	(160)	(320)
Carrying amount	920	840	680
Charge for year	80	80	160

IAS 23 *Borrowing Costs*

FOCUS

This session covers the following content from the *ACCA Study Guide.*

B. Accounting for Transactions in Financial Statements

1. Tangible non-current assets

a) Define and compute the initial measurement of a non-current asset (including a self-constructed asset and borrowing costs).

☐

Session 8 Guidance

- **Know** how to describe and identify qualifying assets as defined in IAS 23 (s.3.1).
- **Learn** the advantages and disadvantages to expensing and capitalising interest (s.1.2).
- **Calculate** the amount of interest which should be capitalised under IAS 23 (s.3).

(continued on next page)

VISUAL OVERVIEW

Objective: To describe the accounting treatment of borrowing costs.

```
┌────────────────────────────────┐
│             IAS 23             │
│  ─────────────────────────────  │
│   • Issue                       │
│   • Arguments                   │
│   • Scope                       │
│   • Terminology                 │
└────────────────────────────────┘
                 │
┌────────────────────────────────┐
│      ACCOUNTING TREATMENT       │
│  ─────────────────────────────  │
│   • Recognition                 │
│   • Disclosure                  │
└────────────────────────────────┘
                 │
┌────────────────────────────────┐
│       CAPITALISATION ISSUES     │
│  ─────────────────────────────  │
│   • Qualifying Assets           │
│   • Borrowing Costs Eligible    │
│   • Commencement                │
│   • Suspension                  │
│   • Cessation                   │
└────────────────────────────────┘
```

Session 8 Guidance

■ **Comprehend** that "Borrowing Costs" is a relatively straightforward topic. Some borrowing costs may be capitalised as a direct cost of constructing a qualifying asset that is then accounted for under IAS 16 (see *Session 7*).

1 IAS 23

1.1 Issue

- Companies borrow to finance their activities. Companies pay interest (finance charges) on the amounts borrowed.
- How should such debits for interest be recognised in the financial statements:
  - always as an expense; or
  - are there circumstances which justify capitalisation as an asset?*

*Capitalising an asset defers recognition in the profit or loss to a later period.

1.2 Arguments

CAPITALISATION OF INTEREST	
Arguments for	**Arguments against**
✔ Accruals: Better matching of cost (interest) to benefit (use of asset).	✗ Accruals: Benefit is use of money. Interest should be reflected in profit or loss in the period for which the company has the use of the cash.
✔ Comparability is improved. Better comparison between companies which buy the assets and those which construct.	✗ Comparability is distorted. Similar assets at different costs depending on the method of finance.
✔ Consistency: Interest treated as any other costs.	✗ Consistency: Interest treated differently from period to period.
	✗ Reported profit distorted.

1.3 Scope

- IAS 23 is applied to account for borrowing costs.
- The standard does not apply to qualifying assets which are measured at fair value (e.g. under IAS 41 *Agriculture*).
- Any inventories manufactured in large quantities and on a repetitive basis are *not* qualifying assets.

1.4 Terminology

Borrowing costs—interest and other costs incurred by an entity in connection with the borrowing of funds.

Qualifying asset—an asset which necessarily takes a substantial period of time to get ready for its intended use or sale.

- The following may fall within the definition of **borrowing costs**:
  - Interest expense calculated using the effective interest method (IFRS 9), which may include:
    - amortisation of discounts or premiums related to borrowings; or
    - amortisation of any directly attributable costs related to borrowings.
  - Finance charges with respect to lease liabilities (IFRS 16).
  - Exchange differences arising from foreign currency borrowings to the extent they are regarded as an adjustment to interest costs (IAS 21).
  - Preference dividend when preference capital is classified as debt.

2 Accounting Treatment

2.1 Recognition

Key Point

Borrowing costs which relate to a **qualifying asset** must be capitalised as part of the cost of *that asset.*

- All other borrowing costs must be recognised as an *expense* in the period in which they are incurred.

2.2 Disclosure

- The amount of borrowing costs capitalised in the period.
- The capitalisation rate used.

3 Capitalisation Issues

3.1 Qualifying Assets

Key Point

Borrowing costs which are *directly attributable* to the acquisition, construction or production of a qualifying asset are capitalised as part of the cost of that asset.

- The amount of borrowing costs eligible for capitalisation is determined in accordance with IAS 23.
- A qualifying asset is an asset which necessarily takes a substantial period of time to get ready for its intended use or sale.

3.1.1 Examples of qualifying assets:

✔ Inventories which require a substantial period of time to bring them to a saleable condition (e.g. whisky)
✔ Manufacturing plant
✔ Power generation facilities
✔ Investment properties.

3.1.2 Examples of assets which do not qualify:

✗ Inventories routinely manufactured or otherwise produced in large quantities on a repetitive basis over a short period of time.
✗ Assets ready for their intended use or sale when acquired.

3.2 Borrowing Costs Eligible for Capitalisation

3.2.1 Specific Borrowings

- When an entity borrows specifically for the purpose of funding an asset the identification of the borrowing costs is straightforward:
  - the amount capitalised is the actual borrowing costs; *less*
  - any income earned on the temporary investment of those borrowings.

3.2.2 Establishing a Direct Relationship

- It is sometimes difficult to establish a direct relationship between asset and funding.*
    - For example:
        - — when financing activity is coordinated centrally;
        - — when a range of debt instruments with varying interest rates are used by a group company and lent to other members of the group; or
        - — when borrowings are in a foreign currency in a high-inflation economy.

*Commentary

*Judgement is therefore required.

3.2.3 Funds Borrowed Generally

Key Point

The amount of borrowing costs eligible for capitalisation is determined by applying a *capitalisation rate* to the expenditures on that asset.

- The capitalisation rate is the weighted average borrowing cost for borrowings during the period, excluding specific borrowing.*
- In some circumstances, it is appropriate to include all borrowings of the parent and its subsidiaries when computing a weighted average borrowing cost; in other circumstances, it is appropriate for each subsidiary to use the weighted average borrowing cost of to its own borrowings.

*Commentary

*The amount capitalised during a period clearly cannot exceed the amount incurred.

Example 1 Capitalisation Rates

An entity has three sources of borrowing in the period.

	Outstanding liability	Interest charge
	$000	$000
7-year loan	8,000	1,000
25-year loan	12,000	1,000
Bank overdraft	4,000 (average)	600

Required:

(a) Calculate the appropriate capitalisation rate if all of the borrowings are used to finance the production of qualifying assets but none of the borrowings relate to a specific qualifying asset.

(b) If the seven-year loan is an amount which can be specifically identified with a qualifying asset, calculate the rate which should be used on the other assets.

3.3 Commencement of Capitalisation

- Capitalisation commences:
    - expenditures for the asset are being incurred;
    - borrowing costs are being incurred; and
    - *activities* which are necessary to prepare the asset for its intended use or sale are *in progress.*

- Expenditures on a qualifying asset include only:
  - payments of cash;
  - transfers of other assets; or
  - the assumption of interest-bearing liabilities.
- Expenditures are *reduced* by any progress payments received and grants received in connection with the asset.
- The average carrying amount of the asset during a period, including borrowing costs previously capitalised, is normally a reasonable approximation of the expenditures to which the capitalisation rate is applied in that period.

Activities Included	Activities Excluded
✔ Physical construction of the asset. ✔ Technical and administrative work before physical construction commences (e.g. obtaining planning permission).	✗ Holding an asset when there is no production or development which changes its condition (e.g. land acquired and held without any associated development activity).

3.4 Suspension of Capitalisation

- Capitalisation is suspended during *extended* periods in which active development is interrupted.
- Capitalisation is not normally suspended:*
  - during a period when substantial technical and administrative work is being carried out; or
  - when a temporary delay is a necessary part of the process of getting an asset ready for its intended use or sale.

3.5 Cessation of Capitalisation

Key Point

Capitalisation ceases when "substantially all" the activities necessary to prepare the qualifying asset for its intended use or sale are completed.

- An asset is normally ready for its intended use or sale when the physical construction of the asset is complete even though routine administrative work might still continue. If minor modifications are all that are outstanding (e.g. interior decoration of a property to the purchaser's or user's specification), this indicates that substantially all the activities are complete.
- When a construction is completed in parts and each part is capable of being used while construction continues on other parts, capitalisation ceases when substantially all the activities necessary to prepare each part are completed.

*Commentary

*For example, capitalisation continues during the extended period needed for inventories to mature or where high water levels delay construction of a bridge, if high waters are common during the construction period in the geographic region involved.

Summary

- Compliance with IAS 23 is not mandatory for:
  - qualifying assets measured at fair value (e.g. IAS 41); or
  - "mass produced" inventories.
- Borrowing costs include:
  - interest expense calculated by the effective interest method (IFRS 9);
  - finance charges (IFRS 16); and
  - exchange differences on foreign currency borrowings.
- A "qualifying asset" takes a substantial amount of time to be ready for its intended use or sale. Includes "made-to-order" inventories.
- Borrowing costs directly attributable to a qualifying asset must be **capitalised**. Other borrowing costs are expensed when incurred.
- For specific funds, costs eligible for capitalisation are actual costs incurred less any income from temporary investment.
- For general funds, apply a capitalisation rate (weighted average borrowing cost) to expenditures.
- Capitalisation:
  - commences when expenditure, borrowing and activities are in progress;
  - is suspended when active development is interrupted; and
  - ceases when substantially all activities are complete.

Session 8 Quiz
Estimated time: 10 minutes

1. Define a qualifying asset in accordance with IAS 23. (1.4)

2. Specify what would be included within the definition of borrowing costs. (1.4)

3. Describe the type of borrowing costs which may be capitalised according to the standard. (3.1, 3.2)

4. State when the capitalisation of borrowing costs should commence. (3.3)

5. A company is required to capitalise borrowing costs relating to the construction of a qualifying asset; state when the borrowing costs can no longer be capitalised. (3.5)

Study Question Bank
Estimated time: 15 minutes

Priority		Estimated Time	Completed
Q13	Dawes	15 minutes	
Additional			
Q14	Apex		

EXAMPLE SOLUTIONS

Solution 1—Capitalisation Rates

(a) Capitalisation rate

$$\frac{1,000,000 + 1,000,000 + 600,000}{8,000,000,+ 12,000,000 + 4,000,000} = 10.8\%$$

(b) Capitalisation rate

$$\frac{1,000,000 + 600,000}{12,000,000 + 4,000,000} = 10\%$$

Session 9

Government Grants

FOCUS

This session covers the following content from the *ACCA Study Guide.*

B. Accounting for Transactions in Financial Statements	
11. Government grants	
a) Apply the provisions of relevant accounting standards in relation to accounting for government grants.	☐

Session 9 Guidance

- **Learn** the definitions of grants (s.1.2).
- **Learn** the recognition criteria (s.2.1) and accounting treatment (s.2.4) of government grants according to IAS 20.

VISUAL OVERVIEW

Objective: To account for the transfer of resources from government, indicating how an entity benefits from such assistance and to treat the transfer in a way that facilitates comparison with prior periods.

IAS 20
- Scope
- Terminology

GOVERNMENT GRANTS
- Criteria
- Forgivable Loans
- Possible Approaches
- IAS 20 Treatment
- Non-monetary Grants
- Asset-Related Grants
- Income-Related Grants
- Repayment

GOVERNMENT ASSISTANCE
- Examples
- Issue
- Loans at Nil or Low Interest Rates

Session 9 Guidance

■ **Note** that there are two acceptable alternatives to the presentation of asset-related grants in the statement of financial position (s.2.6).

■ **Understand** the nature of government assistance (s.3).

1 IAS 20

1.1 Scope

▨ IAS 20 is applied:
 ● to account for and disclose government grants; and
 ● to disclose other forms of government assistance.

▨ IAS 20 does *not* deal with:
 ● accounting for government grants in financial statements which reflect the effects of changing prices or in supplementary information of a similar nature;
 ● income tax benefits (e.g. income tax holidays, investment tax credits, accelerated depreciation allowances and reduced income tax rates);
 ● government participation in the *ownership* of the reporting entity; or
 ● grants covered by IAS 41 *Agriculture*.

1.2 Terminology

Government: refers to government, government agencies and similar bodies, whether local, national or international.

Government grants: assistance by governments in the form of transfers of resources to an entity in return for past or future compliance with certain conditions relating to operating activities. Grants exclude those forms of government assistance which cannot reasonably have a value placed on them and transactions with government which cannot be distinguished from the normal trading transactions of the entity.

Grants related to assets: grants with a primary condition that the qualifying entity will purchase, construct or otherwise acquire long-term assets. Subsidiary conditions may also be attached, restricting the type or location of the assets or the periods during which they are to be acquired or held.

Grants related to income: grants other than those related to assets.

Forgivable loans: loans for which the lender waives repayment under certain prescribed conditions.

Government assistance: government action designed to provide an economic benefit specific to an entity or range of entities qualifying under certain criteria.∗

∗Government assistance takes many forms, varying in the nature of the assistance given and in the conditions attached. Its purpose may be to encourage an entity to embark on a course of action which it would not otherwise have taken.

2 Government Grants

2.1 Criteria

 **Key Point**

Government grants are not recognised until there is *reasonable assurance* that:

- the entity will comply with the conditions attaching to them; and
- the grants will be *received*.

- The receipt of a grant does not of itself provide conclusive evidence that conditions have been or will be fulfilled.
- A grant is accounted for in the same manner whether received in cash or a reduction of a liability to the government.

2.2 Forgivable Loans

- A **forgivable loan** from a government is treated as a grant when there is reasonable assurance that the entity will meet the terms for forgiveness.

2.3 Possible Approaches to Recognition

Immediate "capital" approach	Deferred "income" approach
■ Credit shareholders' interests.	■ Recognise as income (in profit or loss) over one or more periods.

Arguments for	Arguments for
✔ Like any other form of financing, it should be dealt with in the statement of financial position.	✔ Finance from a source other than owners should not be credited directly to shareholders' interests.
✔ No repayment is expected, therefore benefit accrues to owners.	✔ Government grants are rarely gratuitous (i.e. free) but earned through compliance with conditions and meeting obligations.
✔ Grants are not earned income but an incentive without related costs; therefore it is inappropriate to recognise in profit or loss.	✔ To match against the associated costs for which the grant is intended to compensate.
	✔ As an extension of fiscal policies, deal with in the statement of profit or loss and other comprehensive income as for taxes.

2.4   IAS 20 Treatment

Key Point

Systematically recognise government grants in profit or loss over the periods necessary to match them with the related costs they are intended to compensate. Grants related to:

- depreciable assets—over periods in which depreciation is charged; and

- non-depreciable assets—over periods bearing cost of meeting obligations.

- Do **not** credit directly to reserves within equity.

- Compensation for expenses or losses already incurred or for immediate financial support with no future related costs are recognised in profit or loss in the period receivable.*

*Commentary

*The receipts basis does not accord with the accruals concept. Therefore this is only acceptable if no other basis exists.

2.5   Non-monetary Grants

- When a grant takes the form of a transfer of a non-monetary asset for the use of the entity (e.g. land or other resources) it is usual to account for both the grant and the asset at fair value. As an alternative, both the asset and the grant may be recorded at a nominal amount.

2.6   Presentation of Grants Related to Assets

- Acceptable alternatives in the statement of financial position are to:

EITHER	OR
■ Set up the grant as *deferred income*.	■ *Deduct* the grant in arriving at the *carrying amount* of the asset.
■ Income will be recognised on a systematic and rational basis over the estimated useful life.	■ Income will be recognised over the estimated useful life by way of a reduced depreciation charge.

- Disclose separately in the statement of cash flows regardless of the statement of financial position presentation.

- The accounting policy for government grants, including the method of presentation, must be disclosed.

2.7   Presentation of Grants Related to Income

▨ Acceptable alternatives in the statement of profit or loss are to:

EITHER	OR
■ Credit separately or under a general heading (e.g. "Other income").	■ *Deduc*t in reporting related expense.

Argument for	Argument for
✔ Inappropriate to net income and expense item. ✔ Separation of the grant from expense facilitates comparison with other expenses.	✔ Expenses might not have been incurred if the grant had not been available. ✔ Therefore, presentation without offsetting may be misleading.

2.8   Repayment of Government Grants

▨ Account for as a revision to an accounting estimate:

Related to income	Related to an asset
■ Apply first against any unamortised deferred credit; and	■ Increase the carrying amount of the asset (or reduce deferred income balance); and
■ Recognise any excess immediately as an expense.	■ Recognise any cumulative additional depreciation immediately as an expense.

3   Government Assistance

Definition

Government assistance—action designed to provide an economic benefit specific to entity's qualifying under certain criteria.

9-**5**

3.1   Examples

▩ Examples which are excluded from government grants but are included as government assistance:*

Assistance which cannot reasonably have a value placed on it	Transactions which cannot be distinguished from normal trading transactions
■ Free technical or marketing advice.	■ A government procurement policy is responsible for a portion of sales.
■ Providing guarantees.	■ Although a benefit may exist, segregating trading activities from government assistance could be arbitrary.

Commentary

*Government assistance does not include indirect benefits (e.g. provision of transport infrastructure or imposition of trading constraints on competitors).

3.2   Issue

▩ Significance of the benefit may be such that disclosure of the nature, extent and duration of assistance is necessary so the financial statements will not be misleading.

3.3   Loans at Nil or Low Interest Rates

Key Point

Government loans with a below market rate of interest are a form of government assistance.

▩ The benefit of such loans should be accounted for as a government grant—measured as the difference between the initial carrying amount of the loan (determined in accordance with IFRS 9) and the proceeds received.

Illustration 1   Interest-Free Loan

Drago operates in an area where the government provides interest-free loans to aid investment subject to certain criteria being met.

On 1 January, Drago received an interest-free loan of $5 million for investment in new projects. The loan is repayable after four years.

The fair value of the loan has been calculated to be $4 million.

The accounting entries on receipt of the loan are:

		$5m	
Dr	Cash	$5m	
	Cr Loan		$4m
	Cr Government grant (deferred income)		$1m

Commentary

*Drago will charge annual interest to profit or loss (in accordance with IFRS 9) with a matching credit to profit or loss of the deferred income. Total interest for the period of the loan will be $1 million.

Summary

- IAS 20 applies to all government grants (excluding grants covered by IAS 41) and all other forms of government assistance including loans at below-market rate of interest (but excluding income tax benefits).
- Grants are recognised when there is reasonable assurance that:
  - the entity will comply with any conditions attached to them; and
  - the grant will be received.
- Recognise in profit and loss on a systematic basis to match with related costs.
- A grant for costs already incurred or with no future related costs is recognised as income in the period receivable.
- Non-monetary grants (e.g. land) are usually accounted for at fair value (although a nominal amount is permitted).
- An asset-related grant may be presented:
  - as deferred income; or
  - as a deduction from the asset's carrying amount.
- Other grants may be reported separately, or as "other income" or deducted from the related expense.
- A grant which becomes repayable is treated as a change in accounting estimate.
- Assistance which cannot reasonably be valued or distinguished from normal trading transactions is excluded from the definition of government grants.
- Disclosure includes accounting policy (including method of presentation), grants recognised, unfulfilled conditions and contingencies, and forms of assistance from which the entity has directly benefited.

Session 9 Quiz
Estimated time: 10 minutes

1. Explain what would be classified as a government grant for the purposes of IAS 20. (1.2)
2. Name the TWO types of government grants. (2.2, 2.5)
3. Describe TWO ways a capital grant may be presented in the statement of financial position. (2.6)
4. Define government assistance. (1.2, 3)

Study Question Bank
Estimated time: 25 minutes

Priority		Estimated Time	Completed
Q15	Sponger	25 minutes	
Additional			
Q16	Baxen		

IAS 40 *Investment Property*

FOCUS

This session covers the following content from the *ACCA Study Guide.*

B. Accounting for Transactions in Financial Statements

1. Tangible non-current assets

f) Discuss why the treatment of investment properties should differ from other properties. ☐

g) Apply the requirements of relevant accounting standards to an investment property. ☐

Session 10 Guidance

- **Learn** the definition of investment property (s.1.2).
- **Understand** that IAS 40 *Investment Properties* allows companies to value their investment properties using either a fair value model or a cost model based on the cost model in IAS 16 (s.3).
- **Comprehend** that if a company adopts the fair value model, then any change in value of the property is taken to profit or loss, **not** to a revaluation reserve (s.3.1).

(continued on next page)

VISUAL OVERVIEW

Objective: To describe the accounting treatment of investment properties.

```
                        ┌─────────────────────────┐
                        │         IAS 40          │
                        │  • Need for a Standard  │
                        │  • Objective            │
                        │  • Terminology          │
                        └─────────────────────────┘
```

RECOGNITION AND MEASUREMENT	MEASUREMENT AFTER RECOGNITION	DISCLOSURE
• Recognition	• Fair Value Model	• General
• Initial Measurement	• Exceptional Circumstances	• Fair Value Model
• Meaning of Cost	• Cost Model	• Cost Model
• Expenditure After Initial Recognition	• Transfers	
	• Disposals	
	• Change in Method	

Session 10 Guidance

▪ **Learn** when investment properties must be transferred in or out of the investment property classification of assets (s.3.4).

▪ **Work** through *Example 2* paying particular attention to the determination of cost.

▪ **Read** the disclosures required for IAS 40 *Investment Properties* (s.4).

1   IAS 40

1.1   Need for a Standard

- IAS 16 *Property, Plant and Equipment* deals with property in general use but was deemed not to be appropriate for those entities investing in investment properties.

- Investments in this type of property were being made to earn a return from rentals and for capital appreciation.

- IAS 40 was therefore issued and allows investment property companies to measure their properties at fair value, if they wish, and therefore reflect the substance of these transactions.

1.2   Objective

- IAS 40 prescribes the accounting treatment for investment property and the related disclosure requirements.

1.3   Terminology

Investment property: property (land or a building, or part of a building, or both) held (by the owner or by the lessee as a right-of-use asset) to earn rentals or for capital appreciation or both, rather than for:

- use in the production or supply of goods or services or for administrative purposes; or
- sale in the ordinary course of business.

Owner-occupied property: property held by the owner (or by the lessee as a right-of-use asset) for use in the production or supply of goods or services or for administrative purposes.

- Examples of investment property include:
  - land held for long-term capital appreciation rather than for short-term sale in the ordinary course of business;
  - land held for a currently undetermined future use;
  - a building which is vacant but is held to be leased out; and
  - property which is being constructed or developed for future use as an investment property.

- The following do not meet the definition of investment property:
  - property held for sale in the ordinary course of business; and
  - owner-occupied property (IAS 16 *Property, Plant and Equipment applies*).

- A property that is owned by a parent but occupied by a subsidiary, or vice versa, will be treated as investment property (under IAS 40) in the financial statements of the single entity but as property (under IAS 16) in the consolidated financial statements as the asset is owner-occupied from a group perspective.

2 Recognition and Measurement

2.1 Recognition

▦ Investment property is recognised as an asset when:

  • it is probable that the future economic benefits which are attributable to the investment property will flow to the entity; and

  • the cost of the investment property can be measured reliably.

2.2 Initial Measurement

Key Point

An investment property is measured initially at its cost, which is the fair value of the consideration given for it, including any transaction costs.

2.3 Meaning of Cost

▦ The cost of a purchased investment property comprises its purchase price and any directly attributable expenditure (e.g. professional fees for legal services and property transfer taxes).

▦ The initial cost of leased investment property is recognised in accordance with IFRS 16 *Leases*.

2.4 Expenditure After Initial Recognition

▦ Day-to-day costs of running the investment property are expensed as incurred.

▦ If a part of an investment property requires replacement during the useful life of the property, the replacement part is capitalised when the cost is incurred as long as the recognition criteria are met. Any value remaining with respect to the replaced part will be derecognised as the new cost is capitalised.*

*Derecognising the value of the replaced part when the new cost is capitalised follows the replacement-part principle of IAS 16.

3 Measurement After Recognition

Key Point

An entity chooses either the fair value model or the cost model and applies that policy to *all* its investment properties.

3.1 Fair Value Model

- After initial recognition, an entity which has chosen the fair value model must measure all its investment property at fair value (except in exceptional circumstances).

Key Point

Fair value is assessed using the fair value hierarchy in IFRS 13 *Fair Value Measurements* (see *Session 2*).

- A gain or loss arising from a change in the fair value of investment property is included in *profit or loss* for the period in which it arises.

3.2 Exceptional Circumstances

- There is a "rebuttable presumption" that an entity will be able to measure the fair value of an investment property reliably on a continuing basis.*
- If there is clear evidence that fair value cannot be measured on a reliable and continuing basis when a property is first acquired, it is measured in accordance with the cost model (IAS 16).
- However, all other investment properties are measured at fair value.

3.3 Cost Model

- After initial recognition, an entity which has chosen the cost model measures all investment properties using the cost model in IAS 16 *Property, Plant and Equipment* (i.e. at cost less any accumulated depreciation and impairment losses).
- An investment property measured under the cost model and which is subsequently classified as held for sale is measured in accordance with IFRS 5 *Non-current Assets Held for Sale and Discontinued Operations*.*

Do not use the term "revaluation" when discussing the fair value model under IAS 40. Revaluation is an IAS 16/38 accounting policy and fair value is a method of valuing investment property under IAS 40.

*rebuttable presumption means that the entity may present evidence to the contrary to nullify the presumption.

*IFRS 5 requires investment property previously measured under the cost model to be measured at the lower of carrying amount or fair value less costs to sell. Once it is classified as held for sale, an asset is no longer depreciated.

3.4   Transfers

▦ Transfers to and from investment property are made when, and only when, there is a change in use evidenced by:

- ● the commencement of owner-occupation (for a transfer from investment property to owner-occupied property);
- ● the commencement of development with a view to sale (for a transfer from investment property to inventories);
- ● the end of owner-occupation (for a transfer from owner-occupied property to investment property); or
- ● the commencement of an operating lease to another party (for a transfer from inventories to investment property).

3.5   Disposals

▦ An investment property is derecognised:

- ● on disposal; or
- ● when it is permanently withdrawn from use and no future economic benefits are expected from its disposal.

▦ Any gains or losses on the retirement of an asset are calculated as the difference between the carrying amount of the asset and the disposal proceeds and are included in the profit or loss for the period.

3.6   Change in Method

Key Point

A change from either the fair value model or the cost model to the other model may be made only if the change will result in a more appropriate presentation.*

*Commentary

*IAS 40 states that changing from the fair value model to the cost model is highly unlikely to result in a more appropriate presentation.

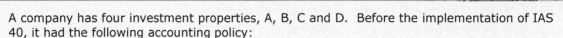

Example 1 Applying IAS 40 Fair Value Model

A company has four investment properties, A, B, C and D. Before the implementation of IAS 40, it had the following accounting policy:

"Investment properties are valued on a portfolio basis at the fair value at year end, with any net gain recognised in the investment property revaluation reserve. Only net losses from revaluation are transferred to statement of profit or loss."

At the beginning of the financial year the carrying amount of each of the four properties was $100m. At the end of the financial year, following a professional appraisal of value, the properties were valued at:

A $140m

B $130m

C $95m

D $90m

Required:

Show how the application of IAS 40 would change the financial statements of the company if the fair value model is chosen.

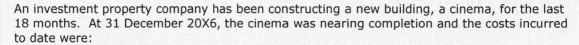

Example 2 Investment Property

An investment property company has been constructing a new building, a cinema, for the last 18 months. At 31 December 20X6, the cinema was nearing completion and the costs incurred to date were:

	$m
Materials, labour and sub-contractors	14.8
Other directly attributable overheads	2.5
Interest on borrowings	1.3

It is the company's policy to capitalise interest on specific borrowings raised for the purpose of financing a construction. The amount of borrowings outstanding at 31 December 20X6 in respect of this project is $18 million and the interest rate is 9.5% per annum.

During the three months to 31 March 20X7 the project was completed, with the following additional costs incurred:

	$m
Materials, labour and sub-contractors	1.7
Other overheads	0.3

The company was not able to determine the fair value of the property reliably during the construction period and so valued it at cost until construction was complete.

On 31 March 20X7, the company obtained a professional appraisal of the cinema's fair value and the valuer concluded that it was worth $24 million. The fee for his appraisal was $100,000 which has not been included in the above costs.

The cinema was taken by a national multiplex chain on an operating lease as at 1 April 20X7, and immediately welcomed capacity crowds. Following a complete valuation of the company's investment properties at 31 December 20X7, the fair value of the cinema was measured at $28 million.

Required:

Set out the accounting entries in respect of the cinema complex for the year ended 31 December 20X7.

4   Disclosure

4.1   General

- The extent to which the fair value is based on an independent valuation.
- The amounts included in the statement of profit or loss for:
  - rental income;
  - direct operating expenses (including repairs) which generated rental income during the period;
  - direct operating expenses (including repairs) which did not generate rental income during the period.

4.2   Fair Value Model

- A reconciliation of the carrying amount at the beginning and end of the period and the movements in the period.

4.3   Cost Model—Additional Disclosures

- The depreciation method used.
- The useful lives or the depreciation rates used.
- A reconciliation of the carrying amount at the beginning and end of the period and the movements in the period.
- The fair value of the property or a note stating that the fair value cannot be measured reliably, giving a description of the property. And, if possible, give a range of estimates for the likely fair value.

Summary

- Investment property is held for rentals and/or capital appreciation. Includes interests held under an operating lease if conditions are met.
- Owner-occupied property is excluded (unless portion is insignificant).
- Property rented to group companies is not investment property in consolidated financial statements.
- Subsequent measurement: fair value or cost model for all properties.
- Change is permitted only for more appropriate presentation (i.e. from cost to fair value model).
- The fair value model:
  - includes fair value gains and losses in profit or loss for the period;
  - reflects actual market circumstances at reporting date;
  - has rebuttable presumption (continuing reliable fair value); and
  - uses fair value until disposal.
- Transfers to/from investment property are only made on a change in use:
  - to owner-occupied or inventory (fair value becomes "cost"); or
  - to investment property (IAS 16 applies to date of reclassification).
- Transfers under the cost model do not change the carrying amount.
- Disclosures include the use of a qualified independent valuer, rental income, contractual obligations, restrictions on sale and reconciliation between carrying amounts (including transfers).

 Session 10 Quiz
Estimated time: 10 minutes

1. Define investment property in accordance with IAS 40. (1.3)
2. Explain how an investment property initially should be measured. (2.2)
3. Explain the measurement options available for investment property. (3)
4. State when a transfer should be made to or from an investment property classification. (3.4)
5. If the cost model is used for valuing investment property, state the disclosures required. (4)

 Study Question Bank
Estimated time: 30 minutes

Priority		Estimated Time	Completed
Q17	Monet	30 minutes	
Additional			
Q18	Fundo		

EXAMPLE SOLUTIONS

Solution 1—Applying IAS 40 Fair Value Model

Under the company's existing accounting policy, the investment properties would be carried in the statement of financial position at the financial year end at a total of $455m. The net gain would be recorded in the revaluation reserve (455 − 400 = 55).

Applying the IAS 40 fair value model, the company would still carry the properties at $455m, but the net gain of $55m would be recorded in the statement of profit or loss.

Solution 2—Investment Property

Costs incurred in the three months to 31 March 20X7

	$m	$m
Dr Asset under construction	1.7	
Cr Cash/Payables		1.7
Dr Asset under construction	0.3	
Cr Cash/Payables		0.3
Dr Asset under construction	0.43	
Cr Interest expense		0.43

Working

Outstanding borrowings = $18m

Interest for 3 months = $18m × $\frac{3}{12}$ × 9.5% = 0.43m

Commentary

*The professional valuation did not improve the profit earning potential of the asset.

Accumulated costs at the date of transfer into investment properties*

	$m
Costs to 31 December 20X6 (14.8 + 2.5 + 1.3)	18.6*
Costs to 31 March 20X7 (1.7 + 0.3 + 0.43)	2.43
Investment property at cost	21.03

Commentary

*On 1 January 20X7, the property would have been valued at its cost of $18.6m as the fair value was not determinable during the period of construction.

	$m	$m
Dr Investment property	2.97	
Cr Profit or loss		2.97

Being the increase from cost to fair value on completion of the property.

At 31 December 20X7

	$m	$m
Dr Investment property (28 − 24)	4	
Cr Profit or loss		4

Being the increase in fair value following the first subsequent re-measurement.

IAS 38 *Intangible Assets*

FOCUS

This session covers the following content from the *ACCA Study Guide.*

B. Accounting for Transactions in Financial Statements

2. Intangible non-current assets

a) Discuss the nature and accounting treatment of internally generated and purchased intangibles. ☐

b) Distinguish between goodwill and other intangible assets. ☐

c) Describe the criteria for the initial recognition and measurement of intangible assets. ☐

d) Describe the subsequent accounting treatment, including the principle of impairment tests in relation to goodwill. ☐

f) Describe and apply the requirements of relevant accounting standards to research and development expenditure. ☐

Session 11 Guidance

■ **Learn** the rules for recognising intangible assets and how to account for them subsequently. IAS 38 *Intangible Assets* is an important standard.

■ **Be able** to distinguish goodwill on a business acquisition from other identifiable intangibles (s.2.2). The examiner frequently includes intangible assets in consolidation questions.

(continued on next page)

VISUAL OVERVIEW

Objective: To explain the accounting rules for intangible non-current assets.

```
                        ┌─────────────────────────┐
                        │          IAS 38          │
                        │   • Scope                │
                        │   • Definitions          │
                        │   • Definition Criteria  │
                        └─────────────────────────┘
```

IAS 38
- Scope
- Definitions
- Definition Criteria

RECOGNITION AND INITIAL MEASUREMENT
- General Criteria
- Goodwill v Other Intangibles
- Initial Measurement
- Subsequent Expenditure

INTERNALLY GENERATED INTANGIBLE ASSETS
- Goodwill
- Other Assets
- Specific Recognition Criteria
- Expenses and Costs

MEASUREMENT AFTER RECOGNITION
- Cost Model
- Revaluation Model
- Accounting for Revaluation

IMPAIRMENT AND DERECOGNITION
- Impairment Losses
- Retirements and Disposals

DISCLOSURE
- Intangible Assets
- Revaluations
- Research and Development

USEFUL LIFE
- Factors
- Finite
- Indefinite

Session 11 Guidance

■ **Understand** the different ways in which intangible assets can arise (s.2.3).

■ **Learn** the criteria that require the capitalisation of internally generated intangibles during the development phase (s.3.3.2).

1 IAS 38

1.1 Scope

■ The standard applies to all intangibles except:

- those covered specifically by other standards (e.g. IAS 2, IAS 12, IAS 19, IAS 32, IFRS 3, IFRS 5 and IFRS 15); and
- mineral rights and expenditure on exploration; development and extraction of minerals, etc.

1.2 Definitions

Definition

Intangible assets—identifiable non-monetary assets without physical substance.

Examples of **intangible assets** include: *

- Patents
- Copyrights (e.g. computer software)
- Licences
- Intellectual property (e.g. technical knowledge obtained from development activity)
- Trademarks including brand names and publishing titles
- Motion picture films and video recordings.

*Commentary

*Some intangibles may be contained in or on a physical medium, e.g. software on a disk or embedded within the hardware. Judgement has to be used to determine which element is more significant, i.e. the intangible or the tangible asset.

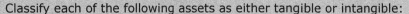

Example 1 Tangible v Intangible Assets

Classify each of the following assets as either tangible or intangible:

Asset	Tangible/Intangible
1. The operating system of a personal computer.	
2. An off-the-shelf integrated publishing software package.	
3. Specialised software embedded in computer-controlled machine tools.	
4. A firewall controlling access to restricted sections of an Internet website.	

1.3   Definition Criteria

1.3.1 "Identifiability"

▓ An intangible asset, whether generated internally or acquired in a business combination, is identifiable when it:

   ◦ is separable; or*

> ***Commentary**
>
> *Separable means capable of being separated or divided from the entity and sold, transferred, licensed, rented or exchanged, either individually or together with a related contract, asset or liability.

   ◦ arises from contractual or other legal rights.*

> ***Commentary**
>
> *Contractual or other legal rights can be identifiable regardless of whether they are transferable or separable from the entity or from other rights and obligations.

▓ These criteria distinguish intangible assets from goodwill acquired in a business combination.

1.3.2 "Control"

▓ Control means:

   ◦ the power to obtain the future economic benefits from the underlying resource; *and**

> ***Commentary**
>
> *Expenditure incurred in obtaining market and technical knowledge, increasing staff skills and building customer loyalty may be expected to generate future economic benefits. Control over the actions of employees and customers, however, is unlikely to be sufficient to meet the definition criterion.

   ◦ the ability to restrict the access of others to those benefits.

▓ Control normally stems from a legal right which is enforceable in a court of law. Legal enforceability, however, is *not* a prerequisite for control as the entity may be able to control the future economic benefits in some other way.

1.3.3 "Future Economic Benefits"

▓ These are net cash inflows and may include increased revenues and/or cost savings.*

*Commentary

*The use of intellectual property in a production process may reduce future production costs rather than increase future revenues.

2 Recognition and Initial Measurement

2.1 General Criteria

▨ An intangible asset should be recognised when it:
- complies with the *definition* of an intangible asset; *and*
- meets the *recognition criteria* set out in the standard.

▨ The recognition criteria are that:
- it is *probable* that future economic benefits specifically attributable to the asset will flow to the entity; and
- the cost of the asset can be *measured reliably*.

▨ The probability of future economic benefits should be assessed using reasonable and supportable assumptions, with greater weight given to external evidence.

▨ The recognition of internally generated intangible assets is covered in section 3.

2.2 Goodwill v Other Intangibles

2.2.1 Nature

▨ "Goodwill", as a general term, describes such things as brand name, reputation, competitive advantage and high employee morale which bring value to a business. It contributes to the generation of revenue.

▨ It is generated over many years with expenditure on promotion, the creation and maintenance of good customer and supplier relations, the provision of high-quality goods and services, skilled workforce and experienced management.

▨ It includes the worth of a corporate identity and is enhanced by such things as corporate image and location. In well-established businesses this worth may be well in excess of that of its physical assets.*

2.2.2 Possible Accounting Treatments

▨ Expenditure can be recognised in only two ways:
- asset; or
- expense.

▨ A business does not incur costs specific to the creation of goodwill but for related activities (e.g. promotion, client services, quality control, etc). Such costs are expensed as incurred.*

 **Key Point**

An entity cannot recognise internally generated goodwill as an asset in its financial statements because it does not meet the definition of an intangible asset—it is not identifiable. In particular, it is clearly inseparable. It only can be disposed of with the business as a whole.

 ***Commentary***

*When acquiring a business, goodwill is commonly valued using an earnings multiple.

 ***Commentary***

*Generally, IFRS does not permit recognition of an asset with respect to an expenditure initially expensed.

However, when a business is acquired as a whole, the buyer will (usually) pay a price in excess of the fair value of all the assets (net of liabilities) which can be separately identified (including other intangible assets such as intellectual property).*

This premium represents not only the future economic benefits expected to arise from the intangible asset which is goodwill in the acquired company but also those which arise from expected synergies (e.g. cost savings) and other benefits of the acquisition.

Possible accounting treatments for goodwill, as a purchased asset, in the consolidated financial statements of an acquirer are:

- immediate write-off;
- carry at cost (with or without annual impairment review);
- carry at cost with annual amortisation; and
- carry at revalued amount.*

*Intangible assets recognised as goodwill by the purchaser is not the same as the goodwill inherent in the business acquired.

*IFRS 3 requires that goodwill is carried as an asset and tested annually for impairment.

2.3 Initial Measurement

Intangible assets should be measured initially *at cost*.

An intangible asset may be acquired:
- separately;
- as part of a business combination;
- by way of a government grant; or
- by an exchange of assets.

2.3.1 Separate Acquisition

The cost of the intangible asset usually can be measured reliably when it has been separately acquired (e.g. purchase of computer software).

As the price paid normally will reflect expectations of future economic benefits, the probability recognition criteria is always considered to be satisfied for separately acquired intangible assets.

"Cost" is determined according to the same principles applied in accounting for other assets. For example:

- Purchase price + import duties + non-refundable purchase tax.
- Deferred payments are included at the cash price equivalent; the difference between this amount and the payments made are treated as interest.

■ As for other assets, expenditures which would not be classified as "cost" include those associated with:

- introducing a new product or service (including advertising and promotion);
- conducting business in a new location or with a new class of customer;
- administration and other general overheads;
- initial operating costs and losses;
- costs incurred while an asset capable of operating in the manner intended has not yet been brought into use; or
- costs incurred in redeploying the asset.

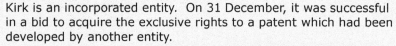

Example 2   Initial Recognition of Intangible Asset

Kirk is an incorporated entity. On 31 December, it was successful in a bid to acquire the exclusive rights to a patent which had been developed by another entity.

The amount payable for the rights was $600,000 immediately and $400,000 in one year's time. Kirk has incurred legal fees of $87,000 in respect of the bid. Kirk operates in a jurisdiction where the government charges a flat rate fee (a "stamp duty") of $1,000 for the registration of patent rights. An appropriate discount rate is 10%.

Required:

Calculate the cost of the patent rights on initial recognition.

2.3.2 Business Combination

■ The cost of an intangible asset acquired in a business combination is its fair value at the date of acquisition, irrespective of whether it had been recognised by the acquiree before the business combination.

■ The fair value of intangible assets acquired can normally be measured with sufficient reliability to be recognised separately from goodwill.

■ The fair value will reflect market participants' expectations at the acquisition date about the probability of future economic benefits.

Example 3 Goodwill Arising From Acquisition

Picard is an incorporated entity. On 31 December it paid $10,000,000 for a 100% interest in Borg.

At the date of acquisition the net assets of Borg as shown on its statement of financial position had a fair value of $6,000,000. In addition, Borg also held the following rights:

1. The brand name "Assimilation", a middle-of-the-range fragrance. Borg had been considering the sale of this brand just prior to its acquisition by Picard. The brand had been valued at $300,000 by Brand International, a reputable firm of valuation specialists, which had used a discounted cash flow technique.

2. Sole distribution rights to a product called "Lacutus". It is estimated that the future cash flows generated by this right will be $250,000 per annum for the next 6 years. Picard has determined that the appropriate discount rate for this right is 10%. The 6-year, 10% annuity factor is 4.36.

Ignore taxation.

Required:

Calculate goodwill arising on acquisition.

2.3.3 Exchanges of Assets

- The cost of an intangible asset acquired in exchange for a non-monetary asset (or a combination of monetary and non-monetary assets) is measured at fair value unless:
  - the exchange transaction lacks commercial substance; or
  - the fair value of neither the asset received nor the asset given up is reliably measurable.

- If the acquired asset is not measured at fair value, its cost is measured at the carrying amount of the asset given up.

- An exchange transaction has commercial substance if, for example, there is a significant difference between the risk, timing and amount of cash flows from the asset received and those of the asset transferred.

2.4 Subsequent Expenditure

2.4.1 Intangible Assets

- In most cases, there are no additions to an intangible asset or the replacement of parts of such assets.

- Most subsequent expenditures maintain the expected future economic benefits embodied in an existing intangible asset and do not meet the definition of an intangible asset and IAS 38 recognition criteria.

- Also, it is often difficult to attribute subsequent expenditure directly to a particular intangible asset rather than to the business as a whole.

- Therefore, only rarely will subsequent expenditure be recognised in the carrying amount of an asset. Normally, such expenditure must be written off through profit or loss.

▓ Subsequent expenditure on brands, mastheads, publishing titles, customer lists, etc (whether internally or externally generated) must always be recognised as an expense.

▓ In the rare circumstances that subsequent expenditure meets the basic asset recognition criteria, it is added to the cost of the intangible asset.

2.4.2 Acquired In-Process Research and Development

▓ Subsequent expenditure on an acquired in-process research and development project is accounted for in the same way as any cost incurred in the research of the development phase of an internally generated intangible asset.

  ● Research expenditure—expense when incurred.

  ● Development expenditure—expense when incurred if it does not satisfy the asset recognition criteria.

  ● Development expenditure which satisfies the recognition criteria—add to the carrying amount of the acquired in-process research or development project.

3 Internally Generated Intangible Assets

3.1 Internally Generated Goodwill

> **Key Point**
>
> Internally generated goodwill is not recognised as an asset.

▓ Although goodwill may exist in any business, its recognition as an asset is precluded because it is not an identifiable resource (i.e. it is not separable nor does it arise from contractual or other legal rights) controlled by the entity which can be measured reliably at cost.

▓ When goodwill is "crystallised" by a business acquisition it is recognised as an asset and accounted for in accordance with IFRS 3.

3.2 Other Internally Generated Assets

▓ It is sometimes difficult to assess whether an internally generated intangible asset qualifies for recognition. Specifically, it is often difficult to:

  ● identify whether there is an identifiable asset which will generate probable future economic benefits; and

  ● determine the cost of the asset reliably.

▓ It is sometimes difficult to distinguish the cost of generating an intangible asset internally from the cost of maintaining or enhancing internally-generated goodwill or running day-to-day operations.

▓ Internally generated brands, mastheads, publishing titles, customer lists and items similar in substance are not recognised as intangible assets.*

*Expenditures related to internally generated brands and similar items cannot be distinguished from the cost of developing the business as a whole.

3.3   Specific Recognition Criteria

In addition to complying with the general requirements for the recognition and initial measurement of an intangible asset, an entity also must apply the following to all internally generated intangible assets.

- Generation of the asset must be classified into:
  - a "research phase"; and
  - a further advanced "development phase".
- If the research and development phases of a project cannot be distinguished they should be regarded as research only and written off as expenditure through profit or loss.

3.3.1 Accounting in the Research Phase

- An entity cannot demonstrate that an intangible asset exists which will generate probable future economic benefits during the research phase.

Key Point

Expenditure on research should be recognised as an expense when it is incurred.

- Examples of research activities are:
  - activities aimed at obtaining new knowledge;
  - the search for, evaluation and final selection of, applications of research findings or other knowledge;
  - the search for alternatives for materials, devices, products, processes, systems or services; and
  - the formulation, design, evaluation and final selection of possible alternatives for new or improved materials, devices, products, processes, systems or devices.

3.3.2 Accounting in the Development Phase

Key Point

An intangible asset arising from development should be recognised if, and only if, an entity can demonstrate specified criteria.

- The criteria to be met by the entity are:
  - the technical feasibility of completing the intangible asset so that it will be available for use or sale;
  - its intention to complete the intangible asset and use it or sell it;
  - its ability to use or sell the intangible asset;
  - how the intangible asset will generate probable future economic benefits;
  - the availability of adequate technical, financial and other resources to complete the development and to use or sell the intangible asset; and
  - its ability to measure reliably the expenditure attributable to the intangible asset during its development.

Examples of development activities are:

- the design, construction and testing of pre-production or pre-use prototypes and models;
- the design of tools, jigs, moulds and dies involving new technology;
- the design, construction and operation of a pilot plant which is not of a scale economically feasible for commercial production; and
- the design, construction and testing of a chosen alternative for new or improved materials, devices, products, processes, systems or services.

Expenditure on an intangible item which was initially recognised as an expense (e.g. research) should not be recognised as part of the cost of an intangible asset at a later date (e.g. after the development phase has commenced). In other words, once the cost has been expensed, it will stay expensed; the charge to profit or loss cannot be reversed.

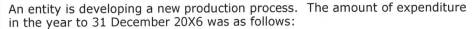

Illustration 1 Development Phase Accounting

An entity is developing a new production process. The amount of expenditure in the year to 31 December 20X6 was as follows:

	$
1 January to 30 November	2,160
1 December to 31 December	240
	2,400

On 1 December the entity was able to demonstrate that the production process met the criteria for recognition as an intangible asset. The amount estimated to be recoverable from the process (including future cash outflows to complete the process before it is available for use) is $1,200.

Analysis

- At 31 December, the production process is recognised as an intangible asset at a cost of $240 (expenditure incurred since 1 December when the recognition criteria were met). The intangible asset is carried at this cost (being less than the amount expected to be recoverable).

- The $2,160 expenditure incurred before 1 December is recognised as an expense because the recognition criteria were not met until that date. This expenditure will never form part of the cost of the production process recognised in the statement of financial position.

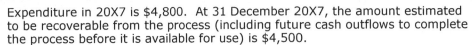

Illustration 1 Development Phase Accounting (continued)

Expenditure in 20X7 is $4,800. At 31 December 20X7, the amount estimated to be recoverable from the process (including future cash outflows to complete the process before it is available for use) is $4,500.

Analysis

- At 31 December, the cost of the production process is $5,040 (240 + 4,800). The entity recognises an impairment loss of $540 to adjust the carrying amount before impairment loss ($5,040) to its recoverable amount ($4,500).

- This impairment loss must be reversed subsequently if the requirements of IAS 36 *Impairment of Assets* are met.

3.4 Recognition of Expenses and Costs

▣ Expenditure on an intangible item is recognised as an expense when *incurred* unless:

- it forms part of the cost of an intangible asset which meets the recognition criteria; or
- the item is acquired in a business combination and cannot be recognised as an intangible asset.

▣ Reliable measurement of costs requires a costing system able to identify costs to particular courses of action.

▣ The cost of an internally generated intangible asset comprises all directly attributable costs necessary to create, produce and prepare the asset to be capable of operating in the manner intended by management.

▣ Examples include:

- costs of materials and services used;
- salaries, wages and other employment related costs;
- fees to register a legal right;
- depreciation of equipment used in the development phase;
- amortisation of patents and licences used to generate the intangible asset;
- other directly attributable costs; and
- overhead costs which can be allocated on a reasonable and consistent basis.

▣ Costs which are not components of the cost of an internally generated intangible asset include:

- selling, administration and other general overhead costs;
- identified inefficiencies and initial operating losses incurred before the asset achieves planned performance;
- costs which have previously been expensed (e.g. during a research phase) must not be reinstated; and
- training expenditure.

▣ Expenditure incurred to provide future economic benefits for which no intangible asset can be recognised is expensed when incurred. Examples include:*

- research costs;
- pre-opening costs for a new facility;
- plant start-up costs incurred prior to full-scale production (unless capitalised in accordance with IAS 16);
- legal and secretarial costs incurred in setting up a legal entity;
- training costs involved in running a business or a product line; and
- advertising and related costs.

*Commentary

*Recognising expenses when incurred does not preclude recognising a pre-payment when payment for goods or services has been made in advance of the delivery of goods or the rendering of services. In particular, a pre-payment asset may be recognised for advertising or promotional expenditure (e.g. mail order catalogues) up to the point at which the entity has the right to access the goods purchased (or the point of receipt of service).

4 Measurement After Recognition

4.1 Cost Model

▓ Cost less any accumulated amortisation and any accumulated impairment losses.

Key Point

An entity can choose either a cost model or a revaluation model.

4.2 Revaluation Model

▓ Revalued amount (i.e. fair value at the date of the revaluation) less any subsequent accumulated amortisation and any accumulated impairment losses.

Key Point

Fair value must be measured by reference to an active market.

▓ Revaluations must be sufficiently regular so that the carrying amount of the asset is not materially different from its fair value.

▓ The revaluation model does *not* allow:

- the revaluation of intangible assets which have not previously been recognised as assets; or
- the initial recognition of intangible assets at amounts other than their cost.

▓ The revaluation is carried out according to the same principles applied in accounting for other assets. For example:

- Surplus is taken directly to revaluation reserve, through other comprehensive income.
- Deficit is expensed unless covered by a previously recognised surplus.
- All intangibles in the class must be revalued, etc.

4.3 Accounting for Revaluation

▓ A surplus is credited to the revaluation reserve (unless reversing a deficit with respect to the same asset which was previously recognised as an expense).

▓ A deficit is recognised as an expense (unless covered by a revaluation surplus with respect to the same asset).

▓ Any balance on the revaluation surplus, which is included in equity, may be transferred to retained earnings when the surplus is realised (e.g. on retirement or disposal).

▓ If some of the surplus is realised as the asset is used by the entity, the difference between amortisation based on the revalued amount and amortisation which would have been charged based on the asset's historical cost is a transfer to retained earnings.*

*Commentary

*The transfer to retained earnings occurs through a movement in reserves reconciliation. The surplus cannot be reclassified through the statement of profit or loss.

5 Useful Life

5.1 Factors

▨ The useful life of an intangible asset should be assessed as finite or indefinite.

▨ A finite useful life is assessed as a period of time or number of production or similar units. An intangible asset with a finite life is amortised. "Indefinite" does not mean "infinite".

▨ Useful life is regarded as indefinite when there is no foreseeable limit to the period over which the asset is expected to generate net cash inflows.*

▨ Factors to be considered in determining useful life include:

  ◦ expected usage of the asset by the entity;

  ◦ typical product life cycles for the asset;

  ◦ public information on estimates of useful lives of similar types of assets similarly used;

  ◦ technical, technological, commercial or other obsolescence;*

  ◦ stability of the industry in which the asset operates;

  ◦ changes in market demand for the output from the asset;

  ◦ expected actions by competitors or potential competitors;

  ◦ the level of maintenance expenditure or funding required and the entity's ability and intent to reach this level;

  ◦ legal or similar limits on the use of the asset, such as the expiry dates of related leases; and

  ◦ whether the useful life of the asset is dependent on the useful life of other assets of the entity.

*Commentary

*Useful life must be based on an analysis of all of the relevant factors. An intangible asset with an indefinite life is not amortised.

*Commentary

*An example of a product susceptible to technological obsolescence is computer software; therefore, it has a short useful life.

5.2 Finite Useful Lives

5.2.1 Contractual or Other Legal Rights

▨ The useful life of an intangible asset arising from contractual or other legal rights should not exceed the period of such rights, but may be shorter.

Illustration 2 Useful Life of a Legal Right

An entity has purchased an exclusive right to operate a passenger and car ferry for 30 years. There are no plans to construct tunnels or bridges to provide an alternative river crossing in the area served by the ferry. It is expected that this ferry will be in use for at least 30 years.

Illustration 3 Useful Life of a Contractual Right

An entity has purchased an exclusive right to operate a wind farm for 40 years. The cost of obtaining wind power is much lower than the cost of obtaining power from alternative sources. It is expected that the surrounding geographical area will demand a significant amount of power from the wind farm for at least 25 years.*

*Commentary

*The wind farm operator in *Illustration 3* amortises the right to generate power over 25 (rather than 40) years.

▨ Where such rights are renewable, the useful life includes renewal periods if there is evidence that the entity will renew without significant cost.*

5.2.2 Amortisation

▨ The depreciable amount of an intangible asset should be allocated on a systematic basis over the best estimate of its useful life.

▨ Amortisation begins when the asset is available for use.

▨ Amortisation ceases at whichever is the earlier of the date that the asset is:*

- classified as held for sale (IFRS 5 applies); or
- derecognised.

▨ The amortisation method used should reflect the pattern in which the asset's economic benefits are consumed by the entity. If that pattern cannot be determined reliably, the straight-line method should be adopted.

▨ The amortisation charge for each period is recognised in profit or loss unless it is permitted to be included in the carrying amount of another asset. For example, amortisation of a patent right exercised to manufacture a product is an inventory cost.

5.2.3 Residual Value

▨ The residual value of an intangible asset is assumed to be *zero* unless the following conditions are met:

- there is a *commitment* by a third party to purchase the asset at the end of its useful life; or
- there is an *active market* (as defined in IFRS 13) for the asset; and*
  - residual value can be measured reliably by reference to that market; and
  - it is probable that such a market will exist at the end of the useful life.

▨ If the residual value of an intangible asset increases to an amount equal to or greater than the asset's carrying amount, the asset's amortisation charge is zero—unless and until its residual value subsequently decreases to an amount below the asset's carrying amount.

▨ An asset with a residual value implies an intention to dispose of it before the end of its economic life. Thus development costs, for example, are unlikely to have a residual value (other than zero).

5.2.4 Review

▨ The amortisation period and the amortisation method should be reviewed at least at each financial year end.

▨ Any changes in period or method are a change in estimate and accounted for in accordance with IAS 8 *Accounting Policies, Changes in Accounting Estimates and Errors.*

*Evidence that the entity will renew without significant cost may be based on past experience or third-party consent. If significant, it represents, in substance, a new intangible asset.

*Amortisation does not cease when an intangible asset is temporarily idle, unless it is fully depreciated.

*IFRS 13 defines an active market as "a market in which transactions for the asset or liability take place with sufficient frequency and volume to provide pricing information on an on-going basis."

Example 4 Research and Development Write-Off

On 1 January, Brook established a new research and development unit to acquire scientific knowledge about the use of synthetic chemicals for pain relief.

The following expenses were incurred during the year ended 31 December.

1. Purchase of building for $400,000. The building is to be depreciated on a straight-line basis at the rate of 4% per annum on cost.

2. Wages and salaries of research staff are $2,355,000.

3. Scientific equipment costing $60,000 is to be depreciated using a reducing balance rate of 50% per annum.

Required:

Calculate the amount of research and development expenditure to be recognised as an expense in the year ended 31 December.

Example 5 Capitalised Development Expenditure

In its first year of trading to 31 December, Eco-chem incurred the following expenditure on research and development, none of which related to the purchase of property, plant and equipment.

1. $12,000 on successfully devising processes to convert the sap extracted from mangroves into chemicals X, Y and Z.

2. $60,000 on developing an analgesic medication based on chemical Z.

No commercial uses have yet been discovered for chemicals X and Y.

Commercial production and sales of the analgesic commenced on 1 September, and are expected to produce steady profitable income during a five-year period before being replaced. Adequate resources exist for the company to achieve this.

Required:

Assuming no impairment, determine the maximum amount of development expenditure which may be carried forward at 31 December under IAS 38.

5.3 Indefinite Useful Lives

An intangible asset with an indefinite useful life is:

- not amortised; but
- tested for impairment:
  - annually; and
  - whenever there is an indication of impairment.

Reassessing a useful life as finite rather than indefinite is an indicator that the asset may be impaired.

The useful life is reviewed each period to determine whether events and circumstances continue to support an indefinite useful life assessment.*

*If an indefinite assessment is no longer supported, the change in accounting estimate is accounted for in accordance with IAS 8.

6 Impairment and Derecognition

6.1 Impairment Losses

Key Point

Goodwill, intangible assets not yet ready for use and intangible assets with an indefinite useful life must be tested annually for impairment.

▦ IAS 36 *Impairment of Assets* contains provisions regarding:

- when and how carrying amounts are reviewed;
- how recoverable amount is determined; and
- when an impairment loss is recognised or reversed.*

▦ The purpose of testing for impairment is to ensure recovery of the carrying amount. Note that the uncertainty about recovering the cost of an intangible asset before it is available for use (e.g. development costs) is likely to be greater than when it is brought into use.

Exam Advice

*Reversals of impairment losses will not be examined.

6.2 Retirements and Disposals

▦ An intangible asset should be derecognised (i.e. eliminated from the statement of financial position):

- on disposal; or
- when no future economic benefits are expected from its use or disposal.

▦ Gains or losses arising are determined as the difference between:

- the net disposal proceeds; and
- the carrying amount of the asset.

Gains or losses are recognised in profit or loss in the period in which the retirement or disposal occurs. Gains are not classified as revenue.

7 Disclosure

7.1 Intangible Assets

7.1.1 General

- The financial statements should disclose the accounting policies adopted for intangible assets and, in respect of each class of intangible assets:
  - whether useful lives are indefinite or finite and, if finite:
    - —the useful lives or the amortisation rates used; and
    - —the amortisation methods used;
  - the gross carrying amount and any accumulated amortisation (including accumulated impairment losses) at the beginning and the end of the period along with a reconciliation of the movement.

7.1.2 Indefinite Useful Life

- Disclose the carrying amount and the reasons supporting the assessment of an indefinite useful life (this includes describing the factors which played a significant role in determining that the asset has an indefinite useful life).

7.1.3 Acquired by Way of Government Grant

- For intangible assets acquired by way of a government grant and initially recognised at fair value, disclose:
  - the fair value initially recognised for these assets;
  - their carrying amount; and
  - whether they are measured after recognition under the cost model or the revaluation model.

7.2 Revaluations

- The following should be disclosed when assets are carried at revalued amounts:
  - The effective date of the revaluation (by class).
  - The carrying amount of the revalued intangible assets (by class).
  - The carrying amount which would have been recognised using the cost model (by class).
  - The amount of the revaluation surplus which relates to intangible assets at the beginning and the end of the period, indicating movements in the period and any restrictions on the distribution of the balance to shareholders.

7.3 Research and Development Expenditure

- Disclose the total cost of research and development recognised as an expense during the period.

Summary

- Intangible assets are *identifiable, non-monetary* assets *without physical substance*. Essential attributes include *control*.

- An intangible is identifiable when it is *separable* or arises from *rights*.

- Intangibles can be acquired by purchase, grant, exchange or internal generation.

- Usual asset recognition criteria. Other costs are expensed when incurred.

- Items expensed include expenditure on own research, brands and internally generated goodwill and costs of start-up, training, advertising and relocation.

- Acquired in-process research and development is an asset.

- Intangible assets are initially measured at cost.

- Subsequent expenditure is expensed when incurred.

- Re-instatement as an intangible asset, at a later date, is *prohibited*.

- For recognition of internally generated intangible assets additional criteria must be *demonstrated*.

- Subsequent measurement: use cost model or revaluation model.

- Revaluation model only if fair value exists in an *active market* (rare).

- Assess useful life as definite (amortise) or indefinite (*not* amortised).

- Amortise to reflect a pattern of consumption, otherwise, straight line.

- Test annually for impairment assets not yet in use.

- Disclosure requirements are comparable to IAS 16, also:

  - basis for determining an indefinite life;

  - description and carrying amount of individually material assets;

  - amount of research and development expensed in the current period.

Session 11 Quiz
Estimated time: 20 minutes

1. Define the term *identifiable* in terms of IAS 38. (1.3)

2. List the recognition criteria which must be satisfied for an intangible asset to be recognised. (2.1)

3. If an intangible asset is acquired as part of a business combination, it must be included in the consolidated statement of financial position at its fair value. Describe how fair value might be determined in this case. (2.3.2)

4. Explain why internally generated goodwill cannot be capitalised. (3.1)

5. List the SIX conditions which must be satisfied for development expenditure to be recognised as an intangible asset. (3.3.2)

6. If an entity wishes to revalue an intangible asset, describe the conditions necessary for revaluation. (4.2)

7. Explain how the extra amortisation charge is treated when an intangible asset is revalued upward. (4.3)

8. When calculating the amortisation of an intangible asset, the expected residual value of the asset should normally be assumed to be zero. State the circumstances under which residual value other than zero may be assumed. (5.2.3)

Study Question Bank
Estimated time: 40 minutes

Priority		Estimated Time	Completed
Q20	Lamond	40 minutes	
Additional			
Q19	Intellectual Individuals		

EXAMPLE SOLUTIONS

Solution 1—Tangible v Intangible Assets

1. **Tangible:** the operating system (e.g. DOS or Windows) is an integral part of the related hardware and should be accounted for under IAS 16 *Property, Plant and Equipment*.
2. **Intangible:** such computer software (e.g. QuarkXpress) is not an integral part of the hardware on which it is used.
3. **Tangible:** specialised software integrated into production line "robots" is similar in nature to answer (1).
4. **Intangible:** companies developing firewall software to protect their own websites may also sell the technology to other companies.

Solution 2—Initial Recognition of Intangible Asset

	$
Cash paid	600,000
Deferred consideration $(400,000 \times \frac{1}{1.1})$	363,636
Legal fees	87,000
Stamp duty	1,000
Cost on initial recognition	1,051,636

Solution 3—Goodwill Arising From Acquisition

Picard will recognise the two intangible assets on consolidation. They are taken into account when the cost of acquisition is allocated in accordance with IFRS 3 *Business Combinations*.

		$000
Cost		10,000
Net assets recognised in Borg's		
statement of financial position:	6,000	
Brand acquired	300	
Distribution rights (250,000 × 4.36)	1,090	
		(7,390)
Goodwill on acquisition		2,610

Solution 4—Research and Development Write-Off

The following costs should be written off:

	$
Building depreciation (400,000 × 4%)	16,000
Wages and salaries of research staff	2,355,000
Equipment depreciation (60,000 × 50%)	30,000
	2,401,000

Solution 5—Capitalised Development Expenditure

Cost

1. This is research expenditure which cannot be capitalised under any circumstances and must therefore be expensed to profit or loss.
2. Initially recognised cost is $60,000. Residual value is presumed to be zero.

Amortisation

Amortise from 1 September for a period of 5 years.

Charge for 4 months is: 4/60 × $60,000 = $4,000

Carrying amount*

$60,000 − $4,000 = $56,000.

*This is the maximum carry forward, assuming no impairment.

IFRS 5 *Non-current Assets Held for Sale and Discontinued Operations*

FOCUS

This session covers the following content from the *ACCA Study Guide.*

B. Accounting for Transactions in Financial Statements	
9. Reporting financial performance	
a) Discuss the importance of identifying and reporting the results of discontinued operations.	☐
b) Define and account for non-current assets held for sale and discontinued operations.	☐

Session 12 Guidance

■ **Recognise** that IFRS 5 requires non-current assets held for sale to be presented separately in the financial statements and also links assets to be disposed with discontinued operations.

■ **Learn** the definition of a discontinued operation and appreciate that it is based on "past events" rather than on "future events" (s.1.2).

■ **Learn** the definition criteria for discontinued operations (s.1.3) and held-for-sale non-current assets (s.2).

(continued on next page)

VISUAL OVERVIEW

Objective: To explain the need for and accounting under IFRS 5 *Non-current Assets Held for Sale and Discontinued Operations.*

```
                    ┌─────────────────────────────┐
                    │           IFRS 5            │
                    ├─────────────────────────────┤
                    │  • Reasons for Issue        │
                    │  • Definitions              │
                    │  • Definition Criteria      │
                    └─────────────────────────────┘
```

```
┌─────────────────────────────┐      ┌─────────────────────────────┐
│       HELD FOR SALE         │      │  PRESENTATION AND DISCLOSURE │
│      CLASSIFICATION         │      ├─────────────────────────────┤
├─────────────────────────────┤      │  • Purpose                  │
│  • Definitions              │      │  • Discontinued Operations  │
│  • Held for Sale Non-current│      │  • Held for Sale Non-current│
│    Assets                   │      │    Assets                   │
│  • Abandoned Non-current    │      │                             │
│    Assets                   │      │                             │
│  • Measurement              │      │                             │
└─────────────────────────────┘      └─────────────────────────────┘
```

Session 12 Guidance

■ **Attempt** *Example 1* to ensure that you can identify a disposal group.

■ **Read** *Illustration 2* and attempt *Example 2* to appreciate how a discontinued operation affects the statement of profit or loss.

1 IFRS 5

1.1 Reasons for Issue

- To establish principles for the classification, measurement and presentation of held for sale non-current assets.

- The information provided enhances the ability of users of financial statements to make projections of an entity's cash flows, earnings-generating capacity and financial position by segregating information about discontinued assets and operations from the information about continuing operations.

- As part of a short-term convergence project with the US Financial Accounting Standards Board (FASB), IFRS 5 was issued to achieve substantial convergence with FASB Statement 144 *Accounting for the Impairment and Disposal of Long-Lived Assets*.

1.2 Definitions

- **Component of an entity**—a portion of the company with operations and cash flows clearly *distinguishable* from the remainder of the entity (both operationally and for financial reporting purposes).*

*Commentary

*A component will have been a cash-generating unit (or a group of cash-generating units) when held for use.

- **Discontinued operation**—a component which has either been disposed of or is classified as held for sale and:*
  - represents a *separate* major line of business or geographical area of operations;
  - is part of a single coordinated plan for its disposal; or
  - is a subsidiary acquired exclusively with a view to re-sale.

*Commentary

*Discontinued operations may qualify as restructurings as defined by IAS 37 *Provisions, Contingent Liabilities and Contingent Assets* but not all restructurings will be treated as discontinued operations.

- **Disposal group**—a group of assets to be disposed of collectively in a single transaction, and directly associated liabilities which will be transferred in the transaction.*

*Commentary

*Disposal may be by sale or otherwise.

▨ The assets in a disposal group include goodwill acquired in a business combination if the group is:

 ◦ a cash-generating unit to which goodwill has been allocated; or

 ◦ an operation within such a cash-generating unit.

1.3   Definition Criteria

1.3.1   "Distinguishable"

▨ A discontinued operation is *distinguishable* operationally and for reporting purposes if:

 ◦ its operating assets and liabilities can be directly attributed to it; *

 ◦ its income (gross revenue) can be directly attributed to it; and

 ◦ at least a majority of its operating expenses can be directly attributed to it.

Commentary

*Elements are directly attributable to a component if they would be eliminated when the component is discontinued.

1.3.2   "Separate"

▨ A discontinued operation must be a *separate:*

 ◦ major line of business (e.g. major product or service line); or

 ◦ geographical area of operations. *

▨ Business entities frequently close facilities, abandon products or even product lines, and change the size of their workforce in response to market forces. These changes are *not* usually discontinued operations but they can occur in connection with a discontinued operation. For example:

 ◦ gradual or evolutionary phasing-out of a product line or class of service;

 ◦ discontinuance of several products in an ongoing line of business;

 ◦ moving some production or marketing activities for a particular line of business from one location to another;

 ◦ closing of a facility to achieve productivity improvements or other cost savings; and

 ◦ sale of a subsidiary whose activities are similar to those of the parent or other subsidiaries or associates within a consolidated group.

Commentary

*An operating segment (or part thereof) would normally satisfy this criterion, however IFRS 8 *Operating Segments* is not examinable.

1.3.3   "A Single Coordinated Plan"

▨ A discontinued operation may be disposed of in its entirety or piecemeal, but always pursuant to an overall coordinated plan to discontinue the entire component.

Example 1 Disposal Groups

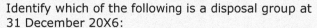

Identify which of the following is a disposal group at
31 December 20X6:

1. On 21 December 20X6, ABC announced the board's intention
to sell its shares in an African company, Sucoma (sugar),
contingent upon the approval of Sucoma's other shareholders.
It seems unlikely that approval will be granted in the near
future and no specific potential buyer has been identified.

2. DEF has entered into a contract to sell the entire delivery fleet
of vehicles operated from its warehouse in Milton Keynes (in
the UK) to a competitor, WheelsRUS, on 14 December 20X6.
The assets will be transferred on 28 January 20X7, from which
date the Group will outsource its delivery activities to another
company, Safe & Sound.

3. On 31 December 20X6, the GHI's management decided
to sell its 50 supermarkets in Germany. The shareholders
approved the decision at an extraordinary general meeting on
19 January 20X7.

4. On 16 October 20X6, JKL's management and shareholders
approved a plan to sell its retail business in Eastern Europe
and a working party was set up to manage the sale. As at
31 December 20X6, heads of agreement had been signed
although due diligence and the negotiation of final terms are
still in process. Completion of the transaction is expected
sometime in the spring of 20X6.

2 Held for Sale Classification

2.1 Definitions

Current asset—an asset which satisfies *any* of the following criteria:

▓ expected realisation, sale or consumption:
  ⊙ in the normal operating cycle; or
  ⊙ within 12 months after the end of the reporting period;
▓ held primarily for trading purposes; or
▓ cash or a cash equivalent.

Non-current asset—an asset which does not meet the definition of a current asset.

▓ A non-current asset (or disposal group) is classified as *held for sale* if its carrying amount will be recovered principally through a sale transaction rather than through continuing use.*

*Commentary

*"Non-current assets (or disposal groups) classified as held for sale" will be referred to more simply as "held for sale non-current assets" in this session.

2.2 Held for Sale Non-current Assets

2.2.1 Recognition Criteria

Key Point

The asset must be available for immediate sale in its present condition.

An asset cannot be classified as held for sale retrospectively.*

▓ The sale must be *highly probable* (i.e. significantly more likely than probable).

2.2.2 Highly Probable

▓ Management must be committed to a plan to sell the asset.
▓ An active programme to locate a buyer and complete the plan must have been initiated.
▓ The asset must be actively marketed for sale at a reasonable price (relative to its current fair value).
▓ The sale is expected to qualify for recognition as a completed sale within one year from the date of classification.*
▓ The actions required to complete the plan should indicate that significant changes to the plan or withdrawal from the plan are unlikely.

*Commentary

*An entity wishing to sell a property which needs renovation must complete the renovation prior to classifying it as held for sale, and the classification cannot be back-dated.

2.2.3 Assets Acquired Exclusively for Disposal

▓ Non-current assets acquired exclusively with a view to subsequent disposal are classified as held for sale at the acquisition date if:
  ⊙ the one-year criterion is met; and
  ⊙ it is highly probable that any other criteria not met at that date will be met within three months.

*Commentary

*However, an extension period does not preclude classification as held for sale if the delay is beyond management's control and there is sufficient evidence of management's commitment to its plan.

2.2.4 Events After the Reporting Period

▨ Assets are not classified as held for sale if the recognition criteria are only met after the end of the reporting period.

▨ However, if the criteria are met before the financial statements are authorised for issue, the notes should disclose the facts and circumstances.*

*The event is non-adjusting (see IAS 10 *Events after the Reporting Period*).

> **Example 2 Discontinued Operation Disclosures**
>
> Assuming all other criteria are met, explain which of the transactions and events in *Example 1* give rise to the classification of non-current assets held for sale at 31 December 20X6.

2.3 Abandoned Non-current Assets

▨ An asset which is to be abandoned is *not* classified as held for sale.*

▨ However, a disposal group which is to be abandoned is treated as a discontinued operation when it ceases to be used, providing that the definition of a "discontinued operation" is met.

▨ Non-current assets (or disposal groups) to be abandoned include those which are to be:

* used to the end of their economic life; and
* closed rather than sold.

▨ An entity does not account for a non-current asset which has been temporarily taken out of use as if it had been abandoned.

*The carrying amount for an asset to be abandoned will be recovered principally through continuing use until it is abandoned.

2.4 Measurement

2.4.1 Principle

> 🔑 **Key Point**
>
> Held for sale non-current assets are carried at the lower of:*
> ■ carrying amount; and
> ■ fair value less costs to sell.

*Immediately before initial classification as held for sale, carrying amount is measured in accordance with applicable IFRSs.

2.4.2 Time Value

▨ If a sale is expected to occur beyond one year, costs to sell are discounted to their present value.*

2.4.3 Subsequent Remeasurement

▨ Assets and liabilities in a disposal group are remeasured in accordance with applicable IFRSs before the fair value less costs to sell of the disposal group is remeasured.

*Any increase in the present value of the costs to sell arising from the passage of time is treated as a financing cost.

2.4.4   Impairment Losses

▨ Impairment losses for initial or subsequent write-downs to fair value less costs to sell must be recognised.

2.4.5   Depreciation

Key Point

Held for sale non-current assets are not depreciated (amortised).*

*Commentary

*Interest and other expenses attributable to the liabilities of a held for sale disposal group will continue to be recognised.

3   Presentation and Disclosure

3.1   Purpose

▨ To enable users of financial statements to evaluate the financial effects of:
  ● discontinued operations; and
  ● disposals of non-current assets (or disposal groups).
▨ Disclosures in IFRSs other than IFRS 5 do *not* apply to non-current assets classified as discontinued operations or held for sale unless such disclosures:
  ● are a specific requirement for such assets when classified as held for sale or discontinued operations; or
  ● relate to information about measurement which is outside the scope of IFRS 5 and not otherwise disclosed in the financial statements.

3.2   Discontinued Operations

3.2.1   A Single Amount

Key Point

A single amount is disclosed in the statement of profit or loss comprising:
■ post-tax profit or loss of discontinued operations;
■ post-tax gain or loss recognised on:
  • the measurement to fair value less costs to sell; or
  • the disposal of the assets (or groups) constituting the discontinued operation.

3.2.2 An Analysis

▨ An analysis of the single amount in the statement of profit or loss or in the *notes* into:

- the revenue, expenses and pre-tax profit or loss of discontinued operations;
- the gain or loss recognised on:
  - the measurement to fair value less costs to sell; or
  - the disposal of the assets or disposal group(s) constituting the discontinued operation.*

▨ If presented in the statement of profit or loss it is identified as relating to discontinued operations separately from continuing operations.

*Related income tax expense should also be recognised for the gain or loss on the discontinued operation.

3.2.3 Net Cash Flows

▨ Net cash flows attributable to the operating, investing and financing activities of discontinued operations must be presented in the financial statements or in the *notes.**

*Comparative information must be re-stated for prior periods presented.

3.3 Held for Sale Non-current Assets

▨ The following requirements also apply to the assets of disposal groups classified as held for sale.

3.3.1 Separate Classification

▨ Non-current assets classified as held for sale are to be shown separately from other assets in the statement of financial position.

▨ The liabilities of a held for sale disposal group are similarly presented separately from other liabilities in the statement of financial position.

▨ The major classes of held for sale assets and liabilities are separately disclosed either in the statement of financial position or in the notes.

▨ Any cumulative income or expense recognised in other comprehensive income relating to a held for sale non-current asset must be presented separately.

▨ Comparative information is not restated.*

Key Point

Offsetting liabilities and assets of a held for sale disposal group is strictly prohibited.

3.3.2 Additional Disclosures*

▨ A description of the non-current asset.

▨ A description of the facts and circumstances of the sale or expected disposal (and the expected manner and timing of that disposal).

▨ Fair value gains or losses.

▨ If held for sale criteria are no longer met, disclose:

- the decision to change the plan to sell the non-current asset;
- the facts and circumstances leading to the decision; and
- the effect of the decision on the results of operations for the period and any prior periods presented.

*Classification as held for sale is reflected in the period when the held for sale recognition criteria are met.

*Note that disclosures are made in the period in which a non-current asset is classified as held for sale or sold.

Illustration 1 Discontinued Operation Disclosures

Entity X has three divisions:

        A   Tobacco

        B   Alcohol

        C   Health foods

The following information relates to the year ended 31 December 20X6:

	A	B	C
	$000	$000	$000
Revenue	200	180	110
Expenses	120	105	115
Taxation (30%)	24	22.5	(1.5)

Division C is thought to be inconsistent with the long-term direction of the Company. Management has decided, therefore, to dispose of this division.

On 5 November 20X6, the board of directors of X voted to approve the disposal and a public announcement was made. On that date, the carrying amount of Division C's assets was $105,000 and it had liabilities of $15,000. The estimated recoverable amount of the assets was determined to be $85,000 and the directors of X concluded that a pre-tax impairment loss of $20,000 should be recognised. This was duly processed in November and is included in the above amounts.

At 31 December 20X6, the carrying amount of Division C's assets was $85,000 and it had liabilities of $15,000. There was no further impairment between 5 November and the reporting date.

X decided to adopt the provisions of IFRS 5 by making the necessary disclosures in the notes to the accounts.

Required:

Show how the above information would be reflected in the financial statements of X for the year ended 31 December 20X6.

Solution

Statement of profit or loss for the year ended 31 December 20X6

	$000
Revenue	490
Expenses	(320)
Impairment loss	(20)
	150
Taxation (30%)	(45)
	105

Note to the financial statements

On 5 November 20X6, the board of directors publicly announced a plan to dispose of the health foods division. The disposal is consistent with the Company's long-term strategy to focus its activities on the manufacture and distribution of cigarettes and alcoholic drinks and to divest unrelated activities. The Company is actively seeking a buyer for the health food division and hopes to complete the sale by the end of September 20X7.

At 31 December 20X6, the carrying amount of the division's assets was $85,000 and its liabilities were $15,000.

During 20X6, the division earned revenues of $110,000 and incurred expenses of $115,000 resulting in a pre-tax operating loss of $5,000, with a related tax benefit to the entity of $1,500.

During 20X6, the division's cash outflow from operating activities was $XX, cash outflow from investing activities was $XX and cash inflow from financing activities was $XX.

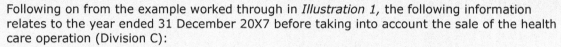

Example 3 Statement Disclosures

Following on from the example worked through in *Illustration 1,* the following information relates to the year ended 31 December 20X7 before taking into account the sale of the health care operation (Division C):

	A	B	C
	$000	$000	$000
Revenue	230	195	90
Expenses	130	115	100
Taxation (30%)	30	24	(3)

On 30 September 20X7, X sold Division C to Z Co for $60,000. The carrying amount of the division's net assets at that date was $70,000. The loss on disposal will attract tax relief at 30%.

The sale contract obliges X to terminate the employment of certain employees of Division C, incurring an expected termination cost of $30,000, to be paid by 31 March 20X8. This has not been accounted for as at the year end and will attract tax relief at 30%.

X has decided to make the disclosures required in respect of the transactions in the statement of profit or loss.

Required:

Show how the above information would be reflected in the financial statements of X for the year ended 31 December 20X7.

Solution

Statement of profit or loss for the year ended 31 December 20X7

	Continuing operations (A and B)		Discontinued operations (C only)		Entity as a whole	
	20X6	*20X7*	*20X6*	*20X7*	*20X6*	*20X7*
	$000	$000	$000	$000	$000	$000
Revenue						
Expenses						
Impairment loss						
Loss on disposal						
Provision for termination of employment						
Taxation (30%)						

Note to the financial statements

Summary

- A "disposal group" is a group of assets (and associated liabilities) to be disposed of in a single transaction.

- An item is classified as held for sale if its carrying amount will be covered principally through *sale* rather than continuing use. This is the case when:
  - the asset is available for *immediate* sale in its present condition; and
  - sale is *highly probable* (i.e. there is management commitment, etc).

- Operations to be wound down or *abandoned* are not held for sale.

- Measurement principles for held for sale items:
  - Before classification: in accordance with applicable IFRSs.
  - After classification: at the *lower* of carrying amount and fair value less costs to sell.

- Impairment must be considered on classification and subsequently.

- Assets held for sale are:
  - *not* depreciated; and
  - presented separately on the statement of financial position.

- A previously consolidated subsidiary now held for sale is consolidated until actually disposed.

- A discontinued operation is a component which has been disposed of or is classified as held for sale and:
  - represents a separate major line of business or a geographical area of operations and is part of a single coordinated plan; or
  - a subsidiary acquired *exclusively* for resale (with disposal of control.)

- Discontinued operations are presented as a *single* amount in the statement of profit or loss and other comprehensive income.

- Detailed disclosure is required either in the notes or in the statement of profit or loss and other comprehensive income distinct from continuing operations.

- Net cash flows attributable to the operating, investing and financing activities of a discontinued operation are presented separately.

- Retrospective classifications of non-current assets held for sale and discontinued operation, when criteria are met after the reporting date, are *prohibited.*

Session 12 Quiz

Estimated time: 10 minutes

1. Define a component of an entity. (1.2)
2. Identify the recognition criteria for held for sale non-current assets. (2.2.1)
3. State the value at which non-current assets held for sale are measured. (2.4.1)
4. State the method of depreciation which may be used for a non-current asset held for disposal. (2.4.5)
5. Identify how discontinued operations should be presented in the statement of profit or loss and other comprehensive income. (3.2)

Study Question Bank

Estimated time: 15 minutes

Priority		Estimated Time	Completed
Q21	Davis	15 minutes	
Additional			
Q22	Manco		

EXAMPLE SOLUTIONS

Solution 1—Disposal Groups

The vehicle fleet (2) and the retail business (4) are disposal groups because each is a collection of assets to be disposed of by sale together as a group in a single transaction.

The sale of the 50 supermarkets is not classified as a disposal group as there is no indication that the supermarkets are to be sold as a package; each could be sold as a separate item.

Solution 2—Discontinued Operation Disclosures

Presented as held for sale

(2) DEF's fleet is classified as held for sale because it constitutes a group of assets to be sold in their present condition and the sale is highly probable at the reporting date (as a contract has been entered into).

(4) JKL's sale of its retail business will not be completed until the final terms (e.g. of purchase price) are agreed. However, the business is ready for immediate sale and the sale is highly probable unless other evidence after the reporting date, before the financial statements are authorised for issue, comes to light to indicate the contrary.

Not presented as held for sale

(1) ABC's shares in Sucoma are not available for an immediate sale as shareholder approval is required. In taking this into account of the assessment of whether the sale is highly probable, it is clearly not highly probable.

(3) GHI's supermarkets are not available for immediate sale at the reporting date as the shareholders' approval was required. The held for sale criteria are only met after the end of the reporting period and the assets cannot be treated retrospectively as held for sale. However, the matter should be disclosed in a note to the financial statements as a non-adjusting event after the reporting period).

Solution 3—Statement Disclosures

Statement of profit or loss for the year ended 31 December 20X7

	Continuing operations (A and B)		Discontinued operations (C only)		Entity as a whole	
	20X6	**20X7**	*20X6*	**20X7**	*20X6*	**20X7**
	$000	**$000**	*$000*	**$000**	*$000*	**$000**
Revenue	*380*	**425**	*110*	**90**	*490*	**515**
Expenses	*(225)*	**(245)**	*(95)*	**(100)**	*(320)*	**(345)**
Impairment loss	*0*	**0**	*(20)*		*(20)*	
Loss on disposal				**(10)**		**(10)**
Provision for termination of employment	*0*	**0**	*0*	**(30)**	*0*	**(30)**
	155	**180**	*(5)*	**(50)**	*150*	**130**
Taxation (30%)	*(46.5)*	**(54)**	*1.5*	**15**	*(45)*	**(39)**
	108.5	**126**	*(3.5)*	**(35)**	*105*	**91**

Note to the financial statements

On 30 September 20X7, the Company sold its health food operations to Z Co for $60,000. The Company decided to dispose of Division C because its operations are in areas apart from the core business areas (cigarette and beverage manufacture and distribution) which form the long-term direction of the Company. Further, Division C's rate of return has not been equal to that of the Company's other two divisions during the period.

The loss on disposal of Division C (before income tax benefit of $3,000) was $10,000.

The Company recognised a provision for termination benefits of $30,000 (before income tax benefit of $9,000) to be paid by 31 March 20X8 to certain employees of Division C whose jobs will be terminated as a result of the sale.

IAS 36 *Impairment of Assets*

FOCUS

This session covers the following content from the *ACCA Study Guide.*

B. Accounting for Transactions in Financial Statements

3. Impairment of assets

a) Define, calculate and account for an impairment loss.

c) Identify the circumstances that may indicate impairment to assets.

d) Describe what is meant by a cash generating unit.

e) State the basis on which impairment losses should be allocated, and allocate an impairment loss to the assets of a cash generating unit.

Session 13 Guidance

■ **Appreciate** the circumstances in which an impairment loss may arise (s.2). IAS 36 *Impairment of Assets* is a very important topic both in real life and for the F7 exam.

■ **Calculate** an asset's recoverable amount. Once an impairment loss has been identified it will need to be accounted for by reducing the value of the asset and charging profits or revaluation surplus, if one exists for that asset (s.3).

(continued on next page)

VISUAL OVERVIEW

Objective: To give guidance on the recognition of impairment losses.

```
                    ┌─────────────────────────┐
                    │          IAS 36          │
                    │   • Objective            │
                    │   • Terminology          │
                    └─────────────────────────┘
                    ┌─────────────────────────┐
                    │       BASIC RULES        │
                    │   • All Assets           │
                    │   • Intangible Assets    │
                    │   • Indications of       │
                    │     Potential            │
                    │     Impairment Loss      │
                    └─────────────────────────┘
   ┌──────────────────────────┐      ┌──────────────────────────┐
   │ MEASUREMENT OF RECOVERABLE│      │   CASH-GENERATING UNITS  │
   │          AMOUNT           │      │   • Basic Concept        │
   │   • General Principles    │      │   • Allocating Shared    │
   │   • Fair Value Less Costs │      │     Assets               │
   │     of Disposal           │      │                          │
   │   • Value in Use          │      │                          │
   └──────────────────────────┘      └──────────────────────────┘
                    ┌─────────────────────────┐
                    │     ACCOUNTING FOR       │
                    │     IMPAIRMENT LOSS      │
                    │   • Basics               │
                    │   • Allocation Within    │
                    │     a CGU                │
                    └─────────────────────────┘
                    ┌─────────────────────────┐
                    │    SUBSEQUENT REVIEW     │
                    │   • Basic Provisions     │
                    │   • Reversals of         │
                    │     Impairment Losses    │
                    └─────────────────────────┘
                    ┌─────────────────────────┐
                    │       DISCLOSURE         │
                    │   • For Each Class of    │
                    │     Assets               │
                    │   • Material Impairment  │
                    │     Losses               │
                    └─────────────────────────┘
```

Session 13 Guidance

■ **Learn** the rules for allocating an impairment loss within a cash-generating unit: goodwill will be the first asset to be reduced in value, and then any remaining loss will be prorated among the remaining assets, with certain exceptions (s.4, s.5.2).

■ **Understand** that an impairment loss on a revalued asset will be charged direct to equity through other comprehensive income (s.5.1).

1 IAS 36

1.1 Objective

- Although most assets are initially accounted for at cost there is a generally accepted accounting principle that any loss in "worth" should be recognised. Historically, such losses were addressed by creating "provisions". Therefore, when IAS 37 *Provisions, Contingent Liabilities and Contingent Assets* was issued (prohibiting such provisions) another specific standard, IAS 36 *Impairment of Assets*, was issued simultaneously to prescribe an acceptable accounting treatment.*

- Some standards (IAS 16 and IAS 28) include a requirement that if the recoverable amount of an asset is less than its carrying amount (i.e. the value of the asset is impaired), then the carrying amount is written down immediately to this recoverable amount.

- IAS 36 prescribes detailed procedures for identifying impairments and accounting for them. It applies to all assets (including subsidiaries, associates and joint ventures) except those covered by the specific provisions of other statements:
  - inventories (IAS 2);
  - contract assets (IFRS 15);
  - deferred tax assets (IAS 12);
  - financial assets included in the scope of IFRS 9;
  - assets arising from employee benefits (IAS 19);
  - investment property which is measured at fair value (IAS 40);
  - biological assets measured at fair value less estimated costs of disposal (IAS 41); and
  - non-current assets classified as held for sale (IFRS 5).

*Commentary

*Prior to these standards the credit entry for a loss was to a provision account. This is not now allowed as there is **no liability.** Under IAS 36 any loss reduces the carrying amount of the **asset.**

1.2 Terminology

Impairment loss: the amount by which the carrying amount of an asset exceeds its recoverable amount.

Recoverable amount: the higher of an asset's fair value less costs of disposal and its value in use.

Fair value: the price which would be received to sell an asset or paid to transfer a liability in an orderly transaction between market participants at the measurement date.

Value in use: the present value of the future cash flows expected to be derived from an asset (or cash-generating unit).

Cash-generating unit: the smallest identifiable group of assets which generate cash inflows that are largely independent of the cash inflows from other assets or groups of assets.*

*Commentary

*The concept of a cash-generating unit is a solution to the problem of measuring value in use and comparison with carrying amount.

2   Basic Rules

2.1   All Assets

 **Key Point**

At the end of each reporting period, an entity should assess whether there is any indication that an asset (or cash-generating unit) may be impaired. If any such indication exists, the entity should estimate the recoverable amount of the asset.

▨ If no indications of a potential impairment loss are present, there is no need to make a formal estimate of recoverable amount, except for intangible assets with indefinite useful lives and those intangible assets which are not yet ready for use.

2.2   Intangible Assets

▨ Irrespective of whether there is any indication of impairment, the following intangible assets must be tested annually for impairment:
  ◦ those with an indefinite useful life;
  ◦ those not yet available for use; and
  ◦ goodwill acquired in a business combination.

▨ The impairment tests for these assets may be performed at any time during an annual period, provided they are performed at the same time every year. Note that all other assets (including intangibles which are amortised) are tested at the end of the financial period.

▨ Where an intangible asset with an indefinite life forms part of a cash-generating unit and cannot be separated, that cash-generating unit must be tested for impairment at least annually, or whenever there is an indication that the cash-generating unit may be impaired.

2.3   Indications of Potential Impairment Loss

▨ An entity should consider the following indications of potential impairment loss—both external and internal—as a minimum.

2.3.1   External Sources of Information

▨ Observable indications are that the asset's value has declined during the period significantly more than would be expected as a result of the passage of time or normal use.

▨ Significant changes with an adverse effect on the entity have taken place during the period, or will take place in the near future, in the technological, market, economic or legal environment in which the entity operates.

▨ Market interest rates or other market rates of return on investments have *increased* during the period, and those increases are likely to affect the discount rate used in calculating an asset's **value in use** and decrease the asset's recoverable amount materially.

▨ The carrying amount of the net assets of the reporting entity is more than its market capitalisation.

2.3.2   Internal Sources of Information

▨ Evidence is available of obsolescence or physical damage.

▨ Significant adverse changes have taken place during the period, or are expected to take place in the near future, in the extent to which, or manner in which, an asset is used or is expected to be used.

▨ Evidence is available from internal reporting which indicates that the economic performance of an asset is, or will be, worse than expected. Such evidence which indicates an asset may be impaired includes the existence of:*

  ⊚ cash flows for acquiring the asset, or subsequent cash needs for operating or maintaining it, which are significantly higher than those originally budgeted;

  ⊚ actual net cash flows or operating profit or loss flowing from the asset which are significantly worse than those budgeted;

  ⊚ a significant decline in budgeted net cash flows or operating profit, or a significant increase in budgeted loss, flowing from the asset; or

  ⊚ operating losses or net cash outflows for the asset, when current period figures are aggregated with budgeted figures for the future.

▨ Where there is an indication that an asset may be impaired, this may indicate that the remaining useful life, the depreciation (amortisation) method or the residual value for the asset needs to be reviewed and adjusted, even if no impairment loss is recognised for the asset.

3   Measurement of Recoverable Amount

3.1   General Principles

🔑 Key Point

The recoverable amount is the higher of the asset's **fair value** less costs of disposal and value in use:

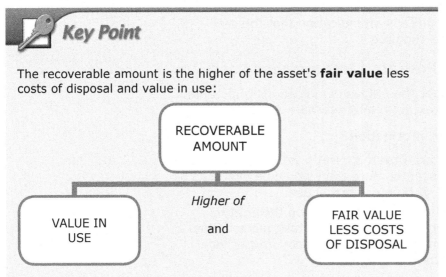

▨ Recoverable amount is determined for an individual asset, unless the asset does not generate cash inflows from continuing use which are largely independent of those from other assets or groups of assets. If this is the case, recoverable amount is determined for the cash-generating unit to which the asset belongs.

Illustration 1 Determining Recoverable Amount

Recoverable amount is the greater of:

Value in use	Fair value less costs of disposal	Therefore recoverable amount is:	Carrying amount	Commentary
900	1,050	1,050	1,000	No impairment
900	980	980	1,000	An impairment loss of $20 must be recognised. The carrying amount of the asset is written down to 980.
960	925	960	1,000	An impairment loss of $40 must be recognised. The carrying amount of the asset is written down to $960.

▨ It is not always necessary to determine both an asset's fair value less costs of disposal and its value in use to determine the asset's recoverable amount if:

  ● either of these amounts exceeds the asset's carrying amount (i.e. the asset is not impaired and it is not necessary to estimate the other amount); or

  ● there is no reason to believe that the asset's value in use materially exceeds its fair value less selling costs (i.e. the asset's recoverable amount is its fair value less selling costs).*

*Commentary

*For example, when an asset is held for imminent disposal the value in use will consist mainly of the net amount to be received for the disposal of the asset. Future cash flows from continuing use of the asset until disposal are likely to be negligible.

3.2 Fair Value Less Costs of Disposal

▨ Fair value is assessed using the fair value hierarchy in IFRS 13 *Fair Value Measurements*.

Definition

Active market—"a market in which transactions for the asset or liability take place with sufficient frequency and volume to provide pricing information on an ongoing basis."

—IFRS 13

Costs of disposal—incremental costs directly attributable to the disposal of an asset, excluding finance costs, income tax expense and any cost which has already been included as a liability. Examples include:*

  ■ legal costs;
  ■ stamp duty; and
  ■ costs of removing the asset.

*Commentary

*Examples of costs which are not costs of disposal include termination benefits and costs associated with reducing or reorganising a business following the disposal of an asset.

Illustration 2 Fair Value Less Costs of Disposal*

X operates in leased premises. It owns a bottling plant which is situated in a single factory unit. Bottling plants are sold periodically as complete assets.

Professional valuers have estimated that the plant might be sold for $100,000. They have charged a fee of $1,000 for providing this valuation.

X would need to dismantle the asset and ship it to any buyer. Dismantling and shipping would cost $5,000. Specialist packaging would cost $4,000 and legal fees $1,500.

Fair value less costs of disposal:	$
Sales price	100,000
Dismantling and shipping	(5,000)
Packaging	(4,000)
Legal fees	(1,500)
Fair value less costs of disposal	89,500

*Commentary

*The professional valuer's fee of $1,000 would not be included in the fair value less costs of disposal as this is not a directly attributable cost of selling the asset.

3.3 Value in Use

▨ **Value in use** is the present value of the future cash flows expected to be derived from an asset. Estimating it involves:

⦾ estimating the future cash inflows and outflows to be derived from continuing use of the asset and from its ultimate disposal; and

⦾ applying the appropriate discount rate.

Key Point

Value in use differs from fair value; value in use is more entity specific, whereas fair value would reflect only the assumptions market participants would use when pricing an asset.

▨ Fair value normally would *not* reflect the following factors:

⦾ additional value derived from the grouping of assets;

⦾ synergies between the asset being measured and other assets;

⦾ legal rights or restrictions specific to the current owner of the asset; and

⦾ tax benefits or burdens specific to the current owner of the asset.

Illustration 3 Value in Use

X holds a patent on a drug. The patent expires in five years. During this period the demand for the drug is forecast to grow at 5% per annum.

Experience shows that competitors flood the market with generic versions of a profitable drug as soon as it is no longer protected by a patent. As a result, X does not expect the patent to generate significant cash flows after five years.

Net revenues from the sale of the drug were $100 million last year.

The entity has decided that 15.5% is an appropriate discount rate for the appraisals of the cash flows associated with this product.

Time	Cash flow $m	Discount factor @15.5%	Present value ($m)
1	$100 \times 1.05 = 105$	0.86580	91
2	$100 \times 1.05^2 = 110.3$	0.74961	83
3	$100 \times 1.05^3 = 115.8$	0.64901	75
4	$100 \times 1.05^4 = 121.6$	0.56192	68
5	$100 \times 1.05^5 = 127.6$	0.48651	62
	Value in use		379

3.3.1 Cash Flow Projections

▨ Projections should be based on reasonable and supportable assumptions which represent management's best estimate of the set of economic conditions which will exist over the remaining useful life of the asset. Greater weight should be given to external evidence.

▨ They should be based on the most recent financial budgets/ forecasts approved by management.

▨ Projections based on these budgets/forecasts should cover a *maximum* period of five years, unless a longer period can be justified.

▨ Beyond the period covered by the most recent budgets/ forecasts, the cash flows should be estimated by extrapolating the projections based on the budgets/forecasts using a steady or declining growth rate for subsequent years, unless an increasing rate can be justified.

▨ The growth rate should not exceed the long-term average growth rate for the products, industries or country (countries) in which the entity operates or for the market in which the asset is used, unless a higher rate can be justified.

▨ Estimates of future cash flows should include:

  ● projected cash inflows including disposal proceeds; and

  ● projected cash outflows which are necessarily incurred to generate the cash inflows from continuing use of the asset.

▓ Estimates of future cash flows should exclude:*

- cash flows relating to the improvement or enhancement of the asset's performance; and
- cash flows which are expected to arise from a future restructuring that is not yet committed;
- cash outflows required to settle obligations which have already been recognised as liabilities;
- cash inflows or outflows from financing activities*; and

*Commentary

*Cash inflows/outflows from financing activities are already taken account of in discounting.

- income tax receipts or payments.

*Commentary

*Future cash flows are estimated based on the asset in its current condition or in maintaining its current condition (e.g. maintenance, or the replacement of components of an asset, to enable the asset as a whole to achieve its estimated current economic benefit).

3.3.2 Discount Rate

▓ The discount rate should be a pre-tax rate which reflects current market assessment of:

- the time value of money; and
- the risks specific to the asset.

Example 1 Relevant Cash Flows

Sumter is testing a machine, which makes a product called a union, for impairment. Sumter has compiled the following information in respect of the machine.

	$
Selling price of a union	100
Variable cost of production	70
Fixed overhead allocation per unit	10
Packing cost per unit	1

All costs and revenues are expected to inflate at 3% per annum.

Volume growth is expected to be 4% per annum. Last year, 1,000 units were sold. This is in excess of the long-term rate of growth in the industry. Sumter's management has valid reasons for projecting this level of growth.

The machine originally cost $400,000 and was supplied on credit terms from a fellow group entity. Sumter is charged $15,000 interest each year on this loan.

Future expenditure:

In two years' time, the machine will be subject to major servicing to maintain its operating capacity. This will cost $10,000.

In three years' time, the machine will be modified to improve its efficiency. This improvement will cost $20,000 and will reduce unit variable cost by 15%.

The asset will be sold in eight years' time. Currently the scrap value of machines of a similar type is $10,000.

All values are given in real terms (to exclude inflation).

Required:

Identify which cash flows should be included, and which excluded, in the calculation of value in use of the machine and explain why.

Example 1   Relevant Cash Flows (continued)

Solution

	Included/Excluded	Explanation
Net revenue:		
Fixed overhead:		
Volume growth:		
Capital cost of the machine:		
Depreciation:		
Loan interest:		
Major servicing:		
Machine modification:		
Scrap proceeds:		

4   Cash-Generating Units

4.1   Basic Concept

- If there is any indication that an asset may be impaired, the recoverable amount must be estimated for the individual asset.
- However, it may not be possible to estimate the recoverable amount of an individual asset because:
  - its value in use cannot be estimated to be close to its fair value less costs of disposal (e.g. when the future cash flows from continuing use of the asset cannot be estimated to be negligible); and
  - it does not generate cash inflows which are largely independent of those from other assets.
- In this case the recoverable amount of the cash-generating unit to which the asset belongs (the asset's cash-generating unit) must be determined.
- Identifying the lowest aggregation of assets which generate largely independent cash inflows may be a matter of considerable judgement.
- Management should consider various factors, including how to monitor operations (e.g. by product lines, individual locations, regional areas, etc) or how to make decisions about continuing or disposing of assets and operations.

Definition

Cash-generating unit—the smallest identifiable group of assets which generates cash inflows which are largely independent of the cash inflows from other assets or groups of assets.

Illustration 4 Cash-Generating Unit: Dry Dock

An entity owns a dry dock with a large crane to support its activities. The crane could only be sold for scrap value, and cash inflows from its use cannot be identified separately from all of the operations directly connected with the dry dock.

It is not possible to estimate the recoverable amount of the crane because its value in use cannot be determined. Therefore, the entity estimates the recoverable amount of the cash-generating unit to which the crane belongs, (i.e., the dry dock as a whole).

▨ Sometimes it is possible to identify cash flows which stem from a specific asset but these cannot be earned independently from other assets. In such cases the asset cannot be reviewed independently and must be reviewed as part of the cash-generating unit.

Illustration 5 Cash-Generating Unit: Airport

An entity operates an airport which provides services under contract with a government which requires a minimum level of service on domestic routes in return for licence to operate the international routes. Assets devoted to each route and the cash flows from each route can be identified separately. The domestic service operates at a significant loss.

Because the entity does not have the option to curtail the domestic service, the lowest level of identifiable cash inflows which are largely independent of the cash inflows from other assets or groups of assets are cash inflows generated by the airport as a whole. This is therefore the cash-generating unit.

▨ If an active market exists for the output produced by an asset or a group of assets, this asset or group of assets should be identified as a cash-generating unit, even if some or all of the output is used internally.

▨ Cash-generating units should be identified consistently from period to period for the same asset or types of assets, unless a change is justified.

4.2 Allocating Shared Assets

▨ The carrying amount of a cash-generating unit should include the carrying amount of only those assets which can be directly attributed or allocated on a reasonable and consistent basis to it.*

4.2.1 Goodwill Acquired in a Business Combination

 *Key Point*

Goodwill acquired in a business combination must be allocated to each of the acquirer's cash-generating units which are expected to benefit from the synergies of the combination, *regardless* of whether other assets or liabilities of the acquiree are assigned to those units.

 *Commentary*

*Goodwill acquired in a business combination and corporate (head office) assets are examples of shared assets which will need to be allocated.

- Each unit (or group of units) to which the goodwill is so allocated must:

  - represent the *lowest* level within the entity at which the goodwill is monitored for internal management purposes; and

  - be no larger than an operating segment (as defined in IFRS 8 *Operating Segments*).

Segment reporting and the definitions associated with IFRS 8 are **not** examinable.

*Commentary

These requirements are necessary to prevent the impairment of one unit being set off against increases in value in another unit (which would be possible if impairment was only assessed at the entity level).

- Once goodwill has been allocated to a cash-generating unit, that unit must be tested for impairment:

  - at least annually; or

  - as soon as there is an indication of impairment of:
    - —goodwill; or
    - —the cash-generating unit.

- Different cash-generating units may be tested for impairment at different times. However, if some or all of the goodwill allocated to a cash-generating unit was acquired in a business combination during the current annual period, that unit is tested for impairment before the end of the current annual period.

4.2.2 Corporate Assets

Definition

Corporate assets—assets, other than goodwill, which contribute to the future cash flows of both the cash-generating unit under review and other cash-generating units.

- The distinctive characteristics of **corporate assets** are that they do not generate cash inflows independently of other assets or groups of assets and their carrying amount cannot be fully attributed to the cash-generating unit under review.*

- Because corporate assets do not generate separate cash inflows, the recoverable amount of an individual corporate asset cannot be determined unless management has decided to dispose of the asset.

- Corporate assets are allocated on a reasonable and consistent basis to each cash-generating unit.

- If a corporate asset cannot be allocated to a specific cash-generating unit, the smallest group of cash-generating units which includes the unit under review must be identified.

- The carrying amount of the unit or group of units (including the portion of corporate assets) is then compared to its recoverable amount. Any impairment loss is dealt with in the same way as dealing with an impairment loss for goodwill.

*Commentary

*Corporate assets include the head office or divisional buildings, a central information system or a research centre.

5   Accounting for Impairment Loss

5.1   Basics

▨ If, and only if, the recoverable amount of an asset is less than its carrying amount, the carrying amount of the asset should be reduced to its recoverable amount. That reduction is an impairment loss.

 **Key Point**

An impairment loss should be recognised as an expense in the profit or loss immediately, unless the asset is carried at revalued amount under another IFRS.

▨ Any impairment loss of a revalued asset is treated as a revaluation decrease under that other IAS, and presented in other comprehensive income.*

 ***Commentary**

*Usually the fall in value of an impaired revalued asset must be charged to the revaluation surplus to the extent that the loss is covered by the surplus. Any amount not so covered is then charged to profit or loss.

Illustration 6   Recognising Impairment Loss

	Carrying amount (1)	Recoverable amount	Profit or loss	Revaluation surplus
Situation 1				
Asset carried at historic cost	100	80	20 **Dr**	—
Situation 2				
Historic cost of asset = 100 but revalued to 150	150	125	—	25 **Dr**
Situation 3				
Historic cost of asset = 100 but revalued to 150	150	95	5 **Dr**	50 **Dr**

(1) Before recognition of impairment loss.

▨ After impairment, the carrying amount of the asset less any residual value is depreciated (amortised) over its remaining expected useful life.

5.2 Allocation Within a Cash-Generating Unit (CGU)

▨ If an impairment loss is recognised for a cash-generating unit, the problem arises as to where to set the credit entry in the statement of financial position.

▨ The impairment loss should be allocated between all assets of the cash-generating unit in the following order:

- goodwill allocated to the cash-generating unit (if any);
- then to the other assets of the unit on a pro rata basis, based on the carrying amount of each asset in the unit.

▨ In allocating an impairment loss, the carrying amount of an asset should not be reduced below the highest of:

- its fair value less costs of disposal (if measurable);
- its value in use (if determinable); and
- zero.

The amount of the impairment loss which would otherwise have been allocated to the asset should be allocated to the other assets of the unit on a pro rata basis.

Example 2 Impairment Loss, Part 1

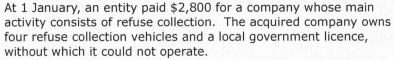

At 1 January, an entity paid $2,800 for a company whose main activity consists of refuse collection. The acquired company owns four refuse collection vehicles and a local government licence, without which it could not operate.

At 1 January, the fair value less costs of disposal of each lorry and of the licence is $500. The company has no insurance cover.

At 1 February, one lorry crashed. Because of its reduced capacity, the entity estimates the value in use of the business at $2,220.

Required:

Show how the impairment loss would be allocated to the assets of the business.

Example 3 Impairment Loss, Part 2

Following on from *Example 2*.

At 22 May, the government increased the interest rates. The entity re-determined the value in use of the business as $1,860. The fair value less costs of disposal of the licence had decreased to $480 (as a result of a market reaction to the increased interest rates). The demand for lorries was hit hard by the increase in rates, and the selling prices were adversely affected.

Required:

Show how the above information would be reflected in the asset values of the business.

Key Point

If assets had included current assets these would not bear any of the impairment loss as they would already be measured at a current value.

6　Subsequent Review

6.1　Basic Provisions

▦ Once an entity has recognised an impairment loss for an asset other than goodwill, it should carry out a further review in later years if there is an indication:

- ● that the asset may be further impaired; or
- ● that the impairment loss recognised in prior years may have decreased.

▦ An entity should consider, as a minimum, the following indications of both external and internal sources of information.

6.1.1　External Sources of Information

▦ Observable indications that the asset's value has increased significantly during the period.

▦ Significant favourable changes during the period, or taking place in the near future, in the technological, market, economic or legal environment in which the entity operates or in the market to which the asset is dedicated.

▦ Decrease in market interest rates or other market rates of return likely to affect the discount rate used in calculating the asset's value in use and materially increase the asset's recoverable amount.

6.1.2　Internal Sources of Information

▦ Significant favourable changes* in the actual or expected extent or manner of use of the asset.

▦ Evidence available from internal reporting indicates that the economic performance of the asset is, or will be, better than expected.

*Commentary

*For example, if capital expenditure incurred improves the asset's performance

6.2　Reversals of Impairment Losses

6.2.1　On Individual Assets, Other Than Goodwill

▦ The carrying amount of an asset, other than goodwill, for which an impairment loss has been recognised is increased to its recoverable amount *only* if there has been a change in the estimates used to determine its recoverable amount since the last impairment loss was recognised.*

▦ The increased carrying amount should not exceed the carrying amount which would have been determined (net of amortisation or depreciation) if the impairment loss had not been recognised.

▦ Any increase above the carrying amount which would have been determined if impairment had not been recognised is a revaluation and must be treated accordingly.

*Commentary

*Any increase in the present value of future cash flows due solely to the passage of time **is not** a reversal of an impairment loss.

Illustration 7 — Reversal of an Impairment Loss

An asset with a carrying amount of $100 and a useful life of 10 years is tested for impairment and the recoverable amount is calculated at $80, giving an impairment loss of $20.

Two years later, the asset's value has recovered and the recoverable amount has been reassessed as $94. The carrying amount would then be $64 (80 − (80 × $\frac{2}{10}$)). The maximum amount that the asset can be measured at, without revaluing it, would be $80 (100 − (100 × $\frac{2}{10}$)), giving a reversal of the impairment loss of $16.

Key Point

If it reverses an impairment previously recognised as an expense in profit or loss, it is recognised in profit or loss to the extent previously recognised as an expense.

- A reversal of an impairment loss is recognised in profit or loss immediately, unless the asset is carried at revalued amount under another IFRS.

- Any reversal of an impairment loss on a revalued asset is treated as a revaluation increase and will usually be recognised in other comprehensive income.

6.2.2 Reversal of an Impairment Loss on Goodwill

- An impairment loss recognised for goodwill **cannot** be reversed in a subsequent period.

- Any increase in the recoverable amount of goodwill in the periods following the recognition of an impairment loss is likely to be an increase in internally generated goodwill, rather than a reversal of the impairment loss recognised for the acquired goodwill.

Key Point

IAS 38 prohibits the recognition of internally generated goodwill.

7 Disclosure

7.1 For Each Class of Assets

- Impairment losses recognised during the period and the line item(s) of the statement of profit or loss and other comprehensive income in which those impairment losses are included.

- The amount of impairment losses recognised against any revaluation surplus during the period.

7.2 Material Impairment Losses Recognised

- The nature of the individual assets or a description of the cash-generating unit (e.g. product line or business operation).

- The events and circumstances which led to the recognition of the impairment loss.

- The amount of the impairment loss recognised.

- Whether the recoverable amount of the asset (cash-generating unit) is its fair value less costs of disposal or its value in use.

Summary

- Indications of impairment (external and internal) must be assessed annually. If indicated, the recoverable amount must be estimated.

- Impairment testing must be measured annually (even if no indication) for certain intangible assets (indefinite life, not available for use, goodwill) and CGUs to which goodwill has been allocated.

- Accounting estimates (useful life, depreciation method and/or residual value) may also need to be reviewed and adjusted.

- If either fair value less costs of disposal or value in use exceed carrying amount there is no impairment.

- If fair value less costs of disposal is indeterminable, the recoverable amount is value in use.

- For assets to be disposed, the recoverable amount is fair value less costs of disposal. If binding sale agreement, use price agreement less costs.

- If an active market exists, use the current bid price or most recent transaction. If no active market, then best estimate.

- Value in use reflects amount/timing of cash flows and time value of money (using pre-tax discount rate).

- Cash flow projections based on supportable assumptions and the asset's current condition exclude cash flows from financing activities or taxation.

- An impairment loss must be recognised when the recoverable amount is below the carrying amount:
  - expense in profit or loss (any excess over revaluation surplus);
  - adjust depreciation for future periods.

- If the recoverable amount for an individual asset cannot be estimated, determine for its CGU.

- In allocating goodwill to CGUs, each CGU must:
  - represent the lowest level at which goodwill is monitored; and
  - be not larger than an operating segment.

- An impairment loss reduces the carrying amount of a CGU's assets. Allocation is firstly to goodwill then other assets (on pro rata basis).

- The carrying amount cannot be less than the higher of fair value less costs of disposal, value in use and zero.

Session 13

Session 13 Quiz
Estimated time: 15 minutes

1. Define the recoverable amount of an asset. (1.2)
2. Identify possible indicators which suggest an impairment loss has occurred. (2.3)
3. Specify the conditions which must exist for there to be an active market in a particular asset. (3.2)
4. When estimating value in use, state which future cash flows should be included and which cash flows should be excluded from projections. (3.3.1)
5. Define a cash-generating unit. (4)
6. Describe how goodwill acquired in a business combination should be allocated. (4.2.1)
7. State the order in which an impairment loss in a cash-generating unit is allocated to its assets. (5.2)

Study Question Bank
Estimated time: 20 minutes

Priority		Estimated Time	Completed
Q23	Justin	20 minutes	
Additional			
Q24	Shiplake		

EXAMPLE SOLUTIONS

Solution 1—Relevant Cash Flows

	Included/Excluded	Explanation
Net revenue:	Included	This is a variable cash flow. 100 – 70 – 1 = 29 in the first year will be inflated each year by 3%.
Fixed overhead:	Excluded	This is a sunk cost and not relevant to the calculation. It will be incurred irrespective of the machine and so is not a direct cost of using the machine.
Volume growth:	Included	Management expects volume to increase by 4% each year and this volume increase should be incorporated in the calculation for the first five years. After this, IAS 36 prohibits the use of a management growth rate that exceeds the industry average. In the absence of further information, zero growth will be assumed.
Capital cost of the machine:	Excluded	This is a sunk cost and therefore not relevant.
Depreciation:	Excluded	This is not a cash flow.
Loan interest:	Excluded	IAS 36 states that cash flows ignore financing costs (and are pre-tax).
Major servicing:	Included	This cost is necessary to maintain operating capacity. This current value will need to be inflated for two years' inflation adjustment.
Machine modification:	Excluded	This cost is an enhancing cost and will not be included, as it does not relate to the present condition of the asset. The resulting savings in variable cost will also be excluded.
Scrap proceeds:	Included	This is a future cash flow relating to the asset. As this amount is a current value it will need to be inflated to a future value, reflecting the expected cash flow in eight years' time.

Solution 2—Impairment Loss, Part 1

	1 January	Impairment loss	1 February
Goodwill	300	(80)	220
Intangible asset	500	—	500
Lorries	2,000	(500)	1,500
	2,800	(580)	2,220

An impairment loss of 500 is recognised first for the lorry which crashed, because its recoverable amount can be assessed individually. (It no longer forms part of the cash-generating unit which was formed by the four lorries and the licence.)

The remaining impairment loss (80) is attributed to goodwill.

Solution 3—Impairment Loss, Part 2

	1 February	Impairment loss	22 May
Goodwill*	220	(220)	—
Intangible asset	500	(20)	480
Lorries*	1,500	(120)	1,380
	2,220	(360)	1,860

*Commentary

*220 is charged to goodwill to reduce it to zero. The balance of 140 must be prorated between the remaining assets in proportion to their carrying amount.

The ratio of the remaining assets to each other is 500:2,000 = 25%. This implies that 25% × 140 = 35 should be allocated to the intangible asset. However, this would reduce its carrying amount to below its fair value less costs of disposal; this is not allowed. The maximum which may be allocated is 20; the remaining 15 must be allocated to the lorries.

*The amount allocated to the lorries is
75% × 140 = 105 + 15 = 120.

IFRS 16 *Leases*

FOCUS

This session covers the following content from the *ACCA Study Guide.*

B. Accounting for Transaction in Financial Statements

6. Leasing

a) Account for right of use assets and lease liabilities in the records of the lessee. ☐

b) Explain the exemption from the recognition criteria for leases in the records of the lessee. ☐

c) Account for sale and leaseback agreements. ☐

Session 14 Guidance

- **IFRS** 16 *Leases* is a very important standard in real life and **is examined regularly.** Note that the syllabus only covers accounting by the lessee—not the lessor.
- **Work** through *Example 1*.

(continued on next page)

VISUAL OVERVIEW

Objective: To describe accounting for leases from the viewpoint of the lessee.

```
                    ┌─────────────────────────────┐
                    │         INTRODUCTION        │
                    │  • Lease v Buy              │
                    │  • Pre IFRS 16             │
                    │  • Scope                   │
                    │  • Terminology            │
                    └─────────────────────────────┘
            ┌──────────────┼──────────────────┐
┌───────────────────────┐ ┌──────────────────┐ ┌──────────────────────┐
│ LEASE IDENTIFICATION  │ │   PRESENTATION   │ │  SALE AND LEASEBACK  │
│  • Inception          │ │  AND DISCLOSURE  │ │  • Recognising sale  │
│  • Separation         │ │  • Presentation  │ │  • Sale not recognised│
│  • Recognition and    │ │  • Disclosure    │ └──────────────────────┘
│    Measurement        │ └──────────────────┘
└───────────────────────┘
```

Session 14 Guidance

■ **Understand** the factors that determine how the lease should be accounted for (s.2).

■ **Be able** to account for any form of sale and leaseback transactions (s.3).

1 Introduction

1.1 Lease v Buy

▓ An entity may choose to buy or lease an asset.

▓ The main advantage of leasing is not having to find the upfront cash for large capital expenditure. Leasing may be cheaper than borrowing funds to buy the asset. Although a leased asset may never be owned outright a lease arrangement may allow for upgrading or replacement of assets without the expense of buying newer models.

▓ Although any kind of equipment can be leased, common examples are vehicles, computers and printers, power tools, etc.

1.2 Pre IFRS 16

▓ IFRS 16 *Leases* was issued by the IASB in 2016 and is effective from 1 January 2019. Before IFRS 16 the relevant standard was IAS 17 *Leases*.

▓ IAS 17 defined two types of lease:

• Operating leases; and

• Finance leases.

▓ If a lease met the definition of a finance lease, the asset and liability were recognised in the statement of financial position. If the lease was an operating lease then no asset or liability were recognised and any lease rental was expensed to profit or loss as incurred.

▓ This accounting model resulted in many leases being excluded from the statement of financial position, even though the lessee (the party using the asset) had a present obligation, and therefore a liability, to make regular payments to the lessor (the party owning the asset).*

Commentary

*Through IFRS 16, the IASB has eliminated such "off balance sheet financing" by requiring entities to account for the substance of the transaction rather than the legal form.

Key Point

Under IAS 17, excluding the asset and liability from the statement of financial position affected key accounting ratios, such as:

■ Return on capital employed (higher); and

■ Gearing (lower).

▓ Papers discussing this less than ideal accounting treatment go as far back as 1999. In 2010, the IASB published its first exposure draft proposing changes to the accounting for leases. It took almost six years for the final standard to be published.

1.3 Scope

▓ IFRS 16 applies to all leases except those that fall within the scope of specific standards (e.g. leases of biological assets covered by IAS 41 *Agriculture*).

1.4 Terminology

Lease: a contract for the right to use an asset for a period of time.

Right-of-use asset: an asset that the lessee has the right to use under the terms of the lease .

Interest rate implicit in the lease: the rate of interest at which the present value of the lease payments and any unguaranteed residual value equals the fair value of the leased asset (including any initial direct costs of the lessor).*

Fair value: the amount for which an asset could be exchanged, or liability settled, between knowledgeable, willing parties in an arm's-length transaction.*

*That is, the internal rate of return of the lessor's cash flows.

*This is not the same as the IFRS 13 definition.

Short-term lease: of 12 months or less. A lease with a purchase option is **not** a short-term lease.

Underlying asset: the subject of a lease.

2 Lease Identification

2.1 Inception

- Whether a contract is a lease or contains a lease is assessed at the earliest of:
  - the date of the lease agreement; and
  - the date of the parties' commitment to the main terms and conditions of the lease.

2.2 Separation

- Each component of a contract must be considered separately (e.g. two distinct buildings rented under the same contract).

- Any non-lease components must also be treated separately (e.g. a cleaning and maintenance contract of leased buildings). The lessee can, however, elect not to separate the non-lease components if this is impractical.

2.3 Recognition and Measurement

2.3.1 Recognition

- On commencement of the lease the lessee recognises:
  - a right-of-use **asset**; and
  - a lease **liability**.
- Exceptions to this are:
  - short-term leases; and
  - leases of assets with a low value (e.g. laptops).*

*Although the standard does not specify a monetary amount, up to $5,000 is indicated in the Basis for Conclusions.

Key Point

The previous standard on leases recognised the *physical* asset leased. IFRS 16 recognises the *right to use* the asset, which will result in more leases being capitalised under IFRS 16.

▨ Rental payments for short-term leases and low-value assets are expensed to profit or loss (normally on a straight-line basis); no asset or liability is recognised other than rent prepayments or accruals.

Illustration 1 Low-Value Assets

Artmap contracted to lease the following:

(1)   20 coffee machines valued at $1,350 each.
(2)   50 vehicles for sales staff with an average cost of $6,800.
(3)   Unspecified tables and chairs for conferences, on an ad hoc basis, paying $1,000 each time.

(1) is a lease of low-value assets, even though the total cost is $27,000. Lease payments will be expensed to profit or loss on a straight-line basis, unless a more systematic basis is appropriate.

(2) Artmap may choose to account for these right-of-use assets as a single portfolio of leases with similar characteristics if the results would not materially differ from accounting for the individual leases.

(3) is not a lease as the contract does not identify the assets.

2.3.2 Liability Measurement

▨ The liability is initially measured at the commencement of the lease at the present value of the future lease payments.

▨ Lease payments are discounted using the interest rate implicit in the lease, if known, or the lessee's incremental cost of borrowing.

▨ Cash flows used in the present value calculation include:

- Fixed payments less any lease incentives;
- Variable payments that are based on a specified index (e.g. a consumer price index) or rate (e.g. LIBOR);
- The value of any purchase option the lessee is likely to exercise; and
- Penalties the lessee expects to pay to cancel the lease.

▨ As time passes, the liability is increased by any interest on the outstanding liability (the so-called "unwinding of the discount") and decreased by the lease payments made.

▨ The liability may require remeasurement if the terms of the lease are modified or the payment schedule is changed.

Illustration 2 Initial Liability

Hick entered into a lease agreement on 1 January to lease a machine for six years. The contract requires an up-front payment of $2,000 on signing the lease plus a further five payments of $2,000 at the end of each year. Hick has an option to buy the asset at the end of year six for $500, which Hick expects to exercise. The rate of interest implicit in the lease is 10%.

The initial amount of liability recognised will be calculated as:

End of year	Cash flow $	10% discount factor	Present value $
1	2,000	0.91	1,820
2	2,000	0.83	1,660
3	2,000	0.75	1,500
4	2,000	0.68	1,360
5	2,000	0.62	1,240
6	500	0.56	280
			7,860

The initial payment of $2,000 is not included in the schedule as it has been paid and therefore is not a liability.

Illustration 3 Interest Allocation

Following on from *Illustration 2* interest is allocated as follows:

Period	Liability $	Interest @ 10% $	Rental $	Closing balance $
1	7,860	786	(2,000)	6,646
2	6,646	665	(2,000)	5,311
3	5,311	531	(2,000)	3,842
4	3,842	384	(2,000)	2,226
5	2,226	223	(2,000)	449
6	449	51*	(500)	—
		2,640		

*Includes rounding difference.

At the end of year 1, the lease liability is $6,646 of which $5,311 is non-current (the amount outstanding at the end of year 2) and $1,335 is current.

2.3.3 Asset Measurement

▦ The right-of-use asset is initially measured at cost which includes:

- The initial amount of the liability recognised;
- Payments made before the lease commenced (e.g. a deposit) less any incentives received;
- Direct costs incurred by the lessee (e.g. installation costs); and
- Decommissioning costs expected to be incurred in dismantling or removing the asset at the end of its economic life.*

▦ The asset is subsequently measured using the cost model. However, it may be revalued if it belongs to a class of assets that are revalued.

▦ Depreciation is charged on the same basis as assets which are owned.

▦ If there is no reasonable certainty that the lessee will obtain ownership at the end of the lease term, the asset is depreciated over the shorter of:

- the lease term; and
- its useful life.

▦ If the lessee will retain ownership at the end of the lease term, the asset is depreciated over its useful life.

▦ If the lessee uses the fair value model of IAS 40 Investment Property, a right-of-use investment property will also be subsequently measured at fair value.

Commentary

*The present value of these costs is recognised as a provision in accordance with *IAS 37*.

Illustration 4 Initial Asset

Following on from *Illustration 2*.

Hick incurs installation costs of $600. Based on the expectation that Hick will exercise the option to buy the asset, Hick will depreciate the asset over eight years on a straight-line basis.

The initial amount capitalised will be:

	$
Initial liability	7,860
Deposit paid	2,000
Installation costs	600
	10,460

Annual depreciation for the asset will be $10,460 ÷ 8 years = $1,308 per annum.

Example 1 Lease Payments in Arrears

Delta entered into a contract to lease an asset on 1 January 20X8. The terms of the lease are six annual payments of $2,000 with the first payment on 31 December 20X8. Delta will incur a further $1,000 installation costs. Delta will return the asset to the lessor at the end of year six.

The initial measurement of the liability has been calculated at $8,710 using the interest rate implicit in the lease of 10%.

Required:

(a) Show the interest allocation over the six-year term of the lease.

(b) Show how the lease should be accounted for in the financial statements of Delta as at 31 December 20X8.

Exam Advice

The interest rate implicit in the lease will always be given in the exam; there will be no requirement to calculate it.

Example 2 Lease Payments in Advance

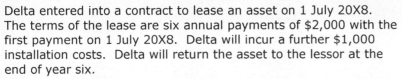

Delta entered into a contract to lease an asset on 1 July 20X8. The terms of the lease are six annual payments of $2,000 with the first payment on 1 July 20X8. Delta will incur a further $1,000 installation costs. Delta will return the asset to the lessor at the end of year six.

The initial measurement of the liability has been calculated at $6,710, being the present value of the remaining five payments, using the interest rate implicit in the lease of 15%.

Required:

(a) Show the interest and depreciation expenses charged to profit and loss for the years ended 31 December 20X8 and 20X9.

(b) Calculate the current and non-current lease liabilities that should be included in the financial statements of Delta as at 31 December 20X8.

3 Sale and Leaseback

3.1 Recognising a Sale

- If the revenue recognition criteria of IFRS 15 are met the seller (lessee) will:
  - Recognise the cash received;
  - Derecognise the asset sold;
  - Recognise a right-of-use asset for the asset leased back;
  - Recognise the lease liability; and
  - Recognise any gain or loss, but only on the portion of the asset transferred to the buyer (lessor).
- If the asset is sold at a price that differs from its fair value the seller must adjust the sale proceeds to fair value by:
  - adding a prepayment, if sold at a below-market price; or
  - deducting additional financing if sold at an above-market price.

Key Point

The treatment of a sale and leaseback of an asset depends on whether the revenue recognition criteria of IFRS 15 have been met.

Illustration 5 Sale and Leaseback

On 1 January 20X8 Juno enters into a sale and leaseback contract to sell for $1,000,000 an asset that has a carrying amount of $600,000 and a fair value of $900,000.

Juno will make 10 annual lease payments of $115,000; the interest rate implicit in the lease is 5%. The cumulative discount factor (annuity factor) for years 1 to 10 is 7.72.

The present value of the 10 payments is $887,800. $100,000 of this relates to the additional finance provided by the buyer (the excess of $1,000,000 over the asset's fair value, $900,000). The remaining $787,800 relates to the lease liability.

The right-of-use asset is measured as a proportion of its carrying amount as follows:

$$\text{Present value of lease liability} \times \frac{\text{Carrying amount}}{\text{Fair value of asset}}$$

$$= 787,800 \times \frac{600,000}{900,000} = \$525,200$$

Although the gain on the sale is $300,000 (900 − 600), only the portion that relates to the rights transferred to the buyer is recognised as follows:

$$\text{Gain} \times \frac{\text{Fair value of asset - lease liability}}{\text{Fair value of asset}}$$

$$300,000 \times \frac{(900,000 - 787,800)}{900,000}$$

In summary, on 1 January 20X8 Juno will account for the sale and leaseback transaction as follows:

	$	$
Cash	1,000,000	
Right-of-use asset	525,200	
Asset sold		600,000
Liability recognised		887,800
Gain on rights transferred		37,400

The right-of-use asset will be depreciated over its 10 year life, usually on a straight-line basis, giving an annual charge of $52,520.

Interest on the liability will be calculated using the interest rate implicit in the lease of 5%. In 20X8 this will lead to a finance charge of $44,390 (5% × 887,800) to profit or loss.

3.2 Sale Not Recognised

- If the criteria of IFRS 15 are not met then no sale can be recognised and the asset **cannot** be derecognised.

- Instead the seller must apply IFRS 9 *Financial Instruments* and recognise a financial liability in respect of the proceeds received (i.e. account for it as a loan).

4   Presentation and Disclosure

4.1   Presentation

4.1.1   Statement of Financial Position

- Right-of-use assets are presented separately from other assets in the statement of financial position or in the disclosure notes.
- A right-of-use asset classified as investment property is included with any other owned investment property.
- The lease liability should be presented separately from all other liabilities in the statement of financial position or the disclosure notes, separated into a non-current and a current liability (in accordance with IAS 1).

4.1.2   Statement of Profit or Loss

- Depreciation of right-of-use assets and rent payments for short-term and low-cost assets are expensed as operating costs.
- Interest relating to a right-of-use asset is presented as a finance cost.

4.1.3   Statement of Cash Flows

- Repayment of the capital element of a lease is classified under financing activities.
- Interest paid may be classified as an operating or financing cash flow (in accordance with IAS 7).
- Payments relating to short-term leases and low-cost assets are classified as an operating cash flow.

4.2   Disclosure

- Extensive disclosure requirements allow users of financial statements to assess how leases affect financial performance, financial position and cash flows.
- Disclosures include:
  - Depreciation of right-of-use assets;
  - Interest expense on lease liabilities;
  - Expense relating to short-term leases and lease of low-cost assets; and
  - Any gains or losses on sale and leaseback contracts.
- Disclosures should also include qualitative information such as the nature of leasing activities and any restrictions or covenants included in leasing contracts.

Summary

- All leases are capitalised except for leases of less than 12 months duration and leases of assets with low value.

- What the lessee is capitalising is the right-of-use asset rather than the physical asset.

- The initial lease liability will be the present value of future lease payments using the interest rate implicit in the lease. Any upfront deposits are not included in the calculation.

- The initial right-of-use asset is measured at the initial lease liability plus any initial deposit plus any direct costs incurred plus any future decommissioning costs.

- Lease payments will be split into the repayment of capital and interest using the interest rate implicit in the lease.

- The right-of-use asset is depreciated over the useful life of the lease, unless it is expected that ownership of the asset will be transferred at the end of the lease term, in which case the asset will be depreciated over the useful life of the asset.

- Short-term leases and leases where the underlying asset is of a low value will expense any rental payments, normally on a straight-line basis.

- The requirements of IFRS 15 *Revenue from Contracts with Customers* will be applied to sale and leaseback transactions.

- If the revenue recognition criteria of IFRS 15 are met in a sale and leaseback, a sale of the asset will be recognised and replaced with a right-of-use asset and a lease liability.

- If the revenue recognition criteria of IFRS 15 are not met in a sales and leaseback, a financial liability is recognised in accordance with IFRS 9 *Financial Instruments*.

Session 14 Quiz
Estimated time: 15 minutes

1. State the effect on Return on Capital Employed and Gearing if a leased asset and liability were excluded from the statement of financial position. (1.2)

2. Define a right-of-use asset. (1.4)

3. Identify the two circumstances when a lessee would not recognise a right-of-use asset and lease liability when entering a lease contract. (2.3.1)

4. Describe how the right-of-use asset is initially measured. (2.3.2)

5. Name the standard which prescribes the initial accounting for a sale and leaseback transaction. (3)

6. Describe what happens to sale proceeds in a sale and leaseback transaction, if the asset is sold at a price that differs from its fair value. (3.1)

7. State the accounting treatment of a sale and leaseback transaction when the asset sold is not derecognised. (3.2)

8. Describe the presentation of a lease liability In the statement of financial position. (4.1.1)

9. State the presentation in the statement of cash flows of payments relating to low-cost assets. (4.1.3)

Study Question Bank
Estimated time: 30 minutes

Priority		Estimated Time	Completed
Q25	Snow	30 minutes	

EXAMPLE SOLUTIONS

Solution 1—Lease Payments in Arrears

(a) Interest allocation

	$
Rentals	12,000
Initial liability recognised	(8,710)
Interest expense	3,290

Year	Amount owed at the start of the year	Interest @ 10%	Rental	Amount owed at the end of the year
1	8,710	871	(2,000)	7,581
2	7,581	758	(2,000)	6,339
3	6,339	634	(2,000)	4,973
4	4,973	497	(2,000)	3,470
5	3,470	347	(2,000)	1,817
6	1,817	183	(2,000)	0
		3,290		

(b) Financial statements
Analysis of payable

Current (2,000 − 758 (W))	1,242	
		= 7,581
Non-current	6,339	

Right-of-use asset	$
Cost (8,710 lease liability + 1,000 installation)	9,710
Depreciation (9,710 ÷ 6)	(1,618)
Carrying amount	8,092

WORKING

Finance lease payable

		1/1/X8 Right-of-use asset	8,710
31/12/X8 Cash	2,000	31/12/X8 Interest	871
31/12/X8 Bal c/d	7,581		
	9,581		9,581
		01/01/X9 Bal b/d	7,581
31/12/X9 Cash	2,000	31/12/X9 Interest	758

Solution 2—Lease Payments in Advance

(a) Interest and depreciation expenses

	$
Profit or loss for year ended 31 December 20X8:	
Interest (W1)	503
Depreciation (1,618 (W2) × $^{6}/_{12}$)	809
Profit or loss for year ended 31 December 20X9:	
Interest (503 + 428 (W1))	931
Depreciation	1,618

(b) Lease liabilities as at 31 December 20X8

	$
Non-current (7,213 − 2,000)	5,213
Current	2,000

WORKINGS

(1) Interest and liability

	$
1 July 20X8	6,710
Interest to 31 December 20X8 (6,710 × 15%) × $^{6}/_{12}$	503
31 December 20X8 Balance	7,213
Interest to 30 June 20X9	503
30 June 20X9 Balance	7,716
1 July 20X9 Cash flow	(2,000)
Interest to 31 December 20X9 (5,716 × 15%) × $^{6}/_{12}$	428
31 December 20X9 Balance	6,144

(2) Right-of-use asset

	$
Initial liability	6,710
Advance payment	2,000
Installation costs	1,000
Initial amount recognised	9,710
Annual depreciation = 9,710 ÷ 6 years	1,618

IAS 37 *Provisions, Contingent Liabilities and Contingent Assets*

FOCUS

This session covers the following content from the *ACCA Study Guide.*

B. Accounting for Transactions in Financial Statements

7. Provisions and events after the reporting period

a) Explain why an accounting standard on provisions is necessary.

b) Distinguish between legal and constructive obligations.

c) State when provisions may and may not be made and demonstrate how they should be accounted for.

d) Explain how provisions should be measured.

e) Define contingent assets and liabilities and describe their accounting treatment and required disclosure.

f) Identify and account for:

    i)   warranties/guarantees

    ii)   onerous contracts

    iii) environmental and similar provisions

    iv) provisions for future repairs or refurbishments.

Session 15 Guidance

■ **Appreciate** the need for a standard on accounting for provision (s.1).

■ **Learn** the definitions of a provision and a contingent liability (s.1.1, s.1.4).

■ **Understand** why a provision is recognised in the financial statements, whereas a contingent liability is only disclosed (s.2).

(continued on next page)

VISUAL OVERVIEW

Objective: To define and explain the recognition and measurement of provisions, contingent liabilities and contingent assets.

```
                        ┌─────────────────────────┐
                        │         IAS 37          │
                        ├─────────────────────────┤
                        │  • Background           │
                        │  • Objective            │
                        │  • Scope                │
                        │  • Terminology          │
                        │  • Provisions v         │
                        │    Contingent Liabilities│
                        └─────────────────────────┘
```

RECOGNITION ISSUES	MEASUREMENT	DISCLOSURES
• Provisions	• General Rules	• Provisions
• Present Obligation	• Specific Points	• Contingent Liabilities
• Past Event	• Changes	• Contingent Assets
• Reliable Estimate	• Self-Insurance	• Serious Prejudice
• Contingent Assets and Liabilities		

APPLICATION TO SPECIFIC CIRCUMSTANCES	REPAIRS AND MAINTENANCE
• Future Operating Losses	• Substantial Expenditure
• Onerous Contracts	• Refurbishment—No Legal Requirement
• Restructuring	• Refurbishment—Legal Requirement
• Decommissioning Costs	

Session 15 Guidance

■ **Work through** the *Illustrations* that apply IAS 37 recognition criteria to practical transactions and events (s.2).

■ **Calculate** expected value as a best estimate of a provision (*Illustration 9*) and the interest expense that arises on "unwinding of the discount" (*Illustration 10*).

1 IAS 37

1.1 Background

▨ Before IAS 37, there were no international accounting standards governing the definition, recognition, measurement, use or presentation of **"provisions"**.

▨ "Provisions" were created with a debit to expense and credit to the statement of financial position. Such credits could increase liabilities (e.g. a "provision" for repairs and renewals) or decrease assets (e.g. a "provision" for irrecoverable debts).

▨ Because of the lack of prescription in this area, provisions could be made, not made or "unmade" to suit management's needs based largely on intent. Provisions were created in a "good" year and later released to "smooth" profits. These "big bath" or "rainy day" provisions were so called because they could be used for any and every purpose.*

*Commentary

*Provisions were often made for one purpose and used for another.

Illustration 1 Use of Provision to Smooth Results

In 1999, an investor considered an investment in one of two comparable companies:

Company A	1996 $000	1997 $000	1998 $000	Company B	1996 $000	1997 $000	1998 $000
Results	2,500	3,200	3,700	Results	6,500	1,100	7,500

The higher profits in 1998 in Company B look more attractive, but a risk averse investor would be influenced by the possible repetition of poor performance in 1997. The trend of rising profits in Company A gives an impression of high-quality earnings which may contribute to supporting a higher share price.

Suppose that instead of publishing its results as above, Company B decided, in 1996, to restructure its operations and provide for potential costs of $3 million. Furthermore, in 1997, Company B decided that restructuring was no longer necessary. Its result would be reported as:

	1996 $000	1997 $000	1998 $000
Original	6,500	1,100	7,500
Provision	(3,000)		
Release of provision		3,000	
Revised results	3,500	4,100	7,500

Now Company B shows the investor the steadily increasing profits he seeks.

▨ Although the usual objective of "creative accounting" is to find accounting policies and treatments which maximise reported profit and reduce reported liabilities, the initial effect of using provisions creatively achieves the opposite.

▨ Diverse approaches to the recognition and measurement of provisions were found in the absence of regulation. This reduced the comparability of financial statements and affected, in particular, earnings per share as a stock market indicator.

Illustration 2 Variety of Accounting Practices

On closure of its surface mines, a mining company reinstated the soil excavated and restored the surface with topsoil replacement and landscaping. In the absence of an accounting standard the company could:

(i)   ignore the costs until the mine is closed;

(ii) make some disclosure about the likelihood of future costs for restoration;

(iii) accrue the expected costs of restoration annually over the expected productive life of the mine; or

(iv) provide for the expected costs in full (at some point).

The most commonly used and accepted accounting practice was (i) on the grounds that it was consistent with accrual accounting.

- As well as creating credit balances (that had the appearance of liabilities), provisions were widely used to reduce the carrying amount of assets (inventory, receivables, non-current assets). This also needed to be addressed when developing a standard on provisions.*

*IAS 36 *Impairment of Assets* was issued simultaneously with IAS 37.

 **Key Point**

Defining a provision as a liability (in accordance with the Framework) made a further standard necessary: to prescribe the accounting treatment for the loss in value ("impairment") of assets which was not otherwise dealt with.

1.2   Objective

- To ensure that appropriate recognition criteria and measurement bases are applied to:
  - provisions;
  - contingent liabilities; and
  - contingent assets.

- To ensure that sufficient information is disclosed in the notes to the financial statements in respect of each of these items.

1.3   Scope

- IAS 37 addresses only provisions which are liabilities (i.e. not allowances for reduction in asset values such as depreciation, inventory obsolescence, irrecoverable debts, etc).

- IAS 37 applies to provisions for restructuring (including discontinued operations).

1.4   Terminology

Provisions: liabilities of uncertain timing or amount.

Liability: a present obligation of the entity arising from past events, the settlement of which is expected to result in an outflow from the entity of resources embodying economic benefits.

Obligating event: an event which creates a legal or constructive obligation which results in an entity having no realistic alternative to settling that obligation.*

Legal obligation: an obligation which derives from:

- a contract;
- legislation; or
- other operation of law.

Constructive obligation: an obligation which derives from an entity's actions where:

- by an established pattern of past practice, published policies or a sufficiently specific current statement, the entity has indicated to other parties that it will accept certain responsibilities; and
- as a result, the entity has created a valid expectation on the part of those other parties that it will discharge those responsibilities.

Contingent liability:

- a *possible* obligation which arises from past events and whose existence will be confirmed only on the occurrence or non-occurrence of one or more uncertain future events which are *not wholly within the control* of the entity; or
- a *present* obligation which arises from past events but is not recognised because:
  - it is not probable that an outflow of benefits embodying economic benefits will be required to settle the obligation; or
  - the amount of the obligation cannot be measured with sufficient reliability.*

Contingent asset: a possible asset which arises from past events and whose existence will be confirmed only on the occurrence or non-occurrence of one or more uncertain future events not wholly within the control of the entity.

Onerous contract: a contract in which the unavoidable costs of meeting the obligations under the contract exceed the economic benefits expected to be received from it.

Restructuring: a programme which is planned and controlled by management, and materially changes either:

- the scope of a business undertaken by an entity; or
- the manner in which that business is conducted.

*Obligating event is a key concept in the IAS 37 approach to the recognition of provisions.

*IAS 37 stresses that an entity will be unable to measure an obligation with sufficient reliability only on very rare occasions.

1.5   Relationship Between Provisions and Contingent Liabilities

▧ In a general sense, all provisions are contingent because they are uncertain in timing or amount.

Key Point

IAS 37 distinguishes between provisions and contingent liabilities by using the term *contingent* for assets and liabilities which are not recognised because their *existence* will be confirmed only on the occurrence or non-occurrence of one or more uncertain future events not wholly within the control of the entity.

▧ The standard distinguishes between:
  ◦ *provisions,* which are present obligations; and
  ◦ *contingent liabilities,* which are not recognised because they are either:
    — only *possible* obligations; or
    — present obligations, which *cannot be measured* with sufficient reliability.

2   Recognition Issues

2.1   Provisions

Key Point

A provision must be recognised when certain conditions have been met.

▧ Those conditions are met when:
  ◦ an entity has a present legal or **constructive obligation** to transfer economic benefits as a result of past events;
  ◦ it is probable that an outflow of resources embodying economic benefits will be required to settle the obligation; and
  ◦ a reliable estimate of the obligation can be made.
▧ If these conditions are not met, a provision should not be recognised.

2.2   Present Obligation

Key Point

A present obligation exists when the entity has no realistic alternative but to make the transfer of economic benefits because of a past event (the "obligating event").

Illustration 3 Providing for Warranties

Scenario

A manufacturer gives warranties at the time of sale to purchasers of its product. Under the terms of the contract for sale, the manufacturer undertakes to make good, by repair or replacement, manufacturing defects which become apparent within three years from the date of sale. Based on past experience, it is probable (i.e. more likely than not) that there will be some claims under the warranties.

Present obligation as a result of a past obligating event?	Sale of the product with a warranty gives rise to a **legal obligation.**
An outflow of resources?	Probable.
Conclusion	Provide for the best estimate of the cost of making good under the warranty of the goods sold by the end of the reporting period.

- A provision should be made only if the liability exists independent of the entity's future actions. The mere intention or necessity to undertake expenditure related to the future is not sufficient to give rise to an obligation.

- If the entity retains discretion to avoid making any expenditure, a liability does not exist and *no provision* is recognised.

Examples include:

- The mere existence of environmental contamination (e.g. even if caused by the entity's activities) itself gives rise to an obligation because the entity could choose not to clean it up.

- A board decision alone is not sufficient for the recognition of a provision because the board could reverse the decision.*

- If a decision was made which commits an entity to future expenditure, no provision needs to be recognised as long as the board has a realistic alternative.

- When, in *rare cases,* it is not clear whether there is a present obligation, a past event should be *deemed* to give rise to a present obligation when it is more likely than not that a present obligation exists at the end of the reporting period.*

2.3 Past Event

- A past event which leads to a present obligation is called an *obligating event*.

- An obligating event exists when the entity has *no realistic alternative* but to transfer economic benefits. This may be due to a legal obligation or constructive obligation.

*Commentary

*Until the board makes public a decision or commits itself in some other way to making repairs, there is no obligation beyond that to satisfy the existing statutory and contractual rights of customers.

*Clearly, recognising a present obligation after a past event requires judgement after taking into account all available evidence.

Illustration 4 Obligating Event

Scenario

After a wedding in 20X6, 10 guests died, possibly as the result of food poisoning from products sold by Tin-Tin. Legal proceedings are seeking damages from Tin-Tin, which disputes liability. Up to the date of approval of the financial statements for the year to 31 December 20X6, Tin-Tin's lawyers advise that it is probable that Tin-Tin will not be found liable. However, when preparing financial statements for the year to 31 December 20X7, the lawyers advise that, because of developments in the case, it is probable that Tin-Tin will be found liable.

At 31 December 20X6

Present obligation as a result of a past obligating event?	On the basis of the evidence available when the financial statements were approved, there is no obligation as a result of past events.
An outflow of resources?	Irrelevant, as no present obligation.
Conclusion	No provision.

At 31 December 20X7

Present obligation as a result of a past obligating event?	On the basis of the evidence available, there is a present obligation.
An outflow of resources?	Probable.
Conclusion	Provision should be recognised.

Illustration 5 Constructive Obligation

A retail store which habitually refunds purchases made by dissatisfied customers even though it is under no legal obligation to do so, but could not change its policy without incurring unacceptable damage to its reputation.

Illustration 6 Constructive Obligation

An entity has identified contamination in land surrounding one of its production sites. It is not legally obliged to clean up. However, because of concern for its long-term reputation and relationship with the local community and its published policies or past actions, it is obliged to do so.

Illustration 7   Refund Policy

Scenario

A retail store has a policy of refunding purchases by dissatisfied customers, even though it is under no legal obligation to do so. Its policy of making refunds is generally known.

Present obligation as a result of a past obligating event?	The obligating event is the sale of the product, which gives rise to a constructive obligation because the conduct of the store has created a valid expectation on the part of its customers that the store will refund purchases.
An outflow of resources?	Probable, a proportion of goods are returned for refund.
Conclusion	A provision is recognised for the best estimate of the costs of refunds.

Illustration 8   Clean-up Costs

Scenario

An entity in the oil industry causes contamination and operates in a country in which there is no environmental legislation. However, the entity has a widely published environmental policy in which it undertakes to clean up any contamination it causes. The entity has a record of honouring this published policy.

Present obligation as a result of a past obligating event?	The obligating event is the contamination of the land, which gives rise to a constructive obligation because the conduct of the entity has created a valid expectation on the part of those affected by it that the entity will clean up contamination.
An outflow of resources?	Probable.
Conclusion	A provision is recognised for the best estimate of the costs of clean-up.

- Provisions are not made for general business risks because they do not give rise to obligations which exist at the end of the reporting period.
- It is not necessary to know the identity of the party to whom the obligation is owed in order for an obligation to exist.

2.4   Reliable Estimate of the Obligation

 **Key Point**

A reasonable estimate can always be made when an entity can determine a reasonable range of possible outcomes.

*Commentary

*In these extremely rare cases, disclosure of the matter would be necessary.

- Only in extremely rare cases will it be genuinely impossible to make any quantification of the obligation and therefore impossible to provide for it.*

2.5   Contingent Assets and Liabilities

- These should not be recognised. They are dependent on the occurrence or non-occurrence of an uncertain future event not wholly within the control of the entity.
- It follows that they are not obligations which exist at the end of the reporting period.
- There is an exception to non-recognition of contingent liabilities. IFRS 3 *Business Combinations* requires a subsidiary's contingent liabilities, which are present obligations, to be recognised and measured at fair value as part of the acquisition process.*

 ***Commentary**

*See *Session 21* for details.

3   Measurement

3.1   General Rules

3.1.1   Best Estimate

- The amount provided should be the best estimate at the end of the reporting period of the expenditure required to settle the obligation. The amount is often expressed as:
  - the amount which could be spent to settle the obligation immediately; or
  - to pay to a third party to assume it.
- It may be derived from management's judgement supplemented by:
  - experience of similar transactions; and
  - expert evidence (in some cases).

3.1.2   Uncertainty

- An entity should take account of any uncertainty surrounding the transaction. This may involve:
  - an *expected value* calculation in situations in which there is a large population (e.g. determining the size of warranty provisions); or
  - the use of the *most likely* outcome in situations in which a single obligation is being measured (as long as there is no evidence to indicate that the liability will be materially higher or lower than this amount).

3.1.3 Factors

▨ The following should be considered when estimating the amount of the obligation:

- The time value of money (i.e. the amount provided should be the present value of the expected cash flows).
- Evidence of expected future events, such as:
  — changes in legislation; or
  — improvements in technology.

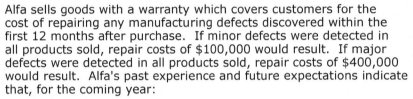

Illustration 9 Estimating Warranty Claims

Alfa sells goods with a warranty which covers customers for the cost of repairing any manufacturing defects discovered within the first 12 months after purchase. If minor defects were detected in all products sold, repair costs of $100,000 would result. If major defects were detected in all products sold, repair costs of $400,000 would result. Alfa's past experience and future expectations indicate that, for the coming year:

  75% of the goods sold will have no defects;

  20% of the goods sold will have minor defects; and

  5% of the goods sold will have major defects.

Required:

Calculate the amount to be provided in the financial statements in respect of the warranty claims.

Solution

The expected value of the cost of repairs is:

$(75\% \times 0) + (20\% \times 100,000) + (5\% \times 400,000) = \$40,000*$

> ***Commentary***
>
> *The weighted average probability formula used assesses the outflow for the warranty obligations as a whole.

3.2 Specific Points

3.2.1 Reimbursement

▨ If some (or all) of the expected outflow is expected to be reimbursed from a third party, the reimbursement should be recognised only when it is *virtually certain* that the reimbursement will be received if the entity settles the obligation.

▨ The expense of the provision may be presented *net* of the amount recognised for a reimbursement.

▨ However, the reimbursement should be treated as a *separate asset* and clearly must not exceed the provision in terms of its value.

3.2.2 Gains on Disposal

Key Point

Gains from an expected disposal should *not* be taken into account when measuring a provision.

3.2.3 Pre-tax

▨ The provision should be measured as a pre-tax amount.

3.3   Changes in Provisions

 **Key Point**

Provisions may be used *only* for expenditures that relate to the matter for which they were originally recognised.

 ***Commentary***

*The increase in the present value of a provision year-on-year (as the discounted amount "unwinds") is a finance cost.

▨ Provisions should be reviewed regularly. If the estimate of the obligation has changed, the amount recognised as a provision should be revised accordingly.

Illustration 10 **Obligating Event Accounting Entries**

An entity becomes subject to an obligating event on 1 January 20X6.

The entity is committed to expenditure of $10 million in 10 years' time as a result of this event.

An appropriate discount factor is 8%.

1 January 20X6
Initial measurement of the provision

$$\$10m \times \frac{1}{(1+0.08)^{10}} = 4{,}631{,}935$$

Dr Profit or loss	4,631,935	
Cr Provision		4,631,935

31 December 20X6
Measurement of the provision

$$\$10m \times \frac{1}{(1+0.08)^{9}} = 5{,}002{,}490$$

	$
Presented as follows:	
Balance brought forward	4,631,935
Borrowing cost ("unwinding" of the discount*) (8% × 4,631,935)	370,555
Carried forward	5,002,490

Provision

Dr Profit or loss	370,555	
Cr Provision		370,555

31 December 20X7
Measurement of the provision

$$\$10m \times \frac{1}{(1+0.08)^{8}} = 5{,}402{,}689$$

	$
Presented as follows:	
Balance brought forward	5,002,490
Borrowing cost (8% × 5,002,490)	400,199
Carried forward	5,402,689

Provision

Dr Profit or loss	400,199	
Cr Provision		400,199

3.4 Self-Insurance

▨ Costs of insurance have become prohibitive for many businesses. Instead, they may choose to "self-insure" rather than take out insurance policies against the various risks that they face.

▨ Rather than pay insurance premiums, they may set aside cash funds to meet future expenses associated with uninsured risks. (There is nothing to prevent an entity "ring-fencing" cash to meet any future uninsured costs.)

▨ IAS 37 does **not** permit the recognition of a provision for such future expenses. Therefore, the cost of being self-insured will only be recognised in the period in which actual expense is incurred.*

▨ If accounting for self-insurance by setting up a provision were permitted, profits could be manipulated.

Commentary

*The cost of self-insurance is a future operating cost.

4 Application to Specific Circumstances

4.1 Future Operating Losses

▨ Provisions should not be recognised for future operating losses because:
- they do not arise out of a past event; and
- they are not unavoidable.

4.2 Onerous Contracts

▨ If an entity has an **onerous contract**, the present obligation under that contract should be recognised as a provision.

Key Point

An expectation of future losses is an indication that the assets of the entity may be impaired. The assets should be tested for impairment according to IAS 36.

Illustration 11   Onerous Contract

ZY Energy has entered into a contract with GasB to purchase units of gas at $50 per unit. The contract allows ZY to pay a penalty of $15 per unit of gas that it does not purchase.

The market price of gas has fallen to $30 per unit and ZY has decided to invoke the penalty clause rather than pay the $50 per unit.

ZY would be required to recognise a provision for the onerous contract at $15 per unit of gas that it has decided not to purchase.

Definition

Onerous contract—one in which the unavoidable costs of meeting the obligations under the contract exceed the economic benefits expected to be received from it.

4.3 Restructuring

4.3.1 Examples

▨ Sale or termination of a line of business.

▨ Closure of business locations in a region.

▨ Relocation from one region to another.

▨ Changes in management structure.

▨ Fundamental reorganisations which have a material effect on the nature and focus of operations.

4.3.2   Application of Recognition Criteria

Commentary

- A constructive obligation to restructure arises only when an entity:
  - has a *detailed formal plan* for the **restructuring**; and
  - has raised a *valid expectation* that it will carry out the restructuring by starting to implement the plan or by announcing its main features to those affected by it.*

- A detailed formal plan must identify, as a minimum:
  - the business or part of a business concerned;
  - the principal locations affected;
  - the location, function and approximate number of employees who will be compensated for terminating their services;
  - the expenditures which will be undertaken; and
  - when the plan will be implemented.

- A management decision to restructure does not give rise to constructive obligation unless the entity has (before the end of the reporting period):
  - started to implement the restructuring plan (e.g. by the sale of assets); or
  - announced the main features of the plan to those affected in a sufficiently specific manner to raise a valid expectation that the restructuring will occur.

- No obligation arises for the sale of an operation until there is a binding sales agreement.

- IFRS 3 *Business Combinations* does not allow a provision to be made for the restructuring of a subsidiary on initial acquisition. The only restructuring provision that can be recognised on acquisition is one made by the subsidiary, in accordance with IAS 37, before acquisition.

*If there is a long delay before implementing the restructuring plan, then it is unlikely that the plan will raise a valid expectation that the entity is committed to the restructuring.

Illustration 12   Provision Not Recognised

Scenario

On 12 December, the board of an entity decided to close down a division. Before the end of the reporting period (31 December), the decision was not communicated to any of those affected and no other steps were taken to implement the decision.

Present obligation as a result of a past obligating event?   No.

An outflow of resources?

Conclusion   No provision is recognised.

Illustration 13 Provision Recognised

Scenario

On 12 December, the board of an entity decided to close down a division making a particular product. On 20 December, a detailed plan for closing down the division was agreed by the board; letters were sent to customers warning them to seek an alternative source of supply. Redundancy notices were sent to the staff of the division. The year end is 31 December.

Present obligation as a result of a past obligating event?	The obligating event is the communication of the decision to the customers and employees. This gives rise to a constructive obligation from that date because it creates a valid expectation that the division will be closed.
An outflow of resources?	Probable.
Conclusion	A provision is recognised at 31 December for the best estimate of the costs of closing the division.

▨ Provisions for restructuring should include only those expenditures which are both:

  ◦ necessarily entailed by a restructuring; and

  ◦ not associated with ongoing activities.

4.4 Decommissioning Costs

▨ Sometimes an entity is committed to spend money when it closes down an asset. These types of costs are called decommissioning costs.*

▨ IAS 37 requires that when an entity has a present obligation to incur these costs then a provision is required. The provision could be set up on the initial recognition of the asset or part way through its life.

Key Point

The provision for decommissioning costs will initially be recognised at the present value of the future expected cash outflow in respect of the obligation. The double entry will be to debit the asset.*

▨ As time passes, the present value of the provision will increase. This increase in the provision is similar to interest, and sometimes it is called "unwinding of the discount"; thus, it is charged as a financing cost to the statement of profit or loss of the period.

Commentary

*Decommissioning costs are very common in the oil industry. Once an oil rig has reached the end of its life the entity must dismantle the rig and put the environment back into a natural condition.

*Refer to IAS 16 for the accounting treatment of the debit entry made for decommissioning costs.

Illustration 14 Accounting for Decommisioning Provision

An entity purchased an asset on 1 January 20X6.

The entity is committed to dismantle the asset in 10 years' time and the estimated cost to dismantle is $10 million. The obligation satisfies the recognition criteria in IAS 37.

An appropriate discount factor is 8%.

1 January 20X6
Initial measurement of the provision

$$\$10m \times \frac{1}{(1+0.08)^{10}} = 4,631,935$$

Dr Asset	4,631,935	
Cr Provision		4,631,935

31 December 20X6
Measurement of the provision

$$\$10m \times \frac{1}{(1+0.08)^{9}} = 5,002,490$$

	$
Presented as follows:	
Balance brought forward	4,631,935
Borrowing cost (8% × 4,631,935)	370,555
Carried forward	5,002,490

Provision

Dr Profit or loss	370,555	
Cr Provision		370,555

Asset

Dr Profit or loss	463,193	
Cr Accumulated depreciation		463,193

To calculate accumulated depreciation:
4,631,935 × 1/10

Profit or loss

370,555

463,193

833,748

5 Repairs and Maintenance

5.1 Substantial Expenditure

- Some assets require, in addition to routine maintenance, substantial expenditure every few years for major "refits" or refurbishment and the replacement of major components.

- IAS 16 *Property, Plant and Equipment* gives guidance on allocating expenditure on an asset to its component parts where these components have different useful lives or provide benefits in a different pattern.

- IAS 37 explains that *no provision* can be made.

5.2   Refurbishment Costs—No Legal Requirement

Illustration 15	No Present Obligation, No Provision

Scenario

A furnace lining needs to be replaced every five years for technical reasons. At the end of the reporting period, the lining has been in use for three years.

Present obligation as a result of a past obligating event?   There is no present obligation.

An outflow of resources?

Conclusion   No provision.

Analysis

- The cost of replacing the lining is not recognised because, at the end of the reporting period, no obligation to replace the lining exists independently of the company's future actions. Even the intention to incur the expenditure depends on the company deciding to continue operating the furnace or to replace the lining.

- Instead of a provision being recognised, the depreciation of the lining takes account of its consumption (i.e. it is depreciated over five years). The re-lining costs then incurred are capitalised with the consumption of each new lining shown by depreciation over the subsequent five years.

5.3   Refurbishment Costs—Legal Requirement

Illustration 16	No Provision for Aircraft Overhaul

Scenario

An airline is required by law to overhaul its aircraft once every three years.

Present obligation as a result of a past obligating event?   There is no present obligation.

An outflow of resources?

Conclusion   No provision.

Analysis

- The costs of overhauling aircraft are not recognised as a provision for the same reasons the cost of replacing a furnace lining is not recognised as a provision in *Illustration 15*.

- Even a legal requirement to overhaul does not make the costs of overhaul a liability, because no obligation exists to overhaul the aircraft independently of the entity's future actions—the airline could avoid the future expenditure by its future actions (e.g. by selling the aircraft).

- Instead of a provision being recognised, the depreciation of the aircraft takes account of the future incidence of maintenance costs (i.e. an amount equivalent to the expected maintenance costs is depreciated over three years).

6 Disclosures

6.1 For Each Class of Provision

▦ The carrying amount at the beginning and end of the period with movements by type, including:

 ◦ additional provisions in the period including increases to existing provisions;

 ◦ amounts used;

 ◦ amounts reversed; and

 ◦ an increase during the period of any discounted amount due to the passage of time or change in rate.

▦ A brief description of the nature of the obligation and expected timing of the expenditure.

▦ An indication of the nature of the uncertainties about the amount or timing of the outflows.

▦ The amount of any expected reimbursement with details of asset recognition.

6.2 For Each Class of Contingent Liability

The following should be disclosed unless the contingency is remote.

▦ A brief description of the nature of the contingency, and where practicable.

 ◦ The uncertainties which are expected to affect the ultimate outcome of the contingency.

 ◦ An estimate of the potential financial effect.

 ◦ The possibility of any reimbursement.

6.3 For Each Class of Contingent Asset

The following should be disclosed when the inflow of economic benefits is probable.

▦ A brief description of the nature of the contingency.

▦ An estimate of the potential financial effect, where practicable.

6.4 Serious Prejudice

▦ In *extremely rare* cases, disclosure of some or all of the information required might seriously prejudice the position of the entity in its negotiations with other parties.

▦ In such cases the information need not be disclosed, but the entity should:

 ◦ explain the general nature of the dispute; and

 ◦ explain the fact and reason why that information has not been disclosed.

Summary

- A provision is recognised only when there is a liability.
- An entity must recognise a provision if, and only if:
  - a *present obligation* has arisen as a result of a past event;
  - payment is probable ("more likely than not"); and
  - the amount can be *estimated reliably*.
- An obligating event creates a legal or constructive obligation which results in no realistic alternative but to settle the obligation.
- A constructive obligation arises if past practice creates a valid expectation.
- A possible obligation is disclosed but not accrued.
- A provision is measured at a best estimate of the expenditure required (using the pre-tax discount rate):
  - for a one-off event—the most likely amount; or
  - for repeated events—at the expected value.
- In measuring a provision, changes in legislation are taken into account only if virtually certain to be enacted.
- A restructuring may include sale, termination, closure or reorganisation.
  - Sale of operation: must have a binding agreement.
  - Closure or reorganisation: requires a publicly announced formal plan.
  - Future operating losses: cannot be provided for.
  - Restructuring on an acquisition: requires an obligation at acquisition.
- Restructuring provisions can include only directly related expenses (must exclude ongoing costs).
- The debit entry for a provision is usually an expense but may be part of the cost of an asset.
- A provision can only be used for the purpose for which it was recognised.
- If it is no longer probable that an outflow of resources will be required to settle the obligation, the provision should be reversed.
- Contingent liabilities are not recognised but disclosed (unless "remote").
- Contingent assets cannot be recognised, only disclosed (when probable).

Session 15 Quiz
Estimated time: 20 minutes

1. Define provision. (1.4)
2. Define contingent liability. (1.4)
3. List THREE conditions a provision must meet to be recognised. (2.1)
4. Explain how a contingent liability should be treated in the statement of financial position. (2.5)
5. Discuss how the value of a provision should be measured. (3.1)
6. State when the amount of a provision should be changed. (3.3)
7. State when future operating losses are recognised as a provision. (4.1)
8. Explain how to treat an onerous contract in the financial statements. (4.2)
9. Specify the method of valuation for the initial decommissioning provision. (4.4)

Study Question Bank
Estimated time: 25 minutes

Priority		Estimated Time	Completed
Q26	Rovers	25 minutes	

IAS 10 *Events After the Reporting Period*

FOCUS

This session covers the following content from the *ACCA Study Guide.*

B. Accounting for Transactions in Financial Statements

7. Provisions and events after the reporting period

g) Events after the reporting date

   i)   distinguish between and account for adjusting and non-adjusting events after the reporting date

   ii) identify items requiring separate disclosure, including their accounting treatment and required disclosures.

Session 16 Guidance

- **Understand** that although IAS 10 is a relatively straightforward standard it has far-reaching implications for many companies. The standard requires either amendments to the accounts or the disclosure of information for events after the reporting period. The treatment will depend on whether the event is adjusting or non-adjusting.

- **Be aware,** in terms of the examination, that IAS 10 is an area which the examiner tends not to examine in a direct manner but quite often will give a scenario in which he expects students to use their knowledge of the standard in answering the question.

(continued on next page)

VISUAL OVERVIEW

Objective: To define events and describe the treatment of events after the reporting period.

```
┌─────────────────────────────────┐
│              IAS 10             │
│  ───────────────────────────── │
│   • Objective                   │
│   • Scope                       │
│   • Definition                  │
└─────────────────────────────────┘
                │
┌─────────────────────────────────┐
│       RECOGNITION AND           │
│         MEASUREMENT             │
│  ───────────────────────────── │
│   • Adjusting Events            │
│   • Non-adjusting Events        │
│   • Dividends                   │
│   • Going Concern               │
└─────────────────────────────────┘
                │
┌─────────────────────────────────┐
│           DISCLOSURE            │
│  ───────────────────────────── │
│   • General                     │
│   • Non-adjusting Events        │
│   • Going Concern               │
└─────────────────────────────────┘
```

Session 16 Guidance

■ **Understand** the difference between adjusting and non-adjusting events (s.1).

■ **Recognise** and be able to measure adjusting events and **understand** the implications for dividend recognition and going concern (s.2).

■ **Learn** the disclosure requirements (s.3).

1 IAS 10

1.1 Objective

▨ The objective of IAS 10 is to describe:

● when an entity should adjust its financial statements for events after the reporting period; and

● the disclosures an entity should give about the date when the financial statements were authorised for issue and about events after the end of the reporting period.

1.2 Scope

▨ IAS 10 should be applied in the accounting for, and the disclosure of, events after the reporting period.

1.3 Definition

Definition

Events after the reporting period—events, both favourable and unfavourable, which occur between the end of the reporting period and the date on which the financial statements are authorised for issue.

Two types of events after the reporting period can be identified:

1. Those which provide further evidence of conditions which existed at the end of the reporting period ("adjusting" events).

2. Those which are indicative of conditions which arose after the end of the reporting period ("non-adjusting" events).

2   Recognition and Measurement

2.1   Adjusting Events

 **Key Point**

An entity should adjust its financial statements for adjusting events after the end of the reporting period.

Examples of adjusting events include:

- The resolution after the end of the reporting period of a court case which, because it confirms that an entity already had a present obligation at the end of the reporting period, requires the entity to recognise a provision instead of merely disclosing a contingent liability or adjusting the provision already recognised.
- The bankruptcy of a customer which occurs after the end of the reporting period and which confirms that a loss already existed at the end of the reporting period on a trade receivable account.
- The discovery of fraud or error which show that the financial statements were incorrect.
- The sale of inventories after the year end at an amount below their cost.

2.2   Non-adjusting Events

 **Key Point**

No adjustment is made in financial statements for non-adjusting events after the end of the reporting period.

- However, non-adjusting events should be disclosed if they are of such importance that non-disclosure would affect the ability of the users of the financial statements to make proper evaluations and decisions.

Examples of non-adjusting events include:

- A major business combination after the end of the reporting period.
- The destruction of a major production plant by a fire after the end of the reporting period.
- Abnormally large changes after the end of the reporting period in asset prices or foreign exchange rates.
- A decline in market value of investments between the end of the reporting period and the date on which the financial statements are authorised for issue.*

 ***Commentary***

*The fall in market value normally does not relate to the condition of the investments at the end of the reporting period, but reflects circumstances which have arisen in the following period. Therefore, an entity does not adjust the amounts recognised in its financial statements for that investment.

2.3   Dividends

Key Point

Dividends proposed or declared after the end of the reporting period cannot be recognised as liabilities (as they do not meet the definition of a liability).

▦ IAS 1 requires an entity to disclose the amount of dividends which were proposed or declared after the end of the reporting period but before the financial statements were authorised for issue. This disclosure must be made in the notes to the accounts, not in the statement of financial position.

2.4   Going Concern

▦ Financial statements should not be prepared on a going concern basis if management determines after the end of the reporting period that:
  • it intends to liquidate the entity or to cease trading; or
  • it has no realistic alternative but to do so.
▦ Deterioration in operating results and financial position after the end of the reporting period may require reconsideration of the going concern assumption.

Key Point

If the going concern assumption is no longer appropriate, the basis of accounting must be changed for the financial statements as a whole.

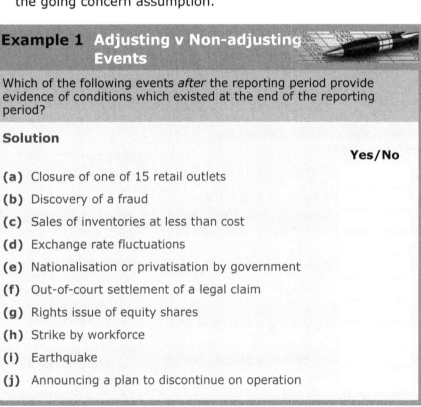

Example 1 Adjusting v Non-adjusting Events

Which of the following events *after* the reporting period provide evidence of conditions which existed at the end of the reporting period?

Solution

		Yes/No
(a)	Closure of one of 15 retail outlets	
(b)	Discovery of a fraud	
(c)	Sales of inventories at less than cost	
(d)	Exchange rate fluctuations	
(e)	Nationalisation or privatisation by government	
(f)	Out-of-court settlement of a legal claim	
(g)	Rights issue of equity shares	
(h)	Strike by workforce	
(i)	Earthquake	
(j)	Announcing a plan to discontinue on operation	

3   Disclosure

3.1   General

- An entity should disclose the date when the financial statements were authorised for issue and the name of the governing body which gives that authorisation.
- If owners (or others) have the power to amend the financial statements after issue, that fact must be stated.*

3.2   Non-adjusting Events

- An entity should disclose the following in respect of non-adjusting events which are of such importance that non-disclosure would affect the ability of the users of the financial statements to make proper evaluations and decisions:
  - the nature of the event; and
  - an estimate of its financial effect or a statement that such an estimate cannot be made.

Commentary

*It is important for users to know when the financial statements were authorised for issue, as the financial statements do not reflect events after this date.

Exhibit 1   DISCLOSURE
The following disclosure describes significant events after the balance sheet date as reported in Deutsche Post AG's Annual Report 2015.
57 Significant events after the reporting date (extract) In January 2016, Deutsche Post DHL Group acquired a minority interest of 27.5% in French e-commerce logistics specialist Relais Colis … Relais Colis will be accounted for using the equity method in the consolidated financial statements.

3.3   Going Concern

- The following disclosures are required by IAS 1 if the accounts are not prepared on the basis of the going concern assumption:
  - a note saying that the financial statements are not prepared on a going concern basis; or
  - management is aware of material uncertainties related to events or conditions, which may cast significant doubt on the entity's ability to continue as a going concern.

Summary

■ Financial statements are adjusted for adjusting events (which provide further evidence of conditions existing at the end of the reporting period).

■ The basis of preparation of financial statements is changed if events indicate that the going concern assumption is **no longer** appropriate.

■ Non-adjusting events (events or conditions which arose after the end of the reporting period) are disclosed if they are of such importance that non-disclosure would affect the ability of users to make decisions. Disclose:

  ● the nature of the event; and

  ● the financial effect (or state that this cannot be estimated).

■ Dividends declared **after** the reporting period is **not** a liability at the end of the reporting period (therefore disclose as a non-adjusting event).

■ The date when the financial statements are authorised for issue (who authorised and who can amend subsequently) must be disclosed.

Session 16 Quiz
Estimated time: 10 minutes

1. State the objective of IAS 10. (1.1)
2. Define "Events after the Reporting Period" according to IAS 10. (1.3)
3. Identify how dividends declared after the year end should be accounted for. (2.3)
4. State the circumstances when an entity would not prepare its financial statements on a going concern basis. (2.4)
5. List the disclosures which should be made in respect of important non-adjusting events. (3)

Study Question Bank
Estimated time: 25 minutes

Priority		Estimated Time	Completed
Q27	Accounting Treatment	25 minutes	

EXAMPLE SOLUTION

Solution 1—Adjusting v Non-adjusting Events

(a) **No**—Going concern assumption is not appropriate for only a part (1/15th) of the entity.

(b) **Yes**—Fraud was perpetrated in the year under review.

(c) **Yes**—Sales of inventories at less than cost (i.e. net realisable value less than cost).

(d) **No**—Movements in foreign exchange rates after the reporting period are in response to changes in economic conditions, etc after the reporting period.

(e) **No**—Government action is after the reporting period.

(f) **Yes**—Out-of-court settlement of a legal claim means the ultimate outcome is known, therefore uncertainty is eliminated.

(g) **No**—Rights not available to shareholders until after the reporting period.

(h) **No**—Strike action is after the reporting period (even if the reason for the action was an event before the end of the reporting period—e.g. sacking of a colleague).

(i) **No**—Natural disaster was not a condition existing at the end of the reporting period.

(j) **No**—The operation was not disposed of as at the end of the reporting period. The operation cannot be classified as held for sale at the end of the reporting period as there is no commitment to a plan at that time. (IFRS 5)

IAS 12 *Income Taxes*

FOCUS

This session covers the following content from the *ACCA Study Guide.*

B. Accounting for Transactions in Financial Statements	
8. Taxation	
a) Account for current taxation in accordance with relevant accounting standards.	☐
b) Explain the effect of taxable temporary differences on accounting and taxable profits.	☐
c) Compute and record deferred tax amounts in the financial statements.	☐

Session 17 Guidance

■ **Work through** the *Illustrations* and *Examples* very carefully in this session.

■ **Understand** when a current tax asset or liability is created (s.2).

■ **Understand** the concept of temporary differences and how they are reflected in deferred tax assets and liabilities (s.4).

(continued on next page)

VISUAL OVERVIEW

Objective: To describe the rules for recognition and measurement of taxes.

```
                        ┌─────────────────────────┐
                        │          IAS 12          │
                        │  • Accounting Concepts   │
                        │  • Terminology           │
                        └─────────────────────────┘
                         /                        \
        ┌──────────────────────────┐   ┌──────────────────────────┐
        │       CURRENT TAX        │   │     DEFERRED TAXATION     │
        │  • Liabilities and Assets│   │  • Underlying Problem     │
        │  • Accounting Entries    │   │  • Illustrating the Concept│
        └──────────────────────────┘   └──────────────────────────┘
                                                    │
                                        ┌──────────────────────────┐
                                        │   ACCOUNTING PRINCIPLES   │
                                        │  • Introduction           │
                                        │  • Calculation of Asset   │
                                        │    or Liability           │
                                        │  • Terminology            │
                                        │  • Accounting Issues      │
                                        └──────────────────────────┘
                                                    │
                                        ┌──────────────────────────┐
                                        │      DETAILED RULES       │
                                        │  • Deferred Tax Liabilities│
                                        │  • Deferred Tax Assets    │
                                        │  • Movement on Deferred Tax│
                                        │  • Complication—Tax Rate  │
                                        │  • Summary of Calculations│
                                        └──────────────────────────┘
```

Session 17 Guidance

■ **Know** the accounting principles which apply to calculation and extinguishment of the asset or liability (s.4).

■ **Work through** *Illustrations 4–9* and **attempt** *Example 1* (s.5).

■ **Learn** the exclusions to creating a deferred tax asset or liability (s.5).

■ **Attempt** the comprehensive example (*Example 4*) without looking at the solution.

1   IAS 12

1.1   Accounting Concepts

- In financial reporting, the financial statements need to reflect the effects of taxation on a company. Tax rules determine the cash flows; these must be matched to the revenues which gave rise to the tax, and tax liabilities must be recognised as they are incurred, not merely when they are paid.

- Consistency must be applied in the presentation of income and expenditure.

1.2   Terminology

Accounting profit: profit or loss for a period *before* deducting tax expense.

Taxable profit (tax loss): the profit (loss) for a period, determined in accordance with the rules established by the taxation authorities, upon which income taxes are payable (recoverable).

Tax expense (tax income): the aggregate amount included in determining profit or loss for the period for current tax and deferred tax.

Current tax: the amount payable (recoverable) in respect of the taxable profit (tax loss) for a period.

Deferred tax liabilities: the amounts payable in future periods in respect of taxable temporary differences.

Deferred tax assets: the amounts recoverable in future periods in respect of:

- deductible temporary differences;
- the carry forward of unused tax losses; and
- the carry forward of unused tax credits.

Temporary differences: differences between the carrying amount of an asset or liability (in the statement of financial position) and its tax base. Temporary differences may be either:

- *taxable* temporary differences; or
- *deductible* temporary differences.

Tax base: the amount attributed to an asset or liability for tax purposes.

2   Current Tax

2.1   Liabilities and Assets

 *Key Point*

A company is a separate legal entity and is therefore liable to income tax. Income tax is based on a company's profits for a period (usually a year).

- IAS 12 requires an entity to recognise current tax liabilities and current tax assets based on the tax legislation of the environment in which the entity is operating.
- Current tax for current and prior periods is recognised as a liability to the extent that it is unpaid.
- If the amount paid exceeds the amounts due, the excess is recognised as an asset.
- Any benefit relating to a tax loss that can be "carried back" to recover current tax for a previous period is also recognised as an asset.

2.2   Accounting Entries

- At the end of each reporting period, management must estimate how much current tax will have to be paid in the following period based on the current year's profits. Assuming a tax expense (rather than a refund) the double entry is:

Dr Profit or loss $x
    Cr   Tax liability $x

- The accounts will be submitted to the tax authority along with tax computations. The tax authority may agree or disagree with management's estimate.
- The entity will pay tax to the body that collects it (e.g. HM Revenue & Customs in the UK). Any difference between the estimated amount and the actual amount paid will be recognised in profit or loss in the period of payment.*
- Any under-provision (under estimate) will result in an additional expense (Dr Profit or loss); an over-provision will result in an expense write-back (Cr Profit or loss).

 *Commentary*

*This is the treatment for any change in accounting estimate.

Illustration 1   Change in Accounting Estimate

In year 1 an estimate of $10,500 was made.

Dr Profit or loss $10,500
    Cr   Tax liability $10,500

The tax authority reviews the accounts and tax computations and raises a payment notice for $10,700. When the amount is paid in year 2:

Dr Tax liability $10,700
    Cr   Cash $10,700

The $200 under-provision will be an additional tax expense in year 2.

3　Deferred Taxation

3.1　Underlying Problem

▦ In most jurisdictions accounting profit and taxable profit differ, meaning that the tax charge may bear little relation to profits in a period.

Key Point

Differences arise because tax authorities follow rules which differ from IFRS rules in arriving at taxable profit.

▦ Transactions which are recognised in the accounts in a particular period may have their tax effect deferred until a later period.

Illustration 2　Timing Differences

Many non-current assets are depreciated.

Most tax authorities will allow companies to deduct the cost of purchasing non-current assets from their profit for tax purposes but only according to a set formula.　If this differs from the accounting depreciation then the asset will be written down by the tax authority and by the company but at different rates.

Thus, the tax effect of the transaction (which is based on the tax laws) will be felt in a different period from the accounting effect.

▦ It is convenient to envisage two separate sets of accounts:

(1)　constructed following IFRS rules; and

(2)　following the tax rules of the jurisdiction in which the company operates (the "tax computation").＊

▦ Differences between the two sets of rules result in different amounts in the financial statements and in the tax computation. These differences may be viewed from the perspectives of:

　● the "balance sheet" (i.e. statement of financial position); or

　● the "income statement" (i.e. statement of profit or loss).

▦ The current tax charge for the period is based on the tax authority's view of profit for the period, not the accounting view.　This means that the relationship between the accounting profit before tax and the tax charge will be distorted.　It will not be the tax rate applied to the accounting profit figure but the tax rate applied to profit according to the tax computation.

＊Commentary

＊Of course, there is not really a full set of tax accounts but there could be.　Tax files in reality merely note those areas of difference between the two accounting systems.

3.2   Illustrating the Concept

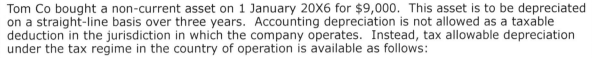

Illustration 3 Deferred Tax Principles

Tom Co bought a non-current asset on 1 January 20X6 for $9,000. This asset is to be depreciated on a straight-line basis over three years. Accounting depreciation is not allowed as a taxable deduction in the jurisdiction in which the company operates. Instead, tax allowable depreciation under the tax regime in the country of operation is available as follows:

20X6	$4,000
20X7	$3,000
20X8	$2,000

Accounting profit for each of the years 20X6 to 20X8 is budgeted to be $20,000 (before accounting for depreciation) and income tax is to be charged at the rate of 30%.

			Differences	
	Carrying amount	**Tax base**	**Financial position**	**Profit or loss**
	$	**$**	**$**	**$**
Cost at 1 Jan 20X6	9,000	9,000		
Charge for the year	(3,000)	(4,000)		(1,000)
Cost at 31 Dec 20X6	6,000	5,000	1,000	
Charge for the year	(3,000)	(3,000)		—
Cost at 31 Dec 20X7	3,000	2,000	1,000	
Charge for the year	(3,000)	(2,000)		1,000
Cost at 31 Dec 20X8	—	—	—	—

3.2.1   Differences Arising

▨ At the end of each reporting period the deferred tax liability can be identified from a "balance sheet" or "income statement" view.

  ◦ The "balance sheet" view identifies the deferred taxation balance which is required in the statement of financial position;

  ◦ The "income statement" approach identifies the deferred tax which arises during the period.*

▨ Clearly the difference in the statement of financial position is the sum of the differences which have gone through the statement of profit or loss.

Commentary

*IAS 12 takes "balance sheet" approach.

3.2.2 Analysis—Balance Sheet Approach

▓ The balance sheet approach calculates the liability (or more rarely the asset) which a company would need to set up in the statement of financial position.

▓ Applying the tax rate to the difference gives the deferred tax balance to be recognised in the statement of financial position.

▓ In summary, the process involves comparing the accounting balance to the tax authority's version of the same transaction and applying the tax rate to the difference.

Illustration 3 Deferred Tax Principles (cont.)

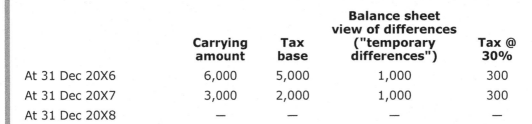

	Carrying amount	Tax base	Balance sheet view of differences ("temporary differences")	Tax @ 30%
At 31 Dec 20X6	6,000	5,000	1,000	300
At 31 Dec 20X7	3,000	2,000	1,000	300
At 31 Dec 20X8	—	—	—	—

■ In 20X6, Tom Co will recognise a deferred tax liability of $300 in its statement of financial position. This will be "released" to profit or loss in later years.

■ $300 is a liability which exists at the end of the reporting period and which will be paid in the future.*

■ The charge to profit or loss is found by looking at the movement on the liability:

	Liability required	Profit or loss entry
20X6	300	Dr 300
20X7	300	Nil
20X8	Nil	Cr 300

---

*Commentary

*In years to come (i.e. looking beyond 20X6), Tom Co will earn profits against which it will charge $6,000 depreciation but tax-allowable depreciation will be only $5,000. Therefore, taxable profit will be $1,000 more than accounting profit. This means that the current tax charge in the future will be $300 (30% × $1,000) more than would be expected from looking at the financial statements. This is because of events which have occurred and have been recognised at the end of the reporting period. This satisfies the definition and recognition criteria for a liability as at the reporting date.

3.2.3 Financial Statements

▨ Accounting for the tax on the differences in profit or loss restores the relationship which exists between the accounting profit and the tax charge. It does this by taking a debit or a credit to the statement of profit or loss. This then interacts with the current tax expense to give an overall figure which is the accounting profit multiplied by the tax rate.

Illustration 3 Deferred Tax Principles (cont.)

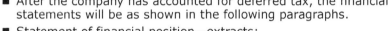

■ After the company has accounted for deferred tax, the financial statements will be as shown in the following paragraphs.

■ Statement of financial position—extracts:

	20X6	20X7	20X8
	$	$	$
Deferred taxation liability	300	300	—

■ Profit or loss:

	20X6	20X7	20X8
	$	$	$
Profit before tax	17,000	17,000	17,000
Income tax @ 30% **(W1)**	4,800	5,100	5,400
Deferred tax	300	—	(300)
	(5,100)	(5,100)	(5,100)
Profit after tax	11,900	11,900	11,900

■ Creating a liability in 20X6 and then releasing it in 20X8 has a "smoothing" effect on profit after tax (i.e. $11,900 each year). A user of the financial statements, therefore, has better information about the relationship between profit before tax and profit after tax.*

W1   Calculations of tax for the periods

	20X6	20X7	20X8
	$	$	$
Accounting profit (after depreciation)	17,000	17,000	17,000
Add back depreciation	3,000	3,000	3,000
Less tax-allowable depreciation	(4,000)	(3,000)	(2,000)
	(1,000)		1,000
Taxable profit	16,000	17,000	18,000
Tax @ 30%	4,800	5,100	5,400

*Commentary

*Accruals and provisions for taxation will affect earnings per share, net assets per share and gearing.

---

4 Accounting Principles

4.1 Introduction

▨ Accounting for deferred taxation involves the recognition of a liability (or more rarely an asset) in the statement of financial position. The difference between the liability at each year end is included in profit or loss.*

Illustration 4	Recognising Changes in the Liability

	$
Deferred taxation balance at the start of the year	1,000
Transfer to the profit or loss (the balancing figure)	500
Deferred taxation balance at the end of the year	1,500

> ***Commentary***
>
> *Most of the effort in accounting for deferred taxation goes into the calculation of the year-end provision. The movement in the balance is analysed later in this session.

4.2 Calculation of the Liability/Asset

▨ The calculation of the balance to be put in the statement of financial position is, in essence, very simple. It involves the comparison of the carrying amounts of items in the accounts to the tax authority's view of the amount (the "tax base"). Each difference is a "temporary difference".

▨ Even though the standard requires the recognition of a future tax liability/asset, the standard does *not* allow or permit the liability/asset to be discounted.

The basic rule in IAS 12 is that deferred taxation must be provided on all taxable temporary differences. (This is a simplification. Complications will be covered later.)

Illustration 5	Calculating the Deferred Tax			

	Carrying amount $	Tax base $	Temporary differences $	Deferred tax at 30% $
Non-current assets	20,000	14,000	6,000	1,800
Other transactions				
A (accrued income)	1,000	—	1,000	300
B (an accrued expense)	(2,000)	—	(2,000)	(600)
			5,000	1,500

The transactions in respect of items A and B are taxed on a cash basis; therefore, the tax authority's statement of financial position would not recognise accrued amounts in respect of these items.

4.3   Terminology

Key Point

- Temporary differences may be either:
  - debit balances in the financial statements compared to the tax computations. These lead to deferred tax credit balances. These are known as *taxable temporary differences*; or
  - credit balances in the financial statements compared to the tax computations. These lead to deferred tax debit balances. These are known as deductible temporary differences.
- **The tax base of an asset** is the amount which will be deductible for tax purposes against any taxable economic benefit which will flow to an entity when it recovers the carrying amount of the asset.

Temporary differences— differences between the carrying amount of an asset or liability and its tax base.

The tax base of an asset or liability is the amount attributed to that asset or liability for tax purposes.

4.4   Accounting Issues

Illustration 6 Illustration 3 Revisited	
	20X6
	$
Carrying amount	6,000
Tax base of the asset	(5,000)
Temporary difference	1,000
Deferred tax balance required (@30%)	300

4.4.1   Temporary Differences

- A temporary difference is so called because it is temporary in nature—it will disappear in time.
- The justification for making a provision now is that ownership of this asset will lead to income of $6,000 in the future but only $5,000 will be expensed for tax purposes. The $1,000 which is not covered will be taxed and so a liability exists.
- Temporary differences may lead to deferred tax credits or debits, although the standard is tougher on the recognition debit (i.e. asset) balances.
- Deferred tax accounting is about accounting for items whose tax effect is deferred to a later period.
- Circumstances under which temporary differences arise mostly include when income or expense is included in accounting profit in one period but is included in the taxable profit in a different period:*
  - items which are taxed on a cash basis but which will be accounted for on an accruals basis;

*Commentary

*IAS 12 does not use the terms "permanent" or "timing" differences; these are terms used by the tax authorities.

Illustration 7 Tax v Accrual Items

The accounts of Bill Co show interest receivable of $10,000. No cash has yet been received and interest is taxed on a cash basis. The interest receivable has a tax base of nil.

Deferred tax will be provided on the temporary difference of $10,000.

- situations in which the accounting depreciation does not equal tax allowable depreciation.

Illustration 8 Tax v Accounting Depreciation

Bill Co has non-current assets at the year end with a cost of $4,000,000. Aggregate depreciation for accounting purposes is $750,000. For tax purposes, depreciation of $1,000,000 has been deducted to date. The non-current assets have a tax base of $3,000,000. The provision for deferred tax will be provided on the taxable temporary difference of $250,000.

- A temporary difference also arises on the revaluation of an asset which the tax authority does not recognise in the tax base.

4.4.2 Exclusions

- Unfortunately the definition of temporary difference captures other items which should not result in deferred taxation accounting (e.g. accruals for items which are *not* taxed or do not attract tax relief).
- The standard includes provisions to exclude such items. The wording of one such provision is as follows:

  "If those economic benefits will not be taxable, the tax base of the asset is equal to its carrying amount."*

 *Commentary

*The wording of the provision seems a little strange but the effect is to exclude such items from the deferred taxation calculations.

Illustration 9 Non-taxable Changes

Bill Co provided a loan of $250,000 to John Co. At the year end, Bill Co's accounts show a loan payable of $200,000. The repayment of the loan has no tax consequences. Therefore the loan payable has a tax base of $200,000. No temporary taxable difference arises.

Example 1 Deferred Tax Provision

The following information relates to Boniek as at 31 December:

	Note	Carrying amount	Tax base
Non-current assets		$	$
Plant and machinery		200,000	175,000
Receivables:			
Trade receivables	1	50,000	
Interest receivable		1,000	
Payables			
Fine		10,000	
Interest payable		2,000	

Note 1: The trade receivables balance is made up of the following:

	$
Balances	55,000
Allowance for irrecoverable debts	(5,000)
	50,000

Further information:

(1) The deferred tax liability balance at the beginning of the year, 1 January, was $1,200.

(2) Interest is taxed on a cash basis.

(3) Allowances for irrecoverable debts are not deductible for tax purposes. Amounts in respect of receivables are only deductible on application of a court order to a specific amount.

(4) Fines are not tax deductible.

(5) Deferred tax is charged at 30%.

Required:

Calculate the deferred tax provision which is required at 31 December and the charge to profit or loss for the year.

Example 1 Deferred Tax Provision (continued)

Solution

	Carrying amount	Tax base	Temporary difference
Non-current assets	$	$	$
Plant and machinery			
Receivables:			
Trade receivables			
Interest receivable			
Payables			
Fine			
Interest payable			

	Temporary differences	Deferred tax @ 30%
Deferred tax liabilities		
Deferred tax assets		
		$
Deferred tax as at 1 January		
Profit or loss (balancing figure)		
Deferred tax as at 31 December		

5   Detailed Rules

5.1   Recognition of Deferred Tax Liabilities

5.1.1   The Rule

Key Point

A deferred tax liability should be recognised for *all taxable temporary differences*, unless the deferred tax liability arises from:

- the initial recognition of goodwill; or
- the initial recognition of an asset or liability in a transaction which:
  - is not a business combination; and
  - at the time of the transaction, affects neither accounting profit nor taxable profit.

▨ If the economic benefits are not taxable, the tax base of the asset is equal to its carrying amount.

5.1.2   Accounting Issues

- ▨ "all taxable temporary differences"
  - ● Temporary differences include all differences between accounting rules and tax rules, not just those which are temporary. The standard contains other provisions to correct this anomaly and excludes items where the tax effect is not deferred but, rather, is permanent in nature.
- ▨ "initial recognition ... not a business combination"
  - ● If the initial recognition is a business combination, deferred tax may arise.
- ▨ "affects neither accounting profit nor loss"
  - ● The rule here is an application of the idea that if an item is not taxable it should be excluded from the calculations.
- ▨ Taxable temporary differences also arise in the following situations:
  - ● Certain IFRSs permit assets to be carried at a fair value or to be revalued:
    - − if the revaluation of the asset is also reflected in the tax base then no temporary difference arises;
    - − if the revaluation does not affect the tax base then a temporary difference does arise and deferred tax must be provided.
  - ● When the cost of acquiring a business is allocated by reference to fair value of the assets and liabilities acquired, but no equivalent adjustment has been made for tax purposes.*

*Commentary

*Basically the same rule applies in a group situation.

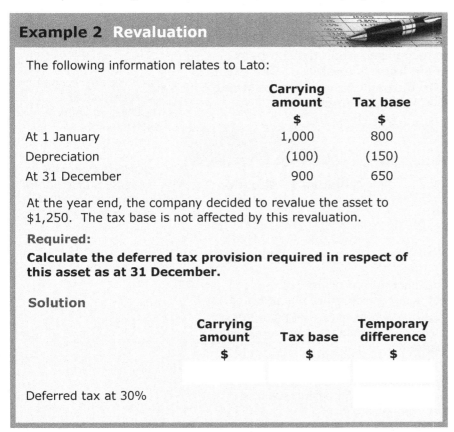

Example 2   Revaluation

The following information relates to Lato:

	Carrying amount $	Tax base $
At 1 January	1,000	800
Depreciation	(100)	(150)
At 31 December	900	650

At the year end, the company decided to revalue the asset to $1,250. The tax base is not affected by this revaluation.

Required:
Calculate the deferred tax provision required in respect of this asset as at 31 December.

Solution

	Carrying amount $	Tax base $	Temporary difference $

Deferred tax at 30%

5.2 Recognition of Deferred Tax Assets

5.2.1 The Rule

Key Point

A deferred tax asset is recognised for all *deductible temporary differences* to the extent that it is probable that taxable profit will be available against which the deductible temporary difference can be utilised, *unless* the deferred tax asset arises from the initial recognition of an asset or liability in a transaction which:

- is not a business combination; and
- at the time of transaction, affects neither accounting profit nor taxable profit (tax loss).

- The carrying amount of a deferred tax asset should be reviewed at the end of every reporting period. The carrying amount of a deferred tax asset should be reduced to the extent that it is no longer probable that sufficient taxable profit will be available to utilise the asset.

5.2.2 Accounting Issues

- Most of the comments made in respect of deferred tax liabilities also apply to deferred tax assets.
- The major difference between the recognition of deferred tax assets and liabilities is in the use of the phrase "to the extent that it is probable that taxable profit will be available against which the deductible temporary difference can be utilised".*
- An asset should only be recognised when the company expects to receive a benefit from its existence. The existence of deferred tax liability (to the same jurisdiction) is strong evidence that the asset will be recoverable.

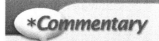

Commentary

*IAS 12 requires that additional criteria be met for the recognition of deferred tax assets. In short, liabilities must always be provided in full (subject to the specified exemptions) but assets may not be recognised in full or, in some cases, at all.

Illustration 10 Asset Recognition

	Situation 1 $	Situation 2 $
Deferred tax liability	10,000	5,000
Deferred tax asset	(8,000)	(8,000)
Net position	2,000	(3,000)

- In situation 1, the existence of the liability ensures the recoverability of the asset and the asset should be provided.
- In situation 2, the company would provide for $5,000 of the asset but would need to consider carefully the recoverability of the $3,000 net debit balance.
- In short, debit balances which are covered by credit balances will be provided (as long as the tax is payable/recoverable to/from the same jurisdiction), but net debit balances will be subject to close scrutiny.

5.3   Movement on Deferred Tax

Key Point

Deferred tax should be recognised as income or an expense and included in profit or loss for the period, except to the extent the tax arises from:

- a transaction or event which is recognised, in the same or a different period, outside of profit or loss; or
- a business combination which is an acquisition.

- Deferred tax should be recognised outside of profit or loss if the tax relates to items which are themselves recognised outside profit or loss.*

*Commentary

*Recognised outside of profit or loss means that the item has either been recognised in other comprehensive income or directly to equity. Basically, the deferred tax will follow wherever the gain or loss itself has been recognised.

Example 3   Outside Profit or Loss

	Carrying amount	Tax base
	$	$
At 1 January	1,000	800
Depreciation	(100)	(150)
At 31 December	900	650

At the year end, the company revalued the asset to $1,250. The tax base is not affected by this revaluation.

	Carrying amount	Tax base	Temporary difference
	$		$
	1,250	650	600
Deferred tax at 30%			180

Required:

Assuming that the only temporary difference that the company has relates to this asset, construct a note showing the movement on the deferred taxation and identify the charge to profit or loss in respect of deferred taxation for the year ended 31 December.

5.4 Complication—Tax Rate

- The tax rate which should be used is the rate which is expected to apply to the period when the asset is realised or the liability is settled, based on tax rates which have been enacted by the end of the reporting period.

Illustration 11   Choice of Tax Rates

The following information relates to Tomaszewski at 31 December 20X6:

	Carrying amount	Tax base
	$	$
Non-current assets	460,000	320,000
Tax losses	90,000	

Further information:

(1) Tax rates (enacted by the 20X6 year end):

20X6	20X7	20X8	20X9
36%	34%	32%	31%

(2) The loss above is the tax loss incurred in 20X6. The company is very confident about the trading prospects in 20X7.

(3) The temporary difference in respect of non-current assets is expected to grow each year until beyond 20X8.

(4) Losses may be carried forward for offset, one third into each of the next three years.

Required:

Calculate the deferred tax provision which is required at 31 December 20X6.

Solution

	Temporary differences
	$
Non-current assets (460,000 − 320,000)	140,000
Losses	(90,000)
Deferred tax liability (31% × 140,000)	43,400
Deferred tax asset	
Reversal in 20X7 (30,000 × 34%)	(10,200)
Reversal in 20X8 (30,000 × 32%)	(9,600)
Reversal in 20X9 (30,000 × 31%)	(9,300)
Deferred tax	14,300

- The tax rate used should reflect the tax consequences of the manner in which the entity expects to recover or settle the carrying amount of its assets and liabilities.

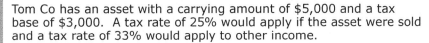

Illustration 12   Tax Rates

Tom Co has an asset with a carrying amount of $5,000 and a tax base of $3,000. A tax rate of 25% would apply if the asset were sold and a tax rate of 33% would apply to other income.

The entity would recognise a deferred tax liability of $500 ($2,000 @ 25%) if it expects to sell the asset without further use and a deferred tax liability of $660 ($2,000 @33%) if it expects to retain the asset and recover its carrying amount through use.

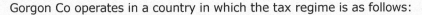

Example 4 Gorgon Co

Gorgon Co operates in a country in which the tax regime is as follows:

- Transactions are only deductible for tax purposes when they are "booked", (i.e. double entered into statutory accounting records). This means that there is often little difference between accounting profit under local GAAP and the taxable profit. It is common practice, however, for large companies to maintain a parallel set of records and accounts for reporting according to IFRS rules. These are notably different from the rules in the domestic tax code and, as a result, the accounting profit under IFRS can be very different from the taxable profit.

- The tax code allows for the general application of accrual accounting but it states the following:

    - tax allowable depreciation is computed according to rules set out in the tax code;

    - expected irrecoverable debts are only deductible under very strict and limited circumstances; and

    - interest is taxable/allowable on a cash basis.

- The government operates a system of incentive through the tax system known as "Investment Relief". Under this system, a company is able to claim a proportion of the costs of qualifying non-current assets as being deductible in excess of the normal depreciation rates which would result from the adoption of IFRSs.

- The tax rate is 30%.

Example 4 Gorgon Co (continued)

The following balances and information are relevant as at 31 December:

Non-current assets	Carrying amount $	Tax base $	Notes
Assets subject to investment relief	63,000		1
Land	200,000		2
Plant and machinery	100,000	90,000	3
Receivables			
Trade receivables	73,000		4
Interest receivable	1,000		
Payables			
Fine	10,000		
Interest payable	3,300		

Note 1: This asset cost the company $70,000 at the start of the year. It is being depreciated on a 10% straight-line basis for accounting purposes. The company's tax advisers have said that the company can claim $42,000 as a taxable expense in this years' tax computation.

Note 2: The land has been revalued during the year in accordance with IAS 16. It originally cost $150,000. Land is not subject to depreciation under IFRS nor under local tax rules.

Note 3: The balances in respect of plant and machinery are after providing for accounting depreciation of $12,000 and tax allowable depreciation of $10,000, respectively.

Note 4: Trade receivables is made up of the following amounts:

	$
Balances	80,000
Expected irrecoverable debt	(7,000)
	73,000

Note 5: The liability balance on the deferred taxation account at the beginning of the year, on 1 January, was $3,600.

Required:

(i) **Identify the tax base of each item listed and then identify the temporary difference.**

(ii) **Calculate the deferred tax provision required at 31 December and the charge to profit or loss and other comprehensive income in respect of deferred taxation for the year.**

5.5   Summary of Deferred Taxation Calculations

(a)   *Debits* in the financial statements compared with the taxman's view give rise to deferred tax *credits*.

Credits in the financial statements compared with the taxman's view give rise to deferred tax *debits.*

(b)   Full provision accounting is easy!

> DT = Tax rate x Temporary difference = Deferred tax asset/Liability

(c)   Steps

Step 1:   Summarise the accounting carrying amounts and the tax base for every asset and liability.

Step 2:   Calculate the temporary difference by deducting the tax base from the carrying amount using the pro forma:

Asset/Liability	Carrying amount	Tax base	Temporary difference
	$	$	$

Step 3:   Calculate the deferred tax liability and asset. To calculate the deferred tax liabilities, sum all positive temporary differences and apply the tax rate. To calculate the deferred tax asset, sum all negative temporary differences and apply the tax rate.

Step 4:   Calculate the net deferred tax liability or asset by summing the two amounts in Step 3. This will be the *asset or liability* carried in the statement of financial position.

Step 5:   Deduct the opening deferred tax liability or asset. The difference will be this year's charge/credit to *profit or loss* (or other comprehensive income).

(d)   Where there has been a change in the tax rate calculate the effect of this change on the opening deferred tax provision. Follow steps 1 through 5 above, calculating the required closing deferred tax liability or asset and the charge/credit to the relevant statement. The charge/credit is then analysed into the amount which relates to the change in the tax rate and the amount which relates to the temporary differences.

The amount which relates to the change in tax rate will equal the amount of the temporary difference in the previous period times the change in the tax rate.

Summary

- Current tax (for current and prior periods) is a liability to the extent that it has not yet been settled, and an asset to the extent that amounts paid exceeds the amount due.

- The benefit of a tax loss which can be carried back to recover current tax of a prior period should be recognised as an asset.

- Current tax assets and liabilities are measured using the rates/laws which have been enacted or substantively enacted by the reporting date.

- Deferred tax *liabilities* should be recognised for all *taxable* temporary differences. Exceptions are liabilities arising from *initial recognition* of:
  - goodwill; or
  - an asset/liability in a transaction which is not a business combination and does not affect accounting or taxable profit.

- A deferred tax *asset* should be recognised for *deductible* temporary differences to the extent that it is probable that taxable profit will be available against which they can be utilised.

- A deferred tax asset is recognised for unused tax losses/credits carried forward to the extent that sufficient future taxable profits are probable.

- Deferred tax assets and liabilities are measured at tax rates expected to apply (enacted or substantively enacted by the end of the reporting period).

- Deferred tax assets and liabilities are *not* discounted.

- Current tax assets and liabilities should only be offset if there is a legal right to offset and intention to settle on a net basis. The same applies for deferred tax where levied by the same tax authority.

- Current and deferred tax is recognised in profit or loss except to the extent that the tax arises from:
  - transactions recognised in other comprehensive income or directly in equity; or
  - a business combination.

Session 17 Quiz
Estimated time: 15 minutes

1. Identify how the taxable profit figure is determined. (1.3)
2. State how deferred tax assets may arise. (1.3)
3. State the type of approach IAS 12 follows when accounting for deferred tax. (3.2.2)
4. Identify under what circumstances temporary differences may arise. (4.3)
5. Explain when a deferred tax asset should be recognised. (5.2.1)
6. Describe how any movement in the deferred tax balance should be accounted for. (5.3)
7. State the tax rate which should be applied when accounting for deferred tax. (5.5)

Study Question Bank
Estimated time: one hour

Priority		Estimated Time	Completed
Q28	Shep (I)	15 minutes	
Q29	Shep (II)	20 minutes	
Q30	Shep (III)	15 minutes	
Q31	Shep (IV)	10 minutes	

EXAMPLE SOLUTIONS

Solution 1—Deferred Tax Provision

Non-current assets	Carrying amount	Tax base	Temporary difference
	$	$	$
Plant and machinery	200,000	175,000	25,000
Receivables:			
Trade receivables	50,000	55,000	(5,000)
Interest receivable	1,000	0	1,000
Payables			
Fine	10,000	10,000	0
Interest payable	2,000	0	(2,000)

	Temporary differences	Deferred tax @ 30%
Deferred tax liabilities	26,000	7,800
Deferred tax assets	(7,000)	(2,100)
		5,700

	$
Deferred tax as at 1 January	1,200
Profit or loss (balancing figure)	4,500
Deferred tax as at 31 December	5,700

Solution 2—Revaluation

	Carrying amount	Tax base	Temporary difference
	$	$	
	1,250	650	600
Deferred tax at 30%			180

Solution 3—Outside Profit or Loss

		Deferred tax @ 30%
		$
Deferred tax as at 1 January	(1,000 – 800) x 30%	60
To other comprehensive income	30% x (1,250 – 900)	105
Profit or loss	Balancing figure (or as (150 – 100) x 30%)	15
Deferred tax as at 31 December		180

Solution 4—Gorgon Co

	Carrying amount	Tax base	Temporary difference
Non-current assets	$	$	$
Assets subject to investment relief	63,000	28,000	35,000
Land	200,000	150,000	50,000
Plant and machinery	100,000	90,000	10,000
Receivables			
Trade receivables	73,000	80,000	(7,000)
Interest receivable	1,000	0	1,000
Payables			
Fine	(10,000)	(10,000)	0
Interest payable	(3,300)	0	(3,300)
			85,700

		Temporary differences	Deferred tax @ 30%
Deferred tax liabilities		96,000	28,800
Deferred tax assets		(10,300)	(3,090)
			25,710

			$
Deferred tax as at 1 January			3,600
To other comprehensive income	30% x 50,000		15,000
Profit or loss	Balancing figure		7,110
Deferred tax as at 31 December			25,710

Financial Instruments

FOCUS

This session covers the following content from the *ACCA Study Guide.*

B. Accounting for Transactions in Financial Statements

5. Financial instruments

a. Explain the need for an accounting standard on financial instruments.

b. Define financial instruments in terms of financial assets and financial liabilities.

c. Explain and account for the factoring of receivables.

d. Indicate for the following categories of financial instruments how they should be measured and how any gains and losses from subsequent measurement should be treated in the financial statements:

   i)   amortised cost

   ii) fair value through other comprehensive income (including where an irrevocable election has been made for equity instruments that are not held for trading)

   iii) fair value through profit or loss

e. Distinguish between debt and equity capital.

f. Apply the requirements of relevant accounting standards to the issue and finance costs of:

   i)   equity

   ii) redeemable preference shares and debt instruments with no conversion rights (principle of amortised cost)

   iii) convertible debt

Session 18 Guidance

■ **Appreciate** that the three standards on financial instruments are difficult standards. However, at the F7 level, only a basic knowledge is required. IFRS 9 is the examinable document for the recognition and measurement of financial assets and liabilities and the impairment of certain financial assets.

■ **Understand** how to account for a compound instrument such as convertible debt (s.2.5), as this topic occurs on a regular basis in the exam.

(continued on next page)

VISUAL OVERVIEW

Objective: To explain the rules on measurement, recognition, presentation and disclosure of financial instruments.

```
┌─────────────────────────────────────────┐
│               INTRODUCTION                │
│  • Traditional Accounting                 │
│  • History                                │
│  • Application and Scope                  │
│  • Terminology                            │
└─────────────────────────────────────────┘

┌──────────────────────────┐   ┌──────────────────────────┐
│   PRESENTATION (IAS 32)   │   │   RECOGNITION (IFRS 9)    │
│  • Liabilities and Equity │   │  • Initial Recognition    │
│  • Offset                 │   │  • Examples               │
│  • Compound Instruments   │   │                           │
└──────────────────────────┘   └──────────────────────────┘

┌────────────────────┐  ┌────────────────────┐  ┌────────────────────┐
│     FINANCIAL      │  │     FINANCIAL      │  │   DERECOGNITION    │
│      ASSETS        │  │    LIABILITIES     │  │  • Financial Asset │
│ • Initial          │  │ • Initial          │  │  • Financial       │
│   Measurement      │  │   Recognition      │  │    Liability       │
│ • Subsequent       │  │ • Subsequent       │  │                    │
│   Measurement      │  │   Measurement      │  │                    │
│ • Amortised Cost   │  │                    │  │                    │
│ • Gains and Losses │  │                    │  │                    │
│ • Reclassification │  │                    │  │                    │
└────────────────────┘  └────────────────────┘  └────────────────────┘

┌────────────────────┐  ┌────────────────────┐
│     IMPAIRMENT     │  │  DISCLOSURE (IFRS 7)│
│ • Terminology      │  │  • Purpose          │
│ • Loss Allowance   │  │  • Rules            │
│ • Credit Risk      │  │                     │
│ • Trade Receivables│  │                     │
└────────────────────┘  └────────────────────┘
```

Session 18 Guidance

■ **Learn** the three categories of financial assets (s.4.3) and the two categories of financial liabilities (s.5) and how each of these instruments is valued and where any changes in valuation are recognised (s.4.3.4).

■ **Read** the technical article "What is a financial instrument—Parts 1 and 2".

1 Introduction

Definition

Financial instrument—any contract which gives rise to both a financial asset of one entity and a financial liability or equity instrument of another entity.

Instruments include:

- primary instruments (e.g. receivables, payables and equity securities); and
- derivative instruments (e.g. financial options, futures and forwards, interest rate swaps and currency swaps).

1.1 Traditional Accounting

- Traditional accounting practices are based on serving the needs of manufacturing companies. Accounting for such entities is concerned with accruing costs to be matched with revenues. A key concept in such a process is revenue and cost recognition.

- The global market for **financial instruments** has expanded rapidly, not only in the sheer volume of such instruments but also in complexity. Entities have moved from using "traditional" instruments (e.g. cash, trade debtors, long-term debt and investments) to highly sophisticated risk management strategies based on derivatives and complex combinations of instruments.

- The traditional cost-based concepts are not adequate to deal with the recognition and measurement of financial assets and liabilities. Specifically:

  - Traditional accounting bases recognition on the transfer of risks and rewards. It is not designed to deal with transactions which divide up the risks and rewards associated with a particular asset (or liability) and allocate them to different parties.

  - Some financial instruments have no or little initial cost (e.g. options) and are not adequately accounted for (if at all) under traditional historical cost-based systems.

- If a transaction has no cost, traditional accounting cannot account for it in terms of Dr and CR. In addition, the historical cost of financial assets and liabilities has little relevance to risk management activities.

1.2 History

- IAS 32 *Financial Instruments: Disclosure and Presentation* was first issued in June 1995.

- IAS 39 *Financial Instruments: Recognition and Measurement* was first issued in December 1998.

▨ IFRS 7 was issued in 2005 to replace IAS 30 *Disclosures in the Financial Statements of Banks and Similar Financial Institutions* and to take over the disclosure issues of IAS 32. IAS 32 is now solely concerned with presentation issues.

▨ This time difference between the initial issue of IAS 32 and IAS 39 reflects the complexity of the recognition and measurement issues. The first exposure draft on financial instruments (issued in 1991) had sought to address disclosure, presentation, recognition and measurement in one standard. The subsequent revisions reflect the "learning process" of dealing with the complexities of financial instruments and new issues which have been raised since the standards were first issued.

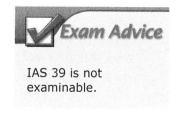

IAS 39 is not examinable.

▨ The IASB's project to replace IAS 39 with a new standard, IFRS 9 *Financial Instruments,* was started in 2009 and was finally completed in July 2014.

▨ IFRS 9 deals with the following:

  ⊙ Recognition and measurement of financial assets and liabilities;

  ⊙ Derecognition of financial assets and liabilities;

  ⊙ Impairment of certain financial assets; and

  ⊙ Hedging and hedge accounting.

▨ IFRS 9 is effective from 1 January 2018, but early adoption is permitted.

1.3 Application and Scope

1.3.1 IAS 32

▨ Classification of financial instruments between:

  ⊙ financial assets;

  ⊙ financial liabilities; and

  ⊙ equity instruments.

▨ Presentation and offset of financial instruments and the related interest, dividends, losses and gains.

1.3.2 IFRS 7

▨ Disclosure of:

  ⊙ factors affecting the amount, timing and certainty of cash flows;

  ⊙ the use of financial instruments and the business purpose they serve; and

  ⊙ the associated risks and management's policies for controlling those risks.

*IFRS 9 "scopes out" 10 items that are accounted for under other standards (e.g. rights and obligations under leases to which IFRS 16 applies).

1.3.3 IFRS 9 Financial Instruments

▨ This standard applies to all financial instruments except those that are specifically scoped out by the standard.*

1.4 Terminology

1.4.1 From IAS 32

■ **Financial asset**: any asset which is:

- cash;
- a contractual right to receive cash or another financial asset from another entity;
- a contractual right to exchange financial instruments with another entity under conditions which are potentially favourable;
- an equity instrument of another entity; or
- certain contracts which will (or may) be settled in the entity's own equity instruments.*

■ **Financial liability:** any liability which is a contractual obligation:

- to deliver cash or another financial asset to another entity;
- to exchange financial instruments with another entity under conditions that are potentially unfavourable; or
- certain contracts that will (or may) be settled in own equity instruments.*

*For this purpose, own equity instruments do not include instruments which are themselves contracts for the future receipt or delivery of own equity instruments.

*Commentary

*Financial instruments do not include physical assets, prepayments, non-contractual liabilities, and contractual liabilities relating to non-financial assets.

Preferred shares which provide for mandatory redemption by the issuer, or which give the holder the right to redeem the share, meet the definition of liabilities and are classified as such even though, legally, they may be equity.

■ **Equity instrument**: any contract which evidences a residual interest in the assets of an entity after deducting all of its liabilities.

■ **Fair value**: the price which would be received to sell an asset or paid to transfer a liability in an orderly transaction between market participants at the measurement date.

1.4.2 From IFRS 9

■ **Derivative:** a financial instrument which:

- changes value in response to the change in a specified interest rate, financial instrument price, commodity price, foreign exchange rate, index of prices or rates, credit rating or credit index, or other variable (sometimes called the "underlying");
- requires little or no initial net investment relative to other types of contracts which would be expected to have a similar response to changes in market conditions; and
- is settled at a future date.

The **amortised cost** of a financial asset or financial liability is:

- the amount at which it was measured at initial recognition;
  minus
- principal repayments;
  plus or minus
- the cumulative amortisation of any difference between that initial amount and the maturity amount; and
  minus
- any write-down (directly or through the use of an allowance account) for impairment or uncollectability.

Effective interest method: a method of calculating the amortised cost of a financial asset or a financial liability, using the *effective interest rate* and of allocating the interest.*

Transaction costs: incremental costs which are directly attributable to the acquisition, issue or disposal of a financial asset (or financial liability).*

*Commentary

*The effective interest rate (also called the "level yield-to-maturity") is the internal rate of return of the financial asset (or liability) for that period.

*An incremental cost is one which would not have been incurred if the entity had not acquired, issued or disposed of the financial instrument (e.g. agents' fees and commissions).

Transaction costs do not include debt premiums or discounts, financing costs, internal administrative and holding costs.

Illustration 1 — Effective Interest Rate Method

A company issues a $100,000 zero coupon bond redeemable in five years at $150,000.

The internal rate of return (the yield) on these flows is 8.45%. This should be used to allocate the expense.

Period	Opening balance	Interest @ 8.45%	Closing balance
1	100,000	8,450	108,450
2	108,450	9,164	117,614
3	117,614	9,938	127,552
4	127,552	10,778	138,330
5	138,330	11,689	150,019

This should be 150,000. The difference of 19 is due to rounding

---

2 Presentation (IAS 32)

2.1 Liabilities and Equity

Some financial instruments may take the legal form of equity but are, in substance, liabilities.

An **equity instrument** is any contract which evidences a residual interest in the assets of an entity after deducting all of its liabilities.

Key Point

On issue, financial instruments should be classified as liabilities or equity in accordance with the **substance** of the contractual arrangement on **initial recognition**.

Illustration 2   Preference Shares

Redeemable preference shares are not classified as equity under IAS 32, as there is a contractual obligation to transfer financial assets (e.g. cash) to the holder of the shares. They are therefore a financial liability.

If such shares are redeemable at the option of the issuer, they would not meet the definition of a financial liability as there is no present obligation to transfer a financial asset to the holder of the shares. When the issuer becomes obliged to redeem the shares, the shares become a financial liability and will then be transferred out of equity.

For non-redeemable preference shares, the substance of the contract would need to be studied. For example, if distributions to the holders of the instrument are at the discretion of the issuer, the shares are equity instruments.

2.2   Offset

- ▥ Financial assets and liabilities must be offset where the entity:*
  - ● has a legal right of offset; *and*
  - ● intends to settle on a net basis or to realise the asset and settle the liability simultaneously.

Commentary

*An offset might be between trade receivables and payables or accounts in debit and credit at a bank.

2.3   Compound Instruments

2.3.1   Presentation

Key Point

Financial instruments which contain both a liability and an equity element are classified into separate component parts.

- ▥ As an example, convertible bonds are primary financial liabilities of the issuer which grant an option to the holder to convert them into equity instruments in the future. Such bonds consist of:
  - ● the obligation to repay the bonds, which should be presented as a liability; and
  - ● the option to convert, which should be presented in equity.
- ▥ The economic effect of issuing such an instrument is substantially the same as issuing simultaneously a debt instrument with an early settlement provision and warrants to purchase ordinary shares.

2.3.2   Carrying Amounts

- ▥ The equity component is the residual amount after deduction of the more easily measurable debt component from the value of the instrument as a whole.
- ▥ The liability is measured by discounting the stream of future payments at the prevailing market rate for a similar liability without the associated equity component.

> ### Example 1 Convertible Debt
>
> An entity issues 2,000 convertible $1,000 bonds at par on 1 January 20X7.
>
> Interest is payable annually in arrears at a nominal interest rate of 6%.
>
> The prevailing market rate of interest at the date of issue of the bond was 9%.
>
> The bond is redeemable 31 December 20X9.
>
> **Required:**
>
> **Calculate the amounts at which the bond will be included in the financial statements on initial recognition and for the first year of issue.**

3 Recognition

3.1 Initial Recognition

- An entity should recognise a financial asset or liability in the statement of financial position when, and only when, it becomes a party to the contractual provisions of the instrument.

- When an entity first recognises a financial asset it is classified as either:

  - fair value through profit or loss;

  - fair value through other comprehensive income; or

  - amortised cost.

- As a consequence of this rule, an entity must recognise all of its contractual rights or obligations under derivatives in its statement of financial position as assets or liabilities.

3.2 Examples

- *A forward contract* (i.e. a commitment to purchase or sell a specified financial instrument or commodity on a future date at a specified price) is recognised as an asset or a liability on the commitment date, rather than waiting until the closing date on which the exchange actually takes place.

- *Financial options* are recognised as assets or liabilities when the holder or writer becomes a party to the contract.

- *Planned future transactions*, no matter how likely, are not assets and liabilities of an entity because the entity, as of the financial reporting date, has not become a party to a contract requiring future receipt or delivery of assets arising out of the future transactions.

4 Financial Assets

4.1 Initial Measurement

- On initial recognition, financial assets (except trade receivables) are measured at **fair value**. If the financial asset is not classified as fair value through profit or loss, any directly attributable transaction costs are adjusted against the fair value.

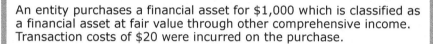

Illustration 3 Transaction Costs

An entity purchases a financial asset for $1,000 which is classified as a financial asset at fair value through other comprehensive income. Transaction costs of $20 were incurred on the purchase.

The asset is initially measured at $1,020.

If the asset had been classified as fair value through profit or loss it would be measured at $1,000 and the $20 would be expensed to profit or loss immediately.

- Trade receivables, which do not have a major financing element, are measured at their transaction price in accordance with IFRS 15.*

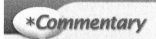

Commentary

*That is, "the amount of consideration expected in exchange for the transfer of promised goods or services to a customer".

4.2 Subsequent Measurement

- Once recognised, a financial asset is subsequently measured at either:
  - amortised cost;
  - fair value through other comprehensive income; or
  - fair value through profit or loss.
- Classification requires consideration of:
  - the entity's **business model**. This refers to how the entity manages its financial assets to generate cash flows. (Does it intend to collect contractual cash flows (i.e. interest and principal repayments), sell financial assets or both?); and
  - the contractual cash flow characteristics of the financial asset.

4.2.1 Amortised Cost

- A financial asset is subsequently measured at **amortised cost** if it meets two conditions:*
  1. It is held within a business model whose objective is achieved through holding financial assets to collect contractual cash flows; and
  2. Its contractual terms give rise to cash flows on specified dates which are solely payments of principal and interest (on the outstanding principal).

Commentary

*These conditions capture simple debt instruments that are intended to be held for the long term, maybe until maturity.

Illustration 4 Amortised Cost

An entity purchased a debt instrument for $1,000. The instrument pays interest of $60 annually and had 10 years to maturity when purchased. The business model test was met and the instrument was classified as a financial asset at amortised cost.

Nine years have passed and the entity is suffering a liquidity crisis and needs to sell the asset to raise funds.

The sale was not expected on initial classification and does not affect the classification (i.e. there is no retrospective reclassification).

4.2.2 Fair Value Through Other Comprehensive Income

A financial asset is subsequently measured at fair value through other comprehensive income if it meets two conditions: *

1. It is held within a business model whose objective is achieved through collecting contractual cash flows **and selling** financial assets; and

2. Its contractual terms give rise to cash flows on specified dates, which are solely payments of principal and interest.

*Commentary

*There is no commitment to keep the asset until maturity. Cash may be realised by selling the asset at any time. This category also captures debt instruments, but without intention to hold until maturity.

Illustration 5 Business Model

Opal anticipates the purchase of a large property in eight years' time. It invests cash surpluses in short and long-term financial assets. Many of the financial assets purchased have a maturity in excess of eight years.

Opal holds the financial assets for their contractual cash flows but will sell them and reinvest the cash for a higher return as and when an opportunity arises.

The objective of the business model is achieved by collecting contractual cash flows and selling the financial assets. Opal's decisions to hold or sell aim to maximise returns from the portfolio of financial assets.

Example 2 Business Model

Johan purchased a loan asset two years ago for $120,000. The loan pays interest annually at 6% of the loan's face value, which was $125,000.

Johan has a business model of holding this type of asset for contractual cash flows and also to sell them if circumstances are favourable. The contractual cash flows are solely the principal and interest on the principal.

Today the asset has a fair value of $127,000 and the amortised cost is $123,000.

Required:

Explain the amount at which the loan asset should be included in the statement of financial position.

The asset is measured at fair value in the statement of financial position, and interest income, based on the amortised cost of the asset, is recognised in the statement of profit or loss. Any difference, after allowing for impairment (see s.5), is recognised in other comprehensive income.

4.2.3 Fair Value Through Profit or Loss

All other financial assets are measured at fair value through profit or loss, with one possible exception:

On **initial recognition** an entity may **elect** to designate an **equity instrument** in **another entity** at fair value through other comprehensive income.

Also, an entity can opt to designate **any** financial asset at fair value through profit or loss in order to eliminate an accounting mismatch (i.e. where a linked financial liability is measured at fair value through profit or loss).*

4.2.4 Classification and Measurement Summary

The diagram below summarises the application of the classification and measurement model for financial assets as described above:

Key Point

This election is irrevocable.

*Commentary

*This so-called "fair value option" is also irrevocable.

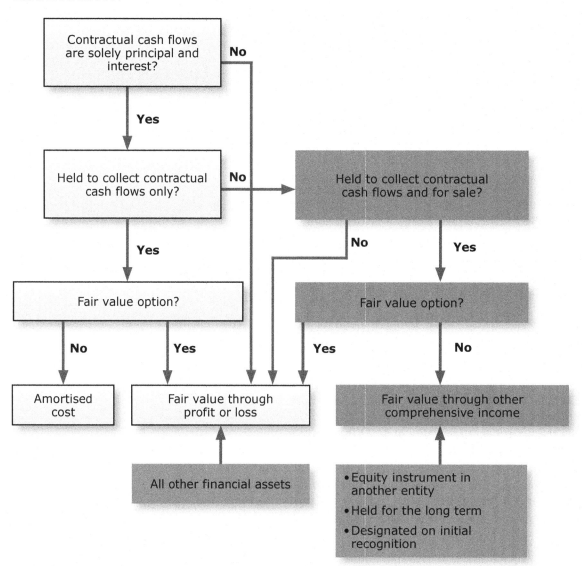

4.3   Amortised Cost

■ Measuring a financial asset at amortised cost means that interest revenue will be calculated using the effective interest method (see s.1.4.2):

- The credit to profit or loss is based on the effective interest rate.
- The cash flow is based on the instrument's coupon (nominal) rate of interest.*

■ Any difference between the interest credited to profit or loss and the cash received is added to the value of the financial asset.

Commentary

*For many instruments the two rates may be the same.

4.4   Gains and Losses

■ Interest income is recognised in **profit or loss** using the instrument's effective interest rate.

■ Dividend income is recognised in **profit or loss** when the right to receive the dividend has been established.

■ Gains and losses on financial assets measured at **amortised cost** are recognised in **profit or loss**.

■ Generally, gains and losses on financial assets that are measured at **fair value** are recognised in **profit or loss** with the following **exceptions**:

- If it is part of a **hedging relationship**.
- If it is an **equity** investment measured at fair value through other comprehensive income.*
- If it is a **debt** instrument measured at fair value through other comprehensive income some fair value changes will be recognised in other comprehensive income:
  — impairment gains and losses and foreign exchange gains and losses are recognised in profit or loss; **but**
  — changes due to the movement in fair value of the instrument are recognised in other comprehensive income.*

Commentary

*Cumulative gains and losses in other comprehensive income are **not reclassified** on derecognition (but can be transferred to retained earnings).

Commentary

*These fair value changes are reclassified through profit or loss on derecognition.

Illustration 6 Accounting for Gains and Losses

An entity purchased a debt instrument at its fair value, $1,000. The entity classified the asset at fair value through other comprehensive income as its business model is to collect contractual cash flows and sell financial assets.

The instrument had five years to maturity and a contractual par value of $1,250. It pays fixed interest of 4.7% and its effective interest rate is 10%.

At the end of the first year the fair value of the instrument is $1,020. The entity has calculated the impairment loss on the asset to be $8.

Dr Cash – interest received ($1,250 x 4.7%)	$ 59
Dr Financial asset (increase in fair value)	$ 20
Dr Profit or loss – impairment (as given)	$ 8
Dr Other comprehensive income (fair value change)	$ 13
Cr Profit or loss – interest income ($1,000 x 10%)	$ 100

The change in fair value recognised in other comprehensive income (in this case a balancing loss of $13) will be reclassified through profit or loss on derecognition.

4.5 Reclassification

- If the entity changes its business model for managing financial assets it must reclassify all affected financial assets **prospectively,** from the date of the change.
- Amounts previously recognised based on the financial assets original classification are **not restated**.

5 Impairment

5.1 Terminology

- **Past due:** a financial asset is past due when the debtor has failed to make a payment that was contractually due.
- **Impairment gain or loss:** gains or losses recognised in profit or loss that arise from the impairment requirements of IFRS 9.
- **Credit loss:** the present value of the difference between all contractual cash flows due to be received and those expected to be received (i.e. all cash shortfalls).*
- **Lifetime expected credit losses:** losses that result from all possible default events over the expected life of a financial instrument.
- **Loss allowance:** the allowance for expected credit losses on:
  - financial assets measured at amortised cost or fair value through other comprehensive income;
  - lease receivables;
  - contract assets (under IFRS 15), loan commitments and financial guarantee contracts.

*Discounted at the original effective interest rate.

5.2 Loss Allowance

- Financial assets measured at amortised cost and financial assets measured at fair value through other comprehensive income according to the business model (see s.4.2.2) are subject to impairment testing.
- A loss allowance for any expected credit losses must be recognised in **profit or loss**.
- The loss allowance is measured at each reporting date. The amount depends on whether or not the instrument's credit risk has *increased significantly* since initial recognition:
  - If significant, the loss allowance is the amount of the lifetime expected credit losses.
  - If not significant, the loss allowance is 12-month expected credit losses.*
- Practical methods may be used to measure expected credit losses as long as they are consistent with the principles prescribed by the standard (e.g. see trade receivables in s.5.4).

*A credit loss can arise even if all cash flows due are expected to be received in full; if receipts are expected to be late the expected present value will fall.

5.3   Credit Risk

- The credit risk associated with a financial asset must be assessed at each reporting date:*
  - If it has increased significantly the loss is measured based on the lifetime of the asset.
  - If it has not increased significantly the loss is measured based on the 12-month expected credit losses.
- The probability of a significant increase in credit risk will be higher for assets with a low credit risk on initial recognition than for those with a high credit risk on initial recognition.
- Factors that could significantly increase credit risk include:
  - An actual or forecast deterioration in the economic environment which is expected to have a negative effect on the debtor's ability to generate cash flows.
  - The debtor is close to breaching covenants which may require restructuring of the loan.
  - A decrease in the trading price of the debtor's bonds and/ or significant increases in credit risk on other bonds of the same debtor.
  - The fair value of an asset has been below its amortised cost for some time.
  - A reassessment of the entity's own internal risk grading of loans given.
  - An actual or expected decline in the debtor's operating results.
- There is a rebuttable presumption that any asset that is more than 30 days past due is an indicator that lifetime expected credit losses should be recognised.*

*Comparison is with the risk of default assessed on initial recognition.

*This presumption can only rebutted if reasonable and supportable information demonstrates that the credit risk is not significantly increased.

Illustration 7   Expected Credit Losses

Amber purchases a debt instrument for $2,000. The Amber business model is to hold financial assets for contractual cash flows and sell them when conditions are favourable. The asset has a coupon rate of 5%, which is also the effective interest rate.

At the end of the first year the fair value of the asset has fallen to $1,920; part of the fall in value is due to 12-month expected credit losses on the asset of $60.

Of the fall in value $60 will be expensed to profit or loss as an impairment loss and $20 will be debited to other comprehensive income.

5.4 Trade Receivables

▦ The standard allows a simplified impairment approach to an entity's trade receivables. The simplification allows the entity to measure the loss allowance as an amount equal to lifetime expected credit losses for trade receivables or contract assets resulting from transactions under IFRS 15 *Revenue from Contracts with Customers.* *

> ### *Commentary
>
> *There is a proviso that the contract does not contain a significant financing element, or if it does the entity has elected an accounting policy that measures the loss allowance at an amount equal to lifetime expected credit losses.

▦ A **provision matrix** is a practical method of calculating expected credit losses on trade receivables. This is based on percentages (using appropriately adjusted historical experience) of the number of days past due. (For example, 1% if not past due, 2% if less than 30 days past due, 5% if more than 30 but less than 90, etc.)

Illustration 8 Provision Matrix

An entity has receivables of $1 million analysed as follows:

	Balance outstanding	Default risk	Expected credit loss
	$	%	$
Current	326,000	0.25	815
1–30 days past due	427,000	1.3	5,551
31–60 days past due	198,000	2.4	4,752
More than 60 days past due	49,000	10.5	5,145
Loss allowance			16,263

>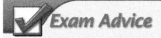
> ### Exam Advice
>
> Calculations of impairment losses for financial assets will not be required. You will, however, need to be able to account for a given impairment loss.

6 Financial Liabilities

6.1 Initial Recognition

▨ A financial liability is recognised only when an entity becomes a party to the contractual provisions of the instrument.

▨ The liability will initially be recognised at fair value less any directly attributable transaction costs.

▨ If the liability is classified at fair value through profit or loss, any relevant transaction costs will be charged immediately to profit or loss.

6.2 Subsequent Measurement

 **Key Point**

Most financial liabilities will subsequently be measured at amortised cost using the effective interest method, with the interest expense being charged to profit or loss.

▨ The groups of financial liabilities that are not measured at amortised cost will include:

⊙ those at fair value through profit or loss (including derivatives); and

⊙ commitments to provide loans at below-market interest rate. These will be measured at the higher of the amount determined under IAS 37 and the initial amount recognised less any cumulative amortisation.

7 Derecognition

7.1 Financial Asset

7.1.1 Basic Derecognition Criteria

▨ An entity should derecognise a financial asset (or a part of it) when, and only when:

⊙ the contractual rights to the cash flows from the financial asset expire; or

⊙ it transfers the financial asset and the transfer qualifies for derecognition.

▨ In many cases derecognition of a financial asset is straightforward; if there no longer are contractual rights, the asset is derecognised. If contractual rights remain, the standard requires three further steps to be considered (i.e. transfer, risks and rewards, control).

7.1.2 Transfer of a Financial Asset

- An entity transfers a financial asset if, and only if, it either:
  - gives the contractual rights to receive the cash flows to a third party; or
  - retains the contractual rights to receive the cash flows, but assumes a contractual obligation to pay the cash to a third party.

7.1.3 Profit or Loss on Derecognition

- On derecognition, profit or loss for the period includes the difference between:
  - the carrying amount of an asset (or portion of an asset) transferred to another party; and
  - the consideration received, adjusted for any new asset received or new liability assumed.

Illustration 9 Factoring of Receivables

An entity has receivables of $1 million which it sells to a factor for $940,000.

If the debtors fail to pay, or have not paid within three months of the sale, the factor can return the debt to the entity.

As the receivables have been sold "with recourse" they cannot be derecognised. Instead, a current liability loan of $940,000 is recognised, with $60,000 finance costs.

If the receivables had been sold "without recourse" they would have been derecognised and $60,000 recognised as an operating cost.

7.2 Financial Liability

- An entity should remove a financial liability from the statement of financial position when, and only when, it is extinguished—that is, when the obligation specified in the contract is discharged, cancelled or expires.
- This condition is met when either:
  - the debtor discharges the liability by paying the creditor, normally with cash, other financial assets, goods or services; or
  - the debtor is legally released from primary responsibility for the liability (or part thereof) either by process of law or by the creditor.*
- If the liability is renegotiated with the original lender at substantially different contractual terms than the original, the liability will be derecognised and a new liability will be recognised.
- Profit or loss for the period includes the difference between:
  - the carrying amount of a liability (or portion) extinguished or transferred to another party (including related unamortised costs); and
  - the amount paid for it, including any non-cash assets transferred or liabilities assumed.

*Commentary

*The fact that the debtor may have given a guarantee does not necessarily mean that this second condition is not met.

8   Disclosure (IFRS 7)

8.1   Purpose

- To enhance understanding of the significance of financial instruments to an entity's financial position, performance and cash flows.
- To assist in assessing the factors affecting the amount, timing and certainty of future cash flows associated with those instruments.
- To provide information to assist users of financial statements in assessing the extent of related risks.

8.2   Rules

8.2.1   Risk Management

- An entity must describe its financial risk management objectives and policies.*

8.2.2   Interest Rate Risk

- An entity must disclose information about its exposure to interest rate risk. Such information includes:
  - contractual re-pricing or maturity dates;
  - effective interest rates; and
  - which financial assets and liabilities are exposed to fair value or cash flow interest rate risk and those which are not directly exposed to interest rate risk.

8.2.3   Credit Risk

- An entity must disclose information about its exposure to credit risk. Such information includes:
  - the maximum credit exposure risk; and
  - significant concentrations of credit risk.

8.2.4   Other Disclosures

- Disclose material items of income, expense, and gains and losses resulting from financial assets and financial liabilities, whether included in profit or loss or as other comprehensive income.
- Disclose the carrying amount of financial assets pledged as collateral and any material terms and conditions relating to such pledged assets.
- If the entity has reclassified a financial asset as one required to be reported at amortised cost rather than at fair value, disclose the reason for that reclassification.
- Disclose the nature and amount of any impairment loss recognised for a financial asset.

*Commentary

*The level of detail to be given needs to strike a balance between excessive detail and over aggregation.

Summary

- Accounting for financial instruments is covered by IAS 32, IFRS 7 and IFRS 9.

- Instruments must be distinguished between equity and liabilities. Convertible instruments which are a mix of equity and liability must be split; the liability is the present value of future cash flows and the equity element is the balancing figure.

- Financial assets are either measured at fair value or amortised cost.

- Any changes in fair value of a financial asset are taken to profit or loss or other comprehensive income (according to initial classification).

- Financial assets and liabilities at amortised cost are measured using the instruments' effective interest rate based on market rates.

- Financial assets measured at amortised cost and those at fair value through other comprehensive income are tested for impairment at the reporting date.

- Trade receivables are derecognised if they are sold "without recourse".

- Disclosure requirements are very extensive and related mostly to related risks.

Session 18 Quiz
Estimated time: 30 minutes

1. Define a financial asset and identify FOUR possible assets which would meet this definition. (1)
2. Summarise the need to issue accounting standards on financial instruments. (1.1)
3. State the formula for amortised cost used to measure certain financial assets and liabilities. (1.4.2)
4. State how preference dividends are accounted for. (2.3)
5. Describe how the carrying amounts of the liability and equity elements are measured, in respect of a compound instrument. (2.3.2)
6. List the THREE classifications of financial assets. (4.2)
7. Identify when an entity may classify a financial asset at fair value through other comprehensive income. (4.2)
8. State how a loss allowance is measured if the credit risk has increased significantly since the instrument was first measured. (5.2)
9. State at what value the majority of financial liabilities will be measured subsequent to initial recognition. (6.2)
10. List the conditions that must be met before an entity can derecognise a financial liability. (7.2)

Study Question Bank
Estimated time: 20 minutes

Priority		Estimated Time	Completed
Q33	Bertrand	20 minutes	
Additional			
Q32	Iota		

EXAMPLE SOLUTIONS

Solution 1—Convertible Debt

On initial recognition	$
Present value of the principal repayable in 3 years' time	
$2,000,000 × 0.772 (3 year, 9% discount factor)	1,544,000
Present value of the interest stream	
$120,000 × 2.531 (3 year, cumulative, 9% discount factor)	303,720
Total liability component	1,847,720
Equity component (taken as a balancing figure)	152,280
Proceeds of the issue	2,000,000

Recognised during first year	
Initial liability recognised	1,847,720
Interest expense for year (to profit or loss)	
$1,847,720 × 9%	166,295
Cash interest paid	
$2,000,000 × 6%	(120,000)
Year-end liability	1,894,015

 **Exam Advice**

A cumulative discount factor (annuity factor) is the sum of simple discount factors. You will not have to calculate discount factors in the examination.

The liability at the end of year 3, the date of maturity, will be $2,000,000.

The standard is silent on what to do with the equity component; an option would be to transfer it to retained earnings over the life of the instrument.

Solution 2—Business Model

 ***Commentary**

As the business model of Johan is to hold such financial assets for both contractual cash flows and the opportunity to sell, it must be classified at fair value through other comprehensive income. The loan asset is therefore valued at $127,000 in the statement of financial position with any changes in fair value being split between profit or loss and other comprehensive income.*

*On derecognition of the asset the cumulative gain or loss in other comprehensive income will be reclassified to profit or loss.

Conceptual Principles of Groups

FOCUS

This session covers the following content from the *ACCA Study Guide.*

A. The Conceptual and Regulatory Framework for Financial Reporting

5. The concept and principles of groups and consolidated financial statements

a) Describe the concept of a group as a single economic unit. ☐

b) Explain and apply the definition of a subsidiary within relevant accounting standards. ☐

c) Identify and outline using accounting standards the circumstances in which a group is required to prepare consolidated financial statements. ☐

d) Describe the circumstances when a group may claim exemption from the preparation of consolidated financial statements. ☐

e) Explain why directors may not wish to consolidate a subsidiary and when this is permitted by accounting standards and other applicable regulation. ☐

f) Explain the need for using coterminous year ends and uniform accounting policies when preparing consolidated financial statements. ☐

Session 19 Guidance

■ **Revise** the definitions relating to business combinations and the principles that underlie consolidation (s.1). This knowledge is assumed from F3 *Financial Accounting*.

■ **Understand** the factors that contribute to power, which is necessary for control to exist (s.2.1.1).

(continued on next page)

VISUAL OVERVIEW

Objective: To describe the provisions of IFRS 10 *Consolidated Financial Statements* and IAS 27 *Separate Financial Statements*.

```
                    ┌─────────────────────────┐
                    │      INTRODUCTION        │
                    │  ─────────────────────   │
                    │   • Terminology          │
                    │   • Truth and Fairness   │
                    └─────────────────────────┘
                       /                    \
                      /                      \
  ┌──────────────────────────┐    ┌──────────────────────────┐
  │         PARENT           │    │   SUNDRY PROVISIONS OF    │
  │      AND CONTROL         │    │          IFRS 10          │
  │  ─────────────────────   │    │  ─────────────────────    │
  │   • Inclusions           │    │   • Intra-group Trading   │
  │   • Exclusions           │    │   • Accounting Year Ends  │
  │   • Exemption            │    │   • Accounting Policies   │
  │   • Separate Financial   │    │   • Date of Acquisition   │
  │     Statements           │    │     or Disposal           │
  │   • Acquisition Method   │    │                           │
  └──────────────────────────┘    └──────────────────────────┘
```

Session 19 Guidance

■ **Learn** the rule that gives exemption from the preparation of consolidated financial statements (s.2.3).

■ **Understand** the issue relating to control (s.2).

■ **Learn** the requirements that relate to different reporting dates (s.3).

1 Introduction

1.1 Terminology

Business combination: a transaction or other event in which the acquirer obtains control of one or more businesses.*

Acquisition date: the date the acquirer obtains control of the acquiree.

Control of an investee: arises when the investor is exposed, or has rights, to variable returns from its involvement with the investee and has the ability to affect those returns through its power over the investee.

Subsidiary: an entity controlled by another entity (the parent).

Parent: an entity which controls one or more entities.

Group: a parent and its subsidiaries.

Consolidated financial statements: the financial statements of a group presented as those of a single economic entity.

Non-controlling interest: the equity in a subsidiary which is not attributable, directly or indirectly, to a parent.

Commentary

*Include a merger.

1.2 Truth and Fairness

- The financial statements of a group of companies should aim to give a true and fair view to the owners of a parent of what their investments represent (i.e. control and ownership of the net assets of subsidiary companies).

- Rules are needed to ensure that the consolidation *includes* all entities controlled by the parent—the definition of subsidiaries attempts to do this (see next section).

- On occasion, no useful purpose is served by a parent company producing group accounts. Thus, in certain circumstances, parent companies are exempt from the general requirement.

2 Parent and Control

2.1 Inclusions

- A parent which issues consolidated financial statements must consolidate **all subsidiaries**, foreign and domestic, other than those excluded for the reasons specified in IFRS 10 *Consolidated Financial Statements*.

Key Point

Control exists when the investor is exposed, or has rights, to variable returns from its involvement with the investee and has the ability to affect those returns through its power over the investee.

- The standard considers the substance of the transaction, being the ability to control, rather than the legal ownership of, shares as the driving force when considering whether control exists.

Exam Advice

The F7 examiner will make it fairly obvious that control exists, normally by giving the parent more than 50% of the equity shares. However, as a five-mark "add-on", the examiner may ask for a discussion of the issues affecting control.

2.1.1   Power

- The investor has power over the investee if the investor has rights giving it the ability to direct activities which significantly affect returns from the investee.

- In many straightforward situations, power is gained by holding more than 50% of the voting rights in the investee (subsidiary).

- But power is not always straightforward and can result from one or more contractual arrangements, without holding a majority of voting rights.

- An investor can have power over an investee even if other entities have rights allowing them to participate in the activities of the investee (e.g. if another investor has *significant influence*).

- The rights could be in the form of voting rights or the rights to appoint, or remove, members of the key management personnel of the investee (e.g. board directors).

- The assessment of rights should take into account any potential voting rights it holds in the investee (e.g. share options or convertible instruments).

Illustration 1   Control

Entity A holds 40% of the voting right in entity B. It also holds share options which, if it were to exercise them, would take its share-holding in entity B to 80%.

Ignoring any other issues, it would be probable that entity A had control over entity B through both its current share-holding and its potential future shares. Entity B would be recognised as a subsidiary of entity A.

2.1.2   Variable Returns

- An investor is exposed to variable returns from the investee when there is potential for variable performance from the investee.

- In other words, the returns, dividends and profits from the investee will depend on the performance of the subsidiary. There will be no fixed right to a specific return.

2.1.3   Link Between Power and Returns

- To have control over the investee, the investor will have power and exposure to variable returns but must also have the ability to use that power to affect the returns from the investee.

- So an investor with decision-making rights determines if it is acting as either a principal or an agent. The investor will only control its investee if it is acting as a principal. An agent would need powers delegated to it by its controlling body.

Example 1 Entities in the Group

Identify the entities to be included in the group, as defined by IFRS 10, in each of the following situations:

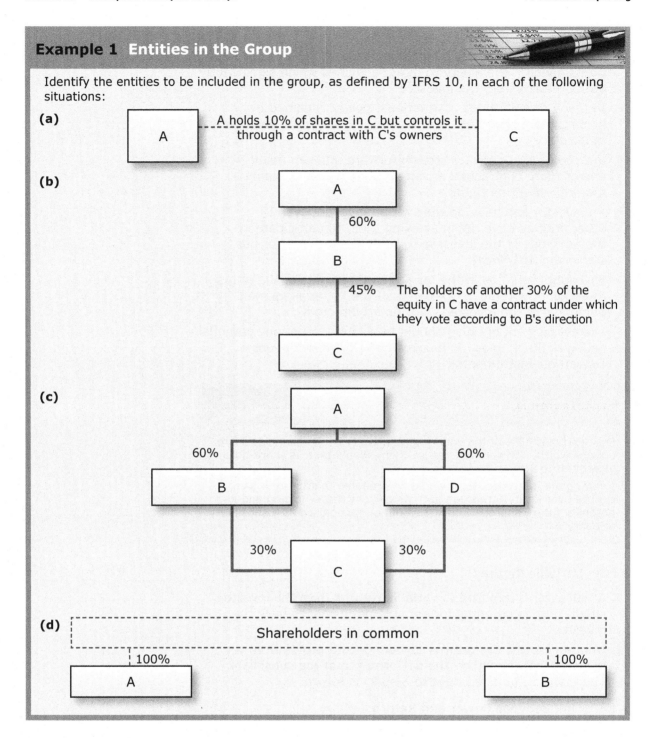

(a)

A

A holds 10% of shares in C but controls it through a contract with C's owners

C

(b)

A

60%

B

45% The holders of another 30% of the equity in C have a contract under which they vote according to B's direction

C

(c)

A

60% B

60% D

30% C 30%

(d)

Shareholders in common

100% A

100% B

2.2 Exclusions

Key Point

A subsidiary which has been acquired **exclusively** with the intention to resell it is not *consolidated* provided that it meets the IFRS 5 criteria of a disposal group *on acquisition*. In this case, it is carried at fair value less costs to sell and disclosed separately.

▨ Previously, and still in some countries, grounds for excluding individual subsidiaries from consolidation have included:

- long-term restrictions over the parent's rights to control a subsidiary;
- a subsidiary having sufficiently different activities from the parent;
- temporary control of a subsidiary;
- subsidiaries being immaterial (separately or in aggregate); and
- disproportionate expense or undue time and effort in obtaining information required.

▨ Clearly, management might want to exclude any subsidiary which reflects poorly on the economic performance and financial position of the group (e.g. a loss-making subsidiary). The IASB has gradually removed all exclusions.

▨ Under IFRS 10 there are *no exclusions* from consolidation of individual subsidiaries which meet the control criteria.

2.3 Exemption

2.3.1 Rule

▨ A parent need not present consolidated financial statements if:

- it is a wholly-owned or partially-owned subsidiary* *(non-controlling shareholders must give their consent)*;
- the parent's debt or equity instruments are not traded on a public market;
- the parent has not filed its financial statements with a recognised stock market;* or
- the ultimate (or intermediate) parent presents consolidated financial statements in accordance with IFRSs.

2.3.2 Rationale

▨ Users of the financial statements of a parent are usually concerned with, and need to be informed about, the financial position, results of operations and changes in financial position of the group as a whole.

▨ This need is served by consolidated financial statements, which present financial information about the group as that of a single entity without regard for the legal boundaries of the separate legal entities.

▨ A parent which is wholly owned by another entity may not always present consolidated financial statements because such statements may not be required by its parent, and the needs of other users may be best served by the consolidated financial statements of the ultimate parent.

2.4 Accounting for Subsidiaries in Separate Financial Statements

▨ When the IASB issued IFRS 10 it amended IAS 27 to deal only with accounting for subsidiaries in the parent's **separate financial statements**. At the same time the IASB issued IFRS 12 *Disclosure of Interests in Other Entities,* which moved disclosure requirements from IAS 27 into IFRS 12.

*"Partially owned" is usually taken to mean 90% in many countries.

*National rules may specify exemptions subject to conditions being met. For example, in the UK a parent which is subject to the "small companies regime" is not required to prepare consolidated financial statements.

IFRS 12 is not an examinable document in the F7 syllabus.

Definition

Separate financial statements—statements presented by a parent (or an investor with joint control of, or significant influence over, an investee) in which the investments are accounted for at cost or in accordance with IFRS 9 *Financial Instruments*.   IAS 27

Key Point

IAS 27 therefore requires that investments in subsidiaries, associates or joint ventures are carried either at cost or fair value (IFRS 9) in the separate financial statements.

▨ If the investment is carried at cost and subsequently the investment is classified as held for sale, then IFRS 5 *Non-current Assets Held for Sale* becomes the relevant standard. If the investment is carried at fair value and then subsequently classified as held for sale, it is still accounted for in accordance with IFRS 9.

Any dividends received from the investment will be included in profit or loss once the investor's right to receive the dividend is established.

2.5   Acquisition Method

Key Point

IFRS 3 requires that all business combinations be accounted for using the acquisition method of accounting.

▨ This involves:
- identifying an acquirer;
- determining the acquisition date;
- recognising and measuring the identifiable assets acquired, the liabilities assumed and any non-controlling interest in the acquiree; and
- recognising and measuring goodwill or a gain from a "bargain purchase".*

See Session 21.

3 Sundry Provisions of IFRS 10

3.1 Results of Intra-group Trading

 **Key Point**

Intra-group balances and intra-group transactions and resulting unrealised profits must be eliminated in full on the consolidation of the subsidiary.*

 ***Commentary***

*See *Session 20* for details.

3.2 Accounting Year Ends

3.2.1 Coterminous Year Ends

▨ The financial statements of the parent and its subsidiaries used in the preparation of the consolidated financial statements are usually drawn up to the same date.

3.2.2 Different Reporting Dates

▨ Either the *subsidiary* must prepare special statements as at the same date as the group;

▨ Or, if it is impracticable to do this, financial statements drawn up to different reporting dates may be used if:
  ◦ the difference is no greater than three months; and
  ◦ adjustments are made for the effects of significant transactions or other events which occur between those dates and the date of the parent's financial statements.

3.3 Accounting Policies

▨ Consolidated financial statements should be prepared using uniform accounting policies for similar transactions and events.

▨ If a member of the group uses different accounting policies in its individual financial statements—perhaps it is a foreign subsidiary using a different GAAP—then the results must be adjusted to reflect the group policy before incorporating the subsidiary's results into the group.

3.4 Date of Acquisition or Disposal

▨ The results of operations of a subsidiary are included in the consolidated financial statements as from the date the parent gains control of the subsidiary.

▨ The date of acquisition and the date of disposal are based on when control passes, not necessarily the legal date of acquisition or date of disposal.

▨ The results of operations of a subsidiary disposed of are included in the consolidated statement of profit or loss and other comprehensive income until the date of disposal, which is the date on which the parent ceases to have control of the subsidiary.

Summary

- In the financial statements of a single entity, investments are accounted for at cost or in accordance with IFRS 9.
- Consolidated financial statements should truthfully reflect the assets and liabilities under the control of the parent.
- Control exists if the parent has power and rights over the subsidiary.
- Control can be achieved through voting rights or control of the board of directors.
- A parent which is part of a larger group may be excluded from preparing consolidated financial statements.
- Consolidated financial statements are prepared using the acquisition method.
- Intra-group balances, transactions and unrealised profits are eliminated on consolidation.
- Accounting policies must be uniform across the group.

Session 19 Quiz
Estimated time: 15 minutes

1. Describe how an investment in a subsidiary may be accounted for in the parent's separate financial statements. (2.4)
2. Explain when control exists in accordance with IFRS. (2.1)
3. Identify the FOUR criteria that must be met that allow the parent not to present consolidated financial statements. (2.3)
4. Describe what must be done when including the subsidiary in the consolidated financial statements, if a subsidiary uses different accounting policies in its single entity accounts. (3.3)

Study Question Bank
Estimated time: 10 minutes

Priority		Estimated Time	Completed
Q34	Danny	10 minutes	
Additional			
Q35	Picant		

EXAMPLE SOLUTION

Solution 1—Entities in the Group

(a) Even though A only holds 10% of the equity in C, it is highly likely that C will be a subsidiary because A has contractual arrangements with the owners of C to control the entity.

(b) A is the parent of B. A is also the parent of C as it has control of 75% of the voting rights of C.

(c) A is the parent of B and D. A may, therefore, appear to control C through a 60% indirect shareholding, in which case A would be the parent. However, A effectively owns only a 36% interest in C. The substance of this relationship would therefore require scrutiny.

(d) There is no group in this situation, as A and B are "shareholders in common", which are scoped out of consolidated accounts.

Consolidated Statement of Financial Position

FOCUS

This session covers the following content from the *ACCA Study Guide*.

A. The Conceptual and Regulatory Framework for Financial Reporting

4. The concept and principles of groups and consolidated financial statements.

g) Explain why it is necessary to eliminate intra-group transactions. ☐

h) Explain the objective of consolidated financial statements. ☐

D. Preparation of Financial Statements

2. Preparation of consolidated financial statements

a) Prepare a consolidated statement of financial position for a simple group (parent and one subsidiary) dealing with pre- and post-acquisition profits, non-controlling interests and consolidated goodwill. ☐

d) Account for the effects in the financial statements of intra-group trading ☐

Session 20 Guidance

- ■ **Revise** the need for consolidated financial statements (s.1) and the calculation of goodwill on acquisition (s.1.4). This is assumed knowledge from F3 Financial Accounting.
- ■ **Work through** *Examples 1–3* to revise the basic approach to the preparation of a consolidated statement of financial position.
- ■ **Learn** the two methods of valuing non-controlling interest and how they affect the goodwill calculation (s.3.4).

(continued on next page)

VISUAL OVERVIEW

Objective: To explain the need for consolidated financial statements and to introduce basic principles of acquisition accounting.

```
┌─────────────────────────────────┐
│   CONCEPTUAL BACKGROUND          │
│                                  │
│   • The Issue                    │
│   • Rule                         │
│   • Substance                    │
└─────────────────────────────────┘
              │
┌─────────────────────────────────┐
│   OVERVIEW OF THE TECHNIQUE      │
│                                  │
│   • Individual Company Accounts  │
│   • Consolidation Adjustments    │
└─────────────────────────────────┘
              │
```

CONSOLIDATED STATEMENT OF FINANCIAL POSITION	**INTRA-GROUP ITEMS**
• Basic Principles	• Intra-group Balances
• Goodwill	• Unrealised Profit
• Post-Acquisition Growth in Reserves	• Inventory
• Non-controlling Interest	• Non-current Asset Transfers
	• Dividends

Session 20 Guidance

▪ **Revise** the effect that intra-group balances have on the preparation of the consolidated statement of financial position (s.4.1).

▪ **Attempt** *Example 7* to revise the accounting adjustment for unrealised profit (s.4.3). Note that you should be able to calculate this based on a profit margin ("on sales") or a mark-up ("on cost").

▪ **Work through** *Illustration 4* to understand the depreciation adjustment that arises on the transfer of a non-current asset (s.4.4).

1 Conceptual Background

1.1 The Issue

▨ Many companies carry on a part of their businesses through the ownership of other companies they control. Such companies are known as *subsidiaries.*

▨ Controlling interests in subsidiaries generally appear at cost in the statement of financial position of the investing company.

▨ Such interests may result in the control of assets of a very different value to the cost of investment.*

*The substance of a parent and subsidiary relationship is not reflected in the accounts.

 **Key Point**

Separate financial statements cannot provide the shareholders of the parent with a true and fair view of what their investment actually represents.

Illustration 1 Reflecting Substance

	Parent	Subsidiary
	$	$
Investment in 80% of Subsidiary*	100	
Other net assets (i.e. assets less liabilities)	900	1,800
	1,000	1,800

*The non-controlling interest (see s.3.4 for definition) is 20%.

■ The investment of $100 in Parent's accounts is, in substance, the cost of owning assets of 80% of $1,800 in Subsidiary (i.e. $1,440).

■ Parent's shareholders cannot see this from looking at the accounts.
 ● The solution is to prepare accounts for the group to reflect the substance of the investment.
 ● The type of group accounts required by IFRS is called **consolidated financial statements.**

1.2 Rule

 **Key Point**

A company with a subsidiary on the last day of its reporting period (i.e. a parent) must prepare consolidated financial statements *in addition* to its own individual accounts.

■ In practice, a parent will usually prepare (and publish):

   ● its own statement of financial position with relevant notes; and

   ● consolidated versions of its statement of financial position, statement of profit or loss and other comprehensive income and statement of cash flows, all with relevant notes.

1.3 Substance

■ Consolidation involves the replacement of cost of investment in the parent's accounts by "what it actually represents", namely:

   ● The net assets of the subsidiary at the end of the reporting period;
     AND

   ● the carrying amount of goodwill which the parent paid for at the date of acquisition.

■ This amount is then adjusted for the net assets that are not owned by the parent (i.e. the non-controlling interest).

■ In addition, the consolidated reserves must be credited with the parent's share of the subsidiary's post-acquisition reserves representing the portion of profit or loss accruing to parent since acquisition).*

*The remainder of this session will build up to an understanding of this.

2   Overview of the Technique

■ The approach may be broadly represented as follows:

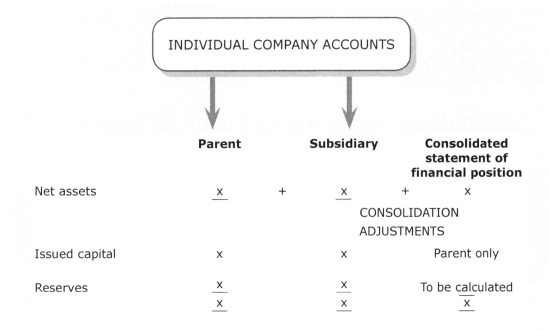

INDIVIDUAL COMPANY ACCOUNTS

	Parent		Subsidiary		Consolidated statement of financial position
Net assets	x	+	x	+	x
			CONSOLIDATION ADJUSTMENTS		
Issued capital	x		x		Parent only
Reserves	x		x		To be calculated
	x		x		x

2.1   Individual Company Accounts

▨ There is no such thing as a separate set of consolidated accounts; the group does not maintain a double-entry accounting system.

▨ The individual members of the group maintain their own financial statements and at the period end, after year-end adjustments, the individual accounts of the members of the group are merged to form the basis of the consolidated financial statements.

▨ It is important that the financial statements of the individual companies are finalised in accordance with IFRS before the consolidation adjustments are made.

2.2   Consolidation Adjustments

TWO TYPES

MAJOR ADJUSTMENTS

Those which "drive" the double entry:

- Goodwill
- Fair value*
- Non-controlling interests
- Consolidated reserves

INTRA-GROUP ADJUSTMENTS

- Intra-group balances
- Unrealised profit
- Inventory
- Non-current asset transfers
- Non-controlling interest

*Commentary

*Fair value adjustments are explained in Session 21.

3   Consolidated Statement of Financial Position

3.1   Basic Principles

▨ This section builds to an understanding of consolidation through a series of examples which will increase in complexity. In each case, it is assumed that any individual company adjustments have already been made.

Example 1 Parent Owns 100%

As at 31 December 20X6	Parent	Subsidiary
Non-current assets:		
Tangibles	2,000	500
Investment in Subsidiary	1,000	
Net current assets	2,000	500
	5,000	1,000
Issued capital	500	1,000
Retained earnings	4,500	
	5,000	1,000

Further information:

Parent bought 100% of Subsidiary on 31 December 20X6.

Features to note:

1. The issued capital of the group is the issued capital of Parent. This is always the case.

2. The cost of investment is to disappear. It is "replaced".

3. The assets and liabilities of the group are simply a line-by-line cross cast of those of Parent and Subsidiary. Parent controls 100% of Subsidiary's net assets. This is always the case.

Required:

Prepare the consolidated statement of financial position

Solution

Consolidated statement of financial position

$

Non-current assets:

Tangibles

Net current assets   _____

                                         _____

Issued capital

Retained earnings **(W3)**   _____

                                         _____

Workings

	Reporting date $	Acquisition $
(1) Subsidiary's net assets		
Issued capital		
Retained earnings	_____	_____
	_____	_____
(2) Goodwill		$
Cost		
Non-controlling interest		
Less: Net assets **(W1)**		_____
		_____
(3) Retained earnings		$
Parent (as given)		
Share of Subsidiary		_____
		_____

■ This is the simplest of examples.
- Parent owns 100% of Subsidiary (so there is no non-controlling interest).
- Consolidation is at the date of acquisition.
- Cost = 100% net assets (i.e. there is no goodwill).*

3.2 Goodwill

Definition

Goodwill—an asset representing the future economic benefits arising from other assets acquired in a business combination which are not individually identified and separately recognised.

■ **Goodwill** is the difference between the value of the business taken as a whole and the fair value of its separate net assets.*
■ It can be calculated as:

Fair value of consideration*	x
Value of non-controlling interest	x
Less: Fair value of net assets at acquisition	(x)
Goodwill at acquisition	x

*Commentary

*The fair value of consideration is the cost of the investment, shown in the financial statements of the parent as "Investment in subsidiary". Goodwill is covered in greater depth in later sessions, but for the time being it is sufficient to consider the relationship here.

*Commentary

*Moving on from *Example 1*, the session will now proceed to relax these simplifications to build towards a realistic example.

*Commentary

*When one company buys an interest in another it will pay a price which reflects both the net assets it buys and the goodwill.

Illustration 2 Goodwill

	Parent's own accounts	Consolidated accounts
	Cost	**Net assets + goodwill**
At the date of acquisition	1,000	800 + 200
		The accounts will continue to balance after the consolidation. *Cost 1,000 has been replaced with 800 + 200*
At the reporting date	1,000	1,200 + 200
		Now the accounts will not balance; *1,000 has been replaced with 1,200 + 200 = 1,400*

The 400 increase in the subsidiary's net assets is attributable to profitable trading since the acquisition. This must be reflected in the consolidated reserves for the consolidated statement of financial position to balance.

Example 2 Acquisition With Goodwill

At 31 December 20X6

	Parent	Subsidiary
	$	$
Non-current assets		
Tangibles	1,000	800
Investment in Subsidiary	1,200	
Net current assets	400	200
	2,600	1,000
Issued capital	100	900
Retained earnings	2,500	100
	2,600	1,000

Further information:

1. Parent bought 100% of Subsidiary on 31 December 20X6.

2. Subsidiary's reserves are $100 at the date of acquisition.

Features to note:

1. to 3. As before.

4. Part of the cost is goodwill. This must be separately identified as a debit (in this case) to help replace the cost of investment.

5. Parent's share of the post-acquisition profits of Subsidiary is included in the consolidated retained earnings. In this case it is zero.

Required:

Prepare the consolidated statement of financial position.

3.3   Post-Acquisition Growth in Reserves

▨ In the period after acquisition (post-acquisition), the subsidiary will either make profits or losses.

▨ The group will include its share of those post-acquisition profits or losses in the consolidated retained earnings.

▨ It is, therefore, necessary for the parent to identify the profits or losses of the subsidiary in the post–acquisition period. This can be achieved using the net assets schedule.

Example 3 Post-Acquisition Profits

At 31 December 20X6	Parent	Subsidiary
	$	$
Non-current assets		
Tangible assets	1,400	1,000
Investment in Subsidiary	1,200	
Net current assets	700	600
	3,300	1,600
Issued capital	100	900
Retained earnings	3,200	700
	3,300	1,600

Further information:

1. Parent bought 100% of Subsidiary two years ago.
2. Subsidiary's reserves were $100 at the date of acquisition.
3. Goodwill has been impaired by $80 since the date of acquisition.

Features to note:

1. to 3. As before.

4. As before, part of the cost is goodwill. This must be separately identified as an asset to help replace the cost of investment.

5. Parent's share of the post-acquisition profits of Subsidiary is included in the consolidated retained earnings.

Required:

Prepare the consolidated statement of financial position.

3.4   Non-controlling Interest

▦ Non-controlling interest represents the proportion of the subsidiary's net assets which are not owned by the parent.

Key Point

Non-controlling interest is valued at the date of acquisition:

1. At the proportionate share of the subsidiary's identifiable net assets (see *Example 4*); OR
2. At fair value (see *Example 5*).

▦ Valuing non-controlling interest at the proportionate share of the subsidiary's identifiable net assets means that it is *not* credited with any goodwill; valuing at fair value on acquisition means non-controlling interest is credited with its share of goodwill.

▦ The amount of goodwill credited to non-controlling interest is not necessarily in the same proportion as the shareholding (ownership).

▦ The increase in value of non-controlling interest will be debited to the value of goodwill.

Example 4 Proportionate Share

	Parent $	Subsidiary $
Non-current assets		
Tangible assets	1,000	600
Investment in Subsidiary	1,200	
Net current assets	500	600
	2,700	1,200
Issued capital	100	50
Retained earnings	2,600	1,150
	2,700	1,200

Further information:

1. Parent bought 80% of Subsidiary two years ago.
2. Subsidiary's reserves are $150 at the date of acquisition.
3. Goodwill has been impaired by $200 since the date of acquisition
4. Non-controlling interest is valued at the proportionate share of the subsidiary's identifiable net assets; it is not credited with its share of goodwill.

Features to note:

1. and 2. As before.

3. As before, the assets and liabilities of the group are simply a cross cast of those of Parent and Subsidiary. Parent's share of Subsidiary's net assets is 100% on a line-by-line basis.

   That part which does not belong to the parent is called "non-controlling interest". It is shown as a credit balance, within equity, in the statement of financial position. This example values non-controlling interest without including any value for goodwill.

4. As before, only this time goodwill is impaired by $200.

5. As before, Parent's share of the post-acquisition profits of Subsidiary is included in the consolidated retained earnings.

Required:

Prepare the consolidated statement of financial position.

Example 5 Fair Value

	Parent $	Subsidiary $
Non-current assets		
Tangible assets	1,000	600
Investment in Subsidiary	1,200	—
Net current assets	500	600
	2,700	1,200
Issued capital (NV $1)	100	50
Retained earnings	2,600	1,150
	2,700	1,200

Further information:

1. Parent bought 80% of Subsidiary two years ago.
2. Subsidiary's reserves are $150 at the date of acquisition.
3. Goodwill has been impaired by $200 since the date of acquisition.
4. Non-controlling interest is valued at fair value on acquisition; it is credited with its share of goodwill. The market price of a share in the subsidiary at the date of acquisition was $29.60.

Features to note:

1. and 2. As before.

3. As before, the assets and liabilities of the group are simply a cross cast of those of Parent and Subsidiary. Parent's share of Subsidiary's net assets is 100% on a line-by-line basis.

That part which does not belong to the parent is called "non-controlling interest". It is shown as a credit balance, within equity, in the statement of financial position. This example measures non-controlling interest at fair value and so includes its share of goodwill. Fair value, in this example, is calculated by using the market price of the subsidiary's share and applying it to the number of shares owned by non-controlling interest.

4. As before, only this time goodwill is impaired by $200. The impairment of goodwill is shared between the parent and non-controlling interest in the proportion of their shareholdings, which is 80%: 20% in this example.

5. Under this method, non-controlling interest is valued based on the fair value on acquisition, plus its share of any post-acquisition profits less its share of goodwill written off.

6. As before, Parent's share of the post-acquisition profits of Subsidiary is included in the consolidated retained earnings.

Required:

Prepare the consolidated statement of financial position.

 Exam Advice

- The full fair value method (*Example 5*) will be the default calculation for questions requiring the preparation of a consolidated statement of financial position.
- The proportionate method (*Example 4*) will only be examined as a comparison to the full fair value method.

4   Intra-group Items

4.1   Intra-group Balances

- Consolidation represents the position and performance of a group of companies as if they were a single entity.

- If the members of the group trade with each other (as is likely), a receivable in one set of accounts will be balanced out by a payable in another.

- Intra-group balances are typically recorded in ledger accounts described as "current accounts" and included in receivables/payables in each individual company's statement of financial position. For the individual entity, it is correct that the balances represent amounts which will be received by/paid to the separate entities.

 **Key Point**

When statements of financial position are consolidated, intra-group balances must be eliminated.

Illustration 3   Intra-group Balances

Parent owns 80% of Subsidiary. Parent sells goods to Subsidiary. At the year end the accounts of the two entities include the following balances:

	Parent	Subsidiary
Receivables		
Amount receivable from Subsidiary	1,000	
Payables		
Amount payable to Parent		1,000

Usually, the assets and the liabilities of the group are a straightforward summation of the individual items in the accounts of the parent and its subsidiaries. If these include intra-group balances, the financial statements of the group would show owed from and to itself. This would clearly be misleading.

To avoid this, the intra-group amounts are cancelled on consolidation.

	Parent	Subsidiary	Consolidation adjustment _Dr_	Consolidated Statement of financial position _Cr_
Receivables				
Amount receivable from Subsidiary	1,000			1,000
Payables				
Amount payable to Parent		1,000	1,000	

- All intra-group amounts in the statement of financial position (receivables and payables) and the statement of profit or loss and other comprehensive income (income and expenses) are cancelled on consolidation. The direction of the sale (Parent to Subsidiary or Subsidiary to Parent) is irrelevant.

- At the end of the reporting period, intra-group trading may result in a group company owning inventory which it purchased from another group company. This is a separate issue.

4.2 Unrealised Profit

4.2.1 Intra-group Trading

- The main reason for intra-group balances arising is intra-group trading.
- If a member of a group sells inventory, at a profit, to another member of the group and that inventory is still held by the buying company at the year end, the company which made:*
  - the seller will show profit in its own accounts; and
  - the purchaser will record the inventory at cost to itself.

*Both of these points are correct from the individual company view. With respect to the sale, however, this profit will not have been realised from the group's perspective and with respect to the purchase, consolidation of this value will result in the inclusion in the financial statements of a figure which is not at cost to the group.

4.2.2 Elimination

"... resulting unrealised profits shall be eliminated in full."
—IFRS 10 *Consolidated Financial Statements*

- This implies that the unrealised profit is eliminated from the inventory value. However, the standard does not rule on the other side of the entry. There are two possibilities:
  1. The **entire** profit adjustment against the parent's shareholders.
  2. **Apportion** between parent's shareholders and non-controlling interest.
- The treatment for the examination is to charge the profits of the selling company with the unrealised profit.
  - If the parent sold the goods then make the adjustment in the retained earnings working and if the subsidary sold the goods then make the adjustment in the net asset schedule working.
  - When it comes to the profit statement then the unrealised profit is added to the costs of the selling company.

4.3 Inventory

4.3.1 Inventory Sold at a Profit Between Group Companies

■ Inventories in the statement of financial position are valued at lower of cost and net realisable value. In the consolidated statement of financial position, where the group is reflected as a single entity, inventories must be at lower of cost and net realisable value to *the group*.

■ Applying the single entity concept, the group has bought and is holding inventory.

Key Point

The group needs to eliminate profit made by the selling company if inventory is still held by the group at the year end, as the group has not yet realised this profit.

4.3.2 Inventory Adjustment

■ Adjustments from *seller* perspective:

 ● Inventory in the statement of financial position.

 ● Closing inventory in the statement of profit or loss/retained earnings of the selling company.

■ In the consolidated financial statements adjust inventory to reflect cost to the *group* by eliminating any profit that has not yet been realised to the group.

 ● Reduce (credit) inventory in the consolidated statement of financial position.*

 ● In the statement of profit or loss reduce the closing inventory of the selling company, thereby increasing its cost of sales.

*Commentary

*As each entity's inventory amounts are totalled, it does not matter which amount is reduced.

Example 6 Unrealised Profit I

Parent owns 80% of Subsidiary. During the current accounting period, Parent transferred goods to Subsidiary for $4,000, which gave Parent a profit of $1,000. These goods were included in the inventory of Subsidiary at the end of the reporting period.

Required:

Calculate the adjustment in the consolidated statement of financial position.

Solution

Dr   Retained earnings

   Cr   Inventory

Example 7 Unrealised Profit II

Parent owns 80% of Subsidiary. During the current accounting period, Subsidiary sold goods to Parent for $18,000, which gave Subsidiary a profit of $6,000. At the end of the reporting period, half of these goods are included in Parent's inventory.

At the end of the reporting period, Parent's accounts showed retained profits of $100,000, and Subsidiary's accounts showed net assets of $75,000, including retained profits of $65,000. Subsidiary had retained profits of $20,000 at acquisition.

Ignore goodwill

Required:

Show the adjustment to eliminate unrealised profits in the consolidation workings for Parent.

Solution

  Dr   Retained earnings

      Cr   Inventory

(1) Subsidiary net assets

	Reporting date $	Acquisition $
Issued capital		
Retained earnings		
As given	_____	
Unrealised profit	_____	_____	_____
	_____	_____

(2) Non-controlling interests

Share of net assets

(3) Retained earnings

                                                               $

Parent (as given)

Share of Subsidiary

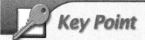

Key Point

- If the subsidiary has sold the goods, the adjustment is made in the *subsidiary's net asset* schedule working.
- If the parent has sold the goods, the adjustment is made in the consolidated retained earnings working.
- The examiner requires that the adjustment be made against the *selling company*.

4.4   Non-current Asset Transfers

- In some situations the asset being acquired may be treated as a non-current asset by the purchasing company; it is for use in the entity rather than being sold onwards.*

In accordance with the single entity concept, the consolidated financial statements should reflect the non-current assets at the amount at which they would have been stated had the transfer not been made.

- On an intra-group transfer, a profit/loss may have been recognised by the selling company. This must be removed on consolidation.
- The buying company will include the asset at cost (which is different from cost to the group) and will depreciate the asset. The expense for the year will be different from what it would have been had no transfer occurred.
- Summary of adjustments needed:
  - eliminate profit; and
  - adjust the depreciation charge.*
- Again, the adjustments may be carried out in the consolidated accounts *or* as individual company adjustments. Note that if they are processed as individual company adjustments:
  - the unrealised profit will be in the accounts of the *selling* company; and
  - the depreciation adjustment will be in the accounts of the buying company.
- *Approach*—Construct a working which shows the figures in the accounts ("with transfer") and shows what would have been in the accounts if no transfer had been made ("without transfer").

*Commentary

*It may be that one entity in the group manufactures computers and sells a computer to another group entity; that entity then uses the computer for administration purposes.

*Commentary

*Once made, the two adjustments will re-establish cost to the group.

Illustration 4 Intra-group Asset Transfer

Parent owns 80% of Subsidiary. Parent transferred an asset to Subsidiary at a value of $15,000 on 1 January 20X6. The original cost to Parent was $20,000 and the accumulated depreciation at the date of transfer was $8,000. The asset had a useful life of five years when originally acquired, with a residual value of zero. The useful life at the date of transfer remains at three years. Full allowance is made for depreciation in the year of purchase and none in the year of sale.

Required:

Calculate the adjustments for the consolidated financial statements at 31 December 20X6.

Solution

		Amounts in the accounts	Amounts if no transfer had occurred	Adjustment
		$	$	$
Cost		15,000	20,000	
Accumulated depreciation (15,000/3 years)		(5,000)	*(12,000)	
		10,000	8,000	2,000
Charge for the year		5,000	4,000	1,000
Profit on disposal				
Proceeds	15,000			
NBV (20 – 8)	(12,000)			
		3,000	–	3,000
Dr "P" profit or loss – profit on disposal			3,000	
Cr Non-current assets				3,000
and				
Dr Non-current assets			1,000	
Cr "S" Profit or loss – depreciation				1,000

*Accumulated depreciation of $12,000 is calculated as 3 years @ 20% per annum based on the original cost of $20,000.

Analysis

By crediting S profit or loss with the depreciation adjustment the $1,000 will be shared between P and the non-controlling interest (in this case, 80% and 20%).

If S had sold the asset to P, the unrealised profit would be adjusted against the profit or loss of S. Thus P and the non-controlling interest would share (80%:20%) the unrealised profit. The depreciation adjustment would be made against the profits of P.

4.5   Dividends

▨ An exam question may present *draft* statements of financial position of group companies and a note that dividends have been declared before the year end but have not yet been recognised in the financial statements.

▨ The final statements of financial position of individual companies need to be consolidated *after* closing adjustments.

 **Key Point**

Process adjustments to finalise the individual statement of financial position before consolidating.

▨ In the books of the company declaring the dividend:

Dr Equity (in statement of changes in equity)   X

    Cr   Current liabilities (dividends payable)   X

▨ If the subsidiary is declaring the dividend, the parent will receive its share. This dividend now represents reserves-in-transit. The parent *must* record its share of the dividend receivable:

Dr   Dividend receivable   X

    Cr   Profit or loss   X

▨ The dividend receivable and liability are intra-group balances and must be cancelled.

▨ Consolidated statement of financial position will reflect in liabilities:

 • the parent's dividends payable; and
 • the non-controlling interest's share of the subsidiary's dividends payable.

Summary

- The cost of an investment in a subsidiary does not reflect the true substance of the transaction.
- Consolidation replaces the equity of the subsidiary with the cost of the investment, creating goodwill as a balancing amount.
- 100% of the net assets of the subsidiary are added to the net assets of the parent.
- Any holding of less than 100% is reflected in the calculation of non-controlling interest. This can be valued at either:
  - a proportion of the fair value of the identifiable net assets; or
  - fair value.
- The difference between these two valuations affects the amount of goodwill identified.
- Post-acquisition profits of the subsidiary are shared between the parent and non-controlling interest.
- Goodwill is tested annually for impairment and any loss allocated to retained earnings and non-controlling interest (depending on the valuation method used).
- All intra-group balances are eliminated on consolidation.
- Unrealised profit is deducted from the profits of the selling company and inventory.
- If goods are treated as a non-current asset by the buyer, then there will also be an adjustment to the consolidated depreciation charge in the buyer's books.
- If goods are treated as a non-current asset by the buyer, then reflect the original cost to the group of the asset after allowing for depreciation adjustment.

Session 20 Quiz
Estimated time: 10 minutes

1. Identify what replaces the cost of investment in a subsidiary in the consolidated financial statements. (1.3)

2. State what must be done annually in respect of goodwill. (3.2)

3. State what non-controlling interest represents. (3.4)

4. Identify which valuation models are allowed for non-controlling interest. (3.4)

5. State how any intra-group balances should be dealt with on consolidation. (4.1)

6. Identify when profit made on the sale of goods between members of a group must be cancelled. (4.2)

7. Give the additional adjustment required if the asset transferred is a non-current asset. (4.4)

Study Question Bank
Estimated time: one hour, 5 minutes

Priority		Estimated Time	Completed
Q36	Consolidations	40 minutes	
Q38	Hammer	25 minutes	
Additional			
Q37	Haggis		

EXAMPLE SOLUTIONS

Solution 1—Parent Owns 100%

Consolidated statement of financial position

	$	
Non-current assets:		
Tangibles (2,000 + 500)	2,500	
		← Cost of investment has disappeared
Net current assets (2,000 + 500)	2,500	
	5,000	
Issued capital	500	← Issued capital of Parent
Retained earnings **(W3)**	4,500	
	5,000	

Workings

(1) Subsidiary's net assets	Reporting date	Acquisition
	$	$
Issued capital	1,000	1,000
Retained earnings	0	0
	1,000	1,000

(2) Goodwill	
	$
Cost	1,000
Non-controlling interest	–
Less: Net assets acquired **(W1)**	(1,000)
	–

(3) Retained earnings	
	$
Parent (as given)	4,500
Share of Subsidiary	–
	4,500

Solution 2—Acquisition With Goodwill

Consolidated statement of financial position

	$
Non-current assets:	
Goodwill **(W2)**	200
Tangibles	1,800
Net current assets	600
	2,600
Issued capital	100
Retained earnings **(W3)**	2,500
	2,600

Workings

(1) Subsidiary's net assets	Reporting date	Acquisition
	$	$
Issued capital	900	900
Retained earnings	100	100
	1,000	1,000

(2) Goodwill	$
Cost	1,200
Non-controlling interest	–
Less: Net assets acquired **(W1)**	(1,000)
	200

(3) Retained earnings	$
Parent (as given)	2,500
Share of Subsidiary **(W1)**	–
100% × (100 − 100)	2,500

Solution 3—Post-Acquisition Profits

Consolidated statement of financial position

	$
Non-current assets:	
Goodwill **(W2)**	120
Tangibles	2,400
Net current assets	1,300
	3,820
Issued capital	100
Retained earnings **(W3)**	3,720
	3,820

Workings

(1) Subsidiary's net assets

	Reporting date	Acquisition
	$	$
Issued capital	900	900
Retained earnings	700	100
	1,600	1,000

(2) Goodwill

	$	$
Cost		1,200
Non-controlling interest		—
Less: Net assets (100% × 1,000)		(1,000)
		200
Impaired	80	
As an asset	120	

(3) Retained earnings

	$
Parent (as given)	3,200
Share of Subsidiary **(W1)** 100% (700 – 100)	600
Goodwill written off **(W2)**	(80)
	3,720

Solution 4—Proportionate Share

Consolidated statement of financial position

	$
Non-current assets:	
Goodwill **(W2)**	840
Tangibles	1,600
Net current assets	1,100
	3,540
Issued capital	100
Retained earnings **(W4)**	3,200
Non-controlling interest **(W3)**	240
	3,540

Workings

(1) Subsidiary's net assets	Reporting date	Acquisition
	$	$
Issued capital	50	50
Retained earnings	1,150	150
	1,200	200

(2) Goodwill	
	$
Cost	1,200
Share of net assets (80% × 200)	(160)
	1,040
To retained earnings (impaired)	200
Asset recognised	840

(3) Non-controlling interests	$
Share of net assets (20 × 1,200 **(W1)**)	240

(4) Retained earnings	$
Parent (as given)	2,600
Share of Subsidiary 80% × (1,150 − 150) **(W1)**	800
Goodwill impairment	(200)
	3,200

Notes:

- Parent now owns only 80% of Subsidiary's shares.
- It must consolidate 80% of 1,200 (i.e. 960).
- This is achieved in two stages: 100% of Subsidiary's net assets are consolidated on a line-by-line basis (as before) and a credit balance representing that part of Subsidiary's net assets not owned is put into the accounts.
- Thus the balances included in the consolidated financial statements are:

  Assets and liabilities   1,200
  (600 in non-current assets/600 in net current assets.)
  Equity section of statement of financial position
  Non-controlling interest
  (20% × 1,200)   240
  Overall effect   960

Solution 5—Fair Value

Consolidated statement of financial position

	$
Non-current assets:	
Goodwill **(W2)**	1,096
Tangibles	1,600
Net current assets	1,100
	3,796
Issued capital	100
Retained earnings **(W4)**	3,240
Non-controlling interest **(W3)**	456
	3,796

Workings

(1) Subsidiary's net assets

	Reporting date	Acquisition
	$	$
Issued capital	50	50
Retained earnings	1,150	150
	1,200	200

(2) Goodwill

		$
Cost		1,200
Fair value of non-controlling interest (10 × $29.60)		296
Less: Net assets on acquisition (100%)		(200)
		1,296
Impaired*	200	
Goodwill recognised	1,096	

(3) Non-controlling interests

	$
Fair value on acquisition **(W2)**	296
Share of post-acquisition profits (1,000 × 20%)	200
Less: Share of goodwill impaired (200 × 20%)	(40)
	456

(4) Retained earnings

	$
Parent (as given)	2,600
Share of Subsidiary (80% × (1,150 – 150)) **(W1)**	800
Goodwill impairment (200 × 80%)	(160)
	3,240

Commentary

*Of the goodwill impaired, 80% is charged to consolidated retained earnings and 20% is debited to non-controlling interest.

Solution 6—Unrealised Profit I

Dr		Retained earnings	$1,000	
	Cr	Inventory		$1,000

Solution 7—Unrealised Profit II

Dr		Retained earnings ($\frac{1}{2} \times 6{,}000$)	$3,000	
	Cr	Inventory		$3,000

Workings

(1) Subsidiary net assets

			Reporting date $	Acquisition $
Issued capital			10,000	10,000
Retained earnings				
	As given	65,000		20,000
	Unrealised profit	(3,000)	62,000	_____
			72,000	30,000

(2) Non-controlling interests

Share of net assets (including the unrealised profit)	
(20% × 72,000)	14,400

(3) Retained earnings

	$
Parent (as given)	100,000
Share of Subsidiary (including the unrealised profit)	
80% × (62,000 − 20,000)	33,600
	133,600

Consolidation Adjustments

FOCUS

This session covers the following content from the *ACCA Study Guide.*

A. The Conceptual and Regulatory Framework for Financial Reporting

4. The concepts and principles of groups and consolidated financial statements

i) Explain why it is necessary to use fair values for the consideration for an investment in a subsidiary together with the fair values of a subsidiary's identifiable assets and liabilities when preparing consolidated financial statements. ☐

B. Accounting for Transactions in Financial Statements

2. Intangible non-current assets

e) Indicate why the value of purchase consideration for an investment may be less than the value of the acquired identifiable net assets and how the difference should be accounted for. ☐

D. Preparation of Financial Statements

2. Preparation of consolidated financial statements

c) Explain and account for other reserves (e.g. share premium and revaluation reserves). ☐

e) Account for the effects of fair value adjustments (including their effect on consolidated goodwill) to: ☐

    i) depreciating and non-depreciating non-current assets

    ii) inventory

    iii) monetary liabilities

    iv) assets and liabilities not included in the subsidiary's own statement of financial position, including contingent assets and liabilities

f) Account for goodwill impairment. ☐

g) Describe and apply the required accounting treatment of consolidated goodwill. ☐

VISUAL OVERVIEW

Objective: To explain the accounting adjustments which must be made before consolidation can proceed.

```
                              ┌─────────────────┐
                              │   ADJUSTMENTS   │
                              └─────────────────┘
                    ┌──────────────────┴──────────────────┐
```

ACCOUNTING POLICIES
- Group Policy
- Investment Property

GOODWILL ON ACQUISITION
- Valuation of Non-controlling Interest
- Cost of Acquisition
- Recognition
- Measurement
- Fair Values
- Bargain Purchase

FAIR VALUE ADJUSTMENTS
- Exam Question Complication
- How Is the Adjustment Accounted For?
- Subsidiary's Reserves

SUBSEQUENT ACCOUNTING
- Asset
- Initial Accounting
- Impairment

CONSOLIDATED WORKINGS

Session 21 Guidance

▦ **Pay attention,** this is the final session about the consolidated statement of financial position; it mainly considers the issues relating to the value of the consideration given and the value of the identifiable net assets acquired. It also looks in greater depth at the accounting for goodwill.

▦ **Attempt** to calculate the fair value of deferred consideration (*Illustration 2*) and a share exchange (s.3.2).

▦ **Be able** to recognise fair value adjustments that need to be made before consolidation (s.5). Attempt *Examples 1 and 2*.

▦ **Be able to formulate** accounting entries for fair value adjustments and goodwill (s.4, s.5).

▦ **Learn** the accounting treatment for "negative" goodwill that arise on a bargain purchase (s.3.6).

1 Adjustments

- Consolidation problems are usually tackled in two stages:

Stage 1 Process any individual company adjustments.

Stage 2 Do the consolidation (introduced in the previous session).*

*Commentary

*With the exception of one or two further complications which, for the most part, are outside the scope of the syllabus, that is all there is to the technique of consolidation.

2 Accounting Policy Adjustments

2.1 Group Policy

Key Point

IFRS 10 requires that the accounts of subsidiaries be drawn up according to the same accounting policies as the parent. If this is not the case, then the accounts of the subsidiary may have to be restated in line with the group policy.

- Such a requirement is rare in practice because a situation which required it would, by definition, be contrary to IFRS.
- It might be needed in the cases of:
  - mid-year acquisition—where the parent has not yet imposed its policies on the subsidiary; or
  - foreign subsidiaries following local GAAP.

2.2 Investment Property

- A property that is owned by a parent but occupied by a subsidiary, or vice versa, will be treated as investment property (under IAS 40) in the financial statements of the single entity but as property (under IAS 16) in the consolidated financial statements as the asset is owner-occupied from a group perspective.

3 Goodwill on Acquisition

3.1 Valuation of Non-controlling Interest

- The non-controlling interest's share of goodwill may be recognised as part of the acquisition process. The option to measure non-controlling interest is allowed on a transaction-by-transaction basis.*

*Commentary

*Non-controlling interest will either be measured at fair value, giving a larger goodwill valuation, or at the proportionate amount of the identifiable net assets, in which case goodwill only reflects the parent's shareholding.

Exam Advice

For exam purposes, it would be expected that the examiner will indicate at what value the non-controlling interest is to be measured, either directly or by the use of a simple valuation model. For example, market price per share times the number of shares attributable to the non-controlling interest.

Illustration 1 Goodwill Measurement

Parent acquires 80% of Subsidiary for $120,000. The fair value of the non-controlling interest's share in Subsidiary is $28,000, while the value of non-controlling interest based on the proportionate share of identifiable net assets acquired would give a value of $25,000. The fair value of the subsidiary's net assets on acquisition has been determined as $125,000.

Goodwill can be calculated as either:

	(a)	(b)
	$	$
Cost of investment	120,000	120,000
Non-controlling interests	28,000	25,000
	148,000	145,000
Fair value of net assets acquired	(125,000)	(125,000)
Goodwill*	23,000	20,000

If non-controlling interest is valued at fair value (a), then the value of goodwill and non-controlling interest will be higher to the extent of the non-controlling interest's share of the fair value of the subsidiary.

*Commentary

*The goodwill calculated in (a) means that goodwill attributable to non-controlling interest is $3,000. The proportion of goodwill attributable to non-controlling interest of 13% ($3/23$) is not necessarily going to be in the same proportion of shares held (20%). This is because the parent is likely to pay a premium for control.

▨ There are several issues to address:
- What is included in cost of acquisition?
- The meaning of the term "identifiability".
- Calculation of the fair value.
- Accounting for the fair valuation in the post-acquisition period.
- Accounting for the goodwill arising on consolidation.

3.2 Cost of Acquisition—Fair Value of Purchase Consideration

Key Point

An acquisition is accounted for at its cost. Cost is:
- the amount of cash or cash equivalents paid; or
- the fair value of the other purchase consideration given.

▨ Any costs directly associated with the acquisition of the subsidiary must be expensed to profit or loss as a period cost.*

*Commentary

*Previously these costs were included in the cost of acquisition, with the effect of increasing the amount of goodwill.

3.2.1 Deferred Consideration

▨ The cost of the acquisition is the present value of the consideration, taking into account any premium or discount likely to be incurred in settlement (and not the nominal value of the payable).

Key Point

If cash is to be paid sometime in the future, then the amount will need to be discounted to present value and that amount included as the fair value in the cost calculation.

▨ The increase in present value, through the passage of time, will be a finance cost charged to profit or loss.

Illustration 2 Deferred Consideration

Parent acquired 60% of Subsidiary on 1 January for $100,000 cash payable immediately and a further $121,000 after two years. The fair value of Subsidiary's net assets at acquisition amounted to $300,000. An appropriate discount rate is 10%.

Non-controlling interest is not credited with goodwill.

Required:

Calculate the goodwill arising on acquisition and show how the deferred consideration should be accounted for in Parent's consolidated financial statements.

Solution:

Cost of investment in Subsidiary at acquisition: $100,000 + $121,000/1.21 = $200,000

Goodwill	$000
Cost	200
Non-controlling interest (40% x 300,000)	120
Share of net assets acquired	(300)
	20

Deferred consideration

Double entry at 1 January:

Dr Cost of Investment in Subsidiary	$100,000	
Cr Deferred consideration		$100,000

On 31 December, due to unwinding of discount, the deferred consideration will equal $121,000/1.1 = 110,000

Dr Parent retained earnings	$10,000	
Cr Deferred consideration		$10,000

■ In the consolidated statement of financial position, the cost of investment in Subsidiary will be replaced by the goodwill of $20,000, and the deferred consideration will be $110,000.

3.2.2   Contingent Consideration

Key Point

When a business combination agreement provides for an adjustment to the cost, contingent on future events, the acquirer includes the acquisition date fair value of the contingent consideration in the calculation of the consideration paid.

Exam Advice

It is likely that the examiner will state the fair value of any contingent consideration.

- If the contingent settlement is to be in cash, then a liability will be recognised.
- If settlement is to be through the issue of further equity instrument the credit entry will be to equity.
- Any non-measurement period changes to the contingent consideration recognised will be accounted for in accordance with the relevant IFRS and will not affect the original calculation of goodwill.

3.2.3   Share Exchange

- It is quite common for a parent to acquire shares in the subsidiary by issuing its own shares to the previous shareholders in a share exchange.
- The cost of acquisition is determined multiplying the number of shares issued by the parent by the market price of the parent's shares at the date of acquisition.

Illustration 3   Share Exchange

Parent acquired 80% of Subsidiary's 100,000 shares in a three-for-five exchange. The market price of one share in P on acquisition was $4 and that of S was $2.20.

Cost of investment = 100,000 × 80% × $\frac{3}{5}$ × $4 = $192,000

The value of S's share is irrelevant.

*Commentary

*This may mean that some assets (especially intangible assets) will be recognised in the consolidated statement of financial position which were not recognised in the subsidiary's single-entity statement of financial position.

3.3   Recognition

3.3.1   Introduction

- The identifiable assets and liabilities acquired are recognised separately as at the date of acquisition (and therefore feature in the calculation of goodwill).*

▧ Any future costs which the acquirer expects to incur in respect of plans to restructure the subsidiary must not be recognised as a provision at the acquisition date. They will be treated as a post-acquisition cost.*

*Expected restructuring costs of an acquisition are not liabilities of the acquiree at the date of acquisition. Therefore, they are not relevant in allocating the cost of acquisition.

Historically, companies recognised large provisions on acquisition, and this had the effect of reducing net assets and thereby increasing goodwill. Goodwill was then charged against profits (through amortisation) over a much longer period than through immediate recognition as an expense. IFRS 3 and IAS 37 have virtually eliminated these so-called big bath provisions.

3.3.2 Contingent Liabilities of the Acquiree

▧ IAS 37 *Provisions, Contingent Liabilities and Contingent Assets* does not permit the recognition of contingent liabilities as liabilities in a statement of financial position.

▧ However, if a contingent liability of the subsidiary has arisen due to a present obligation which has not been recognised (because an outflow of economic benefits is not probable), IFRS 3 requires this present obligation to be recognised in the consolidated financial statements as long as its fair value can be measured reliably.

3.4 Measurement

All assets and liabilities of the subsidiary which are recognised in the consolidated statement of financial position are measured at their acquisition date fair values.

▧ This reflects the amount which would have been paid to acquire the individual assets and liabilities at the acquisition date and correctly identify the value of goodwill acquired.

▧ The non-controlling interest of the subsidiary is measured at either:
- fair value; or
- the non-controlling interest's proportionate share of the subsidiary's identifiable net assets.*

*The choice of measuring the non-controlling interest of the subsidiary can be made for each acquisition, so a parent does not have to be consistent in its measurement of non-controlling interests relating to separate acquisitions.

3.5   Fair Values

An entity should apply IFRS 13 *Fair Value Measurement* when measuring the net assets of the subsidiary on acquisition.

- The fair value must reflect the highest and best use for a non-financial asset even if the parent does not intend to use it in this manner. The parent may be planning to use the asset in a "defensive" manner, to stop competitors from using it. Market participants, though, would not be using it in this manner; they would use it in a manner which gives the best use from the asset and it is this value which should be applied to the asset.

3.6   Bargain Purchase

- If, on initial measurement, the fair value of the acquiree's net assets exceeds the cost of acquisition (excess), then the acquirer reassesses:
  - the value of net assets acquired;
  - that all relevant assets and liabilities have been identified; and
  - that the cost of the combination has been correctly measured.

If an excess still remains after the reassessment, then that excess is recognised immediately in profit or loss.

- This excess (gain) could have arisen as a result of:
  - future costs not being reflected in the acquisition process;
  - measurement of items not at fair value, if required by another standard, such as deferred tax being undiscounted; or
  - bargain purchase.*

*This bargain purchase used to be referred to as "negative goodwill"; the term is still commonly used.

4 Accounting for the Fair Value Adjustments

4.1 Exam Question Complication

- The fair value adjustment will not normally have been reflected in the financial statements of the subsidiary at the date of acquisition.
- If the subsidiary has not reflected fair values in its accounts, this must be done before consolidating.

Key Point

This is not a revaluation exercise under IAS 16 but a fair value exercise in accordance with IFRS 3.

- An increase from carrying amount to fair value of an asset will have the effect of reducing the value of goodwill as value has now been attached to an identifiable asset. A decrease from carrying amount will have the effect of increasing the amount of goodwill.
- At the acquisition date, identify the difference between fair value and carrying amount of the asset, or liability, and include this difference in the schedule of net assets.
- Next, consider the effect of this fair value difference in the post-acquisition period; if the fair value is greater than the carrying amount of a depreciating asset then this will require an adjustment to depreciation in the post-acquisition period.
- In summary, all assets and liabilities, be they monetary or non-monetary, should be valued at fair value on acquisition and any changes to that value in the post-acquisition period will be adjusted against retained earnings.

4.1.1 Depreciating Assets

- Allow for any additional (or reduced) depreciation based on the fair value difference and then show the reporting date figure as a balancing item.

Illustration 4 Depreciating Assets

On acquisition of a subsidiary, the carrying amount of its buildings was $25 million and their fair value $30 million. The buildings had a remaining useful life at the date of acquisition of 20 years. Two years have passed since the acquisition took place.

The fair value difference on the acquisition date is $5 million. The post-acquisition adjustment for depreciation is $500,000 ($5 million × $2/20$ years).

The fair value difference remaining at the reporting date is $4.5 million.

Extract from net assets' schedule:

	Reporting date	Acquisition date	Post-acquisition
Fair value difference	4.5	5	(0.5)

4.1.2 Non-depreciating Assets

▨ Because there will be no depreciation in the post-acquisition period, the fair value difference at the reporting date will be the same as at the acquisition date.

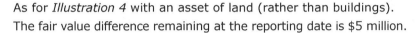

Illustration 5 Non-depreciating Assets

As for *Illustration 4* with an asset of land (rather than buildings). The fair value difference remaining at the reporting date is $5 million.

Extract from net assets' schedule:

	Reporting date	Acquisition date	Post-acquisition
Fair value difference	5	5	0

4.1.3 Inventory

▨ If the inventory has been sold, there will be no fair value difference remaining at the reporting date and so the post-acquisition amount will be the balancing figure.

▨ If the inventory has not been sold, then the fair value difference will be the same at the reporting date as it was on acquisition.

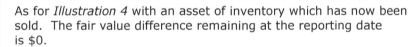

Illustration 6 Inventory

As for *Illustration 4* with an asset of inventory which has now been sold. The fair value difference remaining at the reporting date is $0.

Extract from net assets' schedule:

	Reporting date	Acquisition date	Post-acquisition
Fair value difference	0	5	(5)

4.1.4 Contingent Liabilities

▨ Again, any change in the fair value of the contingent liability between the reporting date and the acquisition date is a post-acquisition adjustment to net asset.

4.2 How Is the Adjustment Accounted For?

▨ IFRS 3 refers to this as "allocation of the cost of acquisition".*

Commentary

*The non-controlling interest shares both the fair value difference and any consequential depreciation adjustment.

Key Point

IFRS 3 requires the entire fair value difference to be reflected in the consolidated financial statements. The amount of non-controlling interest will reflect its share of the difference.

Example 1 Fair Valuation I

As at 31 December 20X6	Parent	Subsidiary
	$	$
Non-current assets:		
Tangibles	1,700	1,000
Cost of investment in Subsidiary	1,100	
Current assets	400	300
	3,200	1,300
Issued capital	100	100
Retained earnings	2,900	1,000
Current liabilities	200	200
	3,200	1,300

Further information:

Parent bought 80% of Subsidiary two years ago.

At the date of acquisition, Subsidiary's retained earnings stood at $600 and the fair value of its net assets were $1,000. The revaluation was due to an asset which had a remaining useful economic life of 10 years as at the date of acquisition.

Goodwill has been impaired by $40 since acquisition.

Non-controlling interest is valued at the proportionate share of the identifiable net assets; it is not credited with its share of goodwill.

Required:

Prepare the consolidated statement of financial position of Group as at 31 December 20X6.

Example 2 Fair Valuation II

Summary statements of financial position for parent and subsidiary are as for Example 1.

Further information:

Parent bought 80% of Subsidiary on 31 December 20X4.

At the date of acquisition, Subsidiary's retained earnings stood at $600 and the fair value of its net assets were $1,000. The revaluation was due to an asset which had a remaining useful economic life of 10 years as at the date of acquisition.

Goodwill has been impaired by $40 since acquisition.

Non-controlling interest are valued at fair value; the market price of a share in the subsidiary can be taken as a measure of fair value; the market price of subsidiary's shares on the date of acquisition was $13.

Required:

Calculate goodwill, non-controlling interest and consolidated retained earnings to be included in the consolidated statement of financial position of Group as at 31 December 20X6.

4.3 Post-acquisition Changes in Subsidiary's Reserves

▨ The parent's share of the subsidiary's post-acquisition retained earnings is included in the consolidated retained earnings.

Key Point

The consolidated revaluation reserve includes the parent's share of the subsidiary's post-acquisition change in revaluation. The non-controlling interest's share is included in non-controlling interest in the statement of financial position.

▨ In the unlikely event that there is a change in the subsidiary's share capital or share premium in the post-acquisition period, due to a bonus or rights issue, then simply reverse the issue to get back to the pre-issue position.

5 Subsequent Accounting for Goodwill

5.1 Asset

▨ Once calculated any positive goodwill is recognised as a consolidated asset; it is not an asset of the parent or subsidiary but an asset of the group.

▨ Subsequent to initial recognition, goodwill is carried at cost less any accumulated impairment losses.*

Key Point

Goodwill is tested annually for impairment; any loss is expensed to profit or loss.

*Commentary

*Refer back to the session on IAS 36 *Impairment of Assets* for the accounting entries. Prior to the issue of IFRS 3, goodwill was capitalised and amortised over its useful life.

5.2 Initial Accounting Determined Provisionally

5.2.1 Provisional Accounting

▨ If accurate figures cannot be assigned to elements of the business combination then provisional values are assigned to those elements at the date of acquisition.

▨ Any new information which becomes available, relating to acquisition date assets and liabilities, is retrospectively adjusted against the initial provisional amounts recognised as long as the information is known during the "measurement period".*

*Commentary

*These retrospective adjustments are an exception to the normal requirement of IAS 8 *Accounting Policies, Changes in Accounting Estimates and Errors*, which normally would require a prospective adjustment.

5.2.2 Measurement Period

▦ The measurement period is the period after the acquisition date during which the parent may adjust the provisional amounts recognised in respect of the acquisition of a subsidiary.

Key Point

The measurement period cannot exceed one year after the acquisition date.

5.2.3 Subsequent Adjustments

▦ Any other adjustments are treated in accordance with IAS 8 *Accounting Policies, Changes in Accounting Estimates and Errors:*

  ● an error in acquisition values is treated *retrospectively*; and

  ● a change in estimate is treated *prospectively*.

Illustration 7 Provisional Accounting

Parent acquires 80% of Subsidiary for $60,000. The subsidiary's net assets at date of acquisition were $62,500. At the end of the first year, goodwill has been impaired by $1,000.

In the year following acquisition, but within 12 months of the acquisition date, it was identified that the value of land was $2,500 greater than that recognised on acquisition. The value of goodwill at the end of year 2 was valued at $7,400.

Year 1:

Cost of investment	60,000
Net assets on acquisition (62,500 × 80%)	50,000
Goodwill	10,000
Goodwill charge to profit or loss	1,000

Year 2:

Cost of investment	60,000
Net assets on acquisition (65,000 × 80%)	52,000
Goodwill on acquisition	8,000
Goodwill at year end	7,400
Goodwill charge to profit or loss	600

Journal

Dr	Land	2,500	
Dr	Profit or loss (goodwill)	600	
Cr	Goodwill (9,000 – 7,400)		1,600
Cr	Non-controlling interest (2,500 × 20%)		500
Cr	Opening retained earnings		1,000
	(adjustment for prior year expense)		

5.3   Impairment of Goodwill

5.3.1   Allocation to Cash-Generating Unit

▨ Goodwill on acquisition must be allocated to a cash-generating unit (CGU) which benefits from the acquisition. A CGU need not necessarily be a unit of the subsidiary acquired; it could be a unit of the parent or another subsidiary in the group.

▨ The assessment of goodwill impairment in a partially-owned subsidiary depends on the valuation of non-controlling interest.

5.3.2   Non-controlling Interest Valued at Proportionate Share of Identifiable Net Assets

▨ Any impairment will firstly be allocated against this grossed-up goodwill figure.

▨ Any impairment in excess of this grossed-up goodwill will then be allocated against the remaining assets of the CGU on a pro rata basis.

Key Point

Goodwill for each CGU must be tested annually for impairment. The test must be carried out at the same time each year, but not necessarily at the year end.

Key Point

Any goodwill in a partially-owned subsidiary must be grossed up to include the non-controlling interest share of goodwill for the purposes of the impairment test.

Illustration 8 Goodwill Impairment

Parent acquires 75% of Subsidiary. The carrying amount of the subsidiary's net assets on 30 June was $1,800; this included $300 of goodwill. The recoverable amount of the subsidiary on the same day was $1,640.

Impairment:

Goodwill grossed up (300 × 100 ÷ 75)	400
Other net assets	1,500
	1,900
Recoverable amount	1,640
Impairment	260

Of this amount, 75% (195) will be allocated against the goodwill recognised in the consolidated financial statements, leaving goodwill included in the consolidated statement of financial position of $105. The carrying amount of the subsidiary's net assets, including goodwill, will now be $1,605.

5.3.3   Non-controlling Interest Valued at Fair Value

▨ There will be no need to gross up goodwill for the impairment test as the non-controlling interest in goodwill has already been recognised and included in the total goodwill figure.

▨ Any impairment of goodwill is shared among the owners of the subsidiary in the same proportion in which the profits of the subsidiary are shared.*

---

*Commentary

*An 80% owned subsidiary will reflect 80% of the impairment loss against consolidated retained earnings and 20% against non-controlling interest.

6   Consolidated Workings

1. Establish group structure   **W1**

2. Process individual company adjustments

- do the double entry on the question paper (as far as possible)

3. Net assets summary   **W2**

- one for each subsidiary
- aim is to show the net assets position at two points in time.

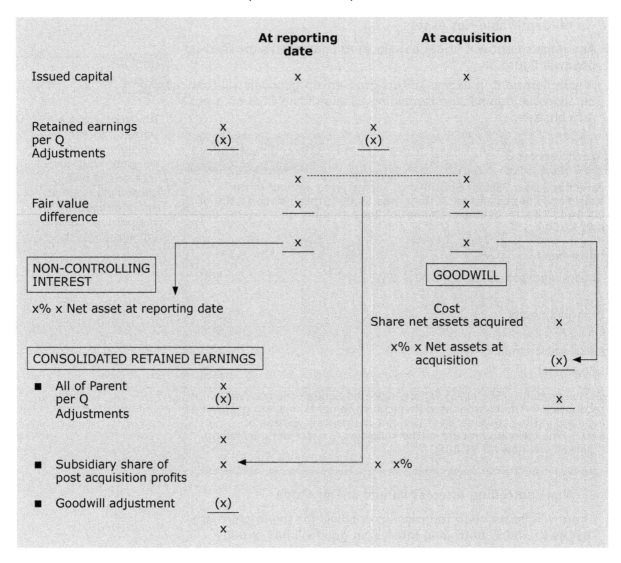

	At reporting date	At acquisition
Issued capital	x	x
Retained earnings per Q	x	x
Adjustments	(x)	(x)
	x	x
Fair value difference	x	x
	x	x

NON-CONTROLLING INTEREST

x% x Net asset at reporting date

CONSOLIDATED RETAINED EARNINGS

- All of Parent   x
  per Q   (x)
  Adjustments
                         x
- Subsidiary share of   x   x x%
  post acquisition profits
- Goodwill adjustment   (x)
                         x

GOODWILL

Cost
Share net assets acquired   x

x% x Net assets at acquisition   (x)

          x

Summary

- Goodwill is the difference between the fair value of the *consideration* given and the fair value of the *net assets acquired.*
- Purchase consideration is valued at fair value; any transaction costs are expensed to profit or loss when incurred.
- Deferred consideration is calculated as the present value of the future cash flows; the unwinding of the discount is charged to profit or loss.
- Contingent consideration is valued at fair value and credited to equity (if settled in shares) or to liabilities (if settled in cash). Any post-acquisition change in fair value is only accounted for if settlement is in cash, and taken to profit or loss.
- The subsidiary's net assets are valued at fair value on acquisition; any fair value difference is reflected in the net asset working schedule.
- Goodwill is tested annually for impairment.
- Goodwill impairment can *never* be reversed.
- Where non-controlling interest is not credited with its share of goodwill the goodwill is grossed up for the impairment test.
- A bargain purchase is credited immediately to profit and loss.
- An entity has 12 months from the acquisition date to measure the subsidiary's net assets at the acquisition date. Any change to provisional values is accounted for retrospectively.

Session 21 Quiz

Estimated time: 30 minutes

1. State why the accounting policies of the subsidiary may be different from those of the parent. (2)
2. Explain the effect on consolidated goodwill if non-controlling interest is valued at fair value. (3.1)
3. State how the increase in the deferred consideration is accounted for. (3.2.1)
4. State how any contingent consideration should be accounted for. (3.2.2)
5. Describe the circumstances under which gain on the acquisition of a subsidiary may occur. (5.2)
6. Identify what period of time is given by IFRS 3 to confirm the value of net assets at the date of acquisition and how any change in fair value should be accounted for. (5.2.2)
7. Explain what happens to goodwill after initial recognition. (5.3.2)

EXAMPLE SOLUTIONS

Solution 1—Fair Valuation I

As at 31 December 20X6

	$
Non-current assets:	
Goodwill	260
Tangibles	
(1,700 + (1,000 + 240))	2,940
Current assets (400 + 300)	700
	3,900
Issued capital	100
Retained earnings	3,132
Non-controlling Interest	268
Current liabilities (200+200)	400
	3,900

Workings

(1) Net assets summary

	At consolidation	At acquisition
	$	$
Issued capital	100	100
Retained earnings As per the question	1,000	600
Fair value adjustments (300 × $^8/_{10}$)	240	300
Net assets	1,340	1,000

(2) Goodwill

	$
Cost	1,100
Non-controlling interest	200
Less: Net assets acquired	(1,000)
	300
Recognise as asset	260
Impaired	40

(3) Non-controlling interest

20% × 1,340	$268

(4) Consolidated retained earnings

	$
Parent	2,900
Share of Subsidiary 80% (1,340 – 1,000)	272
Goodwill	(40)
	3,132

Solution 2—Fair Valuation II

Workings

(1) Goodwill

	$
Cost	1,100
Non-controlling interest	
(100 × 20% × $13)	260
Less: Net assets acquired	(1,000)
	360
Recognise as asset	320
Impaired*	40

> ***Commentary**
>
> *Of the impairment loss, 80% (32) will be charged to consolidated retained earnings and 20% (8) will be charged to non-controlling interest.

(2) Non-controlling interest

	$
Fair value on acquisition	260
Share post-acquisition profits	
(340 × 20%)	68
Goodwill impaired	(8)
	320

If non-controlling interest is valued at fair value then any impairment loss is shared with the parent in the shareholding ratio, even if the percentage of holding of goodwill is not the same as the percentage of shareholding.*

(3) Consolidated retained earnings

	$
Parent	2,900
Share of Subsidiary	
80% (1,340 – 1,000)	272
Goodwill	(32)
	3,140

> ***Commentary**
>
> *Comparing goodwill calculations in *Examples 1* and *2* shows that the parent has $300 of goodwill (*Example 1*) out of a total goodwill of $360 (*Example 2*). Therefore, the parent's share of goodwill is 83% whereas their shareholding is 80%; this should be expected in real life and the exam, as the parent will probably be paying a premium to acquire control.

Consolidated Statement of Comprehensive Income

FOCUS

This session covers the following content from the *ACCA Study Guide.*

D. Preparation of Financial Statements

2. Preparation of consolidated financial statements including an associate

b) Prepare a consolidated statement of profit or loss and consolidated statement of profit or loss and other comprehensive income for a simple group dealing with an acquisition in the period and non-controlling interest. ☐

d) Account for the effects in the financial statements of intra-group trading. ☐

h) Explain and illustrate the effect of the disposal of a parent's investment in a subsidiary in the parent's individual financial statements and/or those of the group (restricted to disposals of the parent's entire investment in the subsidiary). ☐

Session 22 Guidance

■ **Comprehend** how this session brings together all of the relevant adjustments from the previous sessions and considers the effect on the statement of profit or loss and other comprehensive income. The only new item to consider is the treatment of unrealised profits in the opening inventory.

■ **Learn** the components of group income (s.1).

■ **Understand** intra-group transactions and the adjustments required for consolidation (s.2).

(continued on next page)

VISUAL OVERVIEW

Objective: To explain the accounting treatment of subsidiaries in a consolidated statement of profit or loss and other comprehensive income.

```
                          ┌─────────────────────┐
                          │    GROUP INCOME     │
                          ├─────────────────────┤
                          │ • Income Generation │
                          │ • Control and       │
                          │   Ownership         │
                          └─────────────────────┘
```

INTRA-GROUP TRANSACTIONS	NON-CONTROLLING INTEREST	MID-YEAR ACQUISITIONS	DISPOSAL OF A SUBSIDIARY
• Dividends • Other Items	• Recognition • Treatment of Goodwill	• Goodwill • Inclusion of Subsidiary's Results • Dividends From Subsidiary Acquired Mid-year	• Possibilities • Parent's Own Accounts • Consolidated Accounts • Group Profit or Loss • Discontinued Operations

Session 22 Guidance

■ **Learn** the treatment for non-controlling interest's share of subsidiary profits (s.3.1) and the treatment for including subsidiary results from a mid-year acquisition (s.4.1).

■ **Understand** the effect of a mid-year acquisition on the calculation of net assets on acquisition and the resulting calculation of goodwill (s.1.4.1). **Attempt** *Example 3*.

■ **Read** the section "Group disposals" of the technical article "F7 Learning outcomes".

1 Group Income

1.1 Income Generation

- The statement of profit or loss and other comprehensive income shows the income generated by resources (i.e. net assets in the statement of financial position):
  - The parent's own statement of profit or loss and other comprehensive income includes dividend income from its subsidiary.
  - The consolidated statement of profit or loss and other comprehensive income shows the income generated by the group's resources (i.e. net assets in the consolidated statement of financial position).*

*Commentary

*Any following references to consolidated profit or loss also includes consolidated other comprehensive income.

Key Point

The consolidated statement of profit or loss and other comprehensive income is prepared on a basis *consistent* with that used in the preparation of the consolidated statement of financial position.

1.2 Control and Ownership

Consolidated Statement of Profit or Loss

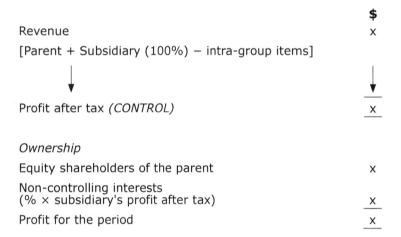

	$
Revenue	x
[Parent + Subsidiary (100%) − intra-group items]	
Profit after tax *(CONTROL)*	x
Ownership	
Equity shareholders of the parent	x
Non-controlling interests (% × subsidiary's profit after tax)	x
Profit for the period	x

- This reflects the profit or loss section of the statement of profit or loss and other comprehensive income; any other gains or losses for the period will be included in other comprehensive income.
- The profit or loss shows the income generated from the net assets under the parent's control.
- Reflect *ownership* by identifying the non-controlling interest's share of the subsidiary's profit after tax, leaving profit attributable to the parent's shareholders.
- Eliminate the effects of transactions between group members (*single-entity concept*).

Key Point

In the profit or loss, dividends from the subsidiary are replaced by the parent's share of the subsidiary's income and expenses (100%) line by line, as far as profit after tax.

2 Intra-group Transactions

2.1 Dividends

▨ Dividends from a subsidiary to its parent are intra-group items:

- Cancel the parent's dividend income from the subsidiary against the subsidiary's dividends paid and payable.
- This "leaves" the non-controlling interest's share of the subsidiary's dividends.

▨ Non-controlling interest in the subsidiary in profit or loss is calculated on profit after tax (before dividends), *and therefore includes the non-controlling interest's share of the subsidiary's dividends and* retained *profits.* *****

▨ In profit or loss, dividend income is from trade investments **only**. Any dividends paid or payable will be dealt with in the statement of changes in equity.

*In short, simply ignore dividends from the subsidiary on consolidation.

2.2 Other Items

2.2.1 Trading

▨ Intra-group trading will be included in the revenue of one group company and the purchases of another. Such inter-company items must be cancelled on consolidation (single entity concept) by taking the following steps:

- add across parent and subsidiary revenue and cost of sales; and
- deduct the value of intra-group sales from revenue and cost of sales. *****

2.2.2 Unrealised Profits in Closing Inventory

Key Point

If any items sold by one group company to another are included in inventories (i.e. have not been sold outside the group by the year end), their value must be adjusted to the lower of cost and net realisable value to the group.

*An adjustment for intra-group trading has no effect on profit and hence will have no effect on the non-controlling interest share of profit.

▨ The adjustment will be made as a consolidation adjustment against the profits of the selling company.

▨ Steps to set up the provision for unrealised profit:

- Calculate the amount of inventory remaining at the year end.
- Calculate the intra-group profit included in it.
- Make an adjustment against the inventory to reduce it to cost to the group (or net realisable value if lower).

Example 1 Group Gross Profit

Whales owns 75% of Porpoise. The trading account for each company for the year ended 31 March is as follows:

	Whales $	Porpoise $
Revenue	120,000	70,000
Cost of sales	(80,000)	(50,000)
Gross profit	40,000	20,000

During the year, Porpoise made sales to Whales amounting to $30,000. Of these sales, $15,000 was in inventory at the year end. Profit made on the year-end inventory items amounted to $2,000.

Required:

Calculate group revenue, cost of sales and gross profit.

Solution

Seller adjustment

	Whales $	Porpoise $	Adjustment $	Consolidated $
Revenue				
Cost of sales – per question				
– unrealised profit				
Gross profit				
Non-controlling interest				

2.2.3 Unrealised Profit in Opening Inventory

▨ Last year's closing inventory will become this year's opening inventory, so any adjustments made in the previous year in terms of the unrealised profit will be reversed in the current year on the presumption that the inventory has been sold in the current period.

 **Key Point**

Any unrealised profit in the opening inventory will be deducted from the costs of the original selling company, thereby increasing the profits for the current year.

▨ All we are doing with unrealised profit is shifting the period in which the profit is recognised, delaying the recognition of the profit by the group until the goods have been sold outside of the group.

▨ This adjustment only ever affects the gross profit calculation, never the statement of financial position.

Illustration 1 Unrealised Profit

In year 1, Parent sells goods to Subsidiary for $100; the cost of these goods was $80. At the end of the year, the goods are still held by the Subsidiary.

In year 2, the Subsidiary sells the goods for $110.

	P	S	Group
Year 1 Profit	$20		0
Year 2 Profit		$10	$30

The profit recognised by the Parent and the Subsidiary over the two years is $30 and the group also recognises profit of $30. The adjustment for unrealised profit merely changes the period of recognition of profit, in this example slipping by one year the recognition of the initial $20 profit.

2.2.4 Non-current Asset Transfers

- The consolidated profit or loss should include depreciation of non-current assets based on cost to the group and should exclude profit/loss on non-current asset transfers between group members. This is consistent with treatment in the consolidated statement of financial position.

  - Eliminate profit or loss on transfer and adjust depreciation in full (control).

  - These adjustments are made in full against the consolidated figures.

*Commentary

*A depreciation adjustment for a non-current asset transfer would be part of the profit after tax of the subsidiary and would therefore be shared with the non-controlling interest.

Illustration 2 Non-current Asset Transfer

Parent owns 80% of Subsidiary. Parent transferred a non-current asset to Subsidiary on 1 January 20X6 at a value of $15,000. The asset originally cost Parent $20,000 and depreciation to the date of transfer was $8,000. The asset had a useful life of five years when originally acquired, with a residual value of zero. The useful life at the date of transfer remains at three years. Both companies depreciate their assets at 20% per annum on cost, making a full year's depreciation charge in the year of acquisition and none in the year of disposal. Total depreciation for 20X6 was $700,000 for Parent and $500,000 for Subsidiary.

Required:

Show the adjustments required for the above transaction in the consolidated statement of profit or loss for the year ended 31 December 20X6.

Solution

	Parent	Subsidiary	Adjustment	Consolidated
	$	$	$	
Per question	700,000	500,000		1,200,000
Asset unrealised profit				
[15,000 − (20,000 − 8,000)]	3,000			3,000
Depreciation adjustment*				
(15,000 ÷ 3 years) − 4,000		(1,000)		(1,000)
				1,202,000

2.2.5 Interest and Other Charges

■ Where a group company lends money to another group company the loan asset is cancelled against the loan liability in the consolidated statement of financial position.

■ Where the loan carries interest payments there will be interest income in one company and interest expense in the other; this interest will also need to be eliminated.

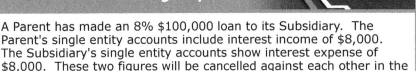

Illustration 3 Intra-group Loan

A Parent has made an 8% $100,000 loan to its Subsidiary. The Parent's single entity accounts include interest income of $8,000. The Subsidiary's single entity accounts show interest expense of $8,000. These two figures will be cancelled against each other in the consolidated accounts and no interest income or interest expense will be recognised.

■ Many companies also make a form of **management charge** against other group companies, normally from the parent to the subsidiary. The parent will reflect other income in its profit or loss while the subsidiary will include the charge as part of operating expenses. On consolidation, these intra-group charges must also be cancelled against each other.

3 Non-controlling Interest

3.1 Recognition

Key Point

The non-controlling interests' share of subsidiary's profit after tax must be shown, leaving the remaining profit as attributable to shareholders of the parent.

3.2 Treatment of Goodwill

■ Goodwill arising on acquisition must be capitalised and tested annually for impairment. Any impairment is recognised as an expense and charged to profit or loss in the period.

Key Point

If non-controlling interest is valued at fair value (i.e. credited with its share of goodwill) any impairment loss relating to goodwill must be allocated between the parent and non-controlling interest in the proportion of their respective share ownerships.

■ Any excess of the fair value of the assets and liabilities acquired over the cost of the acquisition is credited to profit or loss **immediately**.

Example 2 Goodwill Impairment

Pathfinder owns 75% of Sultan. Statements of profit or loss for the two companies for the year ending 30 June are as follows:

	Pathfinder	Sultan
	$	$
Revenue	100,000	50,000
Cost of sales	(60,000)	(30,000)
Gross profit	40,000	20,000
Expenses	(20,000)	(10,000)
Profit for the period	20,000	10,000

During the year, Pathfinder sold goods to Sultan for $20,000, at a gross profit margin of 40%. Half of the goods remained in inventory at the year end.

Non-controlling interest is valued at fair value on acquisition. Goodwill has been impaired by $4,000 in the year ended 30 June.

Required:

Prepare the consolidated statement of profit or loss of the group for the year ended 30 June.

4 Mid-year Acquisitions

Key Point

4.1 Goodwill

- A parent may not acquire a subsidiary only at the start or end of a year. If a subsidiary is acquired mid-year, it is necessary to calculate the net assets at date of acquisition.

> The subsidiary's profit after tax is assumed to accrue evenly over time unless indicated to the contrary.

Example 3 Mid-year Acquisition

Parent acquired 80% of Subsidiary on 31 May 20X6 for $20,000.

Subsidiary's net assets at 31 December 20X5 were:

	$
Issued capital	1,000
Retained earnings:	15,000
	16,000

During the year to 31 December 20X6, Subsidiary made a profit after tax of $600.

Non-controlling interest is valued at the proportionate share of the identifiable net assets; it is not credited with goodwill.

Required:

(1) Calculate Subsidiary's net assets at acquisition.

(2) Calculate goodwill on acquisition.

(3) Show the profits from Subsidiary to be included in the consolidated retained earnings.

Example 3 Mid-year Acquisition
(continued)

Solution

(1) Net assets of Subsidiary at acquisition

	At acquisition	
	$	$
Issued capital		
Retained earnings:		
At 31 December 20X5		
1 January–May 20X6		

(2) Goodwill on acquisition

$

Cost of investment

Less: Share of net assets acquired

(3) Profit from Subsidiary included in consolidation retained earnings reserves

$

Share of post-acquisition reserve of Subsidiary

4.2 Inclusion of Subsidiary's Results

- Consolidated financial statements only include the results of the subsidiary from the date of acquisition, (i.e. when control is gained). If the subsidiary is acquired mid-year:
  - consolidate subsidiary from the date of acquisition;
  - identify net assets at the date of acquisition—opening net assets (equity) plus profit to date of acquisition (see consolidated statement of financial position notes); and
  - assume revenue and expenses accrue evenly over the year (unless the contrary is indicated). Therefore time-apportion totals for revenue and costs, only including the post-acquisition share, then deduct intra-group items.

4.3 Dividends From Subsidiary Acquired Mid-year

- In calculating net assets at acquisition, assume that profit after tax (i.e. before dividends) accrues evenly over the year, unless the contrary is indicated.

Example 4 Mid-year Acquisition

Parent acquired 75% of Subsidiary during the year on 1 April. Extracts from the companies' statements of profit or loss for the year ended 31 December are:

	Parent	Subsidiary
	$	$
Revenue	100,000	75,000
Cost of sales	(70,000)	(60,000)
Gross profit	30,000	15,000

Since acquisition, the Parent has made sales to the Subsidiary of $15,000. None of these goods remain in inventories at the year end.

Required:

Calculate revenue, cost of sales and gross profit for the group for the year ending 31 December.

Solution

Consolidated statement of profit or loss for the year ending 31 December

	Parent	$9/12$ Subsidiary	Adjustment	Consolidated
	$	$	$	$
Revenue				
Cost of sales				
Gross Profit				

5 Disposal

5.1 Possibilities

▨ When a group disposes of all or part of its interest in a subsidiary, the disposal needs to be reflected in the parent's books and, more importantly, in the consolidated financial statements.

▨ Consolidated financial statements reflect:

   • inclusion of results and cash flows of the entity disposed of;

   • calculation and presentation of profit or loss on disposal; and

   • any remaining interest in the company after a part-disposal.

▨ In dealing with these matters in consolidated financial statements, the single entity concept is applied and the effect on the group as a whole is considered.

*Commentary

▨ Disposal may be:

   • full disposal (i.e. sell entire holding);* or

   • part disposal, retaining some interest in the undertaking.

*Only the full disposal is considered in the F7 syllabus.

5.2   Treatment in Parent's Own Accounts

▦ Parent will carry its investment in a subsidiary in its own statement of financial position as a non-current asset investment, usually at cost.

Key Point

The sale of all or part of an investment is recorded as a disposal in the parent's own accounts and will usually give rise to a profit or loss on disposal (i.e. proceeds less cost of investment sold). An accrual may be required for tax on any gain on disposal.

▦ To record disposal:

		$	$
Dr	Cash/receivables (proceeds)	X	
	Cr Investment in S (cost of investment sold)		X
Dr	P or L loss on disposal (*or* Cr profit on disposal)	X	X

If required

		$	$
Dr	P or L tax charge (tax on gain on disposal)	X	
	Cr Tax payable		X

5.3   Treatment in Consolidated Accounts

5.3.1   Consolidated Statement of Financial Position

▦ If at year end the parent has sold its shares in the subsidiary, there will be no reference to the subsidiary in the statement of financial position (even if the subsidiary was sold on the last day of the year).

Key Point

The consolidated statement of financial position reflects the closing position.

5.3.2   Consolidated Statement of Profit or Loss and Other Comprehensive Income

▦ Profit or loss on disposal must be calculated from the group's perspective. This will be different to that recognised by the parent because:

* The group recognises 100% of subsidiary profit (or loss) during the term of ownership whereas the parent recognises only dividends received from the subsidiary; and
* The group will recognise impairment of goodwill (the parent does not).

Key Point

The consolidated statement of profit or loss and other comprehensive income reflects the pattern of ownership in the period.

5.3.3   Pattern of Ownership

Status of Investment		Treatment in Statement of Profit or Loss and Other Comprehensive Income	Treatment in Statement of Financial Position
Before disposal	**After disposal**		
Subsidiary → e.g. 90%	zero 0%	• Consolidate up until the date of disposal	No action needed

Illustration 4   Revenue and Costs

Paper purchased 60% of the shares in Scissors a number of years ago.

On September 30 of the current period, Paper sold all of its shares in Scissors. Paper's year end is 31 December.

Scissors' revenue and costs for the year are $60,000 and $42,000, respectively. Revenue and costs accrue evenly throughout the year.

Revenue and costs of Scissors included in the consolidated profit or loss for the year will be as follows:

Revenue (60,000 x $9/12$)	$45,000
Cost (42,000 x $9/12$)	$31,500
Profit	$13,500

Non-controlling interest would have been calculated at 40% of the above profit to give $5,400.

5.4   Group Profit or Loss on Disposal

Key Point

Any disposal of a shareholding that results in the loss of control will give rise to profit or loss on disposal being recognised in profit or loss.

▦ On the date that control is lost the following adjustments must be made:*

- ◉ Derecognise the carrying amount of assets, including goodwill, liabilities and non-controlling interest from the consolidated statement of financial position.
- ◉ Recognise the fair value of the consideration received on the disposal of the shareholding.
- ◉ Reclassify to profit or loss any amounts that relate to the subsidiary's net assets previously recognised in other comprehensive income, where required.
- ◉ Recognise any resulting difference as a gain or loss in profit or loss attributable to the parent.

Commentary

*Loss of control may result in associate status, a joint venture, an IFRS 9 investment or an entire disposal.

Illustration 5 Profit on Disposal

Plumber purchased 80% of the shares in System a number of years ago for $125 million. On the acquisition date, the non-controlling interest was valued at a fair value of $25 million, the fair value of System's net assets was $140 million, and goodwill of $10 million was recognised.

Since the acquisition, System has made profits of $20 million and goodwill has been impaired by $4 million.

Today, Plumber sells all of its shares in System for $160 million.

Parent and group profit or loss on disposal are calculated as follows:

Parent

	$m
Proceeds on disposal	160
Cost of investment	(125)
Profit on disposal	35

This profit would be included in Plumber's profit or loss in the year of disposal. Tax would be applied to this figure where relevant.

Group

	$m
Proceeds on disposal	160
System net assets on disposal (140 + 20)	(160)
Goodwill remaining (10 − 4)	(6)
Non-controlling interest on disposal (25 + ((20 − 4) x 20%))	28.2
Profit on disposal	22.2

This profit would be included in the consolidated profit or loss in the year of disposal.

Difference in profit

The $12.8-million difference in the two profit figures is System's post-acquisition profit of $20 million less goodwill impaired of $4 million times Plumber's percentage holding of 80%:

($20 − $4) x 80% = $12.8 million

This difference exists because the consolidated statement of profit or loss included Plumber's share of System's profits (less goodwill impaired) during the period of control, while Plumber's own (single entity) statement of profit or loss only included dividends received from System.

The higher profit recognised in the consolidated statement of profit or loss during the term of ownership results in less profit recognised on disposal.

5.5   Discontinued Operations

- It is highly likely that the disposal of a subsidiary will be classified as a discontinued operation.

- IFRS 5 requires that the revenue and costs to the date of disposal and any profit or loss on the actual disposal of the operation are presented as a single item in the profit or loss, and then analysed further either in the profit or loss or in the disclosure notes.

Key Point

In this case, the results for the subsidiary to the date of disposal will be presented separately from the results of the continuing operations.

Exam Advice

A Section C group accounts question will **not** include the disposal of subsidiaries, but aspects of a disposal can be tested elsewhere in the exam, including any analysis and interpretation question.

Example 5 Disposal of Subsidiary

The draft accounts of two companies at 31 March 20X8 were as follows.

Statements of financial position

	Hamble $	Jemima $
Investment in Jemima at cost	3,440	–
Sundry assets	36,450	6,500
	39,890	6,500
Share capital ($1 ordinary shares)	20,000	3,000
Retained earnings	11,000	3,500
	31,000	6,500
Sale proceeds of disposal (suspense a/c)	8,890	–
	39,890	6,500

Statements of profit or loss

	Hamble $	Jemima $
Profit before tax	12,950	3,800
Tax	(5,400)	(2,150)
Profit after tax	7,550	1,650
Retained earnings b/d	3,450	1,850
Retained earnings c/f	11,000	3,500

Hamble had acquired 90% of Jemima when the reserves of Jemima were $700. Goodwill of $90 arose on the acquisition. Goodwill impairment as at 31 March 20X7 was $70; there was no impairment in the current period.

The fair value of the non-controlling interest on acquisition was $350. The carrying amount of Jemima's net assets on disposal and at the year end closely equates to its fair value.

On 31 December 20X7, Hamble sold all its shares in Jemima.

Required:

Prepare extracts from the Hamble Group statement of financial position and Hamble Group statement of profit or loss.

Note: Ignore tax on the disposal.

Summary

- The profit or loss of the parent as a single entity will reflect the dividends received from its subsidiary, whereas the consolidated profit or loss will reflect the parent's share of the subsidiary's profit (or loss).

- Consolidated profit or loss will include 100% of the subsidiary's profits with the non-controlling interest's share shown as an allocation of the profit after tax.

- The same principles are followed for items of other comprehensive income.

- All intra-group revenue (and expenses) is cancelled on consolidation.

- Unrealised profit in closing inventory is added to the costs of the selling company. Unrealised profit in opening inventory is deducted from the costs of the original selling company.

- Consolidated profit or loss must reflect any adjustments for depreciation in respect of fair value differences or intra-group sales treated as non-current assets by the buyer.

- Goodwill impairment for the year is shown as:

  - a subsidiary expense if non-controlling interest is valued at fair value; and

  - an expense against the parent under the alternative model.

- If the subsidiary is acquired part way through the year, only the post-acquisition period income and expenses of the subsidiary are consolidated.

- Profits are assumed to accrue evenly unless told otherwise.

- Only dividends of the parent are reflected in the movement in retained earnings.

- The sale of all or part of an investment is recorded as a disposal in the parent's own accounts and will usually give rise to a profit or loss on disposal.

- If a disposal occurs part way through the year, then the statement of financial position simply reflects the closing position.

- The consolidated statement of comprehensive income must reflect the pattern of ownership for the period.

- Any disposal of a shareholding that results in the loss of control will give rise to profit or loss on disposal, which is recognised in profit or loss.

- Disposal of a subsidiary will usually amount to a discontinued operation, and therefore is presented separately.

Session 22 Quiz
Estimated time: 10 minutes

1. Explain how any dividend received from the subsidiary should be treated in the statement of profit or loss. (2.1)

2. Describe how any unrealised profit in opening inventory should be dealt with. (2.2.3)

3. Explain how any impairment of goodwill should be accounted for when that goodwill is valued to include the non-controlling interest share. (3.2)

4. State when the group should start to include the profits of the subsidiary if a subsidiary is acquired part way through the year. (4.2)

5. Explain how a parent calculates profit on disposal of its shareholding in a subsidiary. (5.2)

6. Describe the difference in the amount of profit calculated from the group perspective compared to the profit calculated from the parent's view. (5.3.2)

7. State how the results of a disposed subsidiary are presented in the consolidated profit or loss. (5.5)

Study Question Bank
Estimated time: 45 minutes

Priority		Estimated Time	Completed
Q42	Premier	45 minutes	
Additional			
Q39	Humphrey		
Q40	Happy		
Q41	RTV		

EXAMPLE SOLUTIONS

Solution 1—Group Gross Profit

Seller adjustment

	Whales	Porpoise	Adjustment	Consolidated
	$	$	$	$
Revenue	120,000	70,000	(30,000)	160,000
Cost of sales — per question	(80,000)	(50,000)	30,000	
— unrealised profit		(2,000)		(102,000)
Gross profit	40,000	18,000		58,000
Non-controlling interest (25% × 18,000)				(4,500)

Solution 2—Goodwill Impairment

Consolidated statement of profit or loss for the year ended 30 June

	$
Revenue	130,000
Cost of sales	(74,000)
Gross profit	56,000
Expenses	(30,000)
Goodwill	(4,000)
Profit	22,000
Non-controlling interest (W3)	(1,500)
Profit for the period	20,500

Workings

(1) Group structure

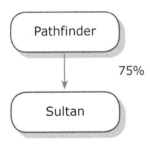

(2) Consolidation schedule

	Pathfinder	Sultan	Adjustment	Consolidated
	$	$	$	$
Revenue	100,000	50,000	(20,000)	130,000
Cost of sales — per question	(60,000)	(30,000)	20,000	
— unrealised profit (W4)	(4,000)			(74,000)
Expenses	(20,000)	(10,000)		(30,000)
Goodwill		(4,000)		(4,000)
Profit				22,000

(3) Non-controlling interest

		$
Sultan (W2) 6,000 × 25% =		1,500

(4) Unrealised profit

	%	$	
Selling price	100	20,000	
Cost	(60)	(12,000)	$
Gross profit	40	8,000 × ½ = 4,000	

Solution 3—Mid-year Acquisition

(1) Net assets of Subsidiary at acquisition

	At acquisition	
	$	$
Issued capital		1,000
Retained earnings:		
At 31 December 20X5	15,000	
1 January − May 20X6 (600 × $\frac{5}{12}$)	250	15,250
		16,250

(2) Goodwill on acquisition

	$
Cost of investment	20,000
Less: Share of net assets acquired	
80% × 16,250 (W1)	(13,000)
	7,000

(3) Profit from Subsidiary included in consolidation retained earnings

	$
Share of post-acquisition reserve of Subsidiary	
80% (15,600 − 15,250)	280

Solution 4—Mid-year Acquisition

Consolidated statement of profit or loss for the year ending 31 December

	Parent	Subsidiary $^{9/12}$	Adjustment	Consolidated
	$	$	$	$
Revenue	100,000	56,250	(15,000)	141,250
Cost of sales	(70,000)	(45,000)	15,000	(100,000)
Gross Profit	30,000	11,250	0	41,250

Solution 5—Disposal of Subsidiary

Consolidated statement of financial position as at 31 March 20X8

	$
Sundry assets	36,450
	36,450
Share capital	20,000
Retained earnings	16,450
	36,450

Consolidated statement of profit or loss for the year ended 31 March 20X8

	$
Operating profit **(W7)**	15,800
Profit on disposal of operations **(W6)**	3,364
Profit before taxation	19,164
Taxation—group **(W8)**	(7,012)
Profit after taxation	12,152
Non-controlling interest **(W9)**	(124)
Profit for the year	12,028
Retained earnings b/f **(W3)**	4,422
Retained earnings c/f	16,450

Workings

(1) Net assets

	Reporting date	Disposal	Acquisition
	$	$	$
Share capital	3,000	3,000	3,000
Retained earnings	3,500	3,088	700
	6,500	6,088	3,700

(2) Retained earnings at date of disposal

	$
B/fwd	1,850
Profit for year to disposal $(1,650 \times \%_{12})$	1,238
	3,088

(3) Retained earnings b/f

	$
Hamble Group	3,450
Jemima 90% (1,850 − 700)	1,035
Less: Goodwill written off (70 × 90%)	(63)
	4,422

(4) Profit on disposal of Jemima (individual company view)

	$
Sale proceeds	8,890
Less: Cost of investment	(3,440)
Profit on disposal	5,450

(5) Consolidated retained earnings

	$
Retained earnings of Hamble	
Per the question	11,000
Profit on disposal **(W4)**	5,450
	16,450

(6) Profit on disposal of Jemima (group view)

		$
Sale proceeds		8,890
Less:		
Net assets at disposal **(W1)**	6,088	
Goodwill remaining	20	
Non-controlling interest **(W10)**	(582)	
		(5,526)
Profit on disposal		3,364

(7) Operating profit

Hamble Group	12,950
Jemima	2,850
	15,800

(8) Taxation—group

	$
Hamble Group	5,400
Jemima	1,612
	7,012

(9) Non-controlling interest in Jemima

Operating profit **(W7)**	2,850
Tax **(W8)**	(1,612)
	1,238
Non-controlling interest share (10%)	124

(10) Non-controlling interest on disposal

	$
Fair value on acquisition	350
Share of profit to 1 April 20X6 (1,850 − 700) × 10%	115
Share of profit for current year **(W9)**	124
Goodwill impaired (70 × 10%)	(7)
	582

IAS 28 *Investments in Associates*

FOCUS

This session covers the following content from the *ACCA Study Guide.*

A. The Conceptual and Regulatory Framework for Financial Reporting	
4. The concepts and principles of groups and consolidated financial statements	
j) Define an associate and explain the principles and reasoning for the use of equity accounting.	☐
D. Preparation of Financial Statements	
2. Preparation of consolidated financial statements including an associate	
a) Prepare a consolidated statement of financial position for a simple group (parent and one subsidiary and associate).	☐

Session 23 Guidance

- ■ **Learn** the factors that contribute to the existence of significant influence (s.1.4).
- ■ **Be able** to measure the amount of investment in the associate to be included in the consolidated statement of financial position (s.2.4) and the amount of income from the associate to be included in the consolidated statement of profit or loss and other comprehensive income (s.2.5).

(continued on next page)

VISUAL OVERVIEW

Objective: To explain the meaning of "an associate" and IFRS accounting for investments in associates.

IAS 28

- Background
- Scope
- Terminology
- Significant Influence
- Separate Financial Statements

ACCOUNTING TREATMENT

- Relationship to a Group
- Basic Rule
- Equity Accounting
- Statement of Financial Position
- Statement of Comprehensive Income
- Accounting Policies and Year Ends
- Impairment
- Exemptions to Equity Accounting

TRANSACTIONS WITH AN ASSOCIATE

- Trading
- Dividends
- Unrealised Profit

Session 23 Guidance

■ **Appreciate** that "goodwill" in respect of an associate is not presented separately but is part of the carrying amount of the investment in associate (s.2.4).

■ **Note** that the test for impairment is against the carrying amount of the investment in an associate (s.2.7).

■ **Understand** the accounting treatment for transactions with an associate (s.3).

Equity Accounting

1.1 Background

■ Where one company has a controlling investment in another company, a parent-subsidiary relationship is formed and accounted for as a group. Companies also may have substantial investments in other entities without actually having control. Thus, a parent-subsidiary relationship does not exist between the two.

> ### Key Point
>
> If the investing company can exert significant influence over the financial and operating policies of the investee company, it will have an active interest in its net assets and results.

■ The nature of the relationship differs from that of a simple investment (i.e. it is not a passive interest).*

■ Equity accounting is used by the investing entity to reflect its interest in the net assets and results of an associate.

1.2 Scope

■ IAS 28 deals with accounting for both associates and joint ventures.

■ IAS 28 is applied in accounting for investments in associates where the investor has *significant influence* over the investee.

1.3 Terminology

Associate: an entity over which an investor has *significant influence*.

Significant influence: the power to participate in the financial and operating policy decisions of the investee without control or joint control over those policies.*

■ **Equity method:** a method of accounting whereby:

- the investment is initially recognised at cost and adjusted thereafter for the post-acquisition change in the investor's share of net assets of the investee;
- the profit or loss of the investor includes the investor's share of the profit or loss of the investee; and
- other comprehensive income of the investor will include its share of other comprehensive income of the investee.

*Including the investment at cost in the company's accounts would not fairly present the investing interest.

This session considers only accounting for associates as joint ventures are excluded from the F7 syllabus.

*Compare the definition of "significant influence" with that of "control" (see *Session 19*).

1.4   Significant Influence

▦ The term *significant influence* means that an investor is involved, or has the right to be involved, in the financial and operating policy decisions of the investee.

▦ The existence of significant influence by an investor is usually evidenced in one or more of the following ways:

- Representation on the board of directors or equivalent governing body.
- Participation in policy-making processes.
- Material transactions between the investor and the investee.
- Interchange of managerial personnel.
- Provision of essential technical information.*

Key Point

A holding of 20% or more of the voting rights of the investee indicates significant influence, unless it can be demonstrated otherwise.

▦ When significant influence is lost, the carrying amount of the investment at that date is regarded as its cost on initial measurement thereafter (and will be accounted for as a financial asset in accordance with IFRS 9).

*Commentary

*A holding of less than 20% presumes that the holder does not have significant influence, unless such influence can be clearly demonstrated (e.g. representation on the board).

1.5   Separate Financial Statements

▦ Investors who are **exempt** from the requirement to equity account may present separate financial statements as their **only** financial statements.*

▦ In the separate financial statements, the investment in the associate should be accounted for:

- under IFRS 5 if classified as held for sale;
- at cost or in accordance with IFRS 9.

*Commentary

*See s.2.8 for details of exemption.

2   Accounting Treatment

2.1   Relationship to a Group

▦ A group is defined as a parent and all of its subsidiaries. An associate is not part of a group as it is not a subsidiary (i.e. it is not controlled by the group).

▦ As such, the accounting treatment of the associate is different from that of subsidiaries.

2.2   Basic Rule

▦ An investment in an associate is accounted for using the equity method.

▦ Associates must be accounted for using the equity method regardless of whether the investor has investments in subsidiaries and does not, therefore, prepare consolidated financial statements.

2.3 Equity Accounting

▤ The cost of the investment in an associate is increased or decreased with the parent's share of the associate's post-acquisition profits or losses. This adjusted carrying amount of the investment in the associate is included as a single line entry in the consolidated statement of financial position.

▤ Distributions received from the associate, normally in the form of a dividend, reduce the carrying amount of the investment.

▤ Adjustments to the carrying amount may also be necessary for changes in the investor's proportionate interest in the associate arising from items of other comprehensive income.

▤ Such changes include those arising from the revaluation of property, plant and equipment and from foreign exchange translation differences.*

▤ The investor's share of the current year's profit or loss of the associate is recognised in the investor's profit or loss.

*These changes will be reflected within the other comprehensive income section of the statement of profit or loss and other comprehensive income.

 **Key Point**

The associate is **not** consolidated line-by-line. Instead:

■ the group's share of the associate's net assets is included in the consolidated statement of financial position in one line; and

■ share of profits (after tax) in the consolidated statement of profit or loss in one line.

2.4 In a Consolidated Statement of Financial Position

▤ The methods described below apply equally to the financial statements of a non-group company which has an investment in an associate as they do to consolidated financial statements.

▤ The amount to be included in the consolidated statement of financial position is the cost of investment plus the parent's share of the associates post-acquisition profits (or less any losses) less any impairment of the investment.

▤ Goodwill is not presented separately; it is included in the carrying amount of the investment (as part of the cost of investment).*

▤ **Do not** consolidate the associate's net assets line-by-line. The associate is not a subsidiary; therefore the net assets are not controlled as they are for a subsidiary.

▤ Include in consolidated reserves the parent's share of the associate's post-acquisition reserves (the same as for a subsidiary).

▤ The fair values of the associate's assets and liabilities must be used when equity accounting for the associate. Any change in reserves, depreciation charges, etc due to fair value adjustments must be taken into account (as they are when dealing with subsidiaries).

▤ Where the share of the associate's net assets acquired at fair value is in excess of the cost of investment, the difference is included as income in determining the investor's share of the associate's profits or losses.

*As for business combinations under IFRS 3, IAS 28 does not permit the amortisation of goodwill.

Key Point

The "investment in associate" is calculated as follows:

	$
Cost of investment	x
Add: % × associate's post-acquisition profits	x
Less: impairment	(x)
	x

Example 1   Investment in Associate

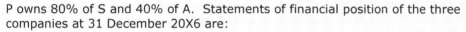

P owns 80% of S and 40% of A. Statements of financial position of the three companies at 31 December 20X6 are:

	P	S	A
	$	$	$
Investment: shares in S	800	–	–
Investment: shares in A	600	–	–
Other non-current assets	1,600	800	1,400
Current assets	2,200	3,300	3,250
	5,200	4,100	4,650
Issued capital – $1 ordinary shares	1,000	400	800
Retained earnings	4,000	3,400	3,600
Liabilities	200	300	250
	5,200	4,100	4,650

P acquired its shares in S seven years ago when S's retained earnings were $520 and P acquired its shares in A on 1 January 20X6 when A's retained earnings were $400.

Non-controlling interest is not credited with goodwill which had been written off after five years.

There were no indications during the year that the investment in A was impaired.

Required:

Prepare the consolidated statement of financial position at 31 December 20X6.

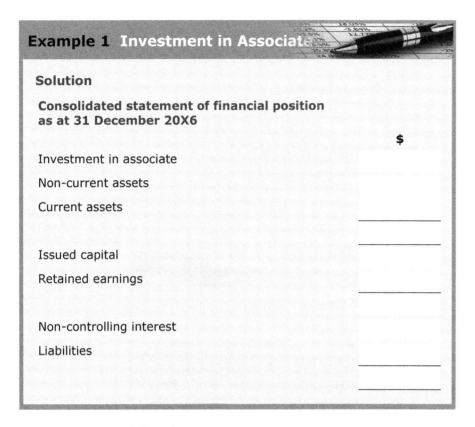

Example 1 Investment in Associate

Solution

Consolidated statement of financial position as at 31 December 20X6

	$
Investment in associate	
Non-current assets	
Current assets	_____
	_____
Issued capital	
Retained earnings	_____
Non-controlling interest	
Liabilities	_____
	_____

2.5 In a Consolidated Statement of Profit or Loss and Other Comprehensive Income

- Treatment is consistent with consolidated statement of financial position and applies equally to a non-group company with an associate:

  - Include the group's share of the associate's profits after tax in the consolidated profit or loss. This replaces dividend income shown in the investing company's own profit or loss.*

  - **Do not** add in the associate's revenue and expenses line by line as this is not a consolidation and the associate is not a subsidiary.

  - Time-apportion the associate's results if acquired mid-year.

Commentary

*This amount of the associate's profit after tax is presented above tax in the consolidated profit or loss.

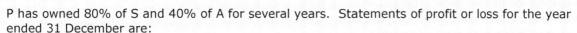

Example 2   Income From Associate

P has owned 80% of S and 40% of A for several years. Statements of profit or loss for the year ended 31 December are:

	P	S	A
	$	$	$
Revenue	14,000	12,000	10,000
Cost of sales	(9,000)	(4,000)	(3,000)
Gross profit	5,000	8,000	7,000
Administrative expenses	(2,000)	(6,000)	(3,000)
	3,000	2,000	4,000
Dividend from associate	400	–	–
Profit before taxation	3,400	2,000	4,000
Income taxes	(1,000)	(1,200)	(2,000)
Profit after taxation	2,400	800	2,000
Dividends (paid)	(1,000)	–	(1,000)
Retained earnings for the period	1,400	800	1,000

Non-controlling interest is not credited with goodwill, which was fully written off three years ago.

Required:
Prepare the consolidated statement of profit or loss for the year ended 31 December.

2.6   Accounting Policies and Year Ends

2.6.1   Accounting Policies

▨ If an associate uses accounting policies other than those of the investor, adjustments must be made to conform the associate's accounting policies to those of the investor in applying the equity method.

2.6.2   Year Ends

▨ The most recent available financial statements of the associate are used by the investor.

▨ When the reporting dates of the investor and the associate are different, the associate prepares, for the use of the investor, financial statements as of the same date as the financial statements of the investor unless it is impracticable to do so.

▨ When it is not practicable to produce statements as at the same date, adjustments must be made for the effects of significant transactions or events that occur between that date and the date of the investor's financial statements.

▨ In any case, the difference between the reporting date of the associate and that of the investor must not be more than three months.

2.7   Impairment

▨ After application of the equity method, including recognising the associate's losses, the investor applies the requirements of IFRS 9 to determine whether there are any indications that impairment may have occurred.

▨ If there are indications that impairment may have occurred the entity then applies the requirements of IAS 36 in measuring the impairment loss.

▨ Because goodwill included in the carrying amount of an investment in an associate is not separately recognised, it is not tested for impairment separately.

▨ In determining the value in use of the investment, an entity estimates:

  ● its share of the present value of the estimated future cash flows expected to be generated by the associate, including the cash flows from the operations of the associate and the proceeds on the ultimate disposal of the investment; or

  ● the present value of the estimated future cash flows expected to arise from dividends to be received from the investment and from its ultimate disposal.

2.8   Exemptions to Equity Accounting

▨ The main exemptions are as follows:

  ● An associate which is classified as held for sale is accounted for under IFRS 5 *Non-current Assets Held for Sale and Discontinued Operations*.*

  ● If the investor is a parent that is exempt from the requirement to prepare consolidated financial statements (see s.2.3 of *Session 19*), the investment in the associate will be measured at cost or in accordance with IFRS 9.

Key Point

Instead, the entire carrying amount of the investment is tested for impairment by comparing its recoverable amount with its carrying amount.

*Commentary

*Under IFRS 5, if an associate is acquired and held with a view to disposal within 12 months, it will be measured at the lower of its carrying amount (e.g. cost) and fair value less costs to sell.

3 Transactions With an Associate

3.1 Trading

▨ Members of the group can sell to or make purchases from the associate. This trading will result in the recognition of receivables and payables in the individual company accounts.

Key Point

Do **not** cancel balances between parent and associate and do **not** adjust sales and cost of sales for trading with associate.

▨ In the consolidated statement of financial position, show balances with associate separately from other receivables and payables.

▨ The associate is not part of the group. It is, therefore, appropriate to show amounts owed to the group by the associate as assets and amounts owed to the associate by the group as liabilities.

3.2 Dividends

▨ Consolidated statement of financial position:
  - Ensure that dividends payable and receivable are fully accounted for in the books of the individual companies.
  - Include receivable in the consolidated statement of financial position for dividends due to the *group* from associates.
  - Do **not** cancel any balances for dividends.
▨ Consolidated statement of profit or loss:
  - Do **not** include dividends from an associate in the consolidated statement of profit or loss. The parent's share of the associate's profit after tax (hence before dividends) is included under equity accounting in the income from the associate.*

*Commentary

*It would be double counting to include dividends in the consolidated statement of profit or loss as well.

3.3 Unrealised Profit

▨ If the parent sells goods to the associate and the associate still has these goods in stock at the year end, their value will include the profit made by the parent and recorded in its books. Hence, profit is included in inventory value in the associate's net assets (profit is unrealised) and in the parent's statement of profit or loss.

▨ If the associate sells to the parent, a similar situation arises, with the profit being included in the associate's statement of profit or loss and the parent's inventory.

▨ To avoid double counting when equity accounting for the associate, this unrealised profit needs to be eliminated.

▨ Unrealised losses should not be eliminated if the transaction provides evidence of impairment in value of the asset which has been transferred.

Key Point

Unrealised profits should be eliminated to the extent of the investor's interest in the associate.

Exam Advice

Both "upstream" and "downstream" transactions should be dealt with as a credit against "Investment in Associate".

Illustration 1 Eliminating Unrealised Profit

Pear has a 40% shareholding in Apple, which gives Pear significant influence over Apple.

Apple's profit for the period was $1,200.

During the year, Pear sold goods to Apple for $2,000 at a mark-up of 25%. Apple still held all these goods in inventory at the year end.

Unrealised profit = $2,000 × $25/125$ = $400

In Pear's consolidated accounts

Pear's share of the realised profit is $320 (40% × (1,200 − 400)). So, to equity account for the associate:

Dr Investment in associate	$320	
Cr Share of profit of associate		$320

The above entry would be exactly the same if the associate had sold goods to parent.

Exam Advice

The adjustment for a question requiring preparation of the consolidated statements of financial position is:

Dr Investment in associate	$320	
Cr Consolidated retained earnings		$320

The adjustment for a consolidated statement of profit or loss is to reduce the share of profit of associate by $160, that is:

Cr Share of profit of associate		$320

Example 3 Eliminating Unrealised Profit

Parent has a 40% associate.

Parent sells goods to associate for $150 which originally cost parent $100. The goods are still in associate's inventory at the year end.

Required:

State how the unrealised profit will be dealt with in the consolidated accounts.

Summary

- Holding 20% or more of the voting power (directly or indirectly) indicates significant influence unless it can be clearly demonstrated otherwise.

- Significant influence is usually evidenced (e.g. board representation).

- Investments in associates are accounted for in consolidated financial statements using the equity method (i.e. initially at cost and subsequently adjusted for share of profit or loss).

- Equity method investments are classified as non-current assets.

- Dividends received reduce carrying amount.

- On acquisition, any difference between cost and share of net fair value of identifiable assets of the associate is accounted for like goodwill.

- The investor's share of post-acquisition profits or losses is adjusted (e.g. for additional depreciation on fair values exceeding carrying amounts).

- If impairment is indicated, the carrying amount is tested for impairment as a single asset (i.e. goodwill is not tested separately).

- Use of the equity method ceases from the date when significant influence ceases.
  The carrying amount at that date is the new cost.

- The investor's share in unrealised profits and losses arising on transactions should be eliminated.

- Unrealised losses should *not* be eliminated to the extent that the transaction provides evidence of an impairment of the asset transferred.

- The associate's financial statements should be adjusted to reflect any differences from the investor's accounting policies.

- The investor's share of changes recognised directly in the associate's other comprehensive income are recognised in other comprehensive income.

Session 23 Quiz
Estimated time: 10 minutes

1. Define significant influence. (1.3)

2. Identify the basic measurement principles used in equity accounting. (2.3)

3. State how much of an associate's revenue is included in the consolidated revenue figure. (2.5)

4. Explain how goodwill is accounted for in respect of the acquisition of the associate. (2.7)

5. State how unrealised profit on transactions with an associate is accounted for. (3.3)

Study Question Bank
Estimated time: 20 minutes

Priority		Estimated Time	Completed
Q43	Haley	20 minutes	
Additional			
Q44	Hamish		

EXAMPLE SOLUTIONS

Solution 1—Investment in Associate

Consolidated statement of financial position as at 31 December 20X6

	$
Investment in associate (W6)	1,880
Non-current assets (1,600 + 800)	2,400
Current assets (2,200 + 3,300)	5,500
	9,780
Issued capital	1,000
Retained earnings (W5)	7,520
	8,520
Non-controlling interest (W4)	760
Liabilities	500
	9,780

Workings

(1) Group structure

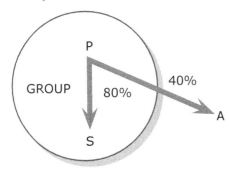

(2) Net assets working

S	Reporting date	Acquisition
	$	$
Issued capital	400	400
Retained earnings	3,400	520
	3,800	920

(3) Goodwill

S

	$
Cost of investment	800
Net assets acquired (80% × 920 (W2))	(736)
	64

(4) Non-controlling interest

	$
S only (20% × 3,800)	760

(5) Retained earnings

	$
P – from question	4,000
Share of S [80% × (3,400 – 520) (W2)]	2,304
Share of A [40% × (3,600 – 400)]	1,280
Less: Goodwill impairment (W3)	(64)
	7,520

(6) Investment in associate

Cost of investment	600
Share of post acquisition profits	1,280
Less: Impairment loss	0
	1,880

Solution 2—Income From Associate

Consolidated statement of profit or loss for the year ending 31 December

	$
Revenue	26,000
Cost of sales	(13,000)
Gross profit	13,000
Administrative expenses	(8,000)
Operating profit	5,000
Income from associate	800
Profit before taxation	5,800
Income taxes	(2,200)
Profit after taxation	3,600
Non-controlling interest (W3)	(160)
Profit for the year	3,440

Statement of Changes in Equity

Dividends paid	1,000

Workings

(1) Group structure

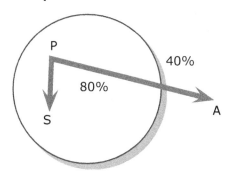

(2) Consolidation schedule

	P	S	A (40%)	Adjustment*	Consolidation
	$	$	$	$	$
Revenue	14,000	12,000			26,000
Cost of sales	(9,000)	(4,000)			(13,000)
Administration expenses	(2,000)	(6,000)			(8,000)
Income from associate					
40% × 2,000			800		800
Tax – group	(1,000)	(1,200)			(2,200)
Profit after tax		800			

(3) Non-controlling interest

	$
S only 20% × 800	160

*Commentary

*The adjustments column is included for completeness (although it is not required in this example).

Solution 3—Eliminating Unrealised Profit

To eliminate unrealised profit:

Deduct $50 from the associate's profit before tax in the statement of profit or loss, to deal with the effect on profit or loss.

Deducted $20 (50 x 40%) from the carrying amount of the associate, to deal with the effect on the consolidated statement of financial position.

Foreign Currency Transactions

FOCUS

This session covers the following content from the *ACCA Study Guide.*

B. Accounting for Transactions in Financial Statements

12. Foreign currency transactions

a) Explain the difference between functional and presentation currency and explain why adjustments for foreign currency transactions are necessary. ☐

b) Account for the translation of foreign currency transactions and monetary/ non-monetary foreign currency items at the reporting date. ☐

Session 24 Guidance

- **Learn** the terminology relevant to IAS 21 (s.1.4) and the recognition rules for individual companies (s.2.1).
- **Work** through *Example 1* (s.2.2).
- **Learn** the factors which drive an entity's functional currency (s.3.2).
- **Read** the section "Foreign currency transactions" of the technical article "F7 Learning outcomes".

VISUAL OVERVIEW

Objective: To prescribe translation rules for transactions in a currency different from the presentation currency and to prescribe the accounting treatment for exchange differences.

```
                        ┌─────────────────────────┐
                        │    ACCOUNTING ISSUES    │
                        │  ─────────────────────  │
                        │   • Introduction        │
                        │   • Key Issues          │
                        │   • Terminology         │
                        └─────────────────────────┘
            ┌───────────────────┼───────────────────┐
┌───────────────────────┐ ┌───────────────────────┐ ┌───────────────────────┐
│  FUNCTIONAL AND       │ │    INDIVIDUAL         │ │                       │
│  PRESENTATION         │ │  COMPANY STAGE        │ │                       │
│  CURRENCY             │ │ ───────────────────── │ │     DISCLOSURE        │
│ ───────────────────── │ │ • Initial Recognition │ │                       │
│ • Functional Currency │ │ • Subsequent          │ │                       │
│ • Presentation Currency│ │   Recognition        │ │                       │
└───────────────────────┘ └───────────────────────┘ └───────────────────────┘
```

1 Accounting Issues

1.1 Introduction

- A company may engage in foreign currency operations in two ways:

  1. Entering directly into transactions which are denominated in foreign currencies.

  2. Conducting foreign operations through a foreign entity (subsidiary or associate).

- Resultant transactions and balances must be translated into the presentation currency of the entity for inclusion in financial statements.

1.2 Key Issues

- Exchange rate to be used for translation.
- Treatment of exchange differences (which arise because exchange rates vary over time).*

1.3 Terminology

Functional currency: the currency of the primary economic environment in which the entity operates.

Presentation currency: the currency in which the financial statements are presented.

Foreign currency: a currency other than the functional currency of the entity.

Closing rate: the spot exchange rate at the end of the reporting period.

Monetary items: money held and assets and liabilities to be received or paid in fixed or determinable number of units of currency.

Spot exchange rate: the exchange rate for immediate delivery.

> ***Commentary***
>
> *F7 does not deal with the translation of the results of foreign subsidiaries; this issue will be covered in P2 studies.

2 Functional and Presentation Currency

2.1 Functional Currency

- An entity should consider the following in determining its functional currency:

  - The currency that mainly influences the selling price of goods or services and the currency of the country whose regulations mainly determine the selling price of goods and services.
  - The currency that affects labour, material and other costs of providing goods and services.

- Secondary factors to are:

  - the currency in which funds from financing activities are generated; and
  - the currency in which monies from operating activities are kept.

> *Key Point*
>
> The functional currency of an entity is dictated by the primary economic environment in which the entity operates.

- The following factors are also to be considered in determining the functional currency of a foreign operation:
  - Are transactions carried out as an extension of the reporting entity or does the foreign operation carry out its activities with a significant degree of autonomy?
  - Are transactions between the reporting entity and foreign operation a high percentage of total transactions?
  - Do cash flows of the foreign operation directly affect the cash flows of the reporting entity and is cash available for remittance to the reporting entity?
  - Is the foreign operation dependent upon the reporting entity to help service debt obligations, both existing and those of the future?
- If the functional currency is not obvious, management must use its judgement in identifying the currency that most faithfully represents the economic effects of the underlying transactions.

Key Point

Once a functional currency has been identified, it should only be changed if there is a change to the economic climate in which it was initially identified.

2.2   Presentation Currency

- The functional currency of most entities will also be the presentation currency.
- However, an entity may choose to present its financial statements in a currency other than its functional currency.
- If an entity chooses to present in a different currency it will need to translate its financial statements each year in accordance with IAS 21.

3   Individual Company Stage

3.1   Initial Recognition

- A **foreign currency** transaction is initially recorded in an entity's **functional currency** using the **spot exchange rate** on the date of the transaction.

Key Point

Exchange differences arising on settlement of a foreign currency transaction in the same reporting period must be recognised in profit or loss for the period.

3.2   Subsequent Recognition

Key Point

At the end of each reporting period, any foreign currency monetary item must be retranslated using the **closing exchange rate.**

- Exchange differences arising on retranslation of a foreign currency balance are recognised in profit or loss for the period.
- Non-monetary items measured at historical cost are translated at the exchange rate at the *date of the transaction*.
- Non-monetary items measured at fair value are translated using the exchange rate when the *fair value was measured*.

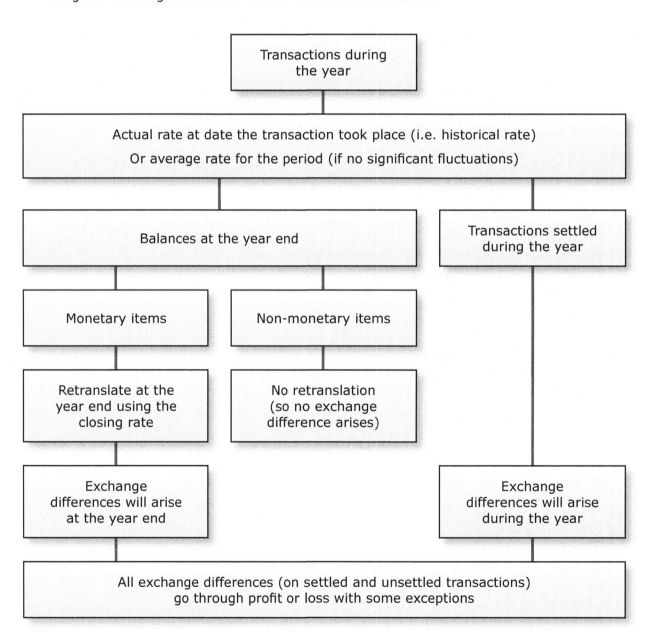

Illustration 1   Purchase of Goods on Credit

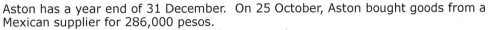

Aston has a year end of 31 December. On 25 October, Aston bought goods from a Mexican supplier for 286,000 pesos.
The goods were still in inventory at the year end.

Exchange rates	Pesos to $
25 October	11.16
16 November	10.87
31 December	11.02

Required:

Show the accounting entries for the transactions in each of the following situations:

(a) on 16 November, Aston pays the Mexican supplier in full;

(b) the supplier remains unpaid at the year end.

Solution

(a) Supplier Paid

		$	$
25 October	Dr Purchases (W1)	25,627	
	Cr Trade payables		25,627
16 November	Dr Trade payables	25,627	
	Dr Profit or loss –		
	other operating expense	684	
	Cr Cash (W2)		26,311

The goods will remain in inventory at the year end at $25,627.

Workings

(1) peso 286,000 ÷ 11.16 = $25,627
(2) peso 286,000 ÷ 10.87 = $26,311

(b) Supplier Unpaid

		$	$
25 October	Dr Purchases (W1)	25,627	
	Cr Trade payables		25,627
31 December	Dr Profit or loss		
	– other operating expense	326	
	Cr Trade payables (W2)		326

The goods will remain in inventory at the year end at $25,627.

Workings

	$
(1) peso 286,000 ÷ 11.16	25,627
(2) peso 286,000 ÷ 11.02	25,953
	326

Example 1 Purchase of Goods on Credit

On 30 October, Barney, a company with the dollar ($) as its functional currency, buys goods from Rubble for £60,000. The contract requires Barney to pay for the goods in sterling, in three equal instalments on 30 November, 31 December and 31 January.

Barney's end of reporting period is 31 December.

Exchange rates	
30 October	$1.90 = £1
30 November	$1.98 = £1
31 December	$2.03 = £1
31 January	$1.95 = £1

Required:

Prepare the journal entries that would appear in Barney's books in respect of the purchase of the goods and the settlement made.

Solution

		US $000	US $000
30 October	Dr Purchases		
	Cr Payables		

Being purchase of goods from UK supplier for £60,000 translated at $1.90 = £1.

		US $000	US $000
30 November	Dr Payables		
	Dr Profit or loss		
	Cr Cash		

Being settlement of £20,000 of balance outstanding translated at $1.98 = £1.
One third of the original payable balance has been settled (114,000/3).

		US $000	US $000
31 December	Dr Payables		
	Dr Profit or loss		
	Cr Cash		

Being settlement of £20,000 of balance outstanding translated at $2.03 = £1.
A further one third of the original payable balance has been settled (114,000/3).

		US $000	US $000
31 December	Dr Profit or loss		
	Cr Payables		

Being restatement of outstanding balance of £20,000 at $2.03 = £1.

		US $000	US $000
31 January	Dr Payables		
	Cr Cash		
	Cr Profit or loss		

Being settlement of £20,000 of balance outstanding translated at $1.95 = £1.

Illustration 2 Loan

Warrior has a year end of 31 December. On 29 November, Warrior received a loan from an Australian bank of AUD 1,520,000.
The proceeds are used to finance in part the purchase of a new office block. The loan remains unsettled at the year end.

Exchange rates	AUD to $
29 November	1.52
31 December	1.66

Required:

Show the accounting entries for these transactions.

Solution

		US $000	US $000
29 November	Dr Cash	1,000	
	Cr Loan		1,000
31 December	Dr Loan	84	
	Cr Profit or loss –		
	other operating income		84

Workings

	US $000
(1) AUD 1,520,000 ÷ 1.52	1,000
(2) AUD 1,520,000 ÷ 1.66	916
	84

4 Disclosure

- The amount of exchange differences included in profit or loss for the period.

- Net exchange differences shown within other comprehensive income and a reconciliation of the amount of such exchange differences at the beginning and end of the period.

- When presentation currency is different to the functional currency, that fact must be stated along with what the functional currency is and the reason for using a different reporting currency.

- Any changes in functional currency and the reasons for the change.

Summary

- Foreign currency transactions are initially recorded using the spot exchange rate.
- Exchange differences arising on settlement in the same reporting period are recognised in profit or loss for the period.
- At each reporting date, any foreign currency monetary item is retranslated using the closing exchange rate.
- An entity's functional currency is dictated by the primary economic environment in which it operates.
- A functional currency can only be changed if there is a change to the economic climate in which it was initially identified.

Session 24 Quiz
Estimated time: 10 minutes

1. Define presentation currency in accordance with IAS 21. (1.4)
2. Discuss the factors an entity should consider when determining its functional currency. (2.1)
3. State how to determine the initial recognition value of a foreign currency transaction. (3.1)
4. Explain what happens at the end of the reporting period to any monetary balances denominated in a foreign currency. (3.2)

Study Question Bank
Estimated time: 20 minutes

Priority		Estimated Time	Completed
Q45	Meridean	20 minutes	

EXAMPLE SOLUTION

Solution 1—Purchase of Goods on Credit

		US $000	US $000
30 October	Dr Purchases	114,000	
	Cr Payables		114,000

Being purchase of goods from UK supplier for £60,000 translated at $1.90 = £1.

		US $000	US $000
30 November	Dr Payables	38,000	
	Dr Profit or loss	1,600	
	Cr Cash		39,600

Being settlement of £20,000 of balance outstanding translated at $1.98 = £1. One third of the original payable balance has been settled (114,000/3).

		US $000	US $000
31 December	Dr Payables	38,000	
	Dr Profit or loss	2,600	
	Cr Cash		40,600

Being settlement of £20,000 of balance outstanding translated at $2.03 = £1. A further one third of the original payable balance has been settled (114,000/3).

		US $000	US $000
31 December	Dr Profit or loss	2,600	
	Cr Payables		2,600

Being restatement of outstanding balance of £20,000 at $2.03 = £1.

		US $000	US $000
31 January	Dr Payables	40,600	
	Cr Cash		39,000
	Cr Profit or loss		1,600

Being settlement of £20,000 of balance outstanding translated at $1.95 = £1.

Analysis and Interpretation

FOCUS

This session covers the following content from the *ACCA Study Guide.*

C. Analysing and Interpreting Financial Statements of Single Entities and Groups

1. Limitations of financial statements

a) Indicate the problems of using historic information to predict future performance and trends. ☐

b) Discuss how financial statements may be manipulated to produce a desired effect (creative accounting, window dressing). ☐

c) Explain why figures in a statement of financial position may not be representative of average values throughout the period. ☐

d) Explain how the use of consolidated financial statements might limit interpretation techniques. ☐

2. Calculation and interpretation of accounting ratios and trends to address users' and stakeholders' needs

a) Define and compute relevant accounting ratios. ☐

b) Explain what aspects of performance specific ratios are intended to assess. ☐

c) Analyse and interpret ratios to give an assessment of an entity's/group's performance in comparison with: ☐

   i)   previous period's financial statements

   ii)   another similar entity/group for the same reporting period

   iii) industry average ratios.

d) Interpret financial statements to give advice from the perspective of different stakeholders. ☐

3. Limitations of interpretation techniques

a) Discuss the limitations in the use of ratio analysis for assessing corporate performance. ☐

b) Discuss the effect that changes in accounting policies or the use of different accounting policies between entities can have on the ability to interpret performance. ☐

c) Indicate other information, including non-financial information, that may be of relevance to the assessment of an entity's performance. ☐

4. Specialised, not-for-profit and public sector entities

a) Explain how the interpretation of the financial statement of a specialised, not-for-profit or public sector organisation might differ from that of a profit-making entity by reference to the different aims, objectives and reporting requirements. ☐

VISUAL OVERVIEW

Objective: To describe the need for analysis of financial statements and the approach to interpreting financial information.

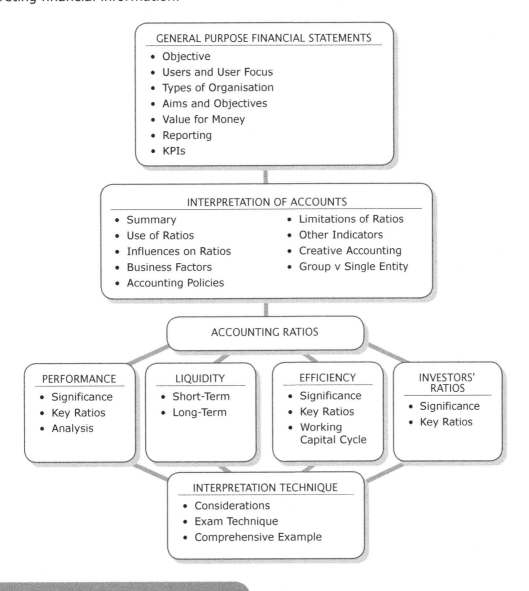

GENERAL PURPOSE FINANCIAL STATEMENTS
- Objective
- Users and User Focus
- Types of Organisation
- Aims and Objectives
- Value for Money
- Reporting
- KPIs

INTERPRETATION OF ACCOUNTS
- Summary
- Use of Ratios
- Influences on Ratios
- Business Factors
- Accounting Policies
- Limitations of Ratios
- Other Indicators
- Creative Accounting
- Group v Single Entity

ACCOUNTING RATIOS

PERFORMANCE
- Significance
- Key Ratios
- Analysis

LIQUIDITY
- Short-Term
- Long-Term

EFFICIENCY
- Significance
- Key Ratios
- Working Capital Cycle

INVESTORS' RATIOS
- Significance
- Key Ratios

INTERPRETATION TECHNIQUE
- Considerations
- Exam Technique
- Comprehensive Example

Session 25 Guidance

■ **Appreciate** that you need to grasp what the ratios are telling you.

■ **Comprehend** that different users have different information needs (s.1).

■ **Understand** the influences on performance information in the business environment and how they affect accounting data and ratios (s.2.3–s.2.5).

■ **Appreciate** the limitations of ratio analysis (s.2.6) and understand that ratios themselves do not give "answers".

■ **Know** various types of ratios, their construction and nuances (s.3–s.7).

■ **Attempt** *Example 2* (s.8).

1 General Purpose Financial Statements

1.1 Objective

Key Point

The objective of financial reporting is to provide information about an entity to external users of its financial statements. The users of financial statements and their information needs are the key issue in financial reporting.

1.2 Users and User Focus

1.2.1 Investors

▦ The providers of risk capital and their advisers are concerned with risk inherent in, and return provided by, their investment. They need information:

  ⚬ to help them determine whether they should buy, hold or sell;

  ⚬ that enables them to assess the performance of management.

1.2.2 Employees

▦ Employees and their representative groups are interested in information about:

  ⚬ the stability and profitability of their employers;

  ⚬ which enables them to assess the ability of the entity to provide remuneration, retirement benefits and employment opportunities.

1.2.3 Lenders

▦ Lenders are interested in information which enables them to determine whether their loans, and the interest attaching to them, will be paid when due.

1.2.4 Suppliers and Other Creditors

▦ Suppliers and other creditors are interested in information which enables them to determine whether amounts owing to them will be paid when due.

▦ Trade suppliers are likely to be interested in an entity over a shorter period than lenders unless they are dependent on the continuation of the entity as a major customer.

1.2.5 Customers

▦ Customers have an interest in information about the continuation of an entity, especially when they have a long-term involvement with, or are dependent on, the entity.

1.2.6   Governments and Their Agencies

- Governments and their agencies are interested in the allocation of resources and, therefore, the activities of an entity.

- They also require information in order to regulate the activities of entities, determine taxation policies and provide a basis for national income and similar statistics.

1.2.7 Public

- Entities affect members of the public in a variety of ways. For example, entities may make a substantial contribution to the local economy in many ways including the number of people they employ and their patronage of the suppliers. Financial statements may assist the public by providing information about the trends and recent developments in the prosperity of the entity and the range of its activities.

1.3   Types of Organisation

1.3.1   Commercial

- Commercial organisations (businesses) are generally profit-seeking (i.e. they aim to maximise the wealth of their owners/shareholders).

- Sub-classifications include:
  - industrial (e.g. extractive, steel, pharmaceuticals, textiles, clothing, electronics, transport, construction, engineering, service);
  - manufacturing (e.g. specific divisions of industrial such as pipes, drugs, fabric, shoes, semiconductors, cars);
  - financial, which can also be considered as a service in managing money (e.g. banking, insurance, investment funds); and
  - service, where no goods or products are produced (e.g. audit and accountancy, consulting, entertainment, advertising, marketing).

- The primary objectives of businesses are to:
  - continue in existence;
  - maintain growth (or at least not decline); and
  - make a profit.

- Other objectives for commercial organisations may include:
  - market standing (e.g. to achieve market share);
  - innovation (e.g. to lead new product developments);
  - productivity (e.g. optimum allocation of resources);
  - managing and sustaining physical and financial resources;
  - manager performance and development;
  - worker performance and attitude; and
  - public responsibility (e.g. waste recycling and local employment).

1.3.2 Not-for-Profit

▨ Not-for-profit organisations do not consider profit to be their primary objective. They aim to satisfy particular needs of their members (they do not have shareholders) or of society in general, and usually consider financial objectives as constraints under which they have to operate.

▨ Examples include:
  ● government departments, local authorities and agencies (exist to implement policy);
  ● educational establishments (but note that private education has a profit motive);
  ● hospitals (note that private hospitals would be classified as profit orientated);
  ● charities (collect money and effectively distribute according to charity's aims);
  ● pressure groups which raise money to follow a given agenda (e.g. Greenpeace); and
  ● clubs and mutual societies that raise money directly from members to be able to provide common services to those members (e.g. golf clubs, tennis clubs, building societies, insurance, trade unions).

1.3.3 Public Sector

▨ The public sector is the part of the economy and the services provided which are controlled by governmental organisations. Typical examples include the police, military, fire and ambulance services, public roads, public transport, public utilities (gas, electricity, water, telephone—although in many countries these may have been privatised into commercial organisations with shareholders), primary healthcare, libraries, refuse collection and local authorities.

▨ Those facilities, businesses and services not controlled by government will be in the private sector.

1.3.4 Non-governmental Organisations (NGOs)

▨ Originally established by the United Nations in the 1950s, the concept of the NGO spread into general usage during the 1970s. Many diverse types of bodies are now described as NGOs.

▨ Generally accepted characteristics of an NGO include:
  ● voluntary formation;
  ● aim to improve circumstances and prospects of disadvantaged people;
  ● independence from the direct control of any government;
  ● not constituted as a political party;
  ● non-profit-making; and
  ● not a criminal group (in particular it is non-violent).

▨ However, some NGOs may be closely identified with a political party; many NGOs generate income from commercial activities (e.g. consultancy contracts or sales of publications); and a small number of NGOs may be associated with politically based protests.

▨ The World Bank classifies NGOs as either operational or
  advocacy:

  ◦ **Operational** NGOs are primarily involved in the design and
    implementation of development (aid) related projects (both
    relief-oriented and development-oriented).

  ◦ **Advocacy** NGOs defend or promote a specific cause,
    typically trying to raise awareness, acceptance and
    knowledge by lobbying, press work and activist events.

▨ For example, Oxfam, although a charity, is an NGO and
  establishes NGOs in many countries to enable funds raised to
  be disbursed to end recipients. Other NGOs may promote a
  country's culture and language in other countries or establish
  health education programmes (e.g. AIDS, birth control).

1.4   Aims and Objectives (non-profit organisations)

▨ Not all organisations are concerned with profitability. Not-for-
  profit organisations and the public sector are more concerned
  with providing a service.

▨ Service users and the general public will want to know how
  these types of organisations have performed and that they are
  providing value for money.

▨ Users are more concerned that the required service is provided
  as economically, efficiently and effectively as possible. Value
  for money audits are frequently carried out within public sector
  organisations to ensure that costs are minimised, outputs are
  maximised and a level of quality is achieved.

▨ Management must be seen as the stewards of the
  organisation's resources and therefore must maintain close
  control of the resources within their domain.

▨ The bottom line for many public sector entities, especially local
  and national governments, is that if they do not perform then
  they will be voted out by the public to whom they should be
  providing a service.

▨ Among their many objectives, national governments seek to
  provide health, education and policing to all members of the
  community; they do not seek to make a profit from giving
  these services.

▨ Other organisations such as charities and many museums do
  not have profit as their primary objective; they again seek
  to provide a service to various groups within the local and
  international community.

▨ Most of the non-profitability ratios can be calculated for these
  specialised organisations, especially the efficiency ratios.

▨ Management and control of cash is also very important
  within these types of organisations; as there is normally no
  profit objective, the management of cash can quite easily be
  forgotten.

1.5 Value for Money

Value for money considers the "3 Es":

1. **Economy**—the organisation looks to minimise the cost of inputs.

2. **Efficiency**—the organisation looks to maximise outputs in proportion to the cost of inputs.

3. **Effectiveness**—the organisation has managed to perform its objectives.

 - Value for money goes further than the calculation of ratios. If an organisation is providing value for money then the organisation is:
   - Effective in accomplishing its aims and objectives;
   - Efficient, using the minimal amount of resources to meet the aims and objectives; and
   - Economical, with input costs as low as possible without being detrimental to the efficiency and effectiveness of the organisation.

1.6 Reporting

Most not-for-profit and public sector organisations use accrual accounting. Cash-based accounting, however, is still used in some public sector institutions.

The International Federation of Accountants (IFAC) has published International Public Sector Accounting Standards prescribing the accounting treatment to be followed by public sector bodies. These standards are derived from IFRS, with adaptations being made to put them in a public sector context when appropriate. The preface to these standards states that the conceptual framework of the IASB is still relevant in public sector accounting.

Charitable organisations cannot do as they please with their funds; they must produce accounting records showing the stewardship of the funds which have been entrusted to them. Reporting must also show exactly where funds are being distributed and that a code of ethics is being followed.

Not-for-profit and public sector organisations must still produce financial statements and report information to respective users. Organisations and their users may include the following:

 - Ministries reporting to heads of government;
 - Schools reporting results to parents and local authorities;
 - Clubs and societies reporting to their membership;
 - Charities reporting to the general public and also trustees; and
 - Hospitals reporting to local community and hospital trusts; these trusts will also be required to report performance upwards to government organisations.

1.7   Key Performance Indicators (KPIs)

▓ The analysis of not-for-profit and public sector organisations should consider indicators other than profit. It should be noted that some of these organisations may actually make a profit, more commonly termed "surplus", as some of their operations will result in profitable transactions.

▓ KPIs enable users to determine whether the organisation is meeting its aims and objectives.

▓ KPIs include some of the following:

  ● For charities—growth in number of donors or a growth in donation per donor;

  ● For schools—number of pupils attaining at least 3 A grades in their exams;

  ● For hospitals—the number of patients readmitted after undergoing surgery;

  ● For golf clubs—the increase in membership; and

  ● For local councils—number of complaints received from public regarding potholes in roads.

2   Interpretation of Accounts

2.1   Summary

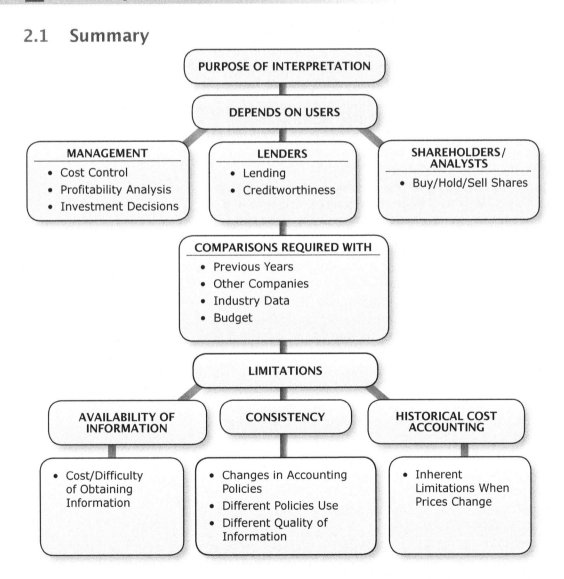

2.2 Use of Ratios

Ratios are of no use in isolation. To be useful, a basis is needed for comparison, for example:

- previous years;
- other companies;
- industry averages; or
- budgeted v actual (for management use).

2.3 Influences on Ratios

The "story" of the performance and position told by a set of financial statements is a function of:

- business factors (including the results of management actions and related party situations)*; and
- accounting policies.

2.4 Business Factors

Type of business (e.g. retailer, manufacturer): This affects the nature of the assets employed and the returns earned; a retailer may have higher asset turnover but lower margins than a manufacturer.

Quality of management: Better-managed businesses are likely to be more profitable and have better working capital management than businesses in which management is weak.

State of economy and market conditions: If a market or the economy in general is depressed, this is likely to adversely affect companies and make most or all of their ratios appear worse.

Management actions: These will be reflected in changes in ratios. For example, price discounting to increase market share is likely to reduce margins but increase asset turnover; withdrawing from unprofitable market sectors is likely to reduce turnover but increase profit margins.

Changes in the business: If the business diversifies into wholly new areas, this is likely to change the resource structure and thus affect key ratios. A new acquisition near the year end will mean that capital employed will include all the assets acquired but profits generated by the new acquisition will only be included in the statement of profit or loss for a small part of the year, thus tending to depress return on capital employed (ROCE).

Related party situations: A parent company and its subsidiaries are related parties and transactions between them may not be on non-commercial terms due to the control that is exercised by the parent.

- There is nothing "wrong" with transactions being other than "at arm's length", for example:
  - sale of raw materials for a production process or goods for distribution at a transfer price that is not a market price;
  - transfer of non-current assets at an undervalue (or overvalue);
  - management charges; or
  - financial support (e.g. loans) at below-market interest rates (e.g. zero finance cost).

Key Point

Ratios are a tool to assist analysis. They focus attention on trends and weaknesses and facilitate comparison over time and between companies.

*Commentary

*Ratios may change over time or differ between companies because of the nature of the business or management actions in running the business.

Exam Advice

IAS 24 *Related Party Disclosures* is not examinable.

- However, although the effects of these transactions will be eliminated on consolidation in the consolidated financial statements, the single entities' financial statements will be distorted. For example, the profits of one may be boosted and those of another dampened.
- To assess the performance of a single entity though the analysis and interpretation of ratios it is therefore necessary to take account of the existence of related-party relationships and the related transactions.
- Relevant disclosures that should be made in published financial statements include:
  - the nature and amounts of transactions;
  - any outstanding balances including terms of settlement, security and guarantees; and
  - whether any allowance has been made for irrecoverability of outstanding balances and any bad debt expense.

2.5 Accounting Policies

- Choice of accounting policies can significantly affect the view presented by the accounts, and the ratios computed, without affecting the business's core ability to generate profits and cash. For example:
  - If assets are depreciated for a whole year in the year of acquisition, accounting profit may be reduced by more than the additional income generated if the acquisition is near the end of the accounting period.
  - Carrying amounts of non-current assets will be greater:
    - if they are depreciated on a reducing balance basis rather than a straight-line basis (over the same useful life);
    - the longer the estimated useful life; and
    - the higher the estimated residual value (i.e. the depreciable amount will be lower).
  - If a business revalues its assets rather than carrying them at historical cost, this will usually increase capital employed and reduce profit before tax (due to higher depreciation). Thus, ROCE, profit margins and gearing are all likely to be lower if a business revalues its assets.
  - In times of rising prices, inventory valuation will be higher under FIFO than under weighted average cost. When inventory volumes are increasing, higher profits will be reported under FIFO.
- Where policies have been chosen to reflect the entity in the best possible light, then the entity could be accused of adopting "creative accounting" policies which do not necessarily reflect a fair presentation of the events and transactions which have occurred in the period (see s.2.8).

2.6   Limitations of Ratios

✗   Ratio analysis is essentially a retrospective examination—not prospective. Ratios use historical data which is unlikely to be predictive as this ignores future actions by management and changes in the business environment. When trying to make forecasts for historical ratios, consider future plans and the impact that these plans will have on the historical data.

✗   Ratios are based on accounting rather than economic data. Making adjustments to historical costs to reflect current economic values may increase relevance but with a loss of reliability.

✗   Usefulness is limited by the limitations of financial statements (e.g. "off balance sheet items").

✗   Ratios may be distorted by differences in accounting policies (see above).

✗   Comparisons between companies in the same industry sector may not provide reliable information. The comparative size of the companies would need to be considered; also, one company might be a new, expanding company and the other might be an old, stagnating company.

✗   A wide range of governmental and commercial organisations publish industry statistics including financial-based information. This information may not, however, be reliable. Factors to be considered when using such industry data include whether:

  ● the information is provided on a voluntary or mandatory basis;
  ● the collection of the data is sponsored by one specific company;
  ● entities contributing to the statistics have the same year end.

✗   Ratios summarise information; information about extreme values and the spread of data is therefore "lost".

✗   Comparisons between different types of business are difficult because of differing resource structures and market characteristics.

✗   Many ratios use figures from the statement of financial position, these figures represent only one point in time. If an entity has seasonal or cyclical trading cycles then the ratios derived from the statement of financial position may not be representative of how the business operates at other times.*

*Commentary

*The use of averages of opening and closing balances may still give rise to distortions. For example, if the reporting date coincides with the end of a "busy season", inventory levels may be lower than the average inventory holding during the year (as inventory levels have not yet been replenished) and trade receivables are likely to be higher than average.

✗   Analysis of consolidated financial statements may mask information relating to an entity within the group.

Illustration 1 Gearing

A group has total debt of $100 and equity of $800, giving a gearing ratio of 12.5%.

If all of the debt was held by one subsidiary in the group, and that subsidiary had equity of $100, then the gearing ratio for that subsidiary would be 100%.

By preparing consolidated financial statements the gearing risk of that subsidiary is hidden in the results of the group as a whole.

The same could be said of a loss-making entity within the group; if the group as a whole is profitable then the loss made by an entity of the group may well be hidden from view.

2.7 Other Indicators*

*Commentary

*Ratios are a key tool of analysis but other sources of information are also available.

- Absolute comparisons can provide information without computing ratios (e.g. comparing statements of financial position between this year and last may show that new shares have been issued to repay borrowings or finance new investment, which may in turn affect gearing and ROCE).
- Background information supplied about the nature of the business may help to explain changes or trends (e.g. if a business has made an acquisition).
- The statement of cash flows provides information as to how a business has generated and used cash so that users can obtain a fuller picture of liquidity and financial adaptability.
- Not all indicators of performance need to be financial in nature. Many other factors and non-financial indicators affect an assessment of performance. For example:
  - employee satisfaction and staff turnover;
  - quality or products or services;
  - manufacturing capability, productivity and flexibility;
  - interaction of the entity within the local community;
  - environmental compliance (as many companies now include an environmental report as part of their annual financial statements); and
  - customer satisfaction and care policy.

Exam Advice

Remember, at F7 there will be more marks available for the interpretation of an entity's results rather than the calculation of a few ratios. You need to look beyond the numbers and think a little bit deeper. You will not earn marks simply by stating that profitability has gone down by 10%; you will need to explain possible reasons for the reduction.

2.8   Creative Accounting

Key Point

▦ Over the past 40 years, companies have tried to be creative in the way they account for certain transactions. This has led to abuses of the accounting entries recording these transactions and the financial statements not reflecting the economic reality of the situation. The following are some of the main areas in which management have been creative in their accounting treatment.

Ratios do not provide answers but focus attention on important areas.

2.8.1   Off Balance Sheet Financing

▦ This is where a company has a present obligation to make a payment but has been able to keep the obligation (debt) off the statement of financial position. A sale and repurchase transaction, if accounted under its legal form, is an example of off balance sheet financing.

2.8.2   Profit Manipulation or Smoothing

▦ Management prefer profits to be increasing at a steady rate, not going up and down each year in an uncontrolled manner. Management will change revenue and cost recognition in order to smooth out the profits. Examples of abuse in this area include early recognition of revenue and incorrect recognition of provisions.

2.8.3   Window Dressing

▦ This is where the financial statements are made pretty for one moment in time, normally the year end. Many ratios are calculated using figures from the statement of financial position. If these figures can be made to look good then it will improve the related ratios and put the company in a much better light. Settling trade payables on the last day of the year only to reinstate them the next day is an example of such abuse.

2.9   Group v. Single Entity

▦ When analysing a set of accounts, the analyst needs to consider whether a single entity or a group is being analysed.

▦ If it is a group the question must be asked, "Has the parent bought or sold a subsidiary during the current period"?

▦ If so, then it is not possible to simply compare current year with previous year, as the two periods are not the same.

▦ If a purchase or disposal took place during the year then the analyst will need to strip out the effects of the transaction in order to make meaningful judgement on the performance of the group.

▦ If a user wishes to analyse a subsidiary within a group then it is no use using the consolidated financial statements, as they may mask the specific performance of a single subsidiary within the group.

3   Accounting Ratios

- Accounting ratios help to summarise and present financial information in a more understandable form. They assist in assessing a business's performance by identifying significant relationships between different figures.
- Ratios divide into five main areas:
  1. Performance
  2. Short-term liquidity
  3. Long-term solvency
  4. Efficiency
  5. Investors' (or stock market) ratios.

4   Performance

4.1   Significance

- Performance ratios measure the rate of return earned on capital employed, and analyse this into profit margins and use of assets. These ratios are frequently used as the basis for assessing management effectiveness in utilising the resources under their control.

4.2   Key Ratios

- Return on (total) capital employed (ROCE):

$$\frac{\text{Profit before interest and tax}}{\text{Share capital + reserves + debt}} \times 100$$

  - Measures overall efficiency of company in employing resources available to it.
- Return on shareholders' funds (ROSF): Measures how efficiently a company is employing funds which shareholders have provided.

$$\frac{\text{Profit before tax}}{\text{Share capital + reserves}}$$

  - Measures how efficiently a company is employing funds which shareholders have provided.

Capital employed may also be calculated as total assets less current liabilities.

*ROSF is also know as Return on Equity (RoE) and can also be calculated using profit after tax.

Consideration 1   ROCE/ROSF

When drawing conclusions from ROCE/ROSF consider:

- target return on capital (company or shareholder);
- real interest rates;
- age of plant;
- leased/owned assets;
- revaluation of assets; and
- R&D policy.

Gross profit percentage:

$$\frac{\text{Gross profit}}{\text{Sales}} \times 100$$

- Measures margin earned by company on sales.

Consideration 2   GP Percentage

When drawing conclusions from ROCE/ROSF consider:

- Variations between years may be attributable to:
  - change in sales prices;
  - change in sales mix;
  - change in purchase/production costs; or
  - inventory obsolescence.

Overheads/sales percentage:

$$\frac{\text{Overheads}}{\text{Sales}} \times 100$$

- Measures margin of overheads (fixed and variable usually = distribution costs + administrative expenses) to sales.
- Ideally should be broken into variable overheads (expected to change with sales) and fixed overheads (likely to move in a more "stepped" fashion).

Consideration 3   Overheads/Sales

May change because of:

- change in the value of sales—investigate whether it is due to price or to volume changes;
- company relocation to new premises.

4.3 Analysis

- ROCE measures return achieved by management from assets which they control, before payments to providers of financing for those assets (i.e. lenders and shareholders. Usually year-end capital employed is used to compute this ratio).

- Consideration needs to be given to the age of an entity's assets; old assets with low carrying amounts will lead to a high ROCE, whereas an entity which has just made a major acquisition of new assets will find that the ROCE will be fairly low as the asset will not have reached its optimum performance levels.

- ROCE can be further subdivided into profit margin and asset turnover (use of assets).

Profit margin	×	Asset turnover	=	ROCE
$\dfrac{\text{PBIT}}{\text{Turnover}}$	×	$\dfrac{\text{Turnover}}{\text{Capital employed}}$	=	$\dfrac{\text{PBIT}}{\text{Capital employed}}$

- Profit margin is often seen as a measure of quality of profits. A high profit margin indicates a high profit on each unit sold. Asset turnover is often seen as a quantitative measure, indicating how intensively the management is using the assets.

 **Key Point**

A trade-off often exists between margin and asset turnover. Low margin businesses (e.g. food retailers) usually have high asset turnover. Conversely, capital-intensive manufacturing industries usually have relatively low asset turnover but higher margins (e.g. electrical equipment manufacturers).

5 Liquidity

5.1 Short Term

5.1.1 Significance

▓ Short-term liquidity ratios are used to assess a company's ability to raise cash to meet payments when due. In practice, information contained in the statement of cash flows is often more useful when analysing liquidity.

5.1.2 Key Ratios

▓ Current ratio:

   ◦ $\dfrac{\text{Current assets}}{\text{Current liabilities}}$ (usually expressed as X:1)

   ◦ Measures adequacy of current assets to cover current liabilities.

▓ Quick ratio (acid test):

   ◦ $\dfrac{\text{Debtors + investments + cash}}{\text{Current liabilities}}$ (usually expressed as X:1)

   ◦ Eliminates the slower-moving item—inventory—from the calculation, thus measuring real short-term liquidity.

Consideration 4   Current and Quick Ratios*

- Indicators:
  - Low ratio may indicate liquidity problems.
  - High ratio may indicate poor use of shareholder/company funds.
- Consider constituent components of ratio—inventory obsolescence (in case of current ratio), recoverability of receivables (in case of both ratios).
- Consider manipulation—if a company has positive cash balances and a ratio greater than 1:1, payment of payables just prior to the year end will improve the ratio.

---

*Commentary

- The current ratio is of limited use as some current assets (e.g. inventory) may not be readily convertible into cash, other than at a large discount. Hence, this ratio may not indicate whether the company can pay its debts as they fall due.
- As the quick ratio omits inventory, this is a better indicator of liquidity but is subject to distortions (e.g. retailers have few receivables and utilise cash from sales quickly but finance their inventory from trade payables; hence, their quick ratios are usually low).

5.1.3 Window Dressing

▨ The illustration below shows how easy it is for an entity to manipulate the ratios simply by writing a cheque to clear some of the payable balance.

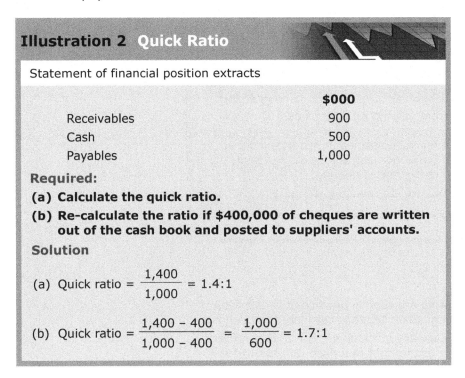

Illustration 2 Quick Ratio

Statement of financial position extracts

	$000
Receivables	900
Cash	500
Payables	1,000

Required:

(a) Calculate the quick ratio.

(b) Re-calculate the ratio if $400,000 of cheques are written out of the cash book and posted to suppliers' accounts.

Solution

(a) Quick ratio $= \dfrac{1,400}{1,000} = 1.4{:}1$

(b) Quick ratio $= \dfrac{1,400 - 400}{1,000 - 400} = \dfrac{1,000}{600} = 1.7{:}1$

5.2 Long Term

5.2.1 Significance

▨ Gearing ratios examine the financing structure of a business. They indicate to shareholders the degree of risk attached to the company and the sensitivity of profits and dividends to changes in profitability and activity level.

5.2.2 Key Ratios

▨ Gearing ratio:

$$\frac{\text{Fixed return capital, preference shares, debentures, loan stock}}{\text{Equity capital and reserves}} \text{; or}$$

$$\frac{\text{Debt}}{\text{Debt + Equity}}$$

- Measures relationship between company's borrowings and its share capital and reserves.
- A company is highly geared if it has a substantial proportion of its capital in the form of preference shares, debentures or loan stock.
- Interest on fixed return capital (and possibly dividends on preference shares) generally has to be paid irrespective of whether profits are earned—this may cause a liquidity crisis if a company is unable to meet its fixed return capital obligations. High gearing, therefore, should be accompanied by stable profits.

- Asset backing—generally loan capital is secured on assets—these should be suitable for the purpose (not fast depreciating or subject to rapid changes in demand and price).
- Interest cover:

$$\frac{\text{Profit before interest}}{\text{Interest}}$$

Consideration 5   Gearing*

When drawing conclusions from gearing ratios consider:

- assets in the statement of financial position at historical cost or revalued amount—revaluation of non-current assets increases shareholders' funds and thus decreases gearing;
- use of "off balance sheet finance" to reduce gearing.

---

*Commentary

- As many measures of gearing are used in practice, it is especially important with gearing ratios that the ratios calculated are defined.
- Preference share capital is usually included as part of debt rather than equity because it carries the right to a fixed rate of dividend which is payable before the ordinary shareholders have any right to a dividend.
- If a business is highly geared, this usually indicates increased risk for shareholders as, if profits fall, debts will still need to be financed, leaving much smaller profits available to shareholders.
- Highly geared businesses are usually more exposed to insolvency if there is an economic downturn. However, returns to shareholders will grow proportionately more in highly geared businesses in which profits are growing.

Illustration 3 Impact of Gearing on Earnings

Consider three situations for the same geared company, ignoring tax.

	(1) $	(2) $	(3) $
Profit before interest	200	100	300
Interest on fixed debt	(100)	(100)	(100)
Profit available to shareholders (earnings)	100	–	200
Compared to situation (1)			
Change in profits before interest		– 50%	+ 50%
Change in earnings		– 100%	+ 100%

▦ Low gearing provides scope to increase borrowings when potentially profitable projects are available. Companies with low gearing are likely to find it easier to borrow and should be able to borrow more cheaply than if gearing is already high.

Key Point

Gearing is also significant to lenders as they are likely to charge higher interest to, and be less willing to lend to, companies which are already highly geared as such companies are more likely to default on the interest or debt repayments.

▦ Interest cover indicates the ability of a company to pay interest out of profits generated. Interest cover of less than two is usually considered unsatisfactory. This indicates that the company may have difficulty financing its debts if its profits fall and also indicates to shareholders that their dividends are at risk as interest must be paid first, even if profits fall.

6 Efficiency

6.1 Significance

Key Point

Working capital ratios are an important indicator of management's effectiveness in running the business efficiently, as for a given level of activity it is most profitable to minimise the level of working capital employed in the business.

6.2 Key Ratios

▓ Inventory turnover:

$$\frac{\text{Cost of sales}}{\text{Average inventory}}$$

(= number of times inventory is turned over each year so the higher the better)

$$\frac{\text{Average inventory}}{\text{Cost of sales}} \times 365$$

(= number of days it takes to turn inventory over once so the lower the better)

- Ideally consider the components of inventory:
  — raw material to volume of purchases;
  — WIP to cost of production; and
  — finished goods to cost of sales.

Consideration 6   Inventory Turnover

- High inventory turnover rate—may be efficient but risk of stock outs increased.
- Low inventory turnover rate—inefficient use of resources and potential obsolescence problems.
- Accurate reflection?
- Does position represent real inventory turnover rate for the year or does year-end inventory holding distort the true picture?

▓ Receivable days:

$$\frac{\text{Average trade receivables}}{\text{Credit sales}} \times 365$$

- Measures period of credit taken by company's customers.
- Ideal approximately 30–40 days, depending on the industry.

Consideration 7 Receivable Days

- A change in the ratio may indicate:
  - bad debt/collection problems;
  - a change in the customer base (big new receivable—slow payer); or
  - a change in settlement terms.
- Accurate reflection?
  - Does year-end receivables give a reasonable indication of the receivable profile for the year as a whole?

Payable days:

$$\frac{\text{Average trade payables}}{\text{Credit purchases}} \times 365$$

- Measures number of days' credit taken by company from suppliers.
- Should be broadly consistent with receivable days.

Consideration 8 Payable Days

- A change in the ratio may indicate:
  - liquidity problems with the company if the figure is high;
  - potential appointment of receiver by aggrieved suppliers.
- Accurate reflection?
  - Do year-end payables give a reasonable indication of payable profile for the year as a whole?

6.3 Working Capital Cycle*

Combining the three efficiency ratios will give the number of days' worth of working capital that an entity needs before it starts to receive cash. The number of days could be negative, common in the retail sector, meaning that cash will be received before the entity has to pay its suppliers.

*Commentary

*The time it takes a transaction to generate cash is also called the cash (conversion) cycle.

	Manufacturing	Retail
Inventory days	120	15
Receivable days	50	Nil
Payable days	(45)	(30)
Working capital cycle	125	(15)

- The manufacturing company will have raw materials, WIP and finished goods, whereas the retail company will have only low levels of finished goods.
- The manufacturers probably will sell their product on credit, whereas the retail outlet will sell goods only for cash.
- Both companies will probably buy their supplies on credit.
- In this example, the manufacturing company needs 125 days' worth of working capital before it receives any cash but the retail outlet receives 15 days' worth of free credit from its supplier.

▦ Inventory turnover, receivable days and payable days give an indication of whether a business is able to generate cash as fast as it uses it. They also provide useful comparisons between businesses (e.g. on effectiveness in collecting debts and controlling inventory levels). The average of opening and closing inventories, receivables and payables is often used to compute these ratios.

Example 1 Ratios and Financial Performance

Virgil has produced the following financial statements:

Statement of profit or loss for the year ended 30 June

	20X7	20X6
	$000	**$000**
Revenue	28,000	25,000
Cost of sales	(15,700)	(18,300)
Gross profit	12,300	6,700
Distribution costs	(3,100)	(2,200)
Administrative expenses	(3,100)	(2,000)
Profit before tax	6,100	2,500
Income tax expense	(1,000)	(500)
Profit after tax	5,100	2,000

Example 1   Ratios and Financial Performance (continued)

Statement of financial position at 30 June

	20X7		20X6	
	$000	$000	$000	$000
Non-current assets		23,000		18,000
Current assets				
Inventory	4,800		2,300	
Trade receivables	3,200		2,500	
Bank and cash	–		1,300	
		8,000		6,100
Total assets		31,000		24,100
Equity and liabilities				
Capital and reserves				
Ordinary share, $1 each.		14,200		13,200
Retained earnings		12,100		7,000
		26,300		20,200
Current liabilities				
Trade payables	3,600		3,900	
Short-term borrowings	1,100		–	
		4,700		3,900
Total equity and liabilities		31,000		24,100

Required:

(a) **State and calculate THREE profitability and THREE liquidity/efficiency ratios for EACH of the two years.**

(b) **Using the information provided by the ratios calculated in (a) comment on the financial performance of Virgil.**

Solution

(a) **Ratios**

	20X7	20X6
ratios		
(1)		
(2)		
(3)		
ratios		
(1)		
(2)		
(3)		

(b) **Comment on financial performance**

7 Investors' Ratios

7.1 Significance

Investors' ratios help to establish characteristics of ordinary shares in different companies. For example:

- Earnings per share (EPS) are important to those investors looking for capital growth.
- Dividend yield, dividend cover and dividends per share are important to those investors seeking income.

7.2 Key Ratios*

*Commentary

- Ideally, investors should use forecast information when making investment decisions. In practice, only historical figures are usually available.
- Dividend yield measures dividend policy rather than performance. A high yield based on recent dividends and current share price may arise because the share price has fallen in anticipation of a future dividend cut. Rapidly growing companies may exhibit low yields based on historical dividends, especially if the current share price reflects anticipated future growth.
- The dividend cover ratio shows how many times a company could have paid its current dividend from available earnings (i.e. an indication of how secure dividends are).
- The PE ratio is used to indicate whether shares appear to be expensive or cheap in terms of how many years of current earnings investors are prepared to pay for.

$$\text{Dividend yield} = \frac{\text{Dividend per share}}{\text{Current market price per share}}$$

$$\text{Dividend cover} = \frac{\text{EPS}}{\text{Dividend per share}}$$

$$\text{Price/earnings (PE) ratio} = \frac{\text{Current market price per share}}{\text{EPS}}$$

EPS is also a very important ratio but it is covered in a later session.

8 Interpretation Technique

8.1 Considerations

```
                    ┌─────────────────────────────────┐
                    │  ANALYSIS AND INTERPRETATION    │
                    └─────────────────────────────────┘
         ┌──────────────────┐            ┌──────────────────┐
         │     ANALYSIS     │            │  INTERPRETATION  │
         └──────────────────┘            └──────────────────┘
```

CALCULATION

of key ratios and statistics

CONSIDERATIONS

- *Who* are you?
- *Who* is the user?
- *What* decision are they taking?
- *What* are the key factors affecting that decision?

COMMENTS

Use the following checklist on each ratio calculated:

- What does the ratio mean?
- What does a change in the ratio mean?
- What is the norm?
- What are the limitations of the ratio?

APPENDICES

- Relegate all workings/ calculations to appendices
- Always show the formulae used

STYLE

FORMAT

- Letter: Formal to third party
- Report: Formal, third party/internal
- Memo: Less formal, internal

BE CONCISE

- Use short, punchy sentences
- Avoid repetition and long paragraphs

STRUCTURE

- Follow the requirements in the question
- Use headings

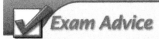 Exam Advice

An interpretation question could include reference to the disposal of a subsidiary during the period. However, calculation of any profit or loss on disposal would **not** be required.

8.2 Exam Technique

- If asked to interpret accounts:
  - make comments pertinent to the users of accounts; therefore we need to identify audience from requirement;
  - only compute ratios if you can make use of them (and always define ratios calculated), make comparisons and suggest reasons;
  - also compare absolute numbers in the accounts to identify differences (e.g. changes year on year);
  - look for the influence of business factors and accounting policies;
  - be able to link different pieces of information and see what they point towards;
  - indicate the need for further information if necessary; and
  - be aware of the limitations of ratios.
- Most marks in the exam are likely to be for specific, relevant comments rather than solely for computations.
- If asked to write a report, put a table of ratios in an appendix and refer to them in the text as appropriate.

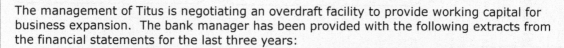

Example 2 Analysis and Interpretation

The management of Titus is negotiating an overdraft facility to provide working capital for business expansion. The bank manager has been provided with the following extracts from the financial statements for the last three years:

Statement of financial position at 31 December

	20X5		20X6	
	$000	$000	$000	$000
Tangible non-current assets		163		153
Current assets				
Inventory	40		52	
Receivables	45		52	
Bank	15		2	
		100		106
Total assets		263		259
Current liabilities (including tax)		45		43

Profit or loss

	20X4	20X5	20X6
	$000	$000	$000
Revenue	360	375	390
Purchases	230	250	280
Profit before tax	32	46	14

The following information is also available:

(1) All sales and purchases are made on credit terms.

(2) The company commenced trading on 1 January 20X4 with capital of 100,000 $1 ordinary shares issued at a premium of 60 cents each.

(3) Income tax amounted to $5,000 in 20X5 and $6,000 in 20X6. There was no income tax charge for 20X4.

(4) Dividends paid amounted to 5 cents per share in 20X4, and 10 cents per share in each of 20X5 and 20X6.

Example 2 Analysis and Interpretation (continued)

			20X5	**20X6**
(i) ROCE	$=$	$\dfrac{\text{Profit before tax}}{\text{Capital employed}} \times 100$	$\dfrac{46}{(263-45)} \times 100$ $= 21.1\%$	$\dfrac{14}{(259-43)} \times 100$ $= 6.5\%$
(ii) Net profit %	$=$	$\dfrac{\text{Profit before tax}}{\text{Turnover}} \times 100$	$\dfrac{46}{375} \times 100$ $= 12.3\%$	$\dfrac{14}{390} \times 100$ $= 3.6\%$
(iii) Receivable days	$=$	$\dfrac{\text{Closing receivables}}{\text{Credit sales}} \times 365$	$\dfrac{45}{375} \times 365$ $= 44$ days	$\dfrac{52}{390} \times 365$ $= 49$ days
(iv) Payment period	$=$	$\dfrac{\text{Closing payables}}{\text{Credit purchases}} \times 365$	$\dfrac{(45-5-10)}{250} \times 365$ $= 44$ days	$\dfrac{(43-6-10)}{280} \times 365$ $= 35$ days

Required:

Analyse the information given and discuss how the information might affect the negotiations for the overdraft.

Example 3 Discontinued Operation

Following on from *Example 2*.

Assume that Titus sold a subsidiary halfway through 20X6.

Required:

Identify and discuss three effects of the disposal on your analysis.

Summary

- The objective of financial reporting is to provide information about an entity to external users of its financial statements.

- Ratios are a tool to assist analysis. They focus attention on trends and weaknesses and facilitate comparison over time and between companies.

- Choice of accounting policies can significantly affect the view presented by the accounts.

- Ratios use historical data which may not be predictive as this ignores future actions by management and changes in the business environment.

- Background information supplied about the nature of the business may help to explain changes or trends.

- Ratios do not provide answers but focus attention on important areas.

- Performance ratios measure rate of return earned on capital employed, and analyse this into profit margins and use of assets.

- A trade-off often exists between margin and asset turnover. Low margin businesses (e.g. food retailers) usually have high asset turnover.

- Short-term liquidity ratios are used to assess a company's ability to raise cash to meet payments when due.

- Working capital ratios are an important indicator of management's effectiveness in running the business efficiently. For a given level of activity, it is most profitable to minimise the level of working capital employed in the business.

- Not all organisations are concerned with profitability. Not-for-profit organisations and the public sector are more concerned with providing a service.

- Analysis of group information may hide issues relating to entities within the group.

Session 25 Quiz
Estimated time: 30 minutes

1. Identify the main users of financial information. (1.2)

2. Describe the limitations of using ratio analysis to compare the performance of companies. (2.6)

3. List FOUR indicators other than ratios that reflect how a company is performing. (2.7)

4. Describe what is meant by "off balance sheet financing". (2.8)

5. Describe other forms which creative accounting may take. (2.8)

6. State which profit figure should be taken when calculating return on capital employed, where capital employed includes non-current liabilities such as long-term debt and debentures. (4.2)

7. Suggest what factors might explain a change in the gross margin of a company when comparing two consecutive years. (4.2)

8. Describe the effect on the current ratio given the following scenario: A company has a current ratio of 1.2:1. The company has a large cash balance, and is considering paying off half of its current liabilities prior to the end of the year. (5.1.2)

9. List the methods available to measure the gearing of a company. (5.2.2)

10. True or false? An inventory holding days ratio of 200 days is acceptable for a supermarket. (6.2)

11. Identify the working capital cycle and explain its meaning. (6.3)

Study Question Bank
Estimated time: 40 minutes

Priority		Estimated Time	Completed
Q46	Rapido	**40 minutes**	
Additional			
Q47	Not-for-profit		

EXAMPLE SOLUTIONS

Solution 1—Ratios and Financial Performance

(a) Profitability ratios

(1)

	20X7	20X6

Gross profit %:

Gross profit/revenue × 100 $\dfrac{12{,}300}{28{,}000} \times 100$ $\dfrac{6{,}700}{25{,}000} \times 100$

= 43.9%   **= 26.8%**

(2)

Net profit %:

PBIT/revenue × 100 $\dfrac{6{,}100}{28{,}000} \times 100$ $\dfrac{2{,}500}{25{,}200} \times 100$

= 21.8%   **= 10%**

(3)

ROCE:

PBIT/Capital employed × 100 $\dfrac{6{,}100}{26{,}300} \times 100$ $\dfrac{2{,}500}{20{,}200} \times 100$

= 23.2%   **= 12.4%**

Liquidity/efficiency ratios

(1)

Current ratio:

Current assets: Current liabilities   8,000:4,700   6,100:3,900

= 1.7:1   **= 1.6:1**

(2)

Inventory turnover (days):

Inventory/cost of sales × 365 $\dfrac{4{,}800}{15{,}700} \times 365$ $\dfrac{2{,}300}{18{,}300} \times 365$

= 112 days   **= 46 days**

(3)

Average collection period:

Trade receivables/sales × 365 $\dfrac{3{,}200}{28{,}000} \times 365$ $\dfrac{2{,}500}{25{,}000} \times 365$

= 42 days   **= 37 days**

(b) Comment on financial performance

- The major trend revealed by the ratios is the significant increase in profitability over the two years (as demonstrated by each of the profit ratios).
- Revenue has increased, maybe in terms of volume and selling price, and the cost of sales has reduced. The reduction in costs may well be due to a reduction in the quality of the goods purchased. Care must be taken that the quality of goods is not reduced, otherwise customers will go elsewhere for the product in the future.
- Regarding liquidity, the position has worsened slightly over the period. The current ratio has increased. This could signal potential future cash flow problems. Virgil has taken on new short-term borrowings during the last 12 months.
- The efficiency ratios have tended to deteriorate. Inventory is taking more than twice as long to be turned over. However, this could be an indication that a wider range of goods is held. This could explain the increase in sales. The increase in the average amount of credit given to customers also may have encouraged sales.

Solution 2—Analysis and Interpretation

Profitability

- ROCE and net profit percentage both fell significantly in 20X6.
- The bank manager will want to know the reasons for the fall in profitability when considering the overdraft application.
- 20X7 could result in a loss if resources cannot be used more efficiently.

Working capital management

- The customers' collection period has lengthened and the suppliers' payment period has shortened.
- Credit control appears to have weakened as customers are being allowed more time to settle their accounts in each successive year (yet suppliers are being paid more quickly).
- This increases the need for working capital. If Titus could reverse these trends (i.e. improve cash flow) then there may be no immediate overdraft requirement.
- The bank manager may be concerned that the company has paid a dividend in excess of profit after tax (i.e. out of reserves).
- At 31 December 20X6, Titus has only $2,000 in the bank and owes $43,000 (including $6,000 to the tax authority). An overdraft facility will enable equity shareholders to be paid a return—this will not expand the business.
- An overdraft providing working capital alone is unlikely to meet the directors' expansion plans. The directors should also be negotiating for medium-/long-term finance.
- As the company has no long-term debt, it is an option for the company to explore. The finance cost of longer-term debt will generally be cheaper than short-term overdrafts.

Solution 3—Discontinued Operation

1. Revenue for the period has increased even though the subsidiary was sold halfway through the year. This may indicate a marketing effort to sell goods relating to the remaining operations within the group.
2. Although revenue has increased, the profit for the period has decreased. This may be due to the subsidiary having been a profitable part of the Titus group, raising the question of why the subsidiary was sold; or it may relate to abnormal disposal cost relating to the sale of the subsidiary.
3. Comparison over the years is not meaningful. For meaningful comments, the results of the disposed subsidiary should be eliminated to enable comparison of the continuing operations.

IAS 7 *Statement of Cash Flows*

FOCUS

This session covers the following content from the *ACCA Study Guide.*

C. Analysing and Interpreting Financial Statements

3. Limitations of interpretation techniques

d) Compare the usefulness of cash flow information with that of a statement of profit or loss or a statement of profit or loss and other comprehensive income. ☐

e) Interpret a statement of cash flows (together with other financial information) to assess the performance and financial position of an entity. ☐

D. Preparation of Financial Statements

1. Preparation of single entity financial statements

c) Prepare a statement of cash flows for a single entity (not a group) in accordance with relevant accounting standards using the direct and the indirect method. ☐

Session 26 Guidance

▪ **Understand** the importance of cash flow in analysing performance (s.1).
▪ **Work through** all examples.
▪ **Learn** the classification of cash flows between operating, investing and financing activities (s.2).

(continued on next page)

VISUAL OVERVIEW

Objective: To prepare a statement of cash flows in order to understand changes in cash and cash equivalents caused by operating, investing and financing activities.

IAS 7

- Applies to All Entities
- Importance of Cash Flow
- Benefits of Cash Flow Information
- Terminology

PRESENTATION OF A STATEMENT OF CASH FLOW

- Classification
- Examples

DISCLOSURES

- Extra Disclosures
- Cash and Cash Equivalents
- Major Non-cash Transactions
- Voluntary Disclosures

OPERATING ACTIVITIES

- Direct Method
- Indirect Method
- Pro Formas
- Choice of Method

INVESTING AND FINANCING ACTIVITIES

- Separate Reporting
- Investing Activities
- Financing Activities

CASH FLOW ANALYSIS

- Operating Cash Flows
- Investing Cash Flows
- Financing Cash Flows

Session 26 Guidance

- **Learn** the format of the statement of cash flows and recognise that it is only concerned with cash flows; look for changes to non-current assets and capital that are not cash flows (s.3.3).
- **Appreciate the use of** cash flow analysis (s.5) and the additional information to be gained from a company's disclosures (s.6).

1 IAS 7

1.1 Applies to All Entities

▦ Users of financial statement are interested in cash generation regardless of the nature of the entity's activities.

▦ Entities need cash for essentially the same reasons:*

- to conduct operations;
- to pay obligations; and
- to provide returns to investors.

1.2 Importance of Cash Flow

▦ Not all profitable companies are successful; many fail due to a lack of cash.

▦ Profit or loss is based on the accruals concept and also includes non-cash items (e.g. depreciation).

▦ A major function of the statement of cash flows is to inform the users of accounts whether or not the reported profits are being realised (e.g. that trade receivables are being recovered).

▦ The statement also helps to identify the availability of cash to:

- pay dividends;
- finance further investment (which will generate more cash).

*Commentary

*Profit is not the same as cash ... and profitability does not mean liquidity (even profitable companies "crash").

1.3 Usefulness of Cash Flow Information

1.3.1 Benefits Suggested by IAS 7

✔ Provides information enabling users to evaluate changes in:

- net assets;
- financial structure (including its liquidity and solvency); and
- ability to affect amounts and timing of cash flows (to adapt to changing circumstances and opportunities).

✔ Useful in assessing ability to generate cash and cash equivalents.

✔ Users can develop models to assess and compare the present value of future cash flows of different entities.

✔ Enhances comparability of operating performance reported by different entities by eliminating the effects of alternative accounting treatments.

✔ Historical cash flow information may provide an indicator of the amount, timing and certainty of future cash flows.

✔ A focus on cash management can improve results (e.g. with lower interest charges) and lead to having cash resources available on a timely basis (e.g. for investment).

1.3.2 Comparison With Profit or Loss

✔ The cash flow statement provides a link between items reported in the statement of profit or loss (or statement of profit or loss and other comprehensive income) and the statement of financial position.

✔ The statement of profit or loss is presented in accordance with accounting policies based on the accruals concept. These policies may involve a degree of judgement in how and when revenue and expenses (and hence profits) are recognised. As cash accounting does not involve such judgements, it provides a more objective reflection of how a company is performing.

✔ Cash flows allow more meaningful comparison between companies. Profits can be manipulated and different accounting policies may lead to different outcomes. It is more difficult, although not impossible, to manipulate cash.

✔ A company generating high profit but "overtrading" will have low or negative cash balances; profits exist currently but there is insufficient cash to support continuation of the business as a going concern.*

✔ Profit or loss does not show whether a company is suffering from a lack of cash (unless it reports losses), whereas the cash flow statement clearly shows whether the change in the level of cash (and cash equivalents) is a net decrease.

✔ Cash is more credible than profit because it has a tangible (physical) aspect, whereas profit is a "made-up" figure. Many users of financial statements who have been affected by company collapses have lost faith in reported profits but may still trust cash as a factual amount.

✔ Profits do not provide funds for investment; cash is needed to finance asset replacement and new investment to grow a business.

✔ Business survival depends on profitability and liquidity. A successful business must therefore have profits and cash.

✔ Cash is more relevant to creditors and providers of loan finance than profits. Creditors are concerned with the availability of cash to meet the debt and interest payments.

*It is commonly said that "cash is king", meaning that cash is more important than profit.

1.4 Terminology

Cash: cash on hand and demand deposits.

Cash equivalents: short-term, highly liquid investments:*

- readily convertible to known amounts of cash;
- subject to an insignificant risk of changes in value;
- excluding equity investments unless they are, in substance, cash equivalents (e.g. preferred shares acquired within a short period of their maturity and a specified redemption date).

Cash flows: inflows and outflows of cash and cash equivalents.

Operating activities: principal revenue-producing activities and other activities which are not investing or financing activities.

Investing activities: acquisition and disposal of long-term assets and other investments not included in cash equivalents.

Financing activities: result in changes in the size and composition of equity capital and borrowings. Bank borrowings are generally included.*

*Cash equivalents are treated as cash because if they were not, the liquidity of entities which manage their cash effectively (e.g. employing overnight deposit facilities, buying bonds etc) would not look as good as it actually was.

*Bank overdraft balances are typically included in cash and cash equivalents.

2   Presentation of a Statement of Cash Flows

Key Point

A statement of cash flows is essentially a list of cash in and cash out reconciling opening and closing cash balances.

2.1   Classification

IAS 7 requires cash inflows and outflows to be analysed across three activities.

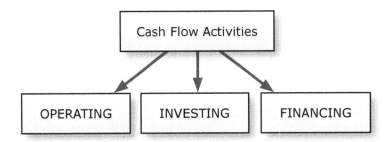

1. Operating Activities or Cash Flow From Operations (CFO)

CFO, without recourse to external sources of finance, is a key indicator of the sufficiency of cash flows to:

- repay loans;
- maintain operating capability;
- pay dividends; and
- make new investments.

It is useful in forecasting future operating cash flows.

Since it is primarily derived from principal revenue-producing activities, it generally results from transactions and events that generate profit or loss.

2. Investing Activities or Cash Flow From Investing (CFI)

Separate disclosure is important—as investing cash flows represent the amount spent on resources that are intended to generate future income and cash flows.

3. Financing Activities or Cash Flow From Financing (CFF)

Separate disclosure is useful in predicting the claims which providers of capital and long-term finance may make on future cash flows.

2.2 Examples

Examples of cash inflows and outflows across the three activities are depicted in the table below.

TRANSACTIONS	CFO	CFI	CFF
Cash Flows From Operations			
1. Cash receipts from sale of goods/ rendering services	x		
2. Cash receipts from royalties, fees and commissions	x		
3. Cash payments to suppliers for goods/ services	x		
4. Cash payments to and on behalf of employees (e.g. pension contributions)	x		
Non-current Asset Transaction			
5. Payments to acquire/receipts from sales of property, plant and equipment, intangibles		x	
6. Payments to acquire/receipts from sales of shares, loan notes, etc of other entities		x	
7. Cash advances and loans made to other parties and repayments thereof		x	
Non-current Liabilities and Equity Transactions			
8. Cash proceeds from issuing shares/equity instruments			x
9. Cash proceeds from debentures, loans, notes, bonds, mortgages, other short-term or long-term borrowings			x
10. Cash payments to owners to acquire or redeem own (i.e. the entity's) shares			x
11. Cash repayments of borrowings			x
Dividends and Interest*			
12. Interest paid			
• when recognised as an expense or capitalised (e.g. in the cost of constructing an asset)	x		
• when it is a cost of obtaining financial resources			x
13. Interest and dividends received			
• when taken into account of in the determination of profit or loss	x		
• when they are returns on investments		x	
14. Dividends paid			
• when they are a cost of obtaining financial resources			x
• when they assist users in determining the company's ability to pay dividends out of operating cash flow	x		

*Commentary

*Management has discretion in classifying cash flows as either CFO, CFI or CFF as appropriate.

Key Point

Cash flows from interest and dividends received and paid should be disclosed **separately** and classified **consistently** from one period to another.

3 Operating Activities

Operating activities can be determined using the indirect or direct method.

3.1 Direct Method

- Discloses major classes of gross cash receipts and gross cash payments.
- Information is obtained either from accounting records or by adjusting sales, cost of sales for:
  - changes in inventories, operating receivables and payables during the period;
  - other non-cash items; and
  - other items for which cash effects are investing or financing cash flows.

Technique	Formula
1. Cash receipts from customers.	Cash receipts from customers
2. Deduct cash paid to suppliers and employees.	– cash paid to suppliers – cash paid to employees
⊃ Cash generated from operations	⊃ Cash generated from operations
3. Payments for interest and income taxes.	– payments for interest – income taxes paid
⊃ Net cash from operating activities	⊃ Net cash from operating activities

3.2 Indirect Method

Adjusts profit or loss for effects of:

- non-cash transactions (e.g. depreciation);
- any deferrals or accruals of past or future operating cash receipts or payments; and
- items of income or expense associated with investing or financing cash flows.

Technique	Formula
1. Start with profit before tax.	Profit before tax
2. Adjust for non-cash items, investing items, and financing items accounted for on the accruals basis (e.g. interest).	+ non-cash expenses/losses – non-cash income/gains
⊃ Operating profit before working capital changes	⊃ Operating profit before working capital changes
3. Make working capital changes.	+ increases (decreases) in operating liabilities (assets) – increases (decreases) in operating assets (liabilities)
⊃ Cash generated from operations	⊃ Cash generated from operations

3.3 Pro Formas

3.3.1 Direct Method

	$	$
Cash flows from operating activities		
Cash receipts from customers	x	
Cash paid to suppliers and employees	(x)	
Cash generated from operations (see next for alternative)	x	
Interest paid	(x)	
Income taxes paid	(x)	
Net cash from operating activities		x
Cash flows from investing activities		
Purchase of property, plant and equipment	(x)	
Proceeds from sale of equipment	x	
Interest received	x	
Dividends received	x	
Net cash used in investing activities		x
Cash flows from financing activities		
Proceeds from issuance of share capital	x	
Proceeds from long-term borrowings	x	
Dividends paid*	(x)	
Net cash used in financing activities		x
Net increase in cash and cash equivalents		x
Cash and cash equivalents at beginning of period		x
Cash and cash equivalents at end of period		x

> ***Commentary***
> *Dividends paid could be shown as an operating cash flow.

3.3.2 Indirect Method

	$
Cash flows from operating activities	
Profit before taxation	x
Adjustments for	
Depreciation	x
Investment income	(x)
Interest expense	x
Operating profit before working capital changes	x
Increase in trade and other receivables	(x)
Decrease in inventories	x
Decrease in trade payables	(x)
Cash generated from operations	x
...remainder as for the direct method	

3.4   Which Method?

Key Point

IASB encourages, but does not require, the use of the direct method.

3.4.1   Advantages of the Direct Method

✔ Reporting the major classes of operating cash receipts and payments better reveals an entity's ability to generate sufficient cash from operations to pay debts, reinvest in operations and make distributions to owners. Thus, it better fulfils information needs for decision-making purposes.*

*Commentary

*In particular, being able to see cash paid is particularly important to many users.

✔ The format is simpler to understand.

3.4.2   Disadvantages of the Direct Method

✗ Many entities do not collect information which would allow them to determine the information necessary to prepare the direct method.

✗ It effectively presents profit or loss information on a cash rather than an accrual basis. This may suggest, incorrectly, that net cash flow from operations is a better measure of performance than profit per the statement of profit or loss.

✗ It requires supplemental disclosure of a reconciliation of net income and net cash. (However, the incremental cost of providing the additional information disclosed in the direct method is not significant.)

3.4.3   Advantages of the Indirect Method

✔ It focuses on the difference between profit per the statement of profit or loss and net cash flow from operations.*

*Commentary

*The indirect method is also sometimes called the reconciliation method.

✔ It provides a useful link between cash flows, the statement of profit or loss and the statement of financial position.

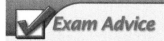

Exam Advice

The indirect method is much more widely used in practice and in the exam.

4 Investing and Financing Activities

4.1 Separate Reporting

- Major classes of gross cash receipts and gross cash payments arising from investing and financing activities should be reported separately.

4.2 Investing Activities

- Purchase of property, plant and equipment—this must represent actual amounts *paid*.*
- Proceeds from sales of tangible assets.

*Commentary

*Only expenditure which results in the recognition of an asset (capital expenditure) can be classified within investing activities.

Example 1 Investing Activity

	20X6	20X5
	$m	$m
Statement of financial position extracts		
Non-current assets	10,000	9,000
Further information		
Depreciation during the year	1,000	
Carrying amount of assets disposed of	100	

Required:
Calculate purchases of non-current assets in the period.

4.3 Financing Activities

▨ Again, the approach is to reconcile the statement of financial position movements to identify the cash element.

Example 2 Financing Activity

	20X6 $m	20X5 $m
Statement of financial position extracts		
Share capital	150	100
Share premium	48	40

During the period the following transactions affected share capital:

1. The entity issued shares with a nominal value of $10m (share premium $2m) to acquire an interest in a subsidiary

2. The entity issued shares for cash. The expense of the issue was $1m. This has been debited to the share premium account.

Required:

Calculate the cash raised from the share issue.

Solution

	Share capital	Share premium
Balances at the year end		
Add: Expenses of the share issue	_____	_____
Less: Non-cash transaction	_____	_____
Less: Balances at the start of the year	_____	_____
Cash raised	_____	_____

Example 3 Cash Flow Statement

Antipodean statements of financial position at

	20X5		20X6	
	$	$	$	$
Non-current assets				
(at carrying amount)				
Premises	37,000		38,000	
Equipment	45,800		17,600	
Motor vehicles	18,930		4,080	
		101,730		59,680
Investments		25,000		17,000
		126,730		76,680
Current assets				
Inventories	19,670		27,500	
Trade receivables	11,960		14,410	
Short-term investments	4,800		3,600	
Cash and bank balances	700		1,800	
		37,130		47,310
Total assets		163,860		123,990
Capital and reserves				
Capital		78,610		75,040
Non-current liabilities				
Interest-bearing borrowings		25,000		28,000
Current liabilities				
Trade payables	32,050		20,950	
Bank overdraft	28,200		–	
		60,250		20,950
		163,860		123,990

Profit for the year ended 31 December 20X6 ($25,200) is after accounting for:

Depreciation	$
Premises	1,000
Equipment	3,000
Motor vehicles	3,000
Profit on disposal of equipment	430
Loss on disposal of motor vehicle	740
Interest expense	3,000

The carrying amount of the assets at date of disposal was:

Equipment	5,200
Motor vehicles	2,010

Interest accrued at 31 December 20X6 is $400.

The company paid a dividend of $21,630 during the year.

Required:

Prepare a statement of cash flows for the year ended 31 December 20X6 in accordance with IAS 7 *Statement of Cash Flows.*

Example 3 Cash Flow Statement (continued)

Solution

	$	$
Cash flows from operating activities		
Profit before taxation		
Adjustments for		
Depreciation		
Net loss on disposals		
Interest expense		
Operating profit before working capital changes	———	
Decrease in trade receivables		
Decrease in inventories		
Increase in trade payables		
Cash generated from operations	———	
Interest paid		
Net cash from operating activities	———	
Cash flows from investing activities		
Purchase of long-term investments		
Purchase of equipment and cars		
Proceeds from sale of equipment and cars		
Net cash used in investing activities	———	
Cash flows from financing activities		
Capital repayment		
Borrowings repayment		
Net cash used in financing activities	———	
		———
Net decrease in cash and cash equivalents		
Cash and cash equivalents at beginning of period		
Cash and cash equivalents at end of period		———
		———

Example 4 Direct Method

Alma has prepared the following financial statements for the year ended 31 December 20X6:

Statement of profit or loss	$000
Revenue	2,880
Cost of sales	(2,016)
Gross profit	864
Expenses	(288)
Profit	576

	20X6	20X5
Statement of financial position (extracts)	**$000**	**$000**
Current assets		
Inventory	384	336
Trade receivables	622	564
Current liabilities		
Trade payables	403	331

You are given the following information:

(1) Expenses include depreciation of $86,000, irrecoverable debts written off of $34,000 and employment costs of $101,000.

(2) During the year, Alma disposed of plant equipment for $58,000 which had a carrying amount of $43,000, the profit being netted off against expenses.

Required:

(a) **Show how the net cash flows from operating activities would be presented in the statement of cash flows using the direct method.**

(b) **Prepare the note reconciling the operating profit to net cash flows from operating activities.**

Example 4   Direct Method (continued)

Solution

(a) Cash flows from operating activities

	$000
Cash received from customers (W1)	
Cash paid to suppliers (W2 + W4)	
Cash paid to employees	
Cash from operating activities	

Workings

(W1)

Trade Receivables			
	$000		$000
Bal b/d		Bad debt	
Revenue		Cash received β	
		Bal c/d	

(W2)

Trade Payables			
	$000		$000
Cash paid β		Bal b/d	
Bal c/d		Purchases (W3)	

(W3)

	$000
Opening inventory	
Purchases β	
Closing inventory	
Cost of sales	

(W4)

	$000
Other cash expenses (from profit or loss)	
Depreciation	
Bad debts	
Profit on disposal	
Less: Employee costs	
Other cash paid to suppliers	

(b) Reconciliation of operating profit to net cash flows from operating activities

	$000
Profit before tax	
Depreciation	
Profit on disposal	
Increase/decrease in inventory	
Increase/decrease in receivables	
Increase/decrease in payables	
Cash from operating activities	

5   Cash Flow Analysis

◾ The statement of cash flows provides additional information which can be used to help analyse the position and performance of a company.

◾ Look at the bottom line. Have cash and cash equivalents increased or decreased during the year? A company cannot maintain a negative cash flow forever. Do consider cash flows of previous years and what was expected from any budgeted cash flows.

5.1   Operating Cash Flows

◾ Comparison of the cash flow from operating activities and operating profit will give some indication as to whether the company is overtrading. Indicators of this overtrading would be if there were high profits but low levels of cash generation or if there were large increases in inventory, receivables and payables.

◾ How does the interest expense compare with the interest paid? If interest paid is much higher, this could indicate a capitalisation of interest and possible over-valuation problems in future years.

◾ Compare the movement on provisions, from the statement of financial position, with any non-cash adjustments made in the operating cash flow calculation. If there is a major difference then this could indicate a manipulation of the profit figure.

Key Point

The cash generated from operations should be sufficient to meet all the obligatory payments to loan providers (interest), government authorities (tax) and shareholders (dividends). A company cannot continue in business if these payments are not met.

5.2   Investing Cash Flows

◾ Compare the depreciation expense with the purchase of non-current assets. If the cash flow is greater than the expense then this is an indication of growth, whereas if the cash flow is less than the depreciation expense then this could mean that the company is not replacing assets when they are taken out of commission.

◾ Is the cash to acquire new assets coming from operating activities or financing? Ideally, growth should be financed internally from a company's operations rather than having to raise new finance for new investments.

◾ Is the company selling non-current assets at a loss? If so, this could indicate that the annual depreciation charge is insufficient leading to an overstatement of profits.

5.3   Financing Cash Flows

◾ How is new capital being raised? If in the form of debt, then this will lead to a higher level of gearing and, therefore, risk in the future.

◾ Compare any dividend paid with the raising of new capital. It is pointless to pay a dividend if the company has to go back to its shareholders and raise additional finance.

6 Disclosures

6.1 Extra Disclosures

- A number of extra disclosures should be made in most cases to support the main statement of cash flows:
  - analysis of cash and cash equivalents;
  - major non-cash transactions;
  - cash and cash equivalents held by the group;
  - reporting futures, options and swaps; and
  - voluntary disclosures.

6.2 Analysis of Cash and Cash Equivalents

- A note should be presented which reconciles amounts held as cash and cash equivalents at the start and end of the period (direct and indirect methods).

Illustration 1 Cash and Cash Equivalents

Cash and cash equivalents consist of cash on hand and balances with banks, and investments in money market instruments. Cash and cash equivalents included in the statement comprise the following amounts.

	20X6	20X5	Change
	$	$	$
Cash on hand and balances with banks	–	1,300	(1,300)
Short-term investments	1,000	2,000	(1,000)
Bank overdraft	(12,000)	–	(12,000)
	(11,000)	3,300	(14,300)

6.3 Major Non-cash Transactions

- Non-cash transactions should be excluded from the main statement. However, some of these do have a major effect on investing and financing activities and should be disclosed in a note.
- Examples of such transactions could include:
  - the issue of shares to acquire assets;
  - the conversion of debt to equity; and
  - the inception of significant lease arrangements.
- In each case, a brief description of the nature and purpose of the transaction should be given.

6.4 Voluntary Disclosures

- The standard encourages the disclosure of other information which may be relevant to users seeking to assess the financial health of a business. This information includes:
  - the amount of undrawn borrowings which are available and any restrictions on their future use; and
  - the amount of cash flows which represent increases in capacity rather than maintenance of existing capacity.

Summary

- The statement of cash flows is a required financial statement.
- Cash equivalents are short-term, highly liquid investments subject to insignificant risk of changes in value.
- Cash flows are classified into operating, investing and financial activities.
- Operating: May be presented using either the direct or indirect methods.
  - Direct method shows receipts from customers and payments to suppliers, etc.
  - Indirect method adjusts accrual basis profit or loss for major non-cash items.
- Investing: acquisition or sale of property, plant and equipment.
- Financing: issue/redemption of equity, debentures etc.

Session 26 Quiz

Estimated time: 20 minutes

1. Give FIVE benefits of cash flow information. (1.3)
2. Define cash equivalents in accordance with IAS 7. (1.4)
3. Name the THREE categories of cash flows used in a statement of cash flows under IAS 7. (2.1)
4. Identify in which section of the statement of cash flows "income taxes paid" appears. (2.2)
5. State the TWO ways a statement of cash flows may be presented. (3)
6. List the bottom THREE lines of a statement of cash flows. (3.3)
7. Explain how the two methods of the statement of cash flows are the same. (3.2)
8. Identify in which sections of the statement of cash flows dividends paid may appear. (3.3)

Study Question Bank

Estimated time: 45 minutes

Priority		Estimated Time	Completed
Q49	Mocha	45 minutes	
Additional			
Q48	Minster		

EXAMPLE SOLUTIONS

Solution 1—Investing Activity

	$m
Balance b/f	9,000
Depreciation	(1,000)
Disposals	(100)
Additions (Balancing figure)	2,100
Balance c/f	10,000

Solution 2—Financing Activity

	Share capital	Share premium
Balances at the year end	150	48
Add: Expenses of the share issue	0	1
	150	49
Less: Non-cash transaction	(10)	(2)
	140	47
Less: Balances at the start of the year	(100)	(40)
	40	7
Cash raised		47

Solution 3—Cash Flow Statement

	$	$
Cash flows from operating activities		
Profit before taxation	25,200	
Adjustments for		
Depreciation	7,000	
Net loss on disposals	310	
Interest expense	3,000	
Operating profit before working capital changes	35,510	
Decrease in trade receivables	2,450	
Decrease in inventories	7,830	
Increase in trade payables $((32,050 − 400) − 20,950)	10,700	
Cash generated from operations	56,490	
Interest paid $(3,000 − 400)	(2,600)	
Net cash from operating activities		53,890
Cash flows from investing activities		
Purchase of long-term investments $(25,000 − 17,000)	(8,000)	
Purchase of equipment and cars $(36,400 (W1) + 19,860 (W2))	(56,260)	
Proceeds from sale of equipment and cars (W3)	6,900	
Net cash used in investing activities		(57,360)
Cash flows from financing activities		
Capital repayment	(21,630)	
Borrowings repayment	(3,000)	
Net cash used in financing activities		(24,630)
Net decrease in cash and cash equivalents*		(28,100)
Cash and cash equivalents at beginning of period		(22,700)
Cash and cash equivalents at end of period		5,400)

***Commentary**

*It is been assumed that short-term investments are cash equivalents.

Workings*

(1)

Equipment

	$000		$000
Bal b/d	17,600	Disposal	5,200
		Depreciation	3,000
Additions (β)	36,400	Bal c/d	45,800
	54,000		54,000

(2)

Motor Vehicles

	$000		$000
Bal b/d	4,080	Disposal	2,010
		Depreciation	3,000
Additions (β)	19,860	Bal c/d	18,930
	23,940		23,940

(3)

Disposals

	$000		$000
Equipment	5,200		
Motor Vehicle	2,010	Loss on disposal (vehicles)	740
Profit on disposal (equipment)	430	Proceeds (β)	6,900
	7,640		7,640

Commentary

*Accounts at carrying amounts.

Solution 4—Direct Method

(a) Cash flows from operating activities

	$000
Cash received from customers (W1)	2,788
Cash paid to suppliers (W2 + W4)	(2,074)
Cash paid to employees	(101)
Cash from operating activities	613

Workings

(W1)

Trade Receivables

	$000		$000
Bal b/d	564	Bad debt	34
Revenue	2,880	Cash received β	2,788β
		Bal c/d	622
	3,444		3,444

(W2)

Trade Payables

	$000		$000
Cash β	1,992β	Bal b/d	331
Bal c/d	403	Purchases (W3)	2,064
	2,395		2,395

(W3)

	$000
Opening inventory	336
Purchases	2,064β
Closing inventory	(384)
Cost of sales	2,016

(W4)

	$000
Other cash expenses (from profit or loss)	288
Depreciation	(86)
Bad debts	(34)
Profit on disposal	15
Employee costs	(101)
Other cash paid to suppliers	82

(b) Reconciliation of operating profit to net cash flows from operating activities

	$000
Profit before tax	576
Depreciation	86
Profit on disposal	(15)
Increase in inventory	(48)
Increase in receivables	(58)
Increase in payables	72
Cash from operating activities	613

Session 27

IAS 33 *Earnings per Share*

FOCUS
This session covers the following content from the *ACCA Study Guide.*

B. Accounting for Transactions in Financial Statements

9. Reporting financial performance

e) Earnings per share (EPS)

   i)   calculate the EPS in accordance with relevant accounting standards (dealing with bonus issues, full market value issues and rights issues)

   ii) explain the relevance of the diluted EPS and calculate the diluted EPS involving convertible debt and share options (warrants)

C. Analysing and Interpreting Financial Statements

3. Limitations of interpretation techniques

f) i)   explain why the trend of EPS may be a more accurate indicator of performance than a company's profit trend and the importance of EPS as a stock market indicator

   ii) discuss the limitations of using EPS as a performance measure.

Session 27 Guidance

■ **Pay attention** as this is an important technique.

■ **Make sure** that you can calculate a basic EPS figure allowing for share issues during the year (s.2).

■ **Know** the rules for adjusting outstanding shares (s.3) and for calculating EPS for various types of dilutive potential ordinary shares (s.4).

(continued on next page)

VISUAL OVERVIEW

Objective: To understand the provisions of IAS 33 and be able to calculate earnings per share (EPS).

```
                        ┌─────────────────────────────┐
                        │           IAS 33            │
                        │  • Earnings Performance     │
                        │  • Scope                    │
                        │  • Terminology              │
                        └─────────────────────────────┘
```

EARNINGS PER SHARE (EPS)	WEIGHTED AVERAGE NUMBER OF SHARES	DILUTED EARNINGS PER SHARE
• Basic EPS • Which Earnings?	• Basic Rule • Issues of Shares— No Consideration	• Purpose • Convertibles • Options

```
                        ┌─────────────────────────────┐
                        │      SIGNIFICANCE OF EPS     │
                        │  • EPS v Earnings           │
                        │  • Performance Measure      │
                        │  • Problems With EPS        │
                        └─────────────────────────────┘

                        ┌─────────────────────────────┐
                        │  PRESENTATION AND DISCLOSURE │
                        │  • Presentation             │
                        │  • Disclosure               │
                        └─────────────────────────────┘
```

Session 27 Guidance

■ **Understand** the significance of EPS and problems with using it as a performance measure (s.5).
■ **Recognise** the requirements for presenting and disclosing basic and diluted EPS (s.6).

1 IAS 33

1.1 Earnings Performance

- Earnings per share (EPS) shows the trend of earnings performance for a company over the years.
- It is felt to be more useful than an absolute profit figure, which will not contain information about the increase in investment which has been made in the period.
- Absolute earnings is *not* useful in comparing companies.

1.2 Scope

Key Point

IAS 33 applies to the separate financial statements of entities whose debt or equity instruments are publicly traded (or are in the process of being issued in a public market).

- IAS 33 also applies to the consolidated financial statements of a group whose parent is required to apply IAS 33 to its separate financial statements.
- An entity which discloses EPS must calculate and present it in accordance with IAS 33.

1.3 Terminology

Ordinary share: an equity instrument which is subordinate to all other classes of equity instruments.

Equity instrument: any contract which evidences a residual interest in the assets of an entity after deducting all of its liabilities.

Potential ordinary share: a financial instrument or other contract which may entitle its holder to ordinary shares. For example:

- convertible instruments;
- share options and warrants;
- share purchase plans; or
- shares which will be issued subject to certain conditions being met.

Options, warrants and their equivalents: financial instruments which give the holder the right to purchase ordinary shares.

Dilution: the *reduction* in EPS (or an increase in loss per share) resulting from the assumption that convertible instruments are converted and that warrants/options are exercised (or that ordinary shares are issued) on the satisfaction of specified conditions.

Anti-dilution: the *increase* in EPS (or a reduction in loss per share) resulting from the assumption that convertible instruments are converted and options are exercised.

Contingently issuable ordinary shares: ordinary shares issuable for little or no cash or other consideration on the satisfaction of specified conditions.

2 Earnings per Share (EPS)

2.1 Basic EPS

▨ An entity is required to present basic earnings per share for:
  ● profit or loss attributable to ordinary shareholders; *and*
  ● profit or loss relating to continuing operations attributable to those ordinary shareholders.

Key Point

The basic EPS calculation is made by dividing the profit (or loss) relating to the ordinary shareholders by the weighted average number of ordinary shares outstanding in the period.

2.2 Which Earnings?

▨ Basic earnings should be:
  ● the profit or loss attributable to ordinary shareholders; and
  ● the profit or loss relating to continuing operations attributable to the ordinary shareholders
▨ Adjusted for:
  ● post-tax effect of preference dividends (and other items relating to preference shares); and
  ● non-controlling interest.

3 Weighted Average Number of Shares

3.1 Basic Rule

▨ The number of ordinary shares will be the *weighted average* number of ordinary shares outstanding during the period.
▨ The number in existence at the beginning of the period should be adjusted for shares which have been issued for consideration during the period.*
▨ Consideration may be received in a number of ways:
  ● issue for cash;
  ● issue to acquire a controlling interest in another entity; or
  ● redemption of debt.

*Such issues may be described as issues at "full market price".

Key Point

In each case, earnings will be boosted from the date of issue. To ensure consistency between the numerator and denominator of the basic EPS calculation, the shares are also included from the date of issue.

Therefore weight the number of shares:

Pro forma

	Number
No before x $\dfrac{3}{12}$ =	x
No after x $\dfrac{9}{12}$ =	$\underline{x}$
	$\underline{x}$

3.2 Issues of Shares Where No Consideration Is Received

▨ The weighted average number of ordinary shares outstanding during the period and for all periods presented should be adjusted for events which have changed the number of ordinary shares outstanding, without a corresponding change in resources. For example:

- bonus issues;
- bonus elements in another issue (e.g. a rights issue);
- share splits; and
- reverse share splits.

3.2.1 Bonus Issues

 **Key Point**

Treat as if the new shares have been in issue for the whole of the period.

▨ Multiply the number of shares in issue by the bonus fraction.

Illustration 1   Bonus Issue of Shares

Bonus issue of 1 for 10:

Bonus fraction: $\dfrac{10+1}{10} = \dfrac{11}{10}$

▨ The EPS will fall (all other things being equal) because the earnings are being spread over a larger number of shares. This would mislead users when they compare this year's figure to those from previous periods.

Key Point

The comparative figure and any other figures from earlier periods which are being used in an analysis must be adjusted. This is done by multiplying the comparative by the *inverse* of the bonus fraction.

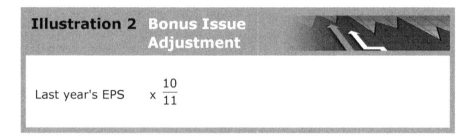

Illustration 2	**Bonus Issue Adjustment**
Last year's EPS	$\times \dfrac{10}{11}$

3.2.2   Rights Issues

▨ A rights issue has features in common with a bonus issue *and* with an issue at full market price. A rights issue gives a shareholder the right to buy shares from the company at a price set below the market value. Thus:

● the company will receive a consideration which is available to boost earnings (like an issue at full price); and

● the shareholder receives part of the share for no consideration (like a bonus issue).

▨ The method of calculating the number of shares in periods when there has been a rights issue reflects the above.

Key Point

A bonus fraction is applied to the number of shares in issue before the date of the rights issue and the new shares issued are prorated as for issues for consideration.

■ The bonus fraction is the cum-rights price per share divided by the theoretical ex-rights price per share ("TERP").

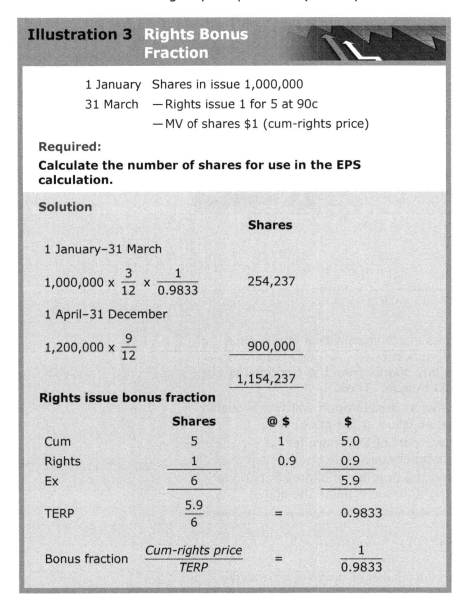

Illustration 3 Rights Bonus Fraction

> 1 January Shares in issue 1,000,000
> 31 March — Rights issue 1 for 5 at 90c
>   — MV of shares $1 (cum-rights price)

Required:
Calculate the number of shares for use in the EPS calculation.

Solution

	Shares
1 January–31 March	
$1,000,000 \times \dfrac{3}{12} \times \dfrac{1}{0.9833}$	254,237
1 April–31 December	
$1,200,000 \times \dfrac{9}{12}$	900,000
	1,154,237

Rights issue bonus fraction

	Shares	@ $	$
Cum	5	1	5.0
Rights	1	0.9	0.9
Ex	6		5.9
TERP	$\dfrac{5.9}{6}$	=	0.9833
Bonus fraction	$\dfrac{Cum\text{-}rights\ price}{TERP}$	=	$\dfrac{1}{0.9833}$

Key Point

For presentational purposes, in order to ensure consistency the comparative figure for EPS must be restated to account for the bonus element of the issue. This is achieved by multiplying last year's EPS by the inverse of the bonus fraction.

4 Diluted Earnings per Share

4.1 Purpose

- Potential ordinary shares may exist whose owners may become shareholders in the future.
- If these parties become ordinary shareholders the earnings will be spread over a larger number of shares (i.e. they will become *diluted*).*
- Potential ordinary shares should be treated as dilutive only if their conversion to ordinary shares would decrease earnings per share *from continuing operations*.

*Commentary

*Diluted EPS is calculated as a warning to existing shareholders of the effects should dilution occur.

4.2 Convertible Instruments

 Key Point

Adjust the profit attributable to ordinary shareholders and the weighted average number of shares outstanding for the effects of all dilutive potential ordinary shares.

- A new EPS is calculated using:
  - a new number of shares;
  - a new earnings figure.

4.2.1 New Number of Ordinary Shares

- This should be the weighted average number of ordinary shares used in the basic EPS calculation plus the weighted average number of ordinary shares which would be issued on the conversion of all the dilutive potential ordinary shares into ordinary shares.

 Key Point

IAS 33 always presumes that the maximum number of ordinary shares is issued on conversion, so if conversion rights differ over time always take the maximum number of shares which could be issued.

- Dilutive potential ordinary shares should be deemed to have been converted into ordinary shares at the beginning of the period or, if later, the date of the issue of the potential ordinary shares.
- New number of shares:

Basic number	x
No of shares which could exist in the future:	
from the later of	
—first day of accounting period	
—date of issue	x
	x

4.2.2 New Earnings Figure

▨ This means adding back:

- ● any dividends on dilutive potential ordinary shares, which have been deducted in arriving at the profit or loss for the period, attributed to ordinary shareholders;
- ● interest after tax recognised in the period for the dilutive potential ordinary shares; and
- ● any other changes in income or expense which would result from the conversion of the dilutive potential ordinary shares.

> **Key Point**
>
> The amount of profit or loss for the period attributable to ordinary shareholder, used in the basic EPS calculation, should be adjusted by the after-tax effect of the potential ordinary shares becoming ordinary shares.

Illustration 4 Diluted EPS– Convertibles

Convertible bonds

1 January	Shares in issue	1,000,000
	Profit for the year ended 31 December	$200,000

31 March Company issues $200,000 6% convertible bonds

Terms of conversion:

100 shares/$100 if within five years
110 shares/$100 if after five years

Tax rate 33%

Basic EPS $\dfrac{200,000}{1,000,000} = \$0.20$

Required:
Calculate diluted EPS.

Solution

	Number of shares	Profit $
Basic	1,000,000	200,000
Dilution		
Shares: $\dfrac{200,000}{100} \times 110 \times \dfrac{9}{12}$	165,000	
Interest		
$\$200,000 \times 6\% \times \dfrac{9}{12} \times 0.67$		6,030
	1,165,000	206,030
EPS		$0.1768

▨ When there has been an actual conversion of the dilutive potential ordinary shares into ordinary shares in the period, a further adjustment has to be made.

▨ The new shares will have been included in the basic EPS from the date of conversion. These shares must then be included in the diluted EPS calculation up to the date of conversion.

4.3   Options

▨ An entity should assume the exercise of dilutive options and other dilutive potential ordinary shares of the entity:
   ● the assumed proceeds from these issues should be considered to be received from the issue of shares at fair value;
   ● the difference between the number of shares issued and the number of shares which would have been issued at fair value should be treated as an issue of ordinary shares for no consideration.

 *Key Point*

Options will be dilutive only when they result in the entity issuing shares at below fair value; this usually will be when the exercise price is lower than the market price of the share.

▨ Each issue of shares under an option is deemed to consist of two elements:

1. A contract to issue a number of shares at a fair value. (This is taken to be the average fair value during the period.)*

2. A contract to issue the remaining ordinary shares granted under the option for no consideration (a bonus issue).*

 *Commentary*

*****1.** These are non-dilutive.

*****2.** These are dilutive.

Illustration 5 Diluted EPS–Options

1 January	Shares in issue	1,000,000
	Profit for the year ended 31 December	$100,000
	Average fair value	$8

The company has in issue options to purchase		200,000 ordinary shares
Exercise price		$6

Required:
Calculate the diluted EPS for the period.

Solution
Diluted EPS:

	Number of shares	Profit $	EPS
Basic	1,000,000	100,000	$0.10
Dilution (**W**)	50,000		
	1,050,000	100,000	$0.095

Working

Proceeds of issue	200,000 × $6	1,200,000

Number that would have been issued at FV	÷ $8 =	150,000
Number actually issued		200,000
Number for "free"		50,000

5   Significance of EPS

5.1   EPS v Earnings

- Prior to 1960, the decision to report EPS, the manner in which it was calculated and where it was reported was left solely to the discretion of company management.

- As expected, management chose to report performance in whole dollar earnings only, which tended to favour large corporations over small companies. EPS became a reporting necessity to create a "level playing field" in performance measurement comparability.

- EPS allows comparison between different-sized companies whereas, if only actual earnings were being compared, the relative size of the company could not be taken into account.

> ### Illustration 6   EPS v Earnings
>
> XYZ's earnings for 20X5 were $10,000. With equity shares of 100,000 in issue this gave an EPS of $0.10 per share.
>
> On 1 January 20X6, XYZ issued a further 100,000 shares. Earnings for 20X6 were $19,000, giving an EPS of $0.095 per share.
>
> Although earnings have almost doubled, EPS has fallen compared with the previous year. The capital injection only generated an additional $9,000 of earnings, which was insufficient to maintain a comparable EPS.

5.2   Performance Measure

- The EPS figure is used by market analysts in the calculation of a company's price/earnings (P/E) ratio. Great emphasis is placed on this measure, which can have a significant effect on the way a company's share price moves.

 **Key Point**

The P/E ratio is also used by investors in assisting in their decisions to buy/hold or sell shares in a company.

5.3   Problems With EPS

- ✗ EPS is affected by a company's choice of accounting policy, so can be manipulated. It also means that comparisons with other companies are not possible if different policies are being used.

- ✗ EPS is a historical figure and should not be used as a prediction of future earnings. A high EPS figure could be achieved through a lack of investment in new assets, but this will have a detrimental effect on future profits as lack of investment will lead to companies falling behind their competitors.

- ✗ EPS is a measure of profitability, but profitability is only one measure of performance.

- Many companies now place much higher significance on other performance measures such as:
  - customer satisfaction;
  - cash flow;
  - manufacturing effectiveness; and
  - innovation.

6 Presentation and Disclosure

6.1 Presentation

- Basic and diluted earnings per share (or loss per share, if negative) should be presented in *the statement of profit or loss and other comprehensive income* for:
  - profit or loss from continuing operations;
  - profit or loss for the period; and
  - each class of ordinary shares which has a different right to share in the profit for the period.
- Basic and diluted earnings per share should be presented with *equal prominence for all periods* presented.

Exhibit 1 PRESENTING BASIC AND DILUTED EPS

The following extract from Nestle Group's 2015 consolidated financial statements presents basic and diluted EPS.

Consolidated income statement for year ended 31 December 2015 (extract)

Earnings per share (in CHF)		2015	2014
Basic earnings per share	16	2.90	4.54
Diluted earnings per share	16	2.89	4.52

6.2 Disclosure

6.2.1 General

- The amounts used as the numerators in calculating basic and diluted earnings per share, and a reconciliation of those amounts to the profit or loss for the period.
- The weighted average number of ordinary shares used as the denominator in calculating basic and diluted earnings per share, and a reconciliation of these denominators to each other.
- Instruments which could potentially dilute basic EPS in the future but they were not included in the diluted EPS because they are anti-dilutive for the period
- A description of ordinary or potential share transactions that occurred after the end of the reporting period which would have significantly changed the number of ordinary shares or potential ordinary shares had the transactions occurred before the end of the period.

Exhibit 2   EPS DISCLOSURES

The following extract from Nestle Group's 2015 consolidated financial statements presents greater detail supporting its calculation of basic and diluted EPS.

16. Earnings per share (extract)

	2015	2014
Basic earnings per share (in CHF)	2.90	4.54
Net profit (in millions of CHF)	9 066	14 456
Weighted average number of shares outstanding (in millions of units)	3 129	3 188
Diluted earnings per share (in CHF)	2.89	4.52
Net profit, net of effects of dilutive potential ordinary shares (in millions of CHF)	9 066	14 456
Weighted average number of shares outstanding, net of effects of dilutive potential ordinary shares (in millions of units)	3 136	3 196

6.2.2   Additional EPS

▨ If an additional EPS figure using a reported component of profit other than profit or loss for the period attributable to ordinary shareholders is disclosed, such amounts should be calculated using the weighted average number of ordinary shares determined in accordance with IAS 33.

▨ A non-standard profit figure can be used to calculate an EPS in addition to that required by IAS 33 but the standard number of shares must be used in the calculation.

▨ If a profit figure is used which is not reported as a line item in the statement of profit or loss, reconciliation should be provided between the figure and a line item, which is reported in the statement of profit or loss.

Key Point

An additional EPS figure *may not be shown* in the statement of profit or loss; it *can only be disclosed* in the notes to the financial statements.

6.2.3   Retrospective Adjustments

▨ If an EPS figure includes the effects of:
- a capitalisation or bonus issue;
- share split; or
- decreases as a result of a reverse share split;

then the calculation of basic and diluted earnings per share for all periods presented should be adjusted retrospectively.

▨ For changes after the end of the reporting period but before issue of the financial statements, the per-share calculations for those and any prior-period financial statements presented should be based on the new number of shares.

▨ Basic and diluted EPS of all periods presented should be adjusted for the effects of errors and for adjustments resulting from changes in accounting policies.

Summary

- IAS 33 applies to entities whose securities are or will be publicly traded.
- If both parent and consolidated statements are presented in a single report, EPS is required only for the consolidated statements.
- Basic and diluted EPS must be presented, with equal prominence for all periods, in the statement of profit or loss, even if negative. This applies to discontinued operations as well as for continuing operations.
- If components of profit or loss are presented in a separate statement of profit or loss, EPS is presented only in that separate statement.
- Basic EPS is calculated as: profit or loss attributable to ordinary shareholders divided by weighted average number of ordinary shares during the period.
- Diluted EPS is calculated by adjusting earnings and number of shares for the effects of dilutive options and other dilutive potential ordinary shares.
- Convertible securities: adjust for the after-tax effects of dividends and interest charged relating to dilutive potential ordinary shares. Include all shares that would be issued on conversion.
- Assume the exercise of outstanding dilutive options and warrants and that proceeds are used to repurchase ordinary shares at the average market price for the period. Any difference between the number of ordinary shares assumed issued on exercise and the number repurchased is treated as an issue of ordinary shares for no consideration.
- Disclosures required:
  - Profit or loss used in calculating basic and diluted EPS with a reconciliation to profit or loss attributable to the parent.
  - Weighted average number of ordinary shares used in calculations.

Session 27 Quiz
Estimated time: 20 minutes

1. Identify to which companies IAS 33 applies. (1.2)
2. Suggest which earnings figure should be used in the basic earnings per share calculation. (2.2)
3. State the adjustments needed in respect of bonus shares issued during the year when calculating the weighted average number of shares. (3.2.1)
4. Explain how the bonus fraction of a rights issue is calculated. (3.2.2)
5. Identify from which date dilutive potential shares should be deemed to have been converted into shares when calculating diluted earnings per share. (4.2.1)
6. List the adjustments made to the earnings figure when calculating diluted earnings per share. (4.2.2)
7. True or false? The P/E ratio is also used by investors in deciding whether to buy/hold or sell shares in a company. (5.2)

Study Question Bank
Estimated time: 30 minutes

Priority		Estimated Time	Completed
Q50	Earnings per share	30 minutes	

INDEX